Charles Cresson
on the
American
Flower Garden

BURPEE EXPERT
GARDENER SERIES

Charles Cresson
on the
American
Flower Garden

PRENTICE HALL GARDENING

New York   London   Toronto   Sydney   Tokyo   Singapore

*To Margaret Detweiler, my aunt. She taught me
to garden as a child, and shares her love of
gardening with me to this day.*

PRENTICE HALL GENERAL REFERENCE
15 Columbus Circle
New York, New York 10023

Text and photographs copyright © 1993 by Charles Cresson
All photographs by Charles Cresson except as noted below
Illustrations copyright © 1993 by Simon & Schuster Inc.

PRENTICE HALL and colophon are registered trademarks
of Simon & Schuster Inc.

Library of Congress Cataloging-in-Publication Data

Cresson, Charles O.
    Charles Cresson on the American flower garden.
        p.   cm.—(Burpee expert gardener)
    Includes bibliographical references and index.
    ISBN 0-671-84720-1
    1. Flower gardening. 2. Flowers. 3. Flower garden-
ing—United States. 4. Flowers—United States. I. Title.
II. Title: American flower garden. III. Series.
SB405.C777 1993
635.9—dc20   92-16748
                                                   CIP

Manufactured in the United States of America

10 9 8 7 6 5 4 3 2 1

First Edition

Photography Credits: W. Atlee Burpee & Co., page 4
Jack Potter, page 37
Scott Arboretum, page 45

Illustrations by Pamela Kennedy
Horticultural editor: Suzanne Frutig Bales

Cover: Spikes of foxgloves (Digitalis purpurea) *take center stage among roses, cottage pinks* (Dianthus plumarius) *and coral
bells* (Heuchera sanguinea) *during June in the author's garden, Hedgleigh Spring.*
*Preceding pages: An American flower garden, circa 1950, as it appears today
(the author's garden)*

ACKNOWLEDGMENTS

Writing a book such as this requires the cooperation and support of friends and colleagues, for which I am very appreciative. This book would probably never have been written without the encouragement and faith of Suzanne Bales. The first eyes to see this manuscript were those of Chela Kleiber, who made the first grammatical and technical edits as it was being written. For her time, interest and dedication, my sincere thanks. Jeff and Liz Ball have stood by me and provided moral and technical support, particularly with regard to computers and the mechanics of organizing a book. My editor at Prentice Hall, Rebecca Atwater, always understood the spirit of this book and strove to preserve and improve it. Her assistant, Rachel Simon, could not have been more helpful and always had my utmost confidence.

But an in-depth knowledge of gardening involves the contributions of many more people. Gertrude Wister taught me the importance of individual plants and how to learn about them. J. Liddon Pennock, Jr., owner of Meadowbrook Farm, improved my eye for design and gave me the opportunity to create a grand flower garden that provided much of the experience reflected in this book. Lynden Miller and Sara Price, at the Conservatory Garden in Central Park, New York, inspired me greatly with their work there, as did Marco Polo Stufano at Wave Hill in the Bronx. The work of Kim Johnson, at Old Westbury Garden on Long Island, appears in many of the photographs. My thanks also to Charles Mewshaw and Mitch Carney, whose work, near Washington, D.C., appears in many photographs in this book.

Pam Kennedy, landscape designer, worked closely with me and drew upon her own invaluable garden experience to make her illustrations for this book accurate and beautiful, particularly those in color.

The following people provided technical advice: Kathy Andersen on lilies and *Narcissus*, Darrel Apps on daylilies, Warren Pollock on hostas, Jack Potter on roses and a variety of other plants, and Steve Scanniello of the Brooklyn Botanical Garden on roses. Rick Darke and Robert Herald of Longwood Gardens answered many questions, particularly taxonomic ones. Dr. J. C. Raulston, Dick Turner, Doug Ruhren and Bill Thomas provided advice on gardening in different regions. Andrew Durham, landscape architect and plantsman, reviewed my comments on garden design. Their generosity is much appreciated. My friends on the staff of the Scott Arboretum of Swarthmore College are knowledgeable and always ready to help in many ways.

Many people and organizations allowed me to photograph and learn from their gardens: Scott Arboretum, J. Liddon Pennock, Jr., Old Westbury Garden, the Conservatory Garden of Central Park, Joanna Reed, Ken Selody of Atlock Flower Farm, George Sherrill, Filoli Center, Woodside, CA, Frank Cabot and Caroline Burgess at Stonecrop, Wayne Winterrowd and Joe Eck, and Geof Beasley and Jim Sampson.

Finally and most of all, I must thank my father, William, and my brother, Richard, partners in my garden, who provide plenty of assistance and who patiently tolerate my obsession with gardening. Without their support and understanding, much of the experience captured in these pages would be absent.

CONTENTS

In early June, herbaceous peonies ('Solange', front; 'Primavera', behind) are backed by clematis 'Niobe' trained on a tripod, in the Conservatory Garden at Wave hill, Bronx, New York.

PREFACE

I've lived nearly all my life with a remarkable garden created during the early years of this century by my grandfather. It features a diversity of habitats and microclimates with nearly two acres of flowers, vegetables, trees, shrubs and a water garden. Family traditions evolved to include intimate knowledge of our land and garden, and we use tools dating back four generations. No wonder I was planting seeds at the age of six.

In my teens, when I worked in a private garden owned by keen gardeners, I learned a very different style of gardening. I brought home new plants and ideas. Later, I spent college summers working in the garden of Dr. John Wister and his wife Gertrude, both exceptional authors and horticulturists with a lifetime of gardening experience. I learned from their naturalistic woodland garden filled with rare plants, including many of their own rhododendron hybrids. Each day the Wisters taught me a new lesson about the particular care of special plants. I brought home bags of extra plants and enough new ideas to boggle the mind. My old family garden was taking on new life while it gracefully absorbed these new influences.

Study in England and travel in Europe revealed new worlds of ideas to me. Horticulture has greater priority for Europeans and above all the British, and this is reflected in their more highly developed skills and appreciation of this art. After study at the University of Bath in England I went to work at the Royal Horticultural Society's Wisley Garden. There I worked alongside old masters and learned the techniques they use to achieve their impeccable results.

Other students and I visited English gardens at every opportunity. We were fascinated by awe-inspiring landscapes with combinations of rare plants (botanical marvels, really) from around the world, so artfully arranged that it seemed the work of nature's own hand. American trilliums proliferated among Chinese rhododendrons under English oaks. Asian primroses meandered in drifts along stream banks. Even the contrived, immaculately maintained flower borders settled comfortably into these enchanted landscapes. I was inspired to learn the subtleties of these design schemes and eager to try them myself. I spent the better part of four years across the Atlantic studying with professional objectives, I was also formulating ideas for my family garden that awaited my return. Since then I have experienced fourteen years of successes and failures as I applied these diverse experiences to my family garden.

In my work I have created and managed large flower gardens other than my own. The biggest problem I've encountered is finding gardeners with the expertise and knowledge to maintain them properly. It is frustrating to see needless mistakes in American gardens because opportunities to learn good garden techniques are so scarce in this country.

Visitors to my garden ask more questions about maintenance than I can possibly answer. Because I know of no practical guide that I can recommend for American flower gardeners, I decided to sit down and write one myself. Here you'll find my approach to flower gardening— not a rehash of the same old stuff from other books, but rather, based on my own experience.

Charles O. Cresson
Hedgleigh Spring
Southeastern Pennsylvania
October 1992

INTRODUCTION

THE MODERN PARADISE AT HOME

Our needs for serenity, tranquility and refuge from the pace and pressures of life are as critical today as they were centuries ago. The soothing greens of foliage and colorful flowers comfort our souls just as they did those of the ancient Babylonians and Persians, makers of some of the earliest gardens. Persian gardens, enclosed by walls, were refuges from the dangers of predatory animals and enemies in a hot, arid climate. Within the protection of garden walls, trees and flowers provided an idyllic, shaded world of tranquility cooled by a fountain—this paradise very like city gardens today.

The connection between heaven, paradise and gardens is deeply rooted in our psyche. The evolution of language traces the concept of the garden as it changed through history. In the Middle East, *Pairidaeza* was the Avestan word for "an enclosure" and *firdaus* meant "paradise" to the Persians. To the Greeks *paradeisos* came to mean "a large and beautifully kept park," whence it was incorporated into the Hebrew concept of the Garden of Eden and heaven. Today gardens need not be symbols, but they are no less an answer to people's need for peace and tranquility in our hustle-and-bustle world. Where better to find this peace than as a part of our own homes?

Would-be gardeners and masterful veterans alike tend to dream. We imagine the ideal garden full of flowers, eagerly read books and pore over their glorious photographs, and envy the owners of those perfect gardens (or at least, envy the skill that creates such beauty). We visit gardens, collecting ideas and fueling enthusiasm. Though gardens are different things to different people, few would argue that gardens add something unique and enviable to the life of anyone fortunate enough to have one. Gardens provide an outlet for artistic and creative expression, as well as a source of healthy and pleasurable exercise. To a dedicated gardener, gardening is neither work nor drudgery, but rather fun.

Gardening is a social activity, too. It is a rare gardener who does not take pride in sharing his or her work with others and thus promote the art in a very personal manner. Gardeners know that there is no end to the varieties of plants to grow, to the challenge and pleasure of experimentation or to the combinations for different effects and moods. Superb compositions can be achieved in the smallest of spaces and most difficult locations.

The majority of American gardeners today have small home gardens, although some people still have the opportunity to garden on a larger or even grand scale. Other gardeners may be professionals working in large public gardens or maintaining private gardens for clients. Whatever the situation, the need today is for a long and reliable display with as little maintenance as possible. Note that I did not say "low maintenance." Such displays require effort, but extravagant displays are possible with less-than-extravagant maintenance, if the gardeners know their stuff. Gardening is an activity most effectively performed with some education. How wrong to believe that any fool can pull weeds and plant flowers!

The method to this glorious madness lies in understanding how to combine the various types of flowers, how they interact as a plant community, and how to manage them so that you work with the community rather than fight it. This book is about how to put together and maintain such a garden, whether it be large or small.

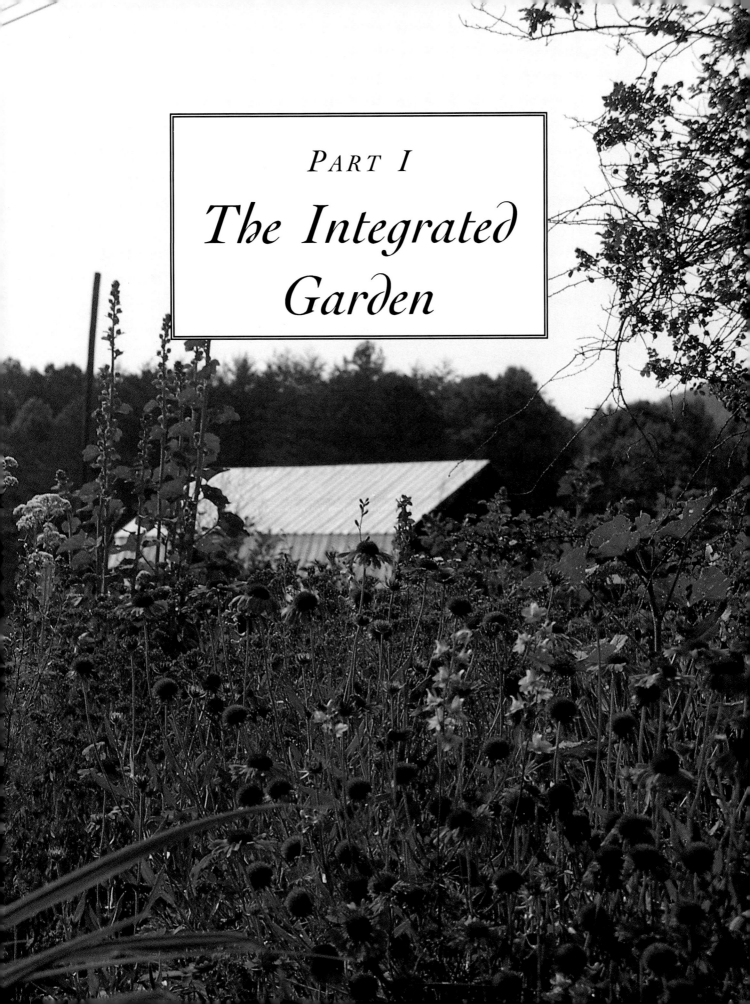

PART I
The Integrated Garden

Small English cottage gardens with lush plantings containing a wide variety of plants gave rise to the mixed flower gardens of today.

Preceding page: This garden in the mountains of western North Carolina features annuals, biennials and perennials in June.

Mixed Flower Gardens in America

American flower gardens have developed their own character as a result of the climate, the plants that can be grown here and our concepts of space and landscape. Indeed, each American region has some characteristics shared by no other. The flower garden movement began in England, and English ideas continue to influence us today. It was the humble English cottage gardens that inspired the flower borders of the large estates where such concepts as color and "garden rooms" developed. Though these concepts flourished on the grand estates, they are applicable to the modest flower gardens of most Americans. A look at the evolution of English gardens can provide ideas for our own.

The tradition of flower gardening stems from the cottage garden in the lush countryside of the British Isles. A wide diversity of plants flourishes there, and the cool, moist summers encourage a long season of bloom. Cottage gardens have always been happy, if unorganized, mixtures of flowers, herbs and even vegetables—in short, of any useful plants that a person of modest means might need or desire.

Cottage gardens have given us many flowers held in high esteem today. Long before genetics was understood, bees were hybridizing different species that grew side by side in these small gardens. Seed fell to

'Maureen' was originally classified as a Cottage tulip, a group that originated in the cottage gardens of England and Ireland. Hybridization has blurred the distinction between the May-flowering Cottage and Darwin tulips and now both are grouped as Single Lates. They bear tall stems with the familiar egg-shaped flowers and are available in a wide range of colors. (Courtesy of W. Atlee Burpee & Co.)

the ground and germinated among the casual plantings. From these self-sown seedlings new and often better sorts grew and were discovered by perceptive cottage gardeners and shared with friends. Many hybrids of *Dianthus plumarius*, for example, arose in this way and it is hardly surprising that they are now commonly referred to as "cottage pinks." Hundreds of garden flowers with cottage garden origins became the important basis upon which the more stylized, grand flower borders were built. Today the common gardener continues to contribute new plants to the ongoing tradition of gardening.

The Grand Tradition

In England the roots of the cottage garden are firmly embedded in the middle and peasant classes, beginning in the Middle Ages. The cottage garden evolved quite separately from the European movements that produced formal Re-

naissance gardens. Aristocratic Italian villas and grand French parks with lavish parterres are both products of great wealth and a drier climate. These landscape styles predominated on the grand English estates, too, until replaced by spacious naturalistic parks of lawns and vistas in the 18th century. During the Victorian era, wealth was also displayed on aristocratic estates with lavish plantings of nonhardy tropicals and annuals. The new technology of the tropical conservatories made artificial outdoor summer displays possible. Spectacular creations often included such bold features as banana and palm trees, planted out for the summer, underplanted with elaborate designs of colorful tropical foliage and flowering annuals. Displays of this type can still be seen today in many of the public parks of England and Europe. The spectacular Victorian bedding schemes were very expensive, labor-intensive and, to some horticulturists of the day, highly artificial, distasteful and even vulgar. The gradual acceptance of a new, simpler style of planting had begun.

The strongest voice in favor of hardy plants adapted to the climate was William Robinson, an influential and opinionated English garden writer and publisher. His best-known books, *The Wild Garden* and *The English Garden* (first published in 1883, retitled *The English Flower Garden* in later editions) advocated choosing plants for their forms and growth habits. His concept of the "wild garden" differed from our concept today of using native plants; rather, Robinson meant "plants of other countries, as hardy as our hardiest wild flowers," used in a "natural" scheme "without further care or cost." This is not to say that he did not appreciate the value of native plants too.

While Robinson liked the natural look, it was his fellow Englishwoman Gertrude Jekyll who promoted color composition in the garden. She had reached the height of her renowned career designing gardens for prominent country estates at the beginning of the 20th century. Jekyll's formal training was as a painter. When she grew nearsighted, painting became difficult and she turned to garden design. Jekyll is credited as the first garden designer to apply the principles of color in fine arts to gardening. Plants and flowers formed the palette with which she painted in the landscape, and cottage gardens provided many of the plants she used.

Jekyll's famous partnership with architect Sir Edwin Lutyens was responsible for many of the finest gardens of the day. Lutyens would design the house and hard landscape features such as walls and pavements. Jekyll designed the plantings, using blends of soft colors carefully coordinated for each season. Of her many books, the most esteemed is *Color in the Flower Garden*, which describes color combinations and the plants used to create them throughout the year.

The Edwardian era, up to World War I, saw the height of the great English flower borders and large estates. There was nothing simple about Jekyll's lavish designs for borders hundreds of feet long and frequently 12 or 15 feet deep. Often, additional mature plants, grown as backups, were sunk in the border at the peak of bloom wherever there was an empty space. Labor was cheap and the larger estates could afford perhaps 100 gardeners.

The gardens of Hidcote Manor elevated the concept of separate garden rooms with different themes to a new level. Located in the Cotswold

Hills of England, Hidcote was begun just after the turn of the century by Lawrence Johnston, an American. Although an expansive garden, it is subdivided by hedges into numerous smaller gardens in both sun and shade, both formal and informal. Each garden has a unique theme depicted through design and color schemes, many of them in the cottage garden style.

Hidcote was an important influence on the garden at Sissinghurst Castle where rich cottage garden plantings occupy a series of small garden rooms. Begun in 1930 by Vita Sackville-West and her husband Sir Harold Nicolson, the garden is made among the ruins of a dilapidated Tudor and Elizabethan manor house. Although the garden grows within the rigid framework of old walls, hedges and paths, the plantings themselves are loose and informal, billowing forth from the beds. Each room has its own theme. The Rose Garden combines mostly old-fashioned roses with perennials in complementary colors. The Cottage Garden is planted with hot reds, oranges, yellows, rusts and creams. The famous

The red borders at Hidcote Manor (England, in May) are famous for combinations of red flowers and reddish foliage.

White Garden combines white flowers with green and silver foliage.

While flower gardening was thriving in England, Americans were catching up. Such avid gardeners as Louise Beebe Wilder were gardening extensively, adapting foreign ideas and techniques and writing of their experiences. Lavish country estates were laid out. Beatrix Farrand created gardens of great substance and sensitivity, most notably at Dumbarton Oaks in Georgetown, Washington, D.C. Old Westbury Mansion with its lavish flower garden was built on Long Island. In the West, Filoli was developing into a masterpiece near San Francisco. These examples and others survive. Although they are American gardens they were strongly influenced by contemporary English gardens and the ideas of Robinson and Jekyll.

The mixed border at Filoli Center, near San Francisco, is a fine example of the use of flower garden plants suitable for the California climate.

Fortunately these gardens can still be seen today, but on both sides of the Atlantic many others of these "dinosaurs" have vanished, and with them have gone many of the skilled professional gardeners, a symptom of changing eco-nomics and times. Examples remain from which we can learn but, regrettably, equivalent skill in flower gardening today is often more scarce than the financial resources required to support it.

The principles of design and maintenance of the grand estates apply equally well to the smaller home gardens of today. Any of us can develop the skills to create and maintain lovely gardens of our own filled with flowers in all but the coldest months. First we must understand the land on which we garden, and the kind of garden that it will support.

FLOWER GARDENS, BEDS AND BORDERS

As an American student in England, I received a withering look from my host at dinner one night. I had referred to his garden as a backyard. After an awkward moment he set me straight. English people have "gardens" around their houses, not "yards." I was told that a "yard" is a utilitarian space, with an unsightly connotation, where the dustbins (trash cans) are often kept. Hardly the word to describe his beautiful garden!

Here in America, the words have slightly different meanings. We often have attractive "yards," which may include a plot or two of flowers or vegetables, and we call that plot "the garden." The garden seldom encompasses the whole yard unless it has also been intensively landscaped with trees, shrubs and groundcovers. The word *garden*, as opposed to *yard*, has a far more restrictive and specific meaning to Americans. When we say "flower garden," the meaning is more universally understood.

Flower gardens—successful ones—differ from other types of gardens and landscapes by their rich combinations of a wide variety of flowers and profusion of color. They are far more colorful and longer blooming than a shrub border (composed of several varieties and perhaps finished off with groundcovers along the front) could ever be. Thoughtfully designed flower gardens provide a woven tapestry of progressive bloom, continuous from late winter or early spring into autumn, even beyond the first frosts. Even in the dead of winter, flower gardens can reflect the richness of the winter landscape. Such gardens may consist of no more than a single flower bed, or may be a series of intricately designed beds.

Traditionally, flower beds have taken the form of borders. That is, they edge or border a lawn, walkway, wall or other structure. On a grand scale a border might be 12 or 15 feet deep and many times longer. A border can be as narrow as a couple of feet wide. In the last 30 years, island beds, championed by English nurseryman and writer Alan Bloom, have become popular. Island beds are just that: islands surrounded by lawn or pavement. The beds are generally irregular in shape, although a rectilinear shape can be effective. Island beds have the advantage of improved light and air circulation as compared with borders backed by a hedge, fence or wall. One benefit of this additional air and light is stronger plant stems and reduced disease, which in turn can result in lower maintenance. Island beds, however, are often more difficult than borders to integrate successfully into the garden plan or landscape, because they do not tie into other elements as easily.

Some garden designs are composed of beds that swell into mass plantings separated only by paths and walkways—not lawn—for a lovely cottage garden effect. Narrow paths in these flower gardens are often paved with brick, stone or gravel because grass would likely suffer excessive wear. Grass paths are also subject to damage by the abundance of flowers spilling over the path.

MIXED FLOWER GARDENS

The idea of combining annuals, bulbs and even shrubs and vines with perennials to create mixed garden plantings is nothing new. Here in America, gardeners free from the pretensions of the latest trends have been growing annuals, perennials and bulbs together all along. (Recently, however, perennials have been all the rage. Trend-following garden snobs have turned up their noses at annuals in the mistaken impression that such attitudes highlight their sophistication. Marigolds, curiously, seem to take the brunt of this discrimination. This is entirely unwarranted.) Annuals, bulbs, shrubs and vines are important elements on the palette of the well-rounded flower gardener. This is particularly true in the United States, where perennials show greater faults and limitations because of our heat and humidity than they do in Europe and the British Isles. So don't fall victim to plant prejudice. Fair enough if you don't like the scent of marigolds—you have good company. But to me, that fragrance is a part of summer; besides, marigolds perform. I make no apologies for marigolds.

There are no rules dictating what to include in what proportions in a mixed garden. A mixed herbaceous border, for example, would include

In Joanna Reed's garden, Longview Farm, in Malvern, Pennsylvania, the plants are allowed to sprawl over the flagstone paths that separate the beds.

Marigolds (center) are an important element of this mixed border, along with creeping zinnia, Sanvitalia *(front),* Crocosmia × crocosmiiflora *(top right), and* Rudbeckia *'Goldsturm' (left).*

only annuals, perennials and bulbs. A full-fledged mixed planting would also include woody shrubs and vines for an added dimension of flowers, foliage and structure that herbaceous plants alone don't provide.

Why have mixed plantings? Imagine that you have an annual garden. Each spring you prepare the entire bed by tilling up the soil and raking it level. Meanwhile, you have been tending seedlings indoors under lights or cluttering up all your windowsills to start masses of annuals for your summer garden. If you haven't grown the plants yourself, you will spend a small fortune annually to purchase these plants. (Never mind that the selection at the local garden center is more limited than if you'd bought seed of the varieties you want and grown them yourself.) The next big job is to plant and mulch the entire area. And then, of course, this sort of garden requires a lot of weeding, to keep looking neat and tidy, until the small plants fill in. Annuals have the reputation of providing a long season of color, but it will be late May or June before the transplants are established enough to give a real show. Before you know it, some of the annuals will be fizzling out by August. Some color continues up until hard frost, although it is of inferior quality. With the need to start everything frantically from scratch each year, I have always been concerned that if my life got crazy for some reason at that critical time in spring, I wouldn't have a garden at all. It takes a lot of work to establish an annual display, if you can get around to it, and it is not necessarily an all-season affair.

Now imagine that you have a perennial garden. You've found that since the plants live from year to year it's not a big job to straighten up the garden in spring for bloom throughout the summer. You notice that some varieties are a bit overgrown; these can easily be divided and replanted on the spot, or if you're too busy in spring, you can handle such jobs in the fall. A perennial garden with a good selection of plants can be in bloom from April, reaching a peak in June, and continuing until after the first frosts. By midsummer, early-blooming varieties may look a bit tired with somewhat sparse bloom, but late-blooming varieties are just coming into flower to fill the spaces and contribute color through September into October. You may never quite have the great mass of color that annuals provide at their peak, but it is a more varied and seasonally interesting display. At least two crops or plantings of annuals would be required to achieve as long a bloom season. Your efforts may seem to fall short of the glorious English perennial garden you've been dreaming about, but it is easier to cope with a perennial garden than one made up exclusively of annuals.

In fact, the "English perennial" garden you once admired in that glossy magazine probably included annuals too. English gardeners aren't averse to using them and realize their value for bolstering lags in the bloom season and generally filling in. Spring bulbs are often included to provide an early burst of color. Thus the three major elements of an integrated garden—perennials, annuals and bulbs—complement each other to provide a well-rounded, season-long display.

SCHEDULING AND RESOURCES

Mixed plantings fit more easily into the gardener's schedule. The different components require different seasons of care, and this allows the gardener to spread maintenance almost throughout the year. You do some work to maintain the garden every season rather than everything frantically at once. Most of what needs to be done to keep perennials in order (such as dividing and reorganizing) can be done in the autumn before the ground freezes, and also serves as a general cleanup. Autumn is an excellent time to prepare some spaces for planting annuals the following spring. (For more about spaces for annuals see page 46). The very last thing to do in autumn is plant your bulbs. If planted before the perennial work is finished, bulbs can be dug up, pierced or even cut in half by your spade. The following spring you can finish the remaining perennials' tasks in a jiffy, plant a few annuals in their prepared spaces and mulch the beds for the summer. With a head start in the fall, spring cleanup is more easily completed and avoids the dreaded spring rush. The plants benefit too, as some have had the chance to become more established over the winter. Routine summer maintenance becomes more of a joy than a chore; it freshens up the display and no longer seems like an exercise in futility.

This mixed border in the terraced gardens at Powis Castle, Wales, is backed by vines and wall shrubs.

The economics of a mixed garden are attractive. While it can cost a small fortune in time and cash each year for the plants in an annual garden, many of the plants in a mixed garden are hardy and live for more than one year, if not virtually forever. If you want more of a particular variety, it is easy to propagate most perennials and many bulbs by division, right out in the garden. And if you garden, you will eventually have gardening friends, and many other plants you may wish to have can be acquired by trade. In this way you'll save your pennies toward buying that tempting new plant in the catalog or a few last-minute annuals for filling some gaps.

I don't mean to imply that there is no cost to flower gardening. There may very well be a considerable initial expense to get started, depending on how you do it, how fast you want results and how grand your vision is. My point is that those of us who use a lot of perennials in our gardens carry on year to year without spending much at all on the essentials, those plants that provide the bulk of the display. This often leaves a good bit of extra pocket money with which to indulge our garden fetishes.

For the artistically inclined, the best excuse for a mixed flower garden is the challenge and satisfaction of creating exciting and subtle combinations of flowers and foliage in an ever-changing picture as the season progresses. Favorite color combinations unite with striking contrasts of bold forms and fine textures, accented by upright spikes and pendant plumes. In early summer, pale pink border carnations contrast with deep blue, spiky salvias or fine sprays of white baby's breath. Later, pink and white Japanese anemones blend with purple aconites or blue asters. Through the growing season, no two months or even weeks are the same, and there is the constant anticipation of the impending bloom of another favorite flower or another combination.

Striking compositions of color, texture and plant forms have been designed by Lynden Miller at the Conservatory Garden in Central Park, New York. Here cool lavender-blue Perovskia and the garnet foliage of barberry catch the eye in a border of interesting foliages.

THE AMERICAN CLIMATE

Novice gardeners quickly get the idea that our American climate does not always cooperate with the garden plans they may have in mind. No matter where you want to cultivate a garden, nature has its arsenal of regional irritations to challenge and frustrate. Accept them and learn how to deal with the local climate. (We can take comfort in the fact that even the moderate climate of the British Isles has its shortcomings.)

Until recently, the general trend in American horticulture has been to introduce superior varieties developed in Europe. Often these European varieties just can't stand up to the rigors of North American continental climates. By the dog days of summer they are no longer decorative, showing crisp, brown-edged or disease-damaged foliage. It's hard to believe that many of these specially selected plants are derived from native American species to begin with. English hybrid phlox are a prime example; their susceptibility

In late summer, the fragrant Oriental lily 'Uchida' captures the leading role among a mass of Anemone hupehensis *and* Aconitum *'Sparks Variety'. The author's garden.*

to mildew, among other problems, makes them difficult candidates in many regions. A notable exception, however, is *Rudbeckia fulgida* 'Goldsturm', one of the finest perennials available today, which was taken to Germany and improved there, then brought back to us. But at last, Americans are developing selections more suited to American climates.

THE REGIONAL NATURE OF AMERICAN GARDENS

Climatic conditions vary greatly across the North American continent, depending on latitude, elevation, and other geographical factors. Temperatures vary from north to south and across the continent according to proximity to such large bodies of water as the oceans and the Great Lakes. These bodies of water keep local temperatures warmer in winter and cooler in summer. Thus coastal areas have more moderate climates than inland areas like the Midwest, which experiences bitterly cold winters and very hot summers. A distinctly moderate maritime climate prevails on the West Coast, because weather for North America tends to move across the continent from the west, carrying the climatic influence of the Pacific Ocean quite far inland.

Remarkable in this respect are the mild winter temperatures in Vancouver, British Columbia, which allow the growth of certain palms and other subtropicals.

Elevation influences climate too. Higher elevations in any region tend to assume climatic conditions that prevail farther north, with cooler summers and colder winters. Humidity is often lower as well. For example, the mountain climate around Asheville, North Carolina, is remarkably similar to that in the vicinity of Philadelphia many miles farther north, but with less sticky summers.

In addition to temperature differences, the time of seasonal change varies. In the South, depending on location, spring may come from 1 to 1½ months earlier than I experience here in Philadelphia, while the same flowers may come into bloom as much as a month later to the north in New England. Inland, away from the coast in western Pennsylvania, winters are much more severe and spring comes later, just as it does farther north. The process works in reverse in the autumn. Southern areas have a growing season that is longer on both ends. Late spring or early fall frosts can significantly shorten the growing season and are particularly damaging to tender, young spring growth. Local geography often creates isolated frost pockets. At night, cold air settles into the bottom of a valley or collects at the bottom of a slope. These low areas also tend to be colder in winter.

Not all areas are suited to mixed flower gardens as described in this book, but good results can be achieved in most areas. The following comments describe the climate of each region in only the most general terms. In each region different advantages and limitations prevail.

The Mid-Atlantic

The Mid-Atlantic states have something in common with the climates of many other regions. Here in the Philadelphia area where I garden, we endure hot, humid and muggy summers often coupled with periods of drought. Where a continuous summer display is desired these conditions can be a challenge to both the gardener and the plants. Many early-summer perennials mature quickly in the heat, passing out of bloom and leaving a "bloom gap" before late summer varieties reach their peak. Annuals help to fill this gap with their continuous summer bloom.

Our winters are cold enough to satisfy the dormancy requirements of most hardy plants, but warm enough to enable a remarkable number of more southern varieties to survive. Local arboreta and botanic gardens have long been known for the richness of their collections, because few regions of North America are suited to growing such a wide range of plants from the North, South and West.

The Northeast

New England gardeners enjoy summers somewhat cooler and moister than those of the Mid-Atlantic. Early perennials overlap with late ones, closing the bloom gap. Delicate, heat-sensitive annuals persist into summer, making rich and varied flower garden displays easier to achieve. Fall displays are cut short by early frosts. Spring is condensed, and spring flowers, which in other regions might be early, mid-, or late-season come into bloom simultaneously. A few plants suffer from the lack of heat, and others can't endure the harsh winters. Most perennials and bulbs, however, are remarkably hardy and thrive, particularly with a snow cover.

The Southeast

Here the mild winters offer great opportunities for winter interest and bloom. In more southern areas, frost-tolerant annuals such as pansies and calendulas can be planted in autumn for bloom all winter long. Spring begins early, allowing an extended progression of spring and early summer bloom. The long period of summer heat makes the selection of heat-tolerant perennials and annuals essential to close the potential bloom gap. Tender varieties unsuitable for the North augment the display. The cool, mild days of autumn foster a long show of such late-blooming varieties of perennials as asters, chrysanthemums and salvias, as well as late-sown annuals. Many plants that withstand full sun in the North require partial or light shade in the heat of the South.

The Midwest

The harsh climate of the midwestern states might seem a real challenge to flower gardeners, but many familiar perennials, such as species of *Rudbeckia, Liatris* and *Echinacea*, are actually native to the prairies. Quite a few perennial nurseries are located in this region, noted for its deep, rich soils. These natives and many other perennials are perfectly hardy and easily endure the cold winters and hot, humid summers. Many annuals thrive here and are useful to fill the summer bloom gap. Many hardy spring-flowering bulbs, such as tulips, thrive as well.

The midwestern climate is characterized by dramatic temperature swings, not only from season to season but often within a single season. During winter, mulches are recommended to moderate soil temperatures and reduce frost heaving. Late spring frosts are common and measures such as delayed removal of mulch and late pruning can be useful to reduce damage.

The Pacific Northwest

The climate of the Pacific Northwest can be compared with the maritime climate of much of Western Europe, although summers are generally without rain with low humidity. The cooler summers in the coastal areas provide an enviable climate for gardening without much of a bloom gap. Winters are mild and wet, with long springs and autumns.

In most areas summer irrigation is essential for flower gardening. Irrigation systems are also used to provide an afternoon misting to temper the dry winds that can singe and dehydrate foliage. Inland, beyond the coastal mountain ranges, summers become progressively hotter, winters colder, and the climate drier, which narrows the range of flowers that can flourish.

California

In California, flower gardening using many of the plants described in this book is possible from the regions around San Francisco north, particularly in the coastal areas. But intense dry heat inland is a limitation in some parts of the state.

With the mild winters of coastal areas and the coming of the winter rainy season, fall becomes a planting season of its own. Many annuals, commonly grown in summer elsewhere, such as nasturtium, calendula, Iceland poppy and the native California poppy, thrive under these conditions. Winter annuals such as pansies are a must for the months of bloom they provide.

Many perennials and woody plants do not perform well without sufficient winter cold to satisfy their dormancy requirements, particularly in southern California. The year-round moderate temperatures of coastal areas change the behavior of other perennials. They may continue to bloom almost year 'round, but last for only a year or two before they exhaust themselves; they function as annuals or short-lived perennials.

In spite of these limitations, the unique Mediterranean climate offers a range of flower garden plants unequaled elsewhere in North America. Many other desirable varieties from Australia, South Africa and southern Europe can be substituted for those that can't be grown in California, offering a wonderful opportunity to the creative gardener.

Irrigation is essential to flower gardens (as discussed in this book) anywhere in this state. Unfortunately, water shortages are increasing in frequency, as demand for this limited resource grows. Future restrictions on water use may mandate the planting of xerophytic gardens, those that make use of plants with lower water requirements.

The Southwest

In very hot and dry regions such as Arizona, New Mexico, Nevada, Utah and much of Texas, flower gardens as outlined in this book are not very suitable and too much in conflict with the climate. I cannot in good conscience recommend flower gardens and lawns for these climates. Water is already critically limited in these regions.

Xerophytic gardens, using plants adapted to arid climates, are a responsible and environmentally sound alternative. Such gardens require much lower maintenance and can be very exciting with a range of uniquely beautiful ornamental plants, whether they be native or from climatically similar regions around the world. In the Southwest, xerophytic gardens achieve a dramatic harmony with the natural landscape.

YOUR CLIMATE CAN WORK FOR YOU

Whatever your region, climatic conditions will limit the range of plants you can grow. It may be too hot, too cold, too dry or yes, even too wet. There are plants, however, that will thrive in every region. Local gardeners, nurseries, horticultural societies and botanical gardens can advise which varieties do best under local conditions. Another approach is to look to the native plants adapted to local conditions. Not all natives make good garden plants, but many simply haven't been given a good try yet.

Wherever you live and garden, mixed plantings of annuals, perennials, bulbs and other flowering plants most adapted to your climate will give the broadest interest and a long bloom season to your garden. The combinations will also diversify the care of your garden throughout the seasons. Of course, the result will be much more successful and fulfilling if you know a little about what you are doing. That's what this book is all about.

June is the best month for lush perennial displays in sunny gardens in much of North America, but integrating annuals helps to maintain an abundance of bloom through the heat of summer.

Your Flower Garden

Before planting a flower garden or making any other changes to your landscape, it is important to evaluate your property for light, soil, climatic conditions and general layout. This includes the location and types of trees present, and the topography of the site, including the position of your house. Think about the design possibilities your property offers and how to use them in an exciting way.

EVALUATING LIGHT AND PLANT NEEDS

Both trees and buildings affect light in a given location. As the sun moves, shade patterns shift. Light can vary even within the space of a few feet. As you look over your property, identify north, south, east and west. When are certain areas sunny? At what times do changes occur? Keep in mind that the angle of the sun changes from spring to fall, and that some locations are much sunnier early in the season because of the absence of leaves on the trees. All these factors influence how well individual plants will do in a given place, and how decorative they will be throughout the year.

Most books divide plants into three groups according to their light requirements: full sun, part shade and full shade. I find it very useful to add two additional categories, part sun and deciduous shade.

"Part sun" means that even though the garden might receive direct sun most of the day, there is some shade cast for part of the time. For example, a garden may get direct sun from 10:00 in the morning until 5:00 in the afternoon, but surrounding trees or buildings block the sun in early morning and late afternoon. "Full sun" exists in a situation such as an open field with wide horizons where no blockage of direct sun occurs. In my experience, most varieties described as requiring full sun in other books will also grow in part sun, but there are a few that will not.

This is how light requirements are defined:

○ Full Sun: Direct sun all day.
◑ Part Sun: From 4 to 6 hours of direct sun.
◐ Part Shade: Less than 4 hours of direct sun, bright high shade or dappled filtered shade.
● Full Shade: No direct sun or bright light; this is dense shade.
◫ Deciduous Shade: Under trees and shrubs that lose their leaves in winter, allowing sun to shine through.

In hot climates morning sun is preferred because it is cooler and reduces heat stress. Most part sun or shade plants will keep a fresher look through the summer when situated out of the hot afternoon sun. They will also be a bit more drought tolerant. Many plants that do best with full sun in the North require part sun or part shade in the South. If you have a plant that looks beaten up and burned in summer, try moving it to a cooler location with more shelter.

No single factor influences the character of a garden more than light. The amount of light dictates what types of plants will grow in a given location. If you want lots of color, you've got to garden in the sun. Sunny gardens, requiring a minimum of four hours of direct sun, offer the greatest possibilities for creative use of color. Although sunny gardens require more maintenance than those in the shade, the result is more than worth the extra effort.

Maintenance should begin with good spring preparation and a mulch to help control weeds

Texture and form assume greater importance in shade. Here bold hosta foliage is backed by the flowers and foliage of climbing hydrangea in a southern Vermont garden.

through the summer. Most plantings require periodic grooming, which includes deadheading (removal of spent flowers) and some staking to maintain order. A certain amount of dividing and replanting of perennials is also necessary, usually during the dormant season. Sometimes dividing is necessary to rejuvenate old clumps (see page 130), but more often, in my garden, it is just because a plant has gotten too large and is crowding its neighbors. I call this policing, the control of unruly or bully plants. No two plants have the same vigor, and sooner or later one begins to spread and overgrow another. Unless you want a monoculture, you've got to get in there and put the offender back into place, dividing and removing the extra. Try to choose the best-behaved varieties and avoid the unruly, spreading ones.

THE NATURE OF SHADE GARDENS

For those people who think gardens in shade have no appeal, I ask: Where would you rather be during the searing heat of summer—out in the sun or keeping cool in the shade? The sad thing is, many people think that they can't grow anything in shade. Remember, there is something to grow in every location.

It is true that shady gardens generally have less bright color. The look is different, more soothing and tranquil, a combination of foliage with some bloom. A wide variety of foliage can be quite dramatic and remarkably colorful. Another appeal of shady gardens is that they usually require lower maintenance. Groundcover-type plants are used in larger groups. Weeds are thus often crowded out, and those that do appear grow less vigorously. Most shade plants don't require staking. Fewer flowers means minimal deadheading, and in fact many types of seed heads have a decorative value of their own, which is more likely to be judged acceptable in a casual, shady setting. The primary effect of foliage lasts all summer. Winter and spring cleanup can be reduced by the greater use of the natural mulch of leaves, quite in keeping with a woodland setting. Even in shade gardens some policing eventually becomes necessary. Again, choose plants with good manners and avoid the rambunctious spreaders. The aim is to establish a relatively stable plant community, which does a lot to take care of itself. Simpler maintenance usually means that larger gardens can be maintained in shade than in sun.

GARDENING UNDER TREES

Trees are an asset to any property as long as they are healthy and of desirable types. They lend an atmosphere of establishment to both house and garden, and they provide the benefits of shade. Plants are protected from the sun's intense summer heat. Foliage usually remains fresher through the summer. Drought stress is also less severe. Even though trees deplete water in the soil, plants under deep-rooted trees seem to tolerate drought more easily, because temperatures are cooler in shade where plants don't lose as much water as in full sun. Trees also provide an annual supply of leaves, which can be used as mulch and to improve the soil. When they fall on plantings below, they are right where you need them—no need to carry them in. Leaves are lightweight and easy to move around if necessary, though. (For more information on those leaves most desirable for mulch, see page 125.)

The best kind of shade is high shade. High shade breaks the severity of the sun, but still allows plenty of bright, diffuse light to enter from the side. This kind of shade can be created by removing some of the lower tree branches, "limbing up," as the professionals say. If you have a crowded stand of trees, particularly young trees, thinning some out might also be necessary, but this is considered a last resort. A better approach is to limb up instead of cut down.

Trees may inhibit the growth of certain plants under them. A classic example is the black walnut (*Juglans nigra*), which gives off a chemical poisonous to a wide variety of plants—a severe limitation in the garden.

Tree Roots

The biggest problem with gardening under trees is dealing with tree roots. The roots of some types of trees are shallow and dense, competing mercilessly for water and nutrients. Norway maple and white pine are among the worst. Many plants have difficulty surviving within the root zones of such trees. Oaks and some pines such as loblolly pine are among the more desirable types with deep roots. I remember noticing as a child that the soil under our white pines was

Long-spurred hybrid columbine (Aquilegia) *flowers in mid- to late spring in partially shaded locations.*

always dry and hard. My explanation was that pines made the soil poor and barren. Since then, some of these pines have been removed, and now the same soil stays moist and new plantings thrive, showing good vigor. The only difference is that the pines aren't there to suck up every drop of water instantly.

Understory plants, those that grow in the shade of trees, vary in their tolerance of tree root competition. English ivy is remarkably tolerant of both drought and heavy shade. Pachysandra is a little less drought-tolerant but doesn't climb over everything in sight. Epimediums are more choice and still remarkably tough under these conditions. Many shade plants such as rhododen-

Barrenwort (Epimedium grandiflorum) is a tough perennial for dry shade and flowers in early to mid-spring.

Deep- and Shallow-rooted Trees

DEEP ROOTS:
Carya species (Hickory)
Liriodendron tulipifera (Tulip tree)
Nyssa sylvatica (Black gum)
Quercus species (Oak)

SHALLOW ROOTS:
Abies species (Fir)
Acer platanoides (Norway maple)
Acer saccharinum (Silver maple)
Chamaecyparis species (False cypress)
Fagus species (Beech)
Picea species (Spruce)
Populus species (Poplar)
Tsuga species (Hemlock)
Ulmus americana (American elm)

GROUNDCOVER PLANTS FOR DRY SHADE:
Aster divaricatus (White wood aster)
Epimedium species and hybrids (Barrenwort)
Geranium macrorrhizum (Hardy geranium)
Hedera helix (English ivy)
Sedum ternatum (Stonecrop)
Symphytum grandiflorum (Large-flowered comfrey)
Vancouveria hexandra (American barrenwort)
Vinca minor (Periwinkle)

Double bloodroot (Sanguinaria canadensis 'Multiplex') flowers in early to mid-spring in a woodland garden. Here it grows with false lily-of-the-valley (Maianthemum canadense) and a woodland stonecrop (Sedum ternatum).

dron and hostas vary somewhat in root tolerance, depending on the specific variety you plant. In gardening there are no guarantees—you've got to experiment under your own conditions to find the answers.

Practical Soil Considerations

If you've gardened, you probably have a fairly good idea of your soil conditions. A common and very discouraging situation is where the builder of a development has "stolen" the topsoil from the land before the individual lots were purchased. Approximately 3 or 4 inches were probably spread back on top of the subsoil, but that won't allow much more than grass to grow well. Even so, the soil can be amended and worked with to provide good results. Local gardeners, public gardens and the county extension service can give information about local soil conditions. Also consult the references at the back of this book for additional information.

Most soils are derived from decomposed rock and are made up of clay, silt, sand and humus. The soil scientist's definition of the first three components is based on size and each has advantages and disadvantages in your garden. Clay has the tiniest particles and they are the most fertile because they hold abundant nutrients and moisture. (This is important because nutrients can be washed out by rain and irrigation.) However, clay is very heavy, sticky when too wet and can be difficult to work. Silt particles are larger and form lighter soils with better drainage that are easier to work. Sand is composed of the largest particles, and makes for relatively infertile soil that dries out quickly due to rapid drainage. Most soils are a mixture of these particles and the proportions determine the character of the mixture. Humus is decomposed organic matter. The best soil is a balanced combination of these four components, and is described as loam.

Most cultivated garden plants require high fertility to thrive, but the roots of many have difficulty penetrating heavy clay. When dry, clay soils become very hard and even crack. If worked when too wet they ball up like putty, then dry to concrete hardness with no aeration. When moist and crumbly, clay soils break up nicely into a friable consistency. Proper treatment and the addition of organic matter encourage these fine clay particles to bond together into larger aggregates with improved tilth, the reason clay soils are treated with such care. Gypsum is often recommended for loosening clay soils because it can increase bonding of clay particles into aggregates. This works only with soils high in sodium, which prevents bonding. Gypsum replaces the sodium with calcium, which encourages bonding. Generally, the alkaline soils of the Southwest are helped by gypsum, but it is ineffective on most of the acid clays in many other regions. Check with your local cooperative extension agent. Sandy soils are the opposite of clay; they dry out rapidly and are not as fertile, but they do have advantages. You can work them and plant at any time. Many plants that tend to rot off in hot muggy weather will do quite well on a well-drained, sandy soil. The limited nutrients also seem to strengthen their constitutions because plants adapted to poor soils become too lush, soft and disease-susceptible under highly fertile conditions. Silty soils have properties between the extremes of sand and clay and are easier to manage.

Soil color is not necessarily a good indication of fertility. While humus does tend to stain soils a dark color, the color is much more dependent on the rock from which it was formed. Light-colored soils can be very fertile too. One way to evaluate your soil is to wet a handful to a claylike consistency, knead it and form it into a ball. Then try to roll it in your palms into a long thin rope. This will be easy with a predominantly clay soil, difficult with a silty loam, and impossible with a sandy soil.

Another method is to do a simple settling test. Half-fill a small jar with soil, add some water and a pinch of water softener (such as Calgon, or try some automatic dishwasher detergent, which should also contain water softeners) to break chemical bonds aggregating soil particles. Use your finger to break up all clods, evenly dispersing the particles in the water. Fill the jar with more water, screw on the lid and shake vigorously. Set the jar down and don't move it until all the particles have settled, which could be a couple of days. The soil will settle out in layers, first sand, then silt, and finally clay. The thickness of the layers will indicate soil type. It is best to have similar quantities of each, but few gardeners are so fortunate. Organic matter will stain the water brown and the darker the color, the better.

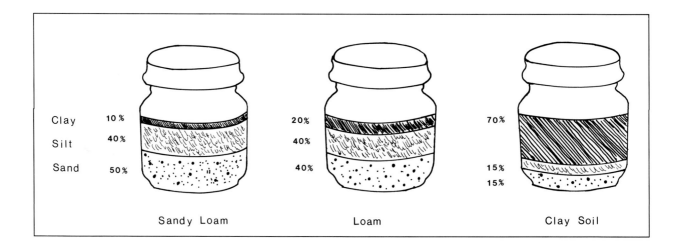

	Sandy Loam	Loam	Clay Soil
Clay	10%	20%	70%
Silt	40%	40%	15%
Sand	50%	40%	15%

Soil Acidity

PH is a measure of acidity and alkalinity, and soil pH affects plant growth. On the pH scale of 1 to 14, 7 is neutral, toward 0 is acid and toward 14 is alkaline. Most soils in North America fall into the range of pH 5 to 9. Arid regions tend to be alkaline and moist regions are generally more acidic (as rain leaches out the alkaline components), but this depends on the rock from which the soils were originally formed. Nutrient availability is affected by pH, with the best balance available in the nearly neutral range of pH 6 to 7. In a shady woodland garden, most suitable plants will be happy in an acid soil, with a pH around 5.5; this is also ideal for rhododendron and azaleas. Acid-loving plants will not grow in an alkaline soil and may eventually become sick when planted near a house or wall that leaches alkaline lime from the mortar into the soil around it. Most sun-loving flower garden plants prefer nearly neutral soil acidity, around pH 6.8, but will also perform well with a mildly alkaline pH up to 7.5 or even higher, depending on the variety.

It is a false savings not to make a soil acidity test and fix your soil before spending money on new plants. Soil tests also provide information on fertility and what fertilizers and nutrients to apply. Tests are available through your local agricultural extension service. Generally you buy a special envelope at a reasonable cost, fill it according to directions and mail it for evaluation by the experts at the agricultural extension.

An easy way to determine the composition of your soil is to shake up a sample with water and a little water softener in a small clear glass jar. (Baby food jars are ideal.) The soil particles settle in layers, first the large sand particles, then the silt and finally the very fine clay particles.

Drainage and Soil Moisture

Slopes by their very nature are well drained, even though the soil may be heavy clay. Beds in flat areas may be well drained, depending on the permeability of the soil, especially the subsoil. Lilies, therefore, notorious for requiring good drainage, may or may not thrive in a level bed. Note how long water sits in puddles on the bed in question after a rain. Puddles should disappear in about half a day.

In areas of poor drainage, plan your garden with raised beds and plants that will tolerate the marshy conditions elsewhere. A raised bed is built up higher than the surrounding soil level, to encourage good drainage; although it can be a simple mound of soil, it is usually surrounded by stones, logs or other material to hold the soil in place. Raised beds built over moist soil are somewhat self-watering, because the root tips of your plants can grow down into the moisture while their crowns remain well drained. However, poorly drained does not necessarily mean always moist, and these areas might dry out during the summer. If you do build raised beds, try to design them to tie in visually with something else in the landscape, such as backing them up to a fence or shrub planting, so they don't stick out like sore thumbs.

Soil is usually moister at the bottom of a slope because water percolates downward. Slopes are not, however, always dry. Underlying rock formations may bring percolating water to the surface on the slope. The requirements of moist and well drained need not always be a contradiction, because a moist spot on a slope may still have excellent drainage.

Organic Matter and Soil Preparation

Whatever your soil condition, organic matter in the form of compost, leaf mold and peat are the best soil conditioners. Peat, though widely available, is less desirable because it is not very nutritious. My best advice is, start composting your leaves and weeds right away. It is difficult to overdo it with compost. It loosens clay, and holds nutrients and moisture in sand. Generally, it makes soils more friable and loamy. Unfortunately, organic matter is not a permanent addition and needs to be continually replaced. Work it in deeply and often. In a permanent planting that can't be constantly dug up, add it to the top and let the worms and bugs carry it down in.

The best time to begin preparing the soil is in late summer or fall. Not only is there more time than in spring, but the soil is usually not too wet to work. Another advantage to fall is that the newly prepared beds have all winter to settle.

Be sure to adjust the pH while turning over the soil. The best soil acidifiers are powdered sulfur and iron sulfate (also called ferrous sulfate or copperas). Aluminum sulfate is less desirable if used often because aluminum can build up to levels toxic to some plants. Very acid soil can be moderated with pulverized limestone. (Hydrated lime is fast acting but short lived, therefore not as good.) Lime, in particular, is much more effective when worked into the soil, as it takes so long to migrate down from the surface. Your soil test will tell you how much to apply.

As a consolation for less-than-perfect soil, keep in mind that many plants are remarkably adaptable, so most gardeners can get away without making management of their soils an exact science. All gardens present a challenge to some plants. There are plants that seem to resent rich soils and pampering and may very well do better for a beginner under less than ideal circumstances. Gardeners have to experiment and endure the occasional failure to find the plants that grow best for them. But one thing is for sure: The more plants you try, the more you will find to fill your garden (and the more you will be the envy of your friends).

CLIMATIC CONSIDERATIONS

Choosing plants suited to your garden's climatic conditions is critical to success. Measures can be taken to improve the survival of less hardy varieties but they require extra effort. The most important factor in plant survival is cold hardiness. The plant's ability to survive the coldest temperatures that may occur in a particular area is rated in hardiness zones. (See the USDA Plant Hardiness Map, pages 234–235.) Other factors can influence hardiness, including the duration of the cold, the speed with which the temperature changes, and such conditions as wind and sun.

The duration of a cold spell can mean the difference between an undamaged plant and a severely damaged one. For instance, the mountains of western North Carolina have similar low temperatures when compared with eastern Pennsylvania, and yet certain plants grow more easily there. The cold spells tend not to last as long at that more southern latitude. Rapid temperature changes cause more damage because the plant's cells don't have the time they need to prepare for the change. This applies to both chilling and warming. To prevent deadly freezing, the cells separate some of the water from the protoplasm into side pockets called "glaciers," where it can freeze safely. This decreases the freezing temperature of the cell, using the same principle as antifreeze in your car. When temperatures rise, the protoplasm reabsorbs this water. If temperatures rise too quickly, this water may be lost, and the cells become dehydrated and die.

Sudden temperature changes occur from rapid changes in the air, but also from the effect of winter sun. After a cold night, bright sun in early morning can warm plant parts in a few minutes and cause serious damage. Evergreen shrubs planted on the eastern side of a house are particularly vulnerable. They will suffer considerably less if evergreen trees provide winter shade. Herbaceous plants are easily protected from rapid changes simply by being mulched.

Dehydration is often a problem for woody plants in exposed windy locations. During extreme cold weather plants experience greater difficulty moving water up from the roots to the stems and leaves. Wind increases the drying effect. The problem is relieved somewhat by mulch to keep the roots warmer so they can function more effectively.

Winter sun and wind are good reasons to place burlap around young shrubs. Burlap breaks the destructive force of both. Evergreen branches can be used for the same purpose, either laid over the top or stuck into the ground around the tender plant to shade and protect the foliage. Mature, well-established plants are acclimatized and have deep root systems. They are better able to withstand stressful variations in the weather than young plants. They also tend to have a slower growth rate, which allows them to harden off their tissues more thoroughly before winter.

Just as cold is a problem up North, lack of cold is a problem down South. Winter-hardy plants usually have a chilling requirement that must be satisfied before the plant can grow normally again in the spring. This mechanism prevents a plant from breaking into growth during a warm spell in midwinter, with disastrous consequences. The requirement is different for each type of plant and variety. (In the laboratory the requirement for each can be defined as the number of hours required below a specific temperature.) The chilling requirement is often the reason many perennials and woody plants cannot be grown in southern climates, such as Florida and southern California. Some southern nurseries sell precooled bulbs. This works for tulips but, unfortunately, not for daffodils, which need

to grow roots in the soil before chilling begins. Southern gardeners must choose daffodil varieties that have minimal chilling requirements.

Hardiness ratings in this book are based on the USDA Plant Hardiness Map of the United States (pages 234–235). Both the northern and southern hardiness zone limits are given for most plants in this book. These ratings are approximate, depending on local conditions as explained above. With extra care and careful siting, hardiness can often be extended by an additional zone.

Summer Temperatures and Heat Tolerance

In the North, some plants are able to survive the winter but don't receive enough summer heat to complete their growth cycle. Either the growing season is too short or the average temperatures are too cool. Tomatoes, for example, are more difficult to grow in the North. Several years ago I was given an aster variety that blooms magnificently in early November in Atlanta, Georgia. It blooms in November here in Philadelphia too, but the weather is usually too cold for the flowers to open well.

A more common problem for flower gardeners is summer heat intolerance. This is more of a problem for ornamentals than for crops. A crop might show some superficial heat stress on the upper leaves but still produce well. In a garden setting, this damage to the upper leaves could destroy the plant's ornamental value. The combination of high temperatures and hot sun causes even higher leaf temperatures, resulting in dried leaves. This is the reason that many plants require more shade in the South than in the North. Some plants can't be grown in areas with hot summers. The famed Himalayan blue poppy (*Meconopsis betonicifolia*) simply will not grow except where summers are cool, as they are in the Pacific Northwest and the mountains of New England. Many primroses do not grow well in the South. They tend to rot off in the heat of summer, even when grown in the shade. Heat-tolerant strains are being selected by a few nurseries and are proving to be tough perennials for the South.

Microclimates

Obviously a plant adapted to shade should not be planted in full sun. Still, subtle factors such as those just discussed combine to create a microclimate unique to each location. Microclimates may change with a distance of only a few feet as trees, buildings and topography influence light, air movement (wind) and temperature.

South-facing sites tend to be warmer and drier as they receive the most direct sun for the longest period. Spring comes earlier to these locations, and this can increase the danger of damage from late spring frosts. During winter, there is danger of sunburn during cold weather unless plants are shaded.

North-facing sites are cooler and moister. They receive less direct sun but, if unshaded, lots of bright, indirect light. Winter temperatures are colder, but plants are protected from the harsh sun, although winds are likely to be more severe. Summer heat is less of a problem.

East-facing sites are prone to damage from winter sun in the morning after a cold night. In summer, heat-sensitive plants have the advantage of the cooler morning sun. Because it is cooler, it is moister.

West-facing sites are better for many tender plants than an eastern location. The west slope is the last to absorb the sun's heat, which is then radiated during the night to provide valuable protection against extreme cold. In the morning, plants are protected from the early sun and can warm up slowly.

Topography also influences temperature. Cold air drains off slopes and settles in such low places as valleys. These "frost pockets" are more subject to early fall and late spring frosts and are colder in winter.

DESIGN

There is no magic rule to determine whether a garden is or should be formal or otherwise. Don't let it hang you up. There are degrees of formality. Before we take the discussion further, let's look at the differences.

A formal garden is generally symmetrical, whether the lines be straight or curved. Strong structural features such as terracing, walls, hedges, and walks and paths add weight and definition. Focal points such as a statue or pot—something nonvegetable—are centered, and serve to draw the eye to a point to accentuate the symmetry of the design. Such structural details can require a good bit of initial work and expense to set up, but if properly designed can help to reduce routine maintenance.

An informal garden is usually asymmetrical and composed of curved lines. If balance is desired it can be achieved by the juxtaposition of various elements (plants, pots, benches and the like). Focal points are usually placed off center; one might get away with drawing the eye to some sort of plant or tree trunk, although it will probably be less effective than a nonplant feature, which would make for better contrast against the mass of other plants. Informal designs are often easier to implement because they can usually be allowed to follow the irregularities of the land and use its natural character to advantage.

The big question is, what's right for you? If you are a highly organized individual who prefers your surroundings to be in order, a design with strong definition may feel most comfortable. Or, perhaps you find that formality just feels too straitlaced and mechanical. Your life-style is more casual and you find an informal garden more relaxing. Informal designs tend to appeal to the gardener with a greater interest in the plants themselves than the design. If the budget is tight, an informal type of design can be less expensive. An indication of the kind of garden appropriate for you is the character of your house. The house and garden should complement each other. More about the relationship of house and garden follows.

Divided Gardens

Unless your garden or property is practically the size of a postage stamp, it probably has more than one section to it. Many people have a backyard and a front yard separated by the house. It is unlikely that you would treat both of these areas in the same way even if the conditions were the same. Various features of the house or the location of trees or shrubs on the property may indicate other logical or natural divisions such as a side yard, a patio, a courtyard, or a subdivision of one of the larger areas. Form, function and use help define different garden areas. These divisions provide opportunities for creating different types of gardens. One might be shady, another sunny. One might be primarily a decorative area viewed through a window, another used for outdoor sitting, and another larger area primarily for recreational use. An important division is a secluded work area for compost, firewood, storage and whatever else.

The value and effectiveness of the various divisions is often increased by separating them even more distinctly. Decorative gardens may need to be protected from recreational areas by a fence—not a chain-link fence, but something that is both attractive and functional. You may want to enclose a garden more completely to in-

The curved path gives focus to this informal residential garden as it disappears among the trees, in Oregon.

crease privacy or develop a theme without the distraction of surrounding areas. Seclusion increases the intimacy of a spot. Hedges, fences, walls and mixed shrub plantings can help to achieve this.

The gentry of England and Europe could afford to build walls, and build they did. On their grand estates they enclosed the kitchen gardens to trap heat, which allowed earlier and later crops of fruits and vegetables. In the cool climate of England, this often made enough of a difference that crops requiring higher summer temperatures could be grown. As times changed, many of these kitchen gardens were converted to flower gardens with the same advantages of a warmer microclimate. In the more distant past, walls served the purpose of protection from enemies and wild animals (ferocious wild animals such as wolves, not the deer that confound many homeowners today). Walled gardens were a place of refuge.

In most parts of North America, save for the northernmost parts, walled gardens don't work like this. Ferocious animals don't roam in most areas and the heat factor works the other way. I have vivid memories of a visit to a walled garden one hot July day several years ago. It was a rather good example of the Sissinghurst style that I was delighted to visit, but really, in the heat all I could think of was getting out of there! The high walls had trapped the heat and cut down on air circulation. Top it off with our typical high humidity and you have a steam bath.

Many plants don't like these steam baths either. In addition to heat stress, the reduced air circulation increases the incidence of all-too-common diseases. If you live in an area of high winds, walls can be more of a problem than a solution. Solid structures can increase wind velocity as it whips around them; the most effective windbreaks allow some air to pass through them while reducing the speed. City gardens have similar problems with wind and heat, but at least tall buildings cast some cooling shade. If I had a garden surrounded by high walls in the South, I think I'd be tempted to lock it up for the summer rather than brave the heat.

By now you may think I disapprove of all garden walls on this side of the Atlantic. Not true. There is no substitute for a good wall in the right situation. Effective walls need not create an enclosure or impeded air circulation. They might be merely the side of a house or other building, or be built out on an angle from such a structure. Fences can serve the same function. Walls and fences provide vertical spaces on which to train roses, various shrubs, and such vines as clematis and honeysuckles. (For more about training shrubs and vines on walls, see Chapter 5.)

Walls are great for creating microclimates. South-facing walls, although hotter in summer, shelter tender plants in winter. North-facing walls are cooler all summer because little direct sun reaches them. Plants of borderline winter hardiness especially benefit from west- or southwest-facing walls; they stay warmer all night because they absorb the last of the sun's rays late in the day, but are not subject to the damaging rapid warming of the morning sun.

High walls are not common features in America and there are many other ways to divide a garden that are more suitable to our climate. In the South, low walls that still allow air to

circulate are common. Open or pierced walls, designed with built-in spaces between the bricks, allow air to pass through. For additional height a lattice can be attached to the top of a low wall.

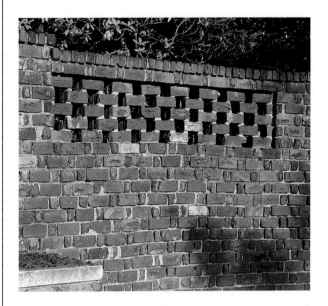

Pierced or honeycombed walls allow air circulation in hot, humid climates while providing enclosure and privacy.

Vegetable Masonry

Peter Thoday, a distinguished English horticulturist and landscape designer, describes plantings used in place of structural elements as "vegetable masonry." The best example would be a hedge used in place of a wall. I prefer evergreens for vegetable masonry because they function more fully as a strong design element than deciduous plants during the winter. Deciduous plants within the garden are most effectively displayed against the rich evergreen background. Vegetable masonry need not be so rigid as a straight-sided hedge. An unclipped row of holly or arborvitae would serve a similar purpose, but must be allowed space to grow. For a more informal effect a mixed shrub border will serve the same function. It can be planned to provide a long progression of seasonal interest by careful selection of different varieties. Such a planting will usually require more space than a single row of plants but will make better use of it.

Naturalized Plantings

"Naturalizing" means using plants in the landscape in such a way that they appear to have grown there naturally, as if Nature had planted them herself. Plants in nature are usually spaced irregularly and in large numbers. Both native and nonnative plants can be used in this way. One of the most well-known and successful types of plants for naturalizing are daffodils, native to Europe. They are most often planted in grass or in woodlands, but also integrate well into meadows.

Naturalized and meadow plantings do not fit within the definition of flower gardening in the scope of this book, due to their larger scales. However, they can provide an excellent background for a garden, helping to create, enhance, or tame a rural setting.

Planning Gardens in Your Landscape

Take a lesson from your house. Unity of design between house and garden is fostered by a similarity of character. You will need to understand the relationship between house and garden to develop an overall scheme for your property. You needn't make a formal master plan, but you should have a sense of what you want to do where. Many of my clients find it interesting to walk around the rooms of their homes with me and look out their windows. Often the design needs and priorities of the garden become defined from the inside of the house. As you look out a window, think of it as a picture in a frame. Be sure to look out from the most important locations in the room. Which are the most important windows? Where do people sit? What is the first view seen on entering the room? Compose the picture in the window from these vantage points.

Using these criteria, you will discover some interesting things about the relationship of house and garden. For example, you might find that you can design your front garden to be attractive from the living room as well as from the street. Outside another room the shady side of the house may be the perfect site for a woodland type of garden with a focal point needed on the far right. The back lawn, although used for recreation and summer entertaining, may be more attractive with shrub and groundcover plantings around the edge. On one side there may be an ideal spot for a small flower border, which would be the focus of the view from the kitchen window, above the sink—someting pretty to see while you prepare meals. Of course, not all schemes can be achieved by the use of plants alone. Some structural elements such as fences, walls or grading may be wanted.

Themes and Locations

Certain gardens lend themselves to particular locations, depending on their purpose and season of use. A typical example would be a cutting garden intended only for providing cut flowers and not for show in itself. Cutting gardens are traditionally located in isolated sections of the garden where there is little concern about decimating the display when all the best flowers are cut. (Most home gardens today don't have the luxury of space for separate cutting gardens, but most flower gardens provide enough for indoors, too.)

A garden of summer flowers might be located near or within view of an outdoor living area. If cleverly placed, it will not be noticeable from inside the house during winter, when many people consider empty herbaceous beds to be unsightly. (I don't share this opinion as many perennials can boast winter interest too.) In another plan, the summer garden might be placed away from the house and screened by a hedge to be enjoyed on a summer stroll or from a secluded garden bench, but be unnoticed in winter when it is seldom visited.

A winter garden with flowers and seasonal interest during the colder months should be located where it is easily enjoyed without the need for long excursions out into the cold. The fragrance of October-blooming osmanthus and February-blooming witch hazel are pleasant surprises near a frequently used door or pathway at these seasons. Outside a window, a mass of the first snowdrops and crocuses will attract attention during

The flower garden is an important part of this living room.

important views? Are deciduous shrubs with winter interest such as witch hazel backed by evergreens to highlight them to best advantage? Many of us live in climates where we spend half the year looking at the winter landscape, so it ought to be pleasing!

Now look at the relationship between the various landscape elements and how they work together. Consider the shapes of the shrub plantings, the flower beds and the lawn. They should fit together like a puzzle. Do these shapes present a harmonious pattern in your garden? All too often the beds have a nice shape but the lawn has become merely an afterthought, filling whatever space is left. If the curves of the lawn are smoothed out it might also improve the shape of the flower beds or shrub borders. Often the lawn is actually the center of the whole design. When it has an awkward shape it destroys the unity of the whole landscape. It is not the square footage of the lawn, but the shape and how it relates to other elements that is critical.

Flower Garden Size

The size of the garden you are contemplating depends on how much time you can spend on it. If you have a shady property, you will be able to care for a larger area of garden space. If you have sun, a more intensive display of color located in a prime spot will have a big impact.

Inexperienced gardeners are best starting out small, expanding as their experience grows. They might experiment with a small bed of about 50 square feet (5 × 10 feet). For those with a little experience, I would recommend planting a flower garden of about 100 square feet. If this sounds a bit large, consider that it will allow you to make a good start using groups of plants without crowding them. Proper spacing is very important for success. Narrow beds—less than 2 feet—seldom work with perennials, unless they are all small varieties, because you can't include enough of them to achieve continuous bloom.

If time and experience are not such critical factors and this is not your first time around, the considerations are somewhat different. For

late winter. Holly berries last through fall into winter and attract birds to the winter landscape.

The farther away a garden feature is located from the viewer, the bolder it must be. Several daffodils up close must be expanded by several dozen if planted on the far side of the lawn to achieve a similar impact. Brighter colors are helpful in creating impact from a distance, but lighter colors will tend to increase the sense of distance. Distant color can be strengthened by use of a contrasting background.

The real proof of a well-conceived landscape is not its appearance in summer, but how it looks in winter. Without the distractions of color and lush foliage the proportions of the major elements of the landscape become fully exposed.

Are you happy with the proportions of evergreen and deciduous trees and shrubs? Are the evergreens strategically placed to hide the neighbor's trash cans and firewood from your most

dramatic effect, you can't beat a spacious bed as much as 12 or even 15 feet deep! This has space for some really striking large perennials and shrubs at the back and room for the smaller flowers at the front. It seems a daunting amount of space initially, but remember that those big plants at the back take quite a bit of space, each one spreading 4 or even 5 feet at maturity. (Spread and spacing distances are given for each variety in the plant reference section, and are explained on page 139.) There won't be room for many of them. You will spend most of your time taking care of the front strip, but the effect will be so much grander than a narrow bed. I've created and cared for some gardens with narrow beds and others with beds 15 feet deep. I can attest to the additional creative and artistic potential of the deeper beds. My own formal perennial beds are about 8 feet deep and at times I yearn to add another 2 feet.

In the shade the beds might be less rigid, and can be a bit larger. Whereas in the sun beds might have more defined shapes such as islands or borders, in the shade you might find it easier to create beds around and among existing shrubs

A small flower border of about 200 square feet, in July, with Coreopsis verticillata *'Grandiflora' at its center.*

and trees, integrating these elements into the design to provide structure. These mature trees and shrubs will immediately lend an air of maturity to the garden.

Whether you garden in sun or shade, the beds can be as formally or informally laid out as you wish. The final consideration for the size and shape of your flower garden is what is right for your property. It should fit in with other structural and landscape features of the property and enhance your use of the place. If you have difficulty making such decisions, a landscape designer or architect can be very helpful to set you on the right track.

Whatever your inspiration and enthusiasm, don't begin work until you set priorities and decide how much you can handle at a time. A little restraint will prevent the frustration of an unfinished project. One of the advantages of visualizing your property in sections is that you can concentrate on one section at a time. Start with

This grand late-spring border is about 15 feet deep.

The same border as shown on page 28, in May with two old-fashioned perennials, Paeonia officinalis *'Rubra Plena' and* Iris *'Loreley'.*

the section that is most important or interesting. It often makes sense to tackle a different section each year. Far more effort is required to create a new garden than to maintain and police an established one. Once one section is established, there will be time available to do another. Before long, the entire property will have become a garden.

This chapter has discussed in very general terms how to understand your property. It is not my purpose to instruct you how to landscape your yard, but rather explain how to create and manage a flower garden within your landscape and provide some guidance in its placement. The following chapters focus on the flower gardens themselves and what happens within the beds.

The bearded Iris 'Loreley' was hybridized in Germany around the turn of the century. Although not as large-flowered as the modern hybrids, it is an excellent garden plant with greater disease resistance and holds its flowers up without staking.

THREE

Knowing Your Garden Plants

Once the location and size of your flower beds have been determined, it is time to think about their content. For most of us, this is where the fun begins. It seems the more you learn, the wider the range of possibilities becomes.

The success of your flower garden will depend on your understanding of plants and how to select them for your conditions. There is no substitution for experience in your own garden, but you need some basics to get started. This chapter is about all the different kinds of plants, how they grow and how to use them in your garden to achieve succession of bloom throughout the season.

Garden design is discussed in the next chapter, but an overview will be helpful here. At the back of the border belong the biggest and most permanent plants (this is true for the middle of an island bed), and progressively smaller plants work toward the front (or outer edge). The big plants tend to be the dominant elements. Larger plants are usually used in small numbers; they allow less flexibility in design and placement. Group plants of moderate size next to the largest, and finally, fill in the front (or edge) with groups of the smallest varieties. When reading about the various types of plants, try to visualize how they might fit together in a design.

The object of good design is to create a dynamic community of plants that grow together harmoniously, each flowering or performing in turn. A good understanding of the different types of plants will enable you to create tightly knit associations, often within the same space, for multiple bloom seasons or spectacular combinations of flowers and foliage together.

SHRUBS

Shrubs can be the largest and most permanent elements in the flower bed. As with perennials and annuals, their use is based on the maximum size they will naturally achieve or be allowed to achieve. Most commonly, shrubs serve as a background to the flower bed, perhaps as vegetable masonry (see page 25). The background might be visually separate, as in the case of a hedge, or more informal so that the natural shape of the shrub blends with the flowers in the bed to the front. A clean transition from shrubs to herbaceous plants need not be apparent.

When I grow shrubs, perennials and annuals together, I use what I call "flower garden shrubs," shrubs that have qualities similar to

Though spectacular in June, as shown here, the Conservatory Garden at Wave Hill, Bronx, New York, is planted to improve throughout the season, reaching its peak display in September.

those of many perennials. They are summer blooming or very long blooming, of moderate size, and in many cases can be pruned rather severely to force vigorous and floriferous growth. In appearance they resemble perennials, which enables them to blend effectively.

Most flower garden shrubs are fairly tall, and are used at the back of the flower bed with other flowers of similar height. You may wonder, why bother with shrubs if they are so similar to perennials? There are three reasons. First, the selection of midsummer-flowering perennials is more limited than the selection for late spring and early summer. Flower garden shrubs help to fill in this gap. Second, many summer-flowering shrubs often have longer bloom seasons than the average perennial. Third, because of their woody stems, shrubs don't need staking, and most tall perennials do. So, flower garden shrubs can save you work.

One of my favorite flower garden shrubs is the butterfly bush (*Buddleia davidii*) because it blends so well with herbaceous plants. Cut it back severely early each spring to remove weak, twiggy, winter-damaged growth and force strong shoots with larger flowers. I always cut it back to 6 to 12 inches from the ground before growth starts. Spring bulbs such as daffodils, planted among the roots, will grow up and hide the stumps until they sprout out. By midsummer the bushes will be at least 6 feet tall and covered with bloom, attracting scads of butterflies. By planting spring bulbs around the base, you'll have two bloom seasons in one spot.

Shrubs are also a useful source of contrasting foliage color. (For more about foliage color, see page 226.) Choices are limited, but purple, golden, and even silvery foliage shrubs are available. Purple foliage can be a useful accent at the back of the border. Purple-foliaged forms of smoke bush (*Cotinus coggygria*) are especially useful. At Hidcote Manor Garden in England, they even use purple-foliaged Norway maples this way as a background. (It is essential to cut these maples back every spring, or they will outgrow their desired size very quickly, as well as losing some of the intensity of foliage color.) If not cut, the smoke bush may soon reach as much as 15 feet; the maple won't stop until it becomes a tree.

Sambucus nigra 'Aurea' provides a striking background for annual larkspur (Consolida orientalis) at England's Herb Farm, Honeybrook, PA.

A fine-textured Abelia grandiflora is enlivened by the drama of Miscanthus sinensis 'Variegata'.

Flower Garden Shrubs

Abelia ×*grandiflora* (Glossy abelia)

Buddleia davidii (Butterfly bush; some with silvery foliage)

Caryopteris ×*clandonensis* (Bluebeard; some with silvery foliage)

Cotinus coggygria (Smoke bush; purple-foliage forms)

Hibiscus syriacus (Rose of Sharon)

Hydrangea paniculata (Panicle hydrangea)

Lagerstroemia indica (Crape myrtle)

Potentilla fruticosa (Bush cinquefoil)

Sambucus nigra 'Aurea' (Golden European elder)

Sorbaria aitchisonii (Kashmir false spirea)

Vitex agnus-castus (Chaste tree)

The intense blue globes of Allium caeruleum *add another dimension to a golden yellow* Potentilla fruticosa.

Buddleia davidii *'Nanho Blue' and* Cimicifuga racemosa *are made extraordinary with the addition of deep purple foliage of* Cotinus coggygria *'Royal Purple' and a touch of deep blue aconite, at the Central Park Conservatory Garden in July.*

Wall Shrubs

Some people would call these espaliers, but to me, wall shrubs are much more. Espaliers are generally thought of as stiff and angular in their branching, too formal and distracting in some situations. Wall shrubs can also be informal in shape, trained flat but maintaining a seminatural form. In any case, wall shrubs and espaliers are useful as backgrounds to a bed against a wall or fence, and they don't take up much space because they are relatively flat. They also make good companions for vines (see page 104).

The choice of plants suitable as wall shrubs is great indeed. Check the suggested reading list at the back of this book for help in making your selection. My primary criterion for choosing appropriate wall shrubs is that they must not be too softwooded and sucker (send out soft shoots) profusely from the base. Softwooded shrubs need constant training as the old stems die out after a few years and new stems are trained back in their place. The multitude of suckers also keep leaning out toward the light and over plantings in front. Hardwooded shrubs can be trained to have one to five trunks that are relatively permanent. Shrubs can often be trained to greater heights when tied to a wall than when standing on their own; the reason for this is not clearly understood.

ROSES

Roses evoke a special romanticism that can be a part of any flower garden. Even the thorns add a defensive mystique to the overgrown tangle of an old rose smothered with fragrant bloom. Americans have voted the rose their national flower. Sadly, most Americans know only of the labor-intensive, pesticide-dependent modern hybrids. The highly touted, ubiquitous Hybrid Teas, Grandifloras and Floribundas are generally the most susceptible to disease and all too often lead to frustration in the home garden. There are very rewarding alternatives.

The appeal of modern roses is that they have been hybridized to the point that now there is a rose suited to almost any need in whatever color (except blue or black) may be desired. The everblooming nature of the Hybrid Tea, Grandiflora and Floribunda roses (often called bush roses) places them among the longest blooming of garden flowers, lasting from late spring to beyond the first frosts of autumn.

The stronger-wooded shrub roses include a wide range of new and old-fashioned hybrids, as well as many charming unhybridized species. Some are everblooming or repeat blooming, oth-

An eye-catching combination of climbing rose 'Blaze' and meadow rue (Thalictrum speciosissimum) at Old Westbury Garden.

A traditional border backed by climbing roses in June at Old Westbury Mansion and Garden, Long Island, New York.

ers bloom only once, but all are charmers. (Repeat bloomers don't rebloom quite as much as the so-called everbloomers and are usually older varieties, although the line between them is a fine one.) The range of flower forms is extensive, from the small clustered polyanthas or tightly quartered old garden roses, to the large single blooms of 'Golden Wings', a modern hybrid. Disease resistance varies too. Once you have taken the time to become familiar with the many kinds of roses, you will want to grow more than you have room for.

The old-fashioned climbing roses are overshadowed today by the newer everblooming climbers. But the abundant annual display of the older climbers in late spring and early summer is still hard to beat. The New English roses comprise a new hybrid group developed by David Austin in England, only recently available to

Old-fashioned June-blooming climbing roses provide an incomparable background to foxgloves, coralbells and cottage pinks, all of which have grown in this garden for decades. The author's garden, Hedgleigh Spring.

Americans. They combine the charm and fragrance of the old-fashioned roses with the everblooming qualities of the modern hybrids in a broad range of colors and growth habits. In the coming years these new roses will win the hearts of most rose growers.

In spite of the popularity of everblooming varieties, June (May in the South) is still the undisputed month of the rose, the very embodiment of the flower garden. Everbloomers put on their first and greatest splash then. This is the season of most other roses too, including the old-fashioned shrub roses with their exquisite perfume. It is the season of rose-draped arbors tangled with clematis, when shrub roses mingle with perennials in a medley of color, texture and fragrance.

The use of roses in flower garden design depends on their size and growth habit. Hybrid Teas and Grandifloras are not as well suited to the mixed garden with their exhibition-quality flowers atop stiff, gawky plants. Keep them separate, in the cutting garden perhaps. Floribundas blend more comfortably with other members of

'Heritage' is a new English rose that combines the old quartered-flower form and fragrance with the everblooming nature of the modern hybrids. (Photograph by Jack Potter.)

the border, bearing a profusion of clustered flowers on plants with a less stiff habit. Climbing roses and ramblers require the support of a trellis, arbor, fence or wall. Some varieties are also suited to climbing into the branches of a tree for a natural effect.

Place freestanding shrub and bush roses in the border according to their height and spread. The larger shrub roses may reach heights of 8 to 10 feet, and are ideal for use as a background. Standard roses (trained atop a single, long, straight stem) are to be discouraged, in my opinion. Except in very formal situations, they usually stick out like a sore thumb, and are not fully hardy in any but southern regions (Zone 8, south).

Commonsense Roses

If you go in for Hybrid Teas, Grandifloras and Floribundas, be prepared to spray them regularly with fungicides and pesticides and fertilize at least twice a year. (Such care is adequately described in numerous rose books; refer to page 240 for some suggestions.) Otherwise, they won't keep up the display and will become defoliated by midsummer, as they fall victim to such diseases as black spot and mildew. If you live in a region where Japanese beetles are a problem, you will be battling them on the everbloomers for most of the summer. After that, you will have lovely flowers throughout the fall. If Japanese beetles are more than you can cope with, there are two choices. One is to grow only the June-blooming roses, which will be finished by the time the beetles emerge; rely on other flowers for summerlong bloom. The alternative is to keep the everbloomers but give up on summer bloom. Several weeks before the beetle season ends give your everblooming roses a good trimming to

---

A Selection of Disease-resistant Roses

'Alba Semiplena' (old garden rose; white, June blooming, hips in fall)

'Chevy Chase' (rambler; dark crimson, June blooming)

'Frau Dagmar Hastrup' (rugosa; pink, repeat blooming, hips in fall)

'Mermaid' (climber; yellow, everblooming)

'New Dawn' (climber; blushed white, everblooming)

'Perle d'Or' (polyantha; peach, everblooming)

'Sea Foam' (shrub; blushed white, everblooming)

'Stanwell Perpetual' (old garden rose; blushed white, repeat blooming)

'Sunflare' (floribunda; yellow, everblooming)

'The Fairy' (polyantha; light pink, everblooming)

'Westerland' (shrub or climber; orange, everblooming)

Rosa rugosa 'Scabrosa', like most rugosa roses, is very pest and disease resistant and blooms through the summer.

'Westerland' is an everblooming climbing rose with good disease resistance.

force new growth. If properly timed this should result in a second flush of bloom to start off the fall season. Here near Philadelphia, we usually see the last of the beetle populations by the end of August, so I prune early in the month.

Discouraged? Don't be. The new landscape roses, such as 'Bonica' and the various other Meidiland roses, are disease-resistant and tough (although they aren't much on fragrance). With minimal care and a sunny site with good air circulation, they do bloom all summer. Many of the shrub roses and old-fashioned roses resist pests and diseases adequately, and many of those that are only once-blooming produce an autumn display of rose hips, which are also attractive to birds. *Rosa rugosa* and its hybrids are particularly trouble free (and salt resistant in coastal gardens). Good disease resistance is now being bred into some of the new hybrids. Insect pests, such as aphids, are less debilitating and easier to control than most other maladies.

By all means, include roses in your garden, but be smart about it. Plant varieties suited to the care you are willing to give them. With careful selection, you can bring roses into your garden without adding a lot of extra work. Then you will be pleased with the result. (For more about types of roses and their garden uses, see page 35.)

PERENNIALS

Discussions of flower gardens inevitably involve perennials. A mixed flower garden is often erroneously referred to as a perennial garden. The "look" of a perennial garden with its varied textures and forms is identifiable to many people; the majority of plants in these gardens are usually perennials, with other plants incorporated as accents or "filler."

If you have difficulty remembering the difference between annuals and perennials, remember that Perennials are Permanent, annuals are not. Perennials grow from roots, rhizomes and tubers, which survive the winter to grow again the following spring. Normally, only nonwoody herbaceous plants that die back to the ground each year are considered perennials. However, some perennials such as Lenten rose (*Helleborus orientalis*) and cottage pinks (*Dianthus plumarius*) are evergreen in southern regions.

Perennials vary in size from giants 8 or more feet tall for the back of the border to mat-forming *Dianthus* for the front and to creeping sedums barely 1 inch high. Those of moderate size fill the middle ground or, in a narrow border, take their place at the back. It's always helpful, from the maintenance point of view, to choose varieties that can stand up on their own, without staking.

Permanent does not mean "planted for once and for all." Although perennials will live year after year, they increase in size. Some are well-behaved, while others can be aggressive and rambunctious if not carefully watched. Whatever the cause, division of most varieties will be required every few years to rejuvenate them, replanting only a piece of the original plant. This won't be necessary as often if you choose well-behaved varieties.

Perennials fall into three basic groups according to behavior:

1. Clumpers form tight masses of rhizomes and roots that, although ever-increasing in size, do keep to themselves. These are the best-behaved perennials for the garden. Examples are purple coneflower (*Echinacea purpurea*) and most daylilies (*Hemerocallis*). Some clumpers, such as New England asters, send out a few short rhizomes when well established. This is usually not a problem, but rather a sign that it is time to divide. A few clumpers, such as the gas plant (*Dictamnus albus*) and balloonflower (*Platycodon grandiflorus*), have very deep roots and once established are best not divided or transplanted at all.

2. Spreaders have rhizomes that spread either underground or on the surface. In the worst cases these rhizomes are very numerous and capable of growing a foot or more in one year. You don't want these in a small garden. I avoid gooseneck (*Lysimachia clethroides*), plume poppy (*Macleaya cordata*), showy evening primrose (*Oenothera speciosa*) and, above all, goutweed (*Aegopodium podagraria*), which is often introduced as a groundcover and never again eradicated (the variegated kind is also risky). Others have very restrained spreading habits that can be tolerated and the shallow rhizomes are easy to remove. I still grow sundrop (*Oenothera tetragona*) and bee balm (*Monarda didyma*), but dig around them each fall to remove what I don't want. (For more about controlling spreaders, see page 106.)

Sundrops (Oenothera tetragona) is one of the more desirable spreaders with shallow rhizomes that are easy to remove when they run too far.

Most daylilies (Hemerocallis) are well-behaved clump-forming perennials that stay in one place.

Beware of these perennials that spread by rhizomes, stolons and runners

Aegopodium podagraria (Goutweed)

Artemisia ludoviciana (Wormwood)

Aster tataricus (Tatarian aster; particularly in the South)

Campanula rapunculoides (Creeping bellflower)

Coreopsis rosea (Coreopsis)

Eupatorium coelestinum (Hardy ageratum)

Lysimachia clethroides (Gooseneck)

Lysimachia punctata (Yellow loosestrife)

Macleaya cordata (Plume poppy)

Monarda didyma (Bee balm)

Oenothera speciosa (Showy evening primrose)

Physalis alkekengi (Chinese lantern)

Physostegia virginiana (Obedient plant)

Polygonum cuspidatum (Japanese knotweed)

3. Self-Sowing Perennials are usually not of great concern. In a few cases, seedlings may be produced in such quantities that they pose a weed problem. Nature seems to have endowed each species with a primary survival mechanism. In the case of perennials, it is usually longevity. Thus, as a rule, only short-lived perennials such as Maltese cross (*Lychnis chalcedonica*) and columbine (*Aquilegia*) are found to be prolific seeders (which turns out to be a convenient means of replacement rather than a nuisance).

*Columbine (*Aquilegia*) is a short-lived perennial that reliably self-sows to provide plenty of young replacement plants.*

Make most of your choices from the clump-forming group, and use the spreaders only when a clump former can't be found to meet your criteria. In very large gardens, or in more natural settings, spreaders might be used to advantage, but even there they can take over and be difficult to control. The idea is to find varieties that grow well under your garden conditions without undue care, but not so well that they overtake their neighbors. Often you discover these by trial and error as you develop your own garden flora.

BIENNIALS

Biennial means "every two years." The basic growth cycle of biennials is that the first year, seeds germinate and form a low rosette of leaves,

*Plume poppy (*Macleaya cordata*) has rampant underground rhizomes that need policing and should not be planted in small gardens.*

then the second year they flower, set seed and die. Most varieties flower during the first half of the summer. For many biennials, a dormant cold period is required to initiate flowering in the second year. Many normally biennial species, such as foxglove (*Digitalis purpurea*), can behave as annuals, blooming in the first year if started early enough in a greenhouse, although these don't get as big as when they bloom in the second year. Varieties such as *D. purpurea* 'Foxy' have been selected to perform more reliably as annuals. Biennials tend to be prolific self-seeders, a means of compensating for their short lives, and this can be worked to the gardener's advantage, as we will see.

I call biennials either "natural" or "functional." The difference is somewhat academic, but it accounts for the fact that some so-called biennials can live longer than two years. Natural biennials, such as the biennial sea holly (*Eryngium giganteum*) and silver thistle (*Onopordum nervosum*), live for only two years and are programmed to die after producing seed. They are what is called monocarpic, meaning that they produce seed only once. Functional biennials are not strictly monocarpic, often surviving into their third or fourth years, but to call them short-lived perennials is stretching it a bit. When they make it to the third year, they are but a shadow of their former selves with a much reduced floral display. Foxgloves belong to this group, along with mullein pink (*Lychnis coronaria*), feverfew (*Chrysanthemum parthenium*) and Moroccan poppy (*Papaver atlanticum*), which seems to be killed off after blooming by the heat of summer. Foxgloves often produce spikes 6 feet tall in the second year but no more than a few short spikes thereafter. I recommend pulling out the whole lot during the second year after they have produced seed, and allowing young plants to replace them for the next year.

Managing Biennials

Biennials depend on strength gained during the first year for a good performance the second. In my garden, most biennials can be planted as late as midsummer and still grow large enough to make a good display the following year. Plant earlier in the shorter northern growing season, and later in the South. The prolific seeding of many types means there are readily available replacements right out in the garden where you need them. After flowering, wait until some seed has matured in midsummer, then pull out the old plants before they drop all of their seed (to avoid overseeding). Transplant young self-sown seedlings where you want them for the following year. Eliminate the extra seedlings (saving a few in reserve) before they get big enough to crowd out other plants. Final adjustments of placement can be done in the fall along with other maintenance.

Using this regime, the prolific nature of biennials can be put to advantage. There is no need for fussing over starting replacement plants in a greenhouse or under lights indoors. Not all biennials are so prolific, and extra effort may be required if those varieties are to remain permanent features in your garden. The temporary nature of biennials means that they can be massed in designated spaces, or used to fill temporary gaps until more permanent plants mature. Fine-textured, shorter varieties such as catchfly (*Silene armeria*) can be allowed to seed among tall perennials where they serve to knit the border together visually. The tall spikes of foxglove are a delight in the middle or back of the border in early sum-

Useful Self-sowing Biennials

Alcea rosea (Hollyhock)
Dianthus barbatus (Sweet William)
Digitalis purpurea (Foxglove)
Eryngium giganteum (Sea holly)
Hesperis matronalis (Sweet rocket)
Lunaria annua (Honesty)
Lychnis coronaria (Mullein pink)
Onopordum nervosum (Silver thistle)
Papaver atlanticum (Moroccan poppy)
Silene armeria (Catchfly)
Verbascum bombyciferum (Mullein)

mer. They are one of the few biennials that can thrive and develop in late summer at the back of the border under the shade of other tall perennials.

Many biennials stay in the garden by seeding themselves and are useful to fill spaces among perennials in early summer. Right: Catchfly (Silene armeria; left), feverfew (Chrysanthemum parthenium; right) and mullein pink (Lychnis coronaria; back) fill the garden with their billowy masses in June and early July. Below: The pale tissue-paper orange of Papaver atlanticum is a delightful filler among Hemerocallis 'Stella de Oro', delphinium, sundrops, Maltese cross and Campanula latifolia.

ANNUALS

Annuals live for only one year. Many have the tremendous advantage of blooming continuously. The long bloom season, heat resistance and easy culture of many varieties have made annuals very popular in America. Annuals can be grown either in association with other flowers or alone in massed plantings. A mass display of such tough annuals as marigolds or petunias can be achieved by a relatively unskilled gardener. The cultural requirements of such massed plantings are uncomplicated—but not necessarily low maintenance. Unskilled labor is cheapest, and that is just what most American city parks departments have. Massed annuals are practical for them, but not for most home gardeners who are better off with mixed plantings that are more permanent and require less concentrated labor at specific seasons.

Some annuals are monocarpic, automatically dying after producing seed. Others, although not technically monocarpic, wear out after several months of bloom and seed production. Deadheading will increase and lengthen flowering of some varieties because it prevents production of seed. Other annuals in our summer gardens are actually tropical perennials. These tropicals grow fast enough to perform during the summer months, but would live longer in a warmer climate. Impatiens and coleus fit into this category and can be grown from cuttings year after year.

Annuals are a diverse group with different growth requirements and bloom seasons. The simplest way to categorize them is either as cool-season bloomers or warm-season bloomers. Some won't take the heat, and some won't take the cold. Planting at the wrong season results in failure. For the purpose of garden planning, it is useful to recognize this; refer to these two groups in the Bloom Seasons lists for annuals (page 223). Alternatively, annuals may be categorized by their cultural requirements. For this purpose annuals are split into three groups: tender, half-hardy and hardy, explained below and referenced in the Encyclopedia of Annuals and Biennials (page 149).

Kinds of Annuals

Of the various ways to categorize annuals, the most important to gardeners is the horticultural classification based on cultural needs. The following categories are based on season and temperature requirements.

1. Tender annuals will tolerate no frost whatsoever. They must not be sown outdoors until all danger of frost is past and the soil is warm. If started earlier indoors, they must not be transplanted outdoors until this time. Many will be set back by cold weather even if not actually frosted. Seeds of a few varieties will be winter hardy and grow the following year, but seed of most must be collected and stored indoors. Irresponsible nurserymen may offer marigolds, impatiens and other tender annuals a month before the last frost date without properly warning the customer.

2. Half-hardy annuals will tolerate light frost in the early stages of growth. It is quite normal for these varieties to germinate during cool weather to get an early start. They may be sown in cool soil after hard frosts are past (2 to 4 weeks before the last expected frost date). Many have winter-hardy seeds that germinate the following spring untended. Varieties such as spider flower (*Cleome hassleriana*) are members of this group and self-sow and persist in the garden year to year.

3. Hardy annuals are remarkable in their ability to withstand heavy frosts and survive the winter. They may be sown in the fall or early spring and often germinate immediately, surviving mild winters as seedlings. Most hardy annuals have limited heat tolerance, completing their growth cycles by late spring or early summer. Except where summers are cool in the North, Pacific coast, and mountain climates, they are a disappointment when grown as summer annuals. They self-sow readily the following year. Larkspur (*Consolida orientalis*), bachelor's button (*Centaurea cyanus*), Shirley poppy (*Papaver rhoeas*) and forget-me-not (*Myosotis sylvatica*) are well-known examples.

Single Late tulip 'Maria Zamora' underplanted with pansy 'Springtime Red and Yellow Bicolor' at Old Westbury Garden.

Pansies (*Viola* × *wittrockiana*) are the best-known hardy annuals. In the Mid-Atlantic states, young pansy plants can be planted in autumn and mulched lightly with salt hay or pine needles for the winter. In the South and along the Pacific coast, mulching is not necessary and they will bloom all winter long. For the longest period of bloom when spring planted, they should be set out as soon as available from garden centers, or just before the daffodils begin to bloom.

For variety, tropical perennials are often brought into the garden as summer annuals. Some, such as the familiar impatiens, are easily grown from seed. Others are more easily grown from cuttings taken from stock plants kept indoors for the winter. Geraniums and coleus have been propagated this way for years, although now seed strains are becoming more common.

Annuals grown from cuttings are more labor-intensive to produce and are consequently more expensive, but they are also more unusual, differing from those that can be grown from seed. These aristocrats are usually reserved for special locations or uses such as container plantings, usually in combinations of several types. A favorite in Europe, gaining popularity here, is licorice plant (*Helichrysum petiolatum*). The trailing stems and gray foliage soften the edges of pots and combine well with most other plants.

*The lily-flowered tulip 'Mariette' is underplanted with forget-me-not (*Myosotis sylvatica 'Victoria'*). Rheum palmatum 'Atrosanguineum' provides a crimson spike.*

English Wallflowers
(Cheiranthus cheiri)

Most Americans have heard of, but never seen, true English wallflowers, one of the finest hardy spring annuals. Their fragrance, height and range of color make them special additions to the garden in spring. In the British Isles and in the Pacific Northwest wallflower transplants are set out in fall. Bulbs are often planted in the same beds. In spring, they both bloom together, although wallflowers have a longer bloom season, lasting for well over one or even two months. In much of North America (north of Zone 8), wallflowers are not hardy enough to be planted outdoors in the fall and must be over-wintered in a coldframe. They are a little more trouble, but those of us who grow them value them all the more for accents and container plants.

Use wallflowers in combination with pansies, forget-me-nots and such bulbs as tulips. Because they reach a height of 18 inches, use them behind short annuals. Interplant them with bulbs. In containers, place them in the center for height.

Growing wallflowers is easy. Sow the seed in July or August. Prick them out (transplant into separate pots), then transplant them twice more, eventually moving them into 4-inch pots by winter. Root disturbance causes branching, resulting in bushy plants. Pinch if needed. Feed regularly. Overwinter them in a coldframe or cold greenhouse, not indoors, as cold is needed to stimulate flowering. (In Zone 6, no artificial heat is required in the cold frame.) Ventilate as often as possible to prevent botrytis mold, but keep closed on frosty nights. Plant outdoors in spring just before the daffodils bloom.

Although the tulips may bloom for only a couple of weeks, the underplanting of forget-me-nots and sweetly fragrant Siberian wallflowers will bloom for months. (Courtesy of Scott Arboretum of Swarthmore College)

Direct Sowing Annuals

Many annuals can be sown directly in the garden. It is an inexpensive, simple and convenient means of growing annuals from seed with minimum effort. They will not bloom as early as those started earlier indoors, but tender annuals sown this way will continue longer into the fall. This method requires a minimum of transplanting, which can delay growth, and is an advantage for such varieties as annual larkspur and nasturtium that resent disturbance to their roots.

Follow package directions for correct sowing time. Note the recommended spacing for mature plants. Prepare the soil and outline the area where the annuals are to grow. Sow seeds thinly in spaced rows within this area according to directions. Space these rows the same distance apart as the recommended final spacing. When seedlings are well established, thin to final recommended spacing within the rows. Transplant extra seedlings to fill gaps. The result will be a properly spaced bed of plants.

1.

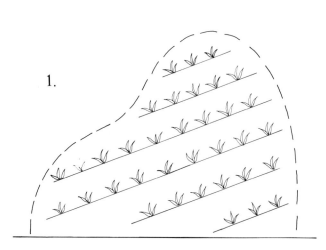

2.

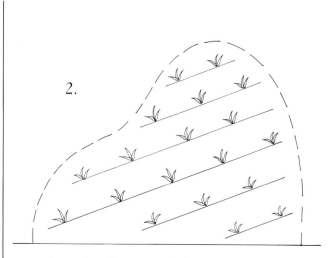

Some annuals resent transplanting, and others are sown directly in the bed for convenience. 1. Determine the final spacing of the annuals desired. Sow the seed closely in rows with that distance between rows. 2. After the seedlings are established, thin to the desired distance within the row for the final spacing.

Using Annuals

Annuals have the one great advantage of continuous bloom within their prescribed season. They are fast growing and short lived. When they are finished, they are replaced. With a little coordination, annuals will give you nearly continuous color from early spring to late fall. A totally annual planting can be a good bit of work, but when you mix annuals with perennials, you stretch the benefits of continuous color to supplement the rest of the display, with minimal extra effort.

Here is a base stategy for using annuals in a mixed planting. A couple dozen transplants will make a big impression. Reserve several spots throughout the bed for annuals. Because many annuals are short or of medium height, these spaces should be near the front where they will show to best advantage. Plant them as follows:

1. In early spring (or late fall, depending on your climate) plant hardy annuals such as pansies or forget-me-nots. These will provide some of the earliest spring color, continue blooming into early summer and complement spring bulbs.

2. When they begin to fade in warm weather, replace the hardy annuals with tender summer annuals such as salvia, impatiens, begonias or marigolds.

3. For fall, plant chrysanthemums or calendulas, followed by ornamental kale. Although they are actually perennials, I prefer to treat chrysanthemums as annuals, grown to maturity in pots and sunk in the bed. They spend relatively little time in the bed because they are removed when the blooms fade and are replaced by ornamental cabbage and kale. They are the last fall annuals and will often stand up into early winter, or longer, depending on your climate.

You can modify the strategy according to your needs. For instance, plant summer annuals where bulbs held a place in the spring. Use only small plants or sow seed, because you can't dig deeply with bulbs underneath. You can even plant between and among the bulb foliage before it dies down. In the back of the bed, plant something tall, like spider flower (*Cleome*). You can probably just move around self-sown seedlings, but do it when they are as young as possible to avoid stunting the plants. At the front, plant something short, such as bedding begonias, or direct sow dwarf nasturtium. Of course, not all annuals are suited to this regimen. Poppies and larkspur do not transplant well and are best sown where they are to bloom, or left where they have sown themselves. Larkspur should be given its own spot at the back because of its height.

As with biennials, many annuals self-sow themselves reliably year to year. Just transplant them to where you want them. Some, such as forget-me-not (*Myosotis sylvatica*) and Johnny-jump-up (*Viola tricolor*), may seed so vigorously that they become pests. You'll have to watch these, and if they become a problem, just keep them all out of the garden for a couple of years. The seeds of many annuals are short lived and there won't be many seedlings after that. In any event, annuals are shallow-rooted and easy to weed out. In my garden, prince's-feather (*Amaranthus hybridus erythrostachyus*), annual larkspur (*Consolida orientalis*), love-in-a-mist (*Nigella damascena*), Shirley poppy (*Papaver rhoeas*) and *Verbena bonariensis* self-sow and add to the display each year.

Euphorbia cyathophora is an unusual self-sowing summer annual related to the familiar poinsettia.

EARLY AND LATE SOWINGS

Garden writers have given much attention to starting annuals early in greenhouses, under artificial lights, in special pots and cells, and so forth. You can learn about the details in many books so I won't get into that here. The advantage is obvious: If the plants are older when set out, they will bloom sooner. The untold truth is that they will also bloom themselves out sooner. Then what do you do?

Astute gardeners have discovered that the odd seedling that comes up late out in the garden looks better in the fall than the older plants. It is younger and more vigorous. Many of these gardeners make a second, late sowing of their favorite annuals, for planting out in July (even later in the South). These young plants outperform their older counterparts, and bloom up until the killing frosts. They lend a lush fullness to the garden when combined with fall-blooming perennials, providing a spectrum of color and variety otherwise unavailable.

Most summer annuals are good for late sowing. As they are planted out during the hottest

Sunset hibiscus (Abelmoschus manihot) is a useful self-sowing annual for late-summer bloom and combines well with the colors of asters.

This September scene at Wave Hill, Bronx, New York, is fresh-ened by the white tubular flowers of Nicotiana sylvestris *and lime-green* Nicotiana alata, *both of which were planted mid-summer. The lavender* Verbena bonariensis *self-sows and blooms all summer long.*

part of the summer, they must be heat-tolerant. Flowering tobacco (*Nicotiana*) and calendula make excellent fall-blooming annuals. The farther south you garden, the longer the summers, and the more useful late-sown annuals are. Cool-season annuals will provide a late fall and winter display if sown in late summer. Such annuals as pansies and violas will bloom until frosts become severe.

BULBS

Bulbs should be included in every garden. They are especially important in spring when they contribute a large share of the bloom, supplemented by a few early perennials and annuals. Among the profusion of summer bloom, they still make a major contribution. Even in fall, bulbs make an impressive display among the autumn colors. In regions with mild winters, there are species that flower during the coldest part of the year.

For simplicity here, the term *bulb* includes tubers, rhizomes and corms as well as the true bulbs, all of which are handled and sold in a dry,

dormant state. The botanical differences between these categories have little bearing on their treatment in the garden. The growth cycle of most hardy bulbs differs from the growth cycle of other hardy plants. Rather than the winter dormancy common to most hardy plants, bulbs are more likely to have a summer dormancy, making their growth during the cool, moist seasons. Must bulbous species are native to regions with a Mediterranean climate, typically very dry in summer. To survive this drought, they go dormant, sheltered from heat and dehydration by the soil. When the rains start in the fall, bulbs begin their growth cycle by forming roots. Flowers and leaves follow, seeds mature, and the cycle is completed before the summer drought begins again in late spring. Bulbs grow underground throughout the winter, but in cold climates, most types don't venture out of the soil until the danger of severe cold is past. Some, however, have adapted to bloom in the autumn, or have leaves that can withstand winter temperatures.

Hardy Spring-flowering Bulbs

Tulips, daffodils, crocuses and most of the other bulbs common to American gardens are examples of spring-flowering bulbs. They are adaptable and hardy in most parts of the United States. Their most remarkable feature is their ability to flower rapidly after they begin growth from pre-formed flowers and stored food contained within the bulb underground. Part of the adaptation for survival is to tolerate severe frosts, at a time of year when most other plants are still dormant. Early varieties under deciduous trees or among herbaceous perennials have the benefit of full sun during their most active period of growth, as the foliage above them hasn't leafed out yet. Bulbs requiring or amenable to deciduous shade are so indicated in the Encyclopedia of Bulbs, page 141.

Because many spring bulbs bloom before other herbaceous plants in the mixed border are in active growth, the rules of placement are slightly different. There are no surrounding plants to hide them. The shortest bulbs are still placed at the front, but at the back a group of

24-inch tulips is quite appropriate next to what will later be a 6-foot perennial. Plant bulbs in the spaces between the large perennials. Plant in loose groups, mark the locations and, of course, be sure to plant them as deeply as possible to avoid digging into them later. Daffodils, for example, massed around the stumps of a butterfly bush, add bloom to an otherwise bare space in early spring and are tall enough to hide the cutback stumps. Later, the lengthening stems of such surrounding perennials as asters, phlox or bee balms will hide the yellowing bulb foliage.

In your mixed border, where you have reserved plots for annuals, try interplanting with bulbs. Use tall spring bulbs, such as tulips and daffodils, with early-blooming annuals such as pansies, forget-me-nots and wallflowers. The annuals will lengthen the bloom season to a month or two, and the bulbs will grow through them and provide a climax of bloom for a couple of weeks. Imagine pink tulips in bloom with blue pansies. Later, the bulbs can be removed with the spring annuals or they can be left in the ground and the summer annuals planted on top. Note that if you expect the bulbs to be permanent, they should be planted as deeply as possible, to avoid damage during digging. Otherwise, shallow planting is recommended for easy removal.

The soft yellow Narcissus 'Hawera' looks best in tight masses in informal perennial plantings.

In these same annual spaces, another popular option is to underplant the tall bulbs with a smaller bulb instead of a hardy annual. The best choice is blue grape hyacinth (*Muscari armeniacum*), which has one of the longest bloom seasons. It won't give as long a display as the annuals, but by the time these flowers are finished it should be warm enough to put the summer annuals in. Note that grape hyacinths can't be deeply planted, and can complicate summer planting if not removed. They can also be a bit weedy, increasing and spreading where you don't want them.

A few 'Angelique' tulips and pansies give spring bloom to this planting of summer-blooming perennials at Old Westbury Garden.

*Blue grape hyacinths (*Muscari armeniacum*) create a pattern among yellow tulips.*

The globes of Allium *'Purple Sensation', Dutch iris, and pansies make a striking late-May display in this Washington, D.C., garden.*

Early small bulbs should be massed in large quantities where they will not be disturbed, such as under deciduous shrubs and in groundcovers. These snowdrops (Galanthus nivalis) *bloom in February and March.*

I don't recommend filling a mixed flower bed with too many bulbs because they tend to get dug up or cut with the spade during maintenance. A few groups go a long way for effect, and are easy enough to keep track of, but too many bulbs can frustrate necessary tasks. I also recommend against using the smaller bulbs like crocuses in an intensively managed bed because they are more shallowly planted and more vulnerable to damage. Smaller bulbs are best used in mass in less intensively managed parts of your landscape, such as under shrubs or in a woodland.

The less formal areas that receive more casual care can have the most spectacular spring displays of all. In beds of groundcover or woodland plantings, where you will be digging less often, daffodils will establish themselves as a permanent feature. Smaller bulbs such as crocus, snowdrop and Siberian squill will also naturalize in masses when planted among low groundcovers such as ajuga, or among deciduous groundcovers such as epimedium. These early-flowering small bulbs should also be planted in masses under the branches of deciduous shrubs. Plant them by the

hundreds for carpets of color. You will never be sorry for the effort of planting them all and they will make a big show every year before there is any other foliage to hide them.

Erythronium *'White Beauty' grows among a groundcover of blue* Pulmonaria angustifolia *in this woodland border in April.*

Controlling Bloom Season

The time of bloom of spring-flowering bulbs can be influenced by the time of planting the previous fall. Late-planted bulbs bloom later in the spring. During subsequent years they will bloom at the normal time if not disturbed. For instance, established hyacinths normally bloom in my garden near Philadelphia in very early April. Late-planted bulbs may bloom as much as a month later. One year, newly planted *Narcissus* 'Ice Follies' daffodils bloomed two weeks later than their established neighbors, and late-planted Dutch crocuses bloomed in mid-April instead of mid-March.

Late planting is not an exact science but it is another technique available to the artful gardener and is worthy of experimentation. My experience indicates that *Narcissus* planted in September or October in the South will flower on a normal schedule. If planted a month later, flowering might be delayed a couple of weeks. If planted two months later, flowering might be delayed a month, but some reduction of vigor might be noticed. The effect of late planting is more pronounced on bulbs that must develop roots before beginning growth, such as daffodils. If the soil

becomes too cold before roots are formed, they will wait until spring to complete the process, with a corresponding delay in growth of leaves and blooms. Tulips are less fussy and seem to be able to jump into growth more rapidly after planting. (In fact, late-planted tulips seem to be more disease resistant.)

The value of delaying bloom of spring-flowering bulbs through late planting is that the bulb bloom season can be condensed to provide a fuller display, timed for some special event, or synchronized with certain annuals and perennials. Imagine having the fragrance of hyacinths a second time with the late-flowering scentless tulips.

Hardy Fall-flowering Bulbs

These are probably the least known of all bulbs, but they can be spectacular and easy to grow. Their growth cycle is essentially the same as that of the spring-flowering varieties, except that they send up flowers in the fall instead of spring. With

In a shady border, Lycoris radiata *blooms in September with caladium.*

the hardier kinds, the leaves wait until spring to appear, avoiding the hazards of winter.

Leafless, fall-blooming bulbs are best planted among a groundcover to provide a green background. *Colchicum*, the hardiest and most common type, thrive in pachysandra or English ivy, where they supply pink blooms in September. *Crocus speciosus* is shorter, and needs to grow in a shorter groundcover. The various species of *Lycoris* bear their flowers on longer stems. The fall-blooming species such as *L. radiata* are hardy only in the South (Zones 8 (7)–9), but *L. squamigera*, blooming July or August, is much hardier (Zones 5–9). In no case should fall-blooming bulbs be planted among plants that are taller than their flowers will be, or they will be hidden.

Fall-blooming bulbs are best used in informal areas in groundcovers that are not much disturbed. I have never seen an example of them used effectively in an intensively managed mixed bed; they just don't fit culturally or aesthetically.

Colchicum byzantinum *flowers in front of the frothy mass of pea shrub* (Lespedeza thunbergii) *in September.*

Colchicum: Order of Bloom of Most Common Varieties

Early (Late August to early September)
    C. *byzantinum*
    C. 'Princess Astrid'
Midseason (Mid- to late September)
    C. *autumnale*
    C. *autumnale album*
    C. *speciosum*
    C. 'The Giant'
    C. 'Violet Queen'
    C. 'Waterlily'
Late (Early October)
    C. 'Lilac Wonder'

Hardy Summer-flowering Bulbs

Most hardy, summer-flowering bulbs fall into one category: the lilies. Over the last 50 years, lilies have been hybridized into a strong, easily grown garden flower. Their requirements are easily met, provided they are given good drain-

Asiatic lily hybrid 'Malta' *grows in front of a fence bedecked with goldflame honeysuckle* (Lonicera ×heckrottii).

Common Fall-flowering Bulbs

Colchicum species and hybrids (Meadow saffron)
Crocus speciosus (Autumn crocus)
Crocus kotschyanus (Autumn crocus)
Sternbergia lutea

This semishaded border of perennials with interesting foliage is accented by regal lily (Lilium regale) *in June. Lungwort* (Pulmonaria saccharata 'Mrs. Moon') *is seen in the foreground, with the purple foliage of* Heuchera 'Palace Purple' *behind.*

age. Few flowers are more beautiful or come in a broader range of colors, often with a delightful fragrance. The bloom season ranges from early summer to early fall, depending on the variety chosen. They will grow in part shade or full sun.

True lilies (not daylilies) are members of the genus *Lilium*. They bloom on a single tall stem, which also bears the leaves. Tall varieties can be placed at the back of the bed between perennials, but don't crowd them too much as they like air circulation. Shorter varieties should, of course, be further forward. If in doubt, plant them toward the front because they don't present a heavy mass of foliage to obstruct the eye. (For more about lily types and bloom seasons, see page 236.)

Tender (or Annual) Summer-flowering Bulbs

Tender bulbs will not survive the winter outdoors except in southern regions. They must be dug up for indoor storage. This is neither time-consuming nor complicated, but when confronted with other gardening activities, you may find it easier to buy new bulbs each year. Because they must be planted yearly, I often call them "annual bulbs."

The most important tender bulbs in the garden are those that bloom in high summer or later to supplement the display. The choice of other flowers is more limited late in the season, with limited colors, forms and textures. Most are used as accents because few bloom so continuously as tender annuals. Those that do bloom continuously, such as cannas and dahlias, can be planned to be an important contribution to the summer and fall display, and may be given prominent locations. Keep in mind that dahlias don't really kick into high gear until quite late in the summer, but excel from early fall until frost.

Cannas have striking blooms borne continuously over a long period from early summer until frost. The bold, tropical, banana-like foliage can be difficult to combine successfully with hardy plants. In regions with Japanese beetles it is best not to plant cannas where the damaged flowers and foliage can be viewed at close range. Massed in the distance, they make a strong statement in the landscape.

Bulbs with shorter bloom seasons, such as gladiolus and tuberose (*Polianthes tuberosa*), are

At Old Westbury Garden, the pure colors of dahlias are an important complement to asters in September and October.

most commonly planted in the cutting garden, but do have limited use in a display bed in what are called "jack-in-the-box" plantings. A group of bulbs is planted in a prepared space between other flowers. They grow up and provide an accent at a time when bloom is scarce. *Gladiolus* are available in practically any color imaginable, and you can time the bloom by when you plant them. Tuberoses, although available only in white, are sweetly fragrant in late summer and early fall. For shade, caladiums are indispensible. Their large leaves last all summer and are a bold contrast to finer-textured annuals, such as impatiens and bedding begonias.

Few flowers can surpass the late-summer fragrance of tuberose (Polianthes tuberosa 'Single Mexican').

VINES

Vines add dimension to a flower garden. Much has been said about their ability to hide unsightly objects in the landscape, but they are less often credited with enhancing an attractive feature, such as a wall or fence, which might otherwise remain blank. Scant mention is made of the sculptural nature of twisted, tangled and gnarled stems and trunks against a wall, nature's own macramé. (Keep the dead wood trimmed out for a clean effect.) Creative gardeners can train vines to enhance the development of the sinuous or ropy nature of their trunks. A vine's suitability for a given purpose is determined by its type and climbing habit. When properly used, vines can add another season of bloom to flowering trees and shrubs without harm. As vines clamber over and through their hosts, they serve to soften and knit various elements of plant combinations together. When well trained, vines can be controlled while giving a perfectly natural appearance. (For training and pruning vines, see page 97.)

While bloom is the primary feature of most vines such as clematis and honeysuckle, others are grown for their attractive foliage. *Actinidia kolomikta* is one of my favorite foliage vines, with pointed leaf tips that appear to have been coated with white paint. English ivy is popular for its evergreen foliage that comes in an almost endless variety of shapes and variegations with white and gold.

Actinidia kolomikta *makes a superb background on a wall or fence. The "white painted" foliage remains attractive for at least two months in early summer as it becomes tinted pink and finally fades to light green.*

Types of Vines

Annual vines are too often overlooked. They develop rapidly from seed sown in the spring and have long seasons of bloom. They are especially useful in a young garden where plenty of virgin space is available in which to develop, space that will be occupied by more permanent woody vines that gradually fill in over the seasons. Some have unique features, such as the hyacinth bean (*Dolichos lablab*) with beet red pods, or the white, night-blooming moon vine (*Ipomoea alba*), lovely near a patio.

Perennial vines die back to the ground each autumn but come up from the root the following spring, when they make rapid growth. The native passion flower, or maypop (*Passiflora incarnata*), bears tropical-looking flowers in my garden from June through September. It grows up on earlier-blooming woody vines and roses, providing them with light shade during the heat of summer.

*Maypop (*Passiflora incarnata*) is a perennial vine native to the southeastern United States. Each winter it dies back to the ground.*

Woody vines are the best-known and most popular types. They range in vigor from wisterias climbing into the tallest trees, to clematis reaching barely 4 or 5 feet. Clematis are by far the most popular of flowering vines and the many species and hybrids have a broad range of bloom seasons. Other woody vines also have a range of bloom seasons. Early-flowering types, such as wisterias, normally have a limited, but spectacular, flowering period (with the possibility of some rebloom), while those that bloom later, such as trumpet vines and many honeysuckles, often flower all summer long.

Climbing Habits

No characteristic has more influence on a vine's use in gardens than its climbing habit. It can spell the difference between success and trouble. **Twiners** twist or wrap around their support. On a flat surface, such as a wall, some sort of mesh, string or wire, must be provided for the twiners to grow on. Their size is limited by the size of the support. They can go no farther than to the

*Hyacinth bean (*Dolichos lablab*) is a fast-growing, twining annual that is happy in any hot, sunny location. It flowers most of the summer and develops attractive, beet red pods.*

top of the support provided on the wall. The disadvantage of woody twiners is that they can strangle plants on which they grow. The thick trunks of wisteria can strangle a large tree. This is not a problem with annual twiners, as their soft stems last only one season.

Lonicera sempervirens 'Sulphurea' is a well-behaved native honeysuckle that flowers all summer.

Grabbers grip their support but don't actually wrap their stems around it. Grapes have tendrils that grab small twigs and branches or trellises and wires. Clematis are similar, but grab by twisting their petioles (leaf stems). As with the twiners, the grabbers are controlled by the size of their support, because they cannot cling to a wall.

Clingers are notorious for climbing all over everything. They can cling to almost any surface. In the wrong location, they can become a mainte-

nance problem if not trimmed regularly. Ivies of all types are clingers. On houses, English ivy constantly overgrows windows and pushes under shingles. Climbing hydrangea is the best-known flowering clinger, with attractive, shredded tan bark in the winter. Contrary to popular belief, clingers normally don't harm trees. The stems grow vertically, rather than around the trunk, and form an expandable matrix that allows the trunk to grow. Use clingers with restraint to avoid high maintenance.

Sprawlers lie on their supports, which in nature are shrubs and trees, sending up progressively taller shoots to arch over higher branches. Jasmine is essentially a sprawler with little ability to twine. All climbing roses are sprawlers and most (a few are thornless) possess the additional adaptation of backward-facing thorns that hook onto branches and prevent the rose stems from slipping out of place. Sprawlers need to be tied to their support in the garden to stay tidy.

Twiners, grabbers and sprawlers are useful on trellises, pergolas and walls where a means of support, such as a wire grid (see page 100), is provided. Under certain circumstances, they can be grown over shrubs. Clingers need no such assistance, merely a vertical surface, such as a blank wall or a stockade fence, to which they will attach themselves.

Silvervein creeper (Parthenocissus henryana) clings to surfaces by means of tendrils fitted with little suction cups. The tendrils can also provide support by grabbing the stems of other plants.

ORNAMENTAL GRASSES

Until their recent surge in popularity, ornamental grasses were seldom seen in gardens. They are invaluable for the bold effects and contrasts that they can create in the landscape and flower garden. The grasses are a remarkably varied group, ranging in height from over 10 feet to just a few inches high. In addition to green foliage, some have striking blue coloration, while others may be variegated with white, gold or red. Grasses are especially appreciated in fall and winter for their plumes, which play in the breeze. The best-known grasses are perennials, but there are annuals too. Most need a sunny location, but a few are useful in shade. Even though sedges and rushes are not truly grasses, they are usually included in this group because of their similar appearance and use. Use grasses for variety and textural contrasts throughout the season and for bringing winter interest to the flower garden.

*The plumes of oriental fountain grass (*Pennisetum orientale*) and* Coreopsis *'Moonbeam' pick up the tones of the wall behind, in this border designed by Edith Edelman at Brookside Gardens, Wheaton, Maryland.*

The varied forms and colors of grasses remain decorative landscape features through the autumn and winter.

CONTAINER PLANTINGS

Potted plants have many uses on decks and patios, in window boxes and as house plants and may consist of single varieties or lavish compositions of many types of plants. Out in the garden, plants in containers should be used sparingly to serve as accents occupying those crucial spots requiring continuous displays of special interest and excellent quality. Such container plantings can be set directly in borders, or may stand alone. Annuals are usually easiest for containers, requiring at least two plantings a year, one for spring and another for summer and fall. Sometimes, the special drainage and soil conditions in pots enable varieties that would not do well in the open garden to be grown.

A big advantage of containers is their mobility. Potted plants can be moved into prime locations when at their peak, and easily replaced when they are past it. This allows the use of a much broader range of plants with shorter bloom periods, spring bulbs and perennials, for example. Of course this approach requires an additional growing area away from the display area, and in some cases, additional muscle for moving pots around.

Don't indulge too many fancy ideas. The container, whether it be a classic urn or contemporary pot, must be bold enough to make a statement. This accent is meant to complement its surroundings, not compete with them. It should be of a quality material such as stone (or concrete), terra-cotta or ceramic. Wood is usually less effective because it lacks contrast with the surrounding plants and flowers. Set the container on a base, such as a slab of stone or a pedestal; even slight elevation will set it off, give definition, and make it look bigger and more important. It's easy for containers to get lost among the foliage of summer. To achieve the necessary boldness, the pot may need to be too large to move easily. Just fill and plant it already in position, or use smaller pots that can be inserted into the container. Plastic inserts are easiest because they are light, thin walled for maximum soil volume, flexible, easily cut to size and retain moisture well. Be sure the insert does not show.

All containers (except those designed for aquatic plantings) must have drainage holes and not sit in saucers when growing outdoors. This rule is not only for the gardener who might overwater; experienced gardeners know that thorough watering requires drainage holes to release the excess. After a rain, excess water must drain away immediately. Accent plants can't perform to perfection with rotten roots.

Containers can be used in almost any environment. I've brightened the end of a shaded walkway with an informal basket-weave terracotta pot filled with an impatiens with white variegated leaves. Another excellent choice would be brightly colored caladium. A classic combination for sun is zonal geranium with variegated vinca (*Vinca major* 'Variegata') trailing over the edge of the pot. A simple, effective accent in one of my borders is a terra-cotta pot with a red variegated *Dracaena marginata* 'Tricolor' underplanted with the chartreuse foliage of *Helichrysum*

Fragrant English wallflowers and dwarf Viola *'Princess Blue' will take light frost to provide early bloom and continue flowering for more than two months.*

A shady spot is brightened by a pot of variegated impatiens.

petiolatum 'Limelight' (a tender perennial grown each year from cuttings) spilling over the edges. In very hot locations, sow portulacca for low-maintenance bloom all summer. The possibilities are almost endless.

The only catch to containers is that they require regular watering and feeding. In the heat of summer, you'll need to water daily. Fertilization is like the throttle on your car. Without feeding, you won't get much bloom after the nutrients

Fuchsia magellanica *'Versicolor' has silvery gray foliage and small, intensely red flowers. In a shaded corner it sits atop a gray stone pedestal surrounded by Impatiens 'Super Elfin Scarlet'.*

run out in early summer; begin feeding and bloom will get up to full speed. Of course, why not feed regularly all summer and have masses of continuous bloom, or better still, use a slow-release fertilizer to save some work? Your container plantings are sure to be some of your most rewarding.

BETTER PLANTS

Of all the good garden plants available, some stand apart from the rest, featuring several superior qualities in just one plant. A prime example is *Coreopsis verticillata* 'Moonbeam', an improvement over other varieties of *Coreopsis verticillata* in many respects. It blooms longer than the other varieties, has shorter stems that don't require staking and is a clumper rather than a spreader; the light yellow flowers are very effectively set off against deeper green foliage and, on top of all that, it's perennial. The flower color is easier to combine with other summer flowers than the deep yellow of the other varieties. It's no wonder *C. v.* 'Moonbeam' has become so popular in just a few years.

Not many plants can boast such a wealth of improved traits, but just two or three good traits can put a variety in the running as a "better plant." Try to include as many of these in your garden as you can because they usually offer a better display and less maintenance. Decide which varieties are truly better plants under your own garden conditions; other gardeners can suggest plants to try.

The superior qualities of some plants have been recognized by the awards of various organizations. Of particular interest to flower gardeners are the All America Selections (AAS). Annuals, roses and vegetables are grown at special trial grounds throughout North America and evaluated by committees of experts for their dependable performance in all regions. The very best varieties are announced and publicized each spring and often noted in plant catalogs thereafter. Regional evaluations also are conducted on a local basis by many organizations. For example, the Pennsylvania Horticultural Society awards its Gold Medal to superior landscape plants for the Delaware Valley (including the climatic region extending from New York City south to Washington, D.C.). The University of British Columbia Botanic Garden has an active program of introducing superior landscape plants for the Pacific Northwest. Even if you don't live in these specific regions, these plants are likely to be better for you too, when hardy. Ask local horticultural organizations and the agricultural extension service about any such schemes in your area.

Some of the Author's "Better Plants"

PERENNIALS:

Achillea 'Moonshine' (Yarrow)

Anemone hupehensis

Artemisia 'Powis Castle' (Wormwood)

Aster ×frikartii 'Monch' (Frikart's aster)

Astermoea mongolica

Coreopsis grandiflora 'Early Sunrise' (Tickseed; AAS)

Coreopsis verticillata 'Moonbeam' (Threadleaf coreopsis)

Echinacea purpurea (Purple coneflower)

Epimedium species and hybrids (Barrenwort)

Filipendula purpurea (Japanese meadowsweet)

Geranium sanguineum striatum (Hardy geranium)

Hemerocallis hybrids (Daylily)

Hosta species and hybrids (Plantain lily)

Miscanthus sinensis 'Strictus' (Porcupine grass)

Rudbeckia fulgida 'Goldsturm Strain' (Orange coneflower)

Sedum 'Autumn Joy' (Stonecrop)

Veronica 'Goodness Grows' (Speedwell)

BULBS:

Allium 'Purple Sensation' (Flowering onion)

Caladium × hortulanum (Fancy-leafed caladium)

Camassia leichtlinii (Camassia)

Colchicum hybrids (Meadow saffron)

Crocus speciosus (Autumn crocus)

Crocus tomasinianus (Snow crocus)

Dahlia hybrids (Dahlia)

Endymion hispanicus (Wood hyacinth)

Narcissus hybrids (Daffodil)

Scilla siberica (Siberian squill)

ANNUALS (selected varieties have received AAS awards):

Begonia × semperflorens-cultorum (Bedding begonia)

Catharanthus roseus (Rose periwinkle)

Dianthus chinensis hybrids (Annual pink)

Impatiens walleriana (Common impatiens)

Pelargonium × hortorum hybrids (Zonal geranium)

Pennisetum setaceum (Crimson fountain grass)

Salvia farinacea (Mealy-cup sage)

Salvia splendens (Scarlet sage)

Tropaeolum minor (Dwarf nasturtium)

SHRUBS:

Berberis thunbergii (Japanese barberry; purple forms)

Buddleia davidii 'Nanho Blue' (Butterfly bush)

Caryopteris × clandonensis 'Longwood Blue' (Bluebeard)

Hibiscus syriacus 'Diana' and 'Helene' (Rose of Sharon)

Hydrangea quercifolia (Oak-leafed hydrangea)

New Versus Old Plant Varieties

In the scramble to have the newest and the best, we often lose sight of what is truly the best, equating "new" with "improved" and therefore better. Don't be fooled. New is not always improved, it is just different. "Different" is marketable, and that appeals to merchandisers. Novice gardeners are particularly susceptible to sensational claims.

Occasionally, "old" becomes stylish. A case in point is old-fashioned garden roses, hot items recently. Not all of them are "best plants," but their resurgence lets us rediscover the best of these forgotten varieties. We can always hope that the best will become popular and stay in the limelight for the benefit of us all. Discriminating gardeners make their selections from both old and new varieties, resisting glossy pictures and hyped descriptions, in favor of proven garden performance.

In all this discussion of how to select the best plants for your garden there is no reason to have to give up growing your favorites or those that have sentimental value. It is to be hoped that you will have proper growing conditions somewhere for each of them. If they are impor-tant to you, that is sufficient to elevate them to the top of the priority list.

Searching for plants for specific needs can be fun. Prioritize your criteria. Suitability to the growing conditions, for instance, is primary. Color might be next in priority, followed by bloom season. In another area, foliage considerations might take on greater importance. Prioritizing your needs allows you to narrow the list of possibilities. Make a separate list for each set of criteria. Criteria I often consider are light requirements, color, bloom season, size (height and spread), foliage type (texture) and persistence, fragrance and type of plant (annual, perennial, and so on).

To assist you in finding the right plant, the reference section at the back of this book is divided into several parts based on plant type. Comments for each plant will help you determine suitability for your needs. In addition, the reference section includes specialized lists of cold- and warm-season annuals subdivided by color and a combined monthly listing subdivided by color for perennials, bulbs, shrubs, and vines. Another list suggests plants with foliage colors other than green, and various foliage textures. Use these lists to find the right plant for your needs when designing your own plantings as described in the next chapter.

This spectacular border near Washington, D.C., combines foxgloves, pansies, blue campanulas and the silver foliage of woolly betany in May.

FOUR

Bringing Plants Together

Approach design by first considering height, color and bloom season rather than a list of specific plants. Although the flowers and foliage are the raison d'être of any flower garden, other issues must be settled first. Consider what it is that you most want the planting to do for you and how it will fit in with the rest of your garden and landscape. When do you want the main bloom season to be? There is no need for spring and fall bloom at a strictly summer home and little need for early spring bloom in a part of the garden that you don't see when it is cold. On the other hand, a bed well in view from the house should be in bloom for as much of the year as possible. Try to imagine how the different types of plants—perennials, bulbs and so forth—will work together in the design. What colors do you want? How tall should the plants be? If too tall, they might block a view or look out of scale. Short plants may not have the desired impact.

Don't try to select your plant varieties before you've settled these broader design issues. Varieties for specific needs will come to mind while you work on design. Make note of them, but don't let them hold you up. Then, when you really are ready to select plants, refer to those notes and search for other varieties too. Select plants because their qualities match your design needs.

Good design requires an awareness of height, spread, bloom season, color and texture—the plant's visual effect in the landscape—and all this can be daunting enough to the beginner without the premature complication of which varieties to pick. These factors are easier to understand when considered separately. In this chapter, we will examine them one at a time, but first, let's take a look at the design process.

1. Make a plot plan. Flower bed design is most easily done on graph paper. Work in as large a scale as possible; you can tape separate sheets together, if you wish. Outline the shape of the bed and note any relevant factors. For example, note which direction is north, so you know the direction of the sun and the influence of microclimates. What is the extent of shade from overhanging trees? What surrounds the bed? Which side of the bed is most important? Make several photocopies of the drawing of the empty bed. That way, you can try out several different ideas and won't have to worry about messing up the original.

2. Plan space for access to the bed. In a large bed, leave space along the back so you can get in to work without disturbing plants and compacting the soil. In small beds, strategically placed stepping-stones direct foot traffic where no harm will be done. (Natural stone rather than concrete slabs or brick blends in best.) Stepping-stones can be added to the plan at a later stage if you are not sure just where they should go.

3. Determine special features. Decide on the location of any special feature or accent such as decorative pots, urns or statuary. Such a feature is a useful way to create a focal point where one is lacking. Pots and urns can showcase special plants, but be cautious, as overuse of these items may attract too much attention away from the rest of the bed.

4. Determine size of plants and plant groupings. All but the largest plants are more effective if planted in groups of more than one. Odd numbers of three, five and seven are preferred; groups of even numbers tend to look regimented. (With groups larger than seven, an irregular effect is easier to achieve, even with even numbers.)

The size of group plantings depends on the size of the plants and of the bed. I prefer to have at least three groups between the back and the front of the bed, because it is easier to organize a progression of bloom and variation of form and texture than with fewer groups. Each group should be large enough to carry about the same weight or mass visually, and take up about the same area on the plan. If the masses at the back are two to three feet wide, then the masses at the front should also be that size. The difference is that the masses at the back may only require one plant and those at the front will need to contain at least five. In a large bed, the groups should be correspondingly large, to keep in proportion. The maximum height of the tallest varieties at the back should be equal to about a third to a half of the distance from back to front. In some cases this height can be stretched to be taller, but it begins to create problems as the large plants shade the smaller ones. Taller plants work best in a south-facing border, where they cast the least shade.

5. Determine plant spacing. Space plants according to their spreads. If a plant has a spread of 18 inches, space it 18 inches from its neighbor of the same variety. When spacing two different varieties with different spreads, take half of the spread of each and add them together for the correct spacing. For instance: Variety A has a spread of 24 inches and variety B has a spread of 18 inches. Adding half of the spread of each, the correct spacing between them would be 21 inches, measured from the stem of A to the stem of B. It is better to crowd plants of the same variety than push different types together. Like varieties compete equally whereas, in the case of different varieties, the stronger will cripple the weaker one.

6. Place largest plants first. Sketch the tallest plants at the back of the bed, then work forward. In the case of island beds, begin in the middle and work out toward the edge.

The first types of plants to place are the largest and most permanent ones: the large shrubs, tallest roses, and largest perennials. Leave space for only those annuals that will be as tall as their neighbors. Place all the plants along the back before working forward, unless a tall one is to be brought forward as an accent.

7. Place middle-size plants. Position plants along the middle section of the bed. These will probably be perennials of moderate height. Plan spaces for groups of annuals regularly through this section. Moderate-size roses and shrubs, such as *Caryopteris* and dwarf crape myrtle, also belong here. Try to arrange groups so that they have an irregular "drop" shape rather than a circle. These shapes will give a sense of movement and flow to the bed, making it look less stiff.

8. Place short plants. Fill in along the front with groups of the shortest varieties of perennials and annuals. Again, try to make irregularly shaped groupings rather than symmetrical ones. Although perennials should continue to be in the majority, the edge is where the long bloom of annuals will have their greatest impact. Today the choice of low-growing bedding annuals is extensive.

9. Add bulbs. This step is most easily done using an overlay of tracing paper. The overlay avoids the confusion of too many ideas on the original plan and keeps the original plan unmarked. You can even use a different overlay for each season.

Use larger bulbs at the back between the large perennials and shrubs. Very early spring bulbs can be massed under deciduous shrubs. Spring bulbs can be used in the annual spaces in conjunction with early annuals. Summer bulbs can be used as "jack-in-the-box" accents in annual spaces with summer annuals. Fall-blooming bulbs should be included only if used along the front and interplanted with a permanent, low groundcover or perennial; this groundcover must not be taller than the bulb flowers.

10. Finally, add vines. If the flower border is backed by a wall or a fence, vines make an excellent addition to it. Grabbers of moderate vigor, such as clematis, can be grown on shrubs and roses and even encouraged to venture out and mingle with a perennial or two. Unless a separate structure is to be included for a vine, it should not be a primary element in the design; rather, it should complement and tie the primary elements together.

The author's red-orange-yellow border remains in bloom through the entire growing season but changes its character and appearance with time. Above: Pastel colors are more available in June with Asiatic lily 'Connecticut Yankee' and Kniphofia 'Springtime' (center). Below: In the same space, September colors are deeper and more intense with red cardinal flower, golden yellow Rudbeckia 'Goldsturm' (center), arching yellow Coreopsis tripteris (upper left) and the purple foliage of Perilla frutescens 'Atropurpurea'.

The well-dressed garden presents a harmonious progression of colors and textures that grow together throughout the year. Each season presents a different interpretation of the same scene, with different players taking the starring roles while others play supporting parts. A well-directed display depends on good staging and choreography. Unless the scheme has a distinctly seasonal intent, plan for a constant show of bloom. During any season, plan to have a good distribution of color throughout the bed and group flowers of similar bloom seasons together. Supplement occasional poor showings and absentees with new additions to fill the gaps temporarily.

Make full use of the assets of each plant. Color, bloom season, form and texture are all factors to consider in associating one variety with another. Generally, the cleanest look is achieved when most varieties maintain their own separate space, but interesting and subtle effects are possible when certain compatible varieties are allowed to grow into each other. Make double use of the same space by interplanting two plants with different bloom seasons.

Above left: At Old Westbury Garden, this bed in the cottage garden features lily-flowered tulip 'Westpoint', pansies and purple bearded iris in May. Above right: In June, the pansies and tulips have been replaced by the summer annuals nasturtium (front left) and Dahlberg daisy (Dyssodia tenuiloba) (front right), which complements Geranium *'Johnson's Blue'*.

Although any flower is a thing of beauty at any time of the year, each kind seems to belong to its own season. (Chrysanthemums at Easter don't make it.) There is a special delight in the anticipation of the growth and bloom of a favorite plant. We yearn for the first crocuses in the spring, look forward to the fragrant oriental lilies of late summer and enjoy brilliant red berries against evergreen holly foliage in December. Seasonal events can be arranged to unfold in the garden all through the year.

The fear of novice gardeners is that after the flowering period of a given plant, the show is over. (This, along with lack of confidence, is the reason novice gardeners plant so many annuals.) But because more than one plant can often occupy the same space, a single location may contribute more than one flush of bloom to the garden's multiseasonal beauty.

DESIGN FACTORS

Height

Height determines a plant's placement in the garden: tall plants at the back, short ones at the front. To many people it is just that simple, and their gardens are always left with a few awkward spots. To solve these problems, make the distinction between flower height and foliage height. Flower height is the height at which the blooms are held. In most cases, such as with phloxes, asters and bee balms, the stems are well clothed with foliage right up to the flowers; thus the fo-

Coralbells (Heuchera) should be placed at the front of the border with other low plants because of its low foliage height.

Cimicifuga simplex is a perennial with tall flower spikes and low foliage. When placed with other plants, its foliage height should be considered.

liage height is approximately the same as that of the flowers. Foliage height in plants such as daylilies, *Kniphofia* and hostas is usually lower than flower height, as the blooms are held atop tall, bare stems. These stems don't block the eye. When placed toward the back of the border with other plants of similar flower height, a "foliage hole" is created, made even more severe when plants are out of bloom (which is much of the time). For a unified composition, put plants like daylilies farther forward where the foliage height matches that of surrounding plants. When in bloom, the long-stemmed flowers become an accent, as if taking center stage for their "big number" in the show. Foliage height is actually more important than flower height in design.

In the reference section that begins on page 137, mature or functional flower heights are given. Foliage height will be given separately, in parentheses, when the foliage height differs from the flower height. Perennials and bulbs usually reach their maximum heights in the first or second year. Shrubs may take two or three years to become fully established. When cut back in spring, summer-blooming shrubs will reach the same size each summer.

Spread

Spread is synonymous in many ways with spacing. The difference is that spread describes the horizontal size of the plant, whereas spacing describes the distance between individuals. The object is to place plants far enough apart that they don't crowd each other, but close enough that the foliage touches. When the plants are close enough for the foliage to touch, weeds are shaded out, and the foliage acts as a groundcover to cool the roots and conserve water.

Because the spread of a plant changes as it grows, a functional mean size is given for planning purposes in the reference section (Part III). In the "Encyclopedia of Perennials," spread is given for a mature plant, usually about three years old. For slower growers that rarely need replanting, spread is given for an older plant. Spreads in the "Encyclopedia of Annuals" are given for the size achieved by mature plants about midseason.

Coordinating Bloom

Bloom season varies in both timing and duration. As discussed earlier, annuals tend to have a very long period of bloom, whereas perennial bloom tends to be more seasonal and of shorter duration. This is not always so, however. Although the average duration of bloom for a perennial is three weeks, many last longer than a month and some flower almost continuously, particularly if deadheaded. These include *Coreopsis verticillata* 'Moonbeam', *Gaillardia grandiflora*, *Salvia* 'East Friesland' and *Aster* ×*frikartii* 'Monch'.

For planning purposes, you may think of perennials in terms of the months in which they bloom. Fine-tuning—whether they bloom early or late in the month—comes with experience. You may find it even easier to break the bloom season into four major periods. Include a good representation of each of these bloom seasons in your plan, and the garden should have a continu-ous display: early to midspring, late spring to early summer, midsummer and late summer to early fall. I normally give the most prominent positions to the longer-blooming perennials, placing those with shorter bloom periods around them. Where a really long period of bloom is required, a patch of annuals may be more appropriate.

In this book, bloom period is given as the average months of bloom. This will be a national average (typical for Zone 6) and can be expected to be earlier in the South and later in the North or at higher altitudes. The reason for giving months is that it is more specific than seasons and gives a more helpful correlation of the plants that are likely to bloom together. For instance, in Zone 8 many plants specified as June-flowering will probably bloom together in May. In Zones 4 and 5, these same plants will probably flower together in late June or early July.

Form and Texture

Form and texture are as important to the finished composition as color. They are more subtle, but ultimately make the difference between an interesting display and a dull one. Contrasting shapes and sizes of flowers enhance the effectiveness of color and provide added interest when used properly. Plant shape and size work in a similar fashion though on a larger scale and can tie a planting together or fragment it; they provide contrast and even drama, as in the case of delphinium spikes among the bushier forms of other plants. When bloom is sparse, good compositions of form and texture are there to carry the show and fill the gaps. In shade, form and texture become even more important as foliage plays a more important role. To make the best use of form and texture, I find it useful to group plants according to their appearance. These are not scientific groupings, but rather aesthetic assessments. There are no rules. Create your own groupings as needed.

This partially shaded bed in the author's garden is a rich combination of various foliage sizes and textures.

Spiky foxgloves contrast with the billowy form of Geranium *'Johnson's Blue'.*

*The arching form of Solomon's seal (*Polygonatum commutatum*) stands above other plants in this shade garden.*

Form refers to the overall shape and habit of a plant.

Spiky, as in the cases of foxglove and cardinal flower.

Creeping, as in *Phlox subulata.*

Mounded, as in dwarf marigolds and dwarf asters.

Arching, as in Solomon's seal.

Texture refers to the size and shape of plant parts and how they affect the plant's appearance in the landscape. Plants with large leaves or flowers are coarse in appearance. Those with small leaves or flowers have a much finer and softer texture. Sprays of tiny baby's breath flowers are light and airy. The other aspect of texture is the shape of leaves and flowers.

Flowers:

Sprays, as in the cases of coralbells and baby's breath.

Spikes, as in lupine.

Plumes, as in astilbe.

Clusters, as in phlox and aster.

Flat heads, as in yarrow.

Daisies, as in aster and *Rudbeckia*.

Plumy white Aruncus dioicus *provides a background for the clustered small flowers of* Anchusa azurea.

The ferny foliage and flat flower heads of Achillea 'Coronation Gold' *bring the eye down from the spikey stems of Russian sage (*Perovskia*) and blue annual larkspur behind.*

*Clustered small flowers of feverfew (*Chrysanthemum parthenium*) create a foil for a soft yellow daylily.*

Foliage:

Grassy or straplike, as in the cases of iris and *Kniphofia*.

Ferny, as in astilbe, bleeding heart and yarrow.

Whorled, as in pachysandra and sweet woodruff.

Large rounded, as in hosta and *Ligularia* 'Desdemona'.

Small rounded, as in coralbells and European ginger.

Palmate, as in hardy geranium and *Delphinium*.

Palmately compound, as in lupine.

Pinnately compound (similar to ferny), as in Jacob's ladder and *Baptisia australis* (note that compound leaves impart the effect of finer texture).

Common (undistinguished leaf shape), as in phlox, aster and zinnia.

The key to successful form and texture compositions is to create contrast and variety. Avoid placing two types of plants with the same form and texture next to each other. Instead, place a ferny leaf on one side of a plant with large, rounded foliage, and on the other side use something from the grassy group. Behind it, something taller from the common group would be appropriate.

Effective contrast can be achieved using size too. Place large leaves next to small, even when both have the same shape. Compound leaves appear smaller because they are divided into smaller segments. A mass of small, rounded leaves works well planted around large, rounded leaves, particularly if the small leaf has a pattern or variegation on it. I've done this with a planting of *Bergenia crassifolia* surrounded by the variegated, small-leafed strawberry saxifrage (*Saxifraga stolonifera*)—handsome and uncomplicated.

Foliage color and shape mingle for summer-long interest: deep shiny green European ginger, light green "grassy" crested iris—with a filler of fine-textured, deep green Sedum sexangulare—and silvery Japanese painted fern.

At the Central Park Conservatory Garden this spherical, sheared purple barberry is a striking contrast to the otherwise frothy plant forms. This and hedges are among the rare situations where sheared plants can be effectively used in a flower garden.

Color

Color can be a complicated subject—it has great snob appeal. Truly skillful use of color though, is simple and magical in effect. Unfortunately, I am not as skillful at creating masterful color combinations as I'd like to be. As color has always been a bit of a mystery to me, I feel unqualified to elaborate at length on color theory. For those who wish to study the subject more deeply, I enthusiastically recommend *Color in Your Garden* by Penelope Hobhouse for its straightforward approach.

Having absolved myself of the responsibility of instruction in color theory, I will admit that I have managed to cope with the subject in my garden by making use of my own simple principles. What is more, I would guess that it gets the approval of 90 percent of my guests, and I get some awfully tough critics. A friend once remarked that the first place she was exposed to the thoughtful manipulation of color in the landscape was in my garden.

The point is that I've managed to develop my own means of working with color, and so can you. If you are a beginner, and the very

A cool, soothing combination of pastels: rose foxglove, silver woolly betany, and lemon yellow and lavender pansies.

task of growing plants successfully is enough of a challenge, then let the color issue rest for a while and enjoy your other successes. The most important thing is to do what you like in your garden because, after all, you're the one living with it. Do you want a carnival effect with lots of bright colors, or will you aim for a more subtle and focused scheme? Whatever you do, if it doesn't work, admit it and change it. Most of us are actually comforted by a little imperfection.

It is easier to explain color in the garden if flower color and foliage color are considered separately. Flower color can either harmonize or contrast. Garden designers can choose from the multitude of plant varieties to obtain the right colors for their compositions. A casual look at a catalog reveals that bearded irises, for instance,

The "carnival effect" is successfully achieved in this spring planting of red tulips interplanted with golden yellow English wallflowers and edged with red English daisies.

Purple Salvia superba *and red* Verbena *'Blaze' are an electric combination.*

Making new combinations with plants already growing in your garden is a bit easier. You are already familiar with how they grow for you and how their bloom periods correspond, and they are right there in front of you in living color—no surprises. To test color compatibility, cut one flower and lay it in with another. You can also make flower arrangements for the house; after all, arrangements are a microcosm of the garden. Make notes on what you like and make changes in the garden during the fall or spring for the following season.

The Single Late tulip 'Palestrina' was chosen to pick up the color of the 'Coral Bells' azalea behind.

are available in a wide range of color shades, heights, and early and late bloom times. Other highly hybridized groups such as dahlias, gladiolas, daffodils, tulips and roses have similar ranges, each at its own season. These endless varieties make up the designer's plant palette.

In developing a color scheme, first look at the background of the area. What are the colors of any buildings, fences and the like? If there are background plants, do they have light green, dark green or colored foliage? When do background plants flower, and what is the color? Is the background in shadow or bright light?

It will take more than one year to get your colors right in your garden. If many of the plants are new, you will find that some of them are not exactly what you had imagined. The color may not really be what the catalog shows or describes. (It is hard for the printer to get flower colors just right.) Bloom periods may not match up precisely either. And, some plants just won't be happy where you put them, so you'll have to move and replace them. The bottom line is, some adjustments will be necessary.

Use colors to best effect. I like hot, bright reds, oranges and yellows in the sun. Cool colors like pinks, mauves and whites seem to be soothing in the shade. Curiously, red is remarkably effective in shade too. Pale yellow and blue tend to cool down hot colors. Blends of pastels are delightfully easy to look at. Blends of brighter, deeper colors are festive.

Some colors clash, but even this is subjective. I once went to a lecture by Pamela Harper, when she presented slides of different color schemes and asked for a show of hands indicat-

June is the easiest month in which to achieve delicate color schemes in mixed borders. Here are two facing beds in the author's garden. Above left: pink, mauve, white and pale yellow. Above right: red, orange and yellow.

ing whether the audience liked or disliked them. There was not a single instance where everyone agreed. In my garden, I dislike orange and mauve together, especially the ubiquitous mauve summer phloxes with mustard yellow *Heliopsis* and *Rudbeckia*. A few gardeners combine them to their satisfaction, but not I. I put the two colors in separate beds where they can't fight. Another good tactic for avoiding clashes is to separate offending colors with a moderator such as white flowers or gray foliage. Pale yellow and chartreuse also make good moderators.

Color affects the perception of space and distance. Hot colors come forward visually and appear closer. They can make a small garden look even smaller and more crowded. Cool colors recede and look farther away. They give a sense of greater space and distance.

There are times when bloom is distinctly scarce, and you've got to make the best of the bloom you've got. If you plan your foliage textures and colors well, this will go a long way to fill the void. In a well-planned border, lack of bloom just means changing gear. This brings us to the subject of foliage color.

Foliage color is less evident than that of flowers. If you try to make subtle color harmonies, the result is likely to be so subtle as to be a nonstatement. Foliage colors need to contrast to create interest. Most foliage is really a shade of green, but the greens of foliage are often touched

with other tints too. "Blue" is not truly blue, and "red" is not truly red. Still, it is helpful to imagine the following foliage color groupings:

Dark green, as in European ginger.

Light green, as in feverfew.

Blue, as in *Hosta* 'Blue Skies' and blue fescue.

Gray or silver, as in artemisia.

Purple or red, as in purple basil and perilla.

Golden, as in *Filipendula ulmaria* 'Aurea'.

Variegated, as in many hostas.

Don't get hung up on not putting two of the same foliage color group next to each other; in the case of texture you want adjacent plants to come from different texture groups, but this isn't necessary for foliage color. Use the nongreen shades as accents and rely on texture for variation among the greens. Too many strong foliage colors can be garish.

Whatever you do, don't put light green and gold foliages next to each other. Each makes the other look sick! Gold foliage looks nice with blue foliage, blue flowers, pink flowers and purple foliage. Light green is best used with other greens. Keep in mind that many golden foliage plants sunburn easily, which indicates that they'll look fresher in partial shade. A good purple foliage is a very strong statement and makes a striking contrast to surrounding plants. It is so strong that it should be treated with the respect a flower color demands. Use it with gray foliage and red, deep pink and yellow flowers. Purple foliage normally needs sun to develop good color. Perilla, however, is a useful annual that will develop effective purple color in partial shade. Gray foliage seems to go with almost any color. It cools hot colors and brightens cool ones. As a rule, gray foliage plants resent excess moisture and poor drainage. Most need sun. Lamb's ears (*Stachys byzantina*) is one that performs well in moderate shade.

Not all foliage will last through the entire growing season. Most spring bulb foliage dies

Yellow tulips are cleverly placed next to the reddish spring foliage of Astilbe *'Fanal' at Old Westbury garden.*

This annual border features the reddish foliage of Pennisetum setaceum *'Cupreum' and* Hibiscus *'Red Shield' along with red* Salvia splendens. *Cerise and white* Cosmos bipinnatus *provides visual relief.*

The golden foliage of Coleus 'Golden Bedder' *is brought to life by dark green foliage and pink* Malva *flowers.*

down in late spring and will not contribute to the display after June. *Doronicum* and oriental poppy foliage also die back in late spring. The tall stems of bee balms become unsightly in midsummer after flowering, and should be cut down. Regrowth from the bottom is much shorter. The tall spikes of foxgloves with their bold leaves are finished by midsummer too. Even when foliage does hold up for the entire season, the color may change. The blue tends to wear off hosta leaves by late summer. Purplish foliage of some varieties may fade to nearly green as it matures. Gold foliage may "green up" in time, as well. The yellow variegation in *Iris pseudacorus* 'Variegata' fades to the same green as the rest of the leaf by late spring.

To combine flowers and foliage successfully, a knowledge of the effective seasons of both is essential. Season of bloom is easily researched, but seasonal peculiarities of foliage are more elusive. Books may or may not provide such details.

Take the large blue-leafed *Hosta sieboldiana elegans*. A good companion would be the yellow, June-flowering *Chrysogonum virginianum* with its small flowers and leaves. A less successful choice would be the yellow, September-blooming *Kir-*

Gray Artemisia 'Silver King' *lights up the surrounding colors in this mixed border.*

The stripes in the foliage of Iris pseudacorus 'Variegata' *pick up the color of creamy yellow primroses,* Primula ×polyantha, *and are intensified by blue* Ajuga.

engeshoma palmata, because by late summer the blue color of the hosta has faded and an element of contrast has been lost.

There are measures to prolong one plant's effective period so that it overlaps with the season of another. Deadheading (see page 112) will prolong bloom, and deadleafing (see page 114) can revive foliage displays. Unfortunately the effect is rarely as good as the first flush, and it is best to synchronize the initial effect of both plants for the greatest impact.

THE SECRET OF PLANT COMMUNITIES

Plant communities in nature achieve stability because the species growing together reach a balance at which they do not overgrow or crowd out one another, whether they are neighbors or share the same space. Such communities resist invasion by foreigners and change in composition only very slowly over a period of years. With the turn of the seasons, however, a rich and varied community can change its appearance dramatically.

The ultimate achievement in the garden is to create a plant community with a balance of its own by selecting plants adapted to the site and with similar vigor. Interplant using plants with complementary growing habits for multiple bloom seasons and foliage combinations. Plant fully to avoid empty space. Mother Nature always tries to fill empty spaces herself and in the garden it is usually with weeds. Stable, balanced plantings are attractive for a period of years and require less maintenance.

The degree of stability that can be achieved depends on how close your garden is to the natural vegetation of your region. In eastern North America, a shade garden will be likely to be the most stable, because forest is the natural vegetation for the region. In California, a sunny garden of plants that can withstand summer drought will be more stable. The more the garden varies from the local ecotype, the more maintenance will be required to keep it in order.

Wherever you garden, the most successful plant communities can be made in informal, natu-ralistic gardens, and these will require less maintenance than flower gardens designed to provide maximum bloom for the longest possible period. For this reason, it is best to concentrate such intensive gardens in the most important locations as accents and make more naturalistic plantings in the other areas. Even so, always use the plant community concept to design plantings in which the plants co-exist successfully and take care of themselves as much as possible. Balance can't be achieved immediately, but will improve with time.

In nature's plant communities plants seldom grow alone in pure colonies. In the garden, however, multiple plantings everywhere would be too complicated and messy. It is difficult to appreciate the beauty of each type when they are all crowded together. Carefully placed interplantings of two (or occasionally three) species, however, add extra bloom and interest. For instance, plant such early bulbs as snowdrops and crocuses among the roots of hosta, which emerges as the bulbs are becoming dormant. Hardy begonia (*Begonia grandis*) makes an excellent companion when grown on top of a clump of daffodils. The daffodils bloom in spring but then the matted leaves must remain until they mature in June. Many perennials have difficulty fighting their way through this mass of foliage but the begonia shoots effortlessly poke through. After the daffodil foliage has died away for the summer, the begonias provide light green foliage and sprays of small pink flowers from July into October. Both of these interplanting combinations work because of complementary growth cycles, and they thrive in moderate shade.

Sometimes short plants can fill in as groundcovers under taller plants and suppress weeds. Creeping phlox will spread under sparsely foliaged Solomon's seal. Plant large variegated hostas in a groundcover of deep green periwinkle. Both these groundcovers provide an attractive contrast of texture. In the flower garden, plant tall lilies among the lower-growing perennials for bloom at either the same or different seasons.

You can expand the concept into a full plant community. Imagine a weed-free groundcover of

Crocus chrysanthus 'E. A. Bowles' blooms in late winter and early spring among the roots of hosta. Last year's hosta flower stalks are still visible.

Begonia grandis is a perennial that blooms in late summer. In this shaded border, daffodils bloom in the same spot in spring.

leadwort (*Ceratostigma plumbaginoides*) blooming with deep blue flowers in fall. During the winter, it dies to the ground, leaving an open space for crocuses, snowdrops and Siberian squill to bloom in spring. By the time these spring bulbs go dormant, the leadwort resumes growth and covers the space for the rest of the year. If this groundcover scheme is used around summer-blooming shrubs, such as butterfly bush or rose of Sharon, or summer-blooming perennials, bloom will occur during each growing season. For even more bloom, add daffodils and wood hyacinths to bloom after the earlier spring bulbs. *Colchicum* can add to the fall display as their pink flowers pop up through those of the blue leadwort.

It's not just what each plant does on its own that counts, but what plants do together. A well-conceived design presents a community of plants that have an aesthetic relationship, as well as a biological harmony. Add to this the element of time, and gardening becomes complex because the relationship needs to hold up to seasonal

changes throughout the year. When a design is "right," it unfolds year in and year out as part of your landscape. The result is immensely satisfying. Here are the principles to consider in bringing a plant community together:

1. Use plants adapted to the microclimate of the location.
2. Allow each plant to express its natural habit and beauty.
3. Interplant plants with complementary growth cycles.
4. Use plants with compatible vigor.
5. Begin with the largest, most dominant plants, and work the others in around and among them.

Plant Communities Working for You

If the plant community mentioned above sounds too good to be true, you're probably wondering what the catch is concerning maintenance. Actually maintenance is not a big deal. Weeding is scarcely necessary once the community is established because the plants will fill the spaces that the weeds would occupy. What is needed is a little policing in case the leadwort wanders too far, and the garden will look better if the dead stems are cut down in winter so the crocus bloom on a clean surface. Otherwise this plant community is ideal, simple and stable, one you just enjoy. Similarly, any established well-planned community will be easier to care for than a bed of miscellaneous plants with a lot of bare soil.

Not Starting From Scratch

If you already have a garden, don't feel you need to rip it all out and start over. Work with and learn from what is there. Consider what you need to achieve your goals. Most gardens will benefit from soil improvement. Soil can be improved in the empty spaces, and whenever a plant is transplanted. Add compost, and dig it deeply into as large an area as possible. If the bed is in need of greater renovation, all the soil can be improved at once. Remove all the plants when they are dormant and set them aside, or heel them in elsewhere. (Heeling in is a method of temporarily holding plants until the permanent planting site is ready. Place the plants closely in a shallow trench and cover the roots with soil or mulch.)

You will probably want to rearrange things to enhance plant combinations and create spaces for new varieties. Remember to make a plan on paper first; it's easier to work it out beforehand. Beds can be reshaped at any time of year in preparation for planting in the fall and spring. (Soil is often easier to work in the fall when it isn't too wet.) Mature clumps of most perennials can be moved while dormant. This is also a good time to divide others that are overmature (see page 130).

Most gardens in need of renovation are too crowded. Before replanting, divide and replant only what is needed, using the most vigorous divisions. You should put back no more than a third of what was taken out. To give the renovated garden an established look, the divisions can be bigger than those you would buy. Renovation is not pretty, but when done neatly during the dormant season, the plants will grow in as though they had never been disturbed. Most of the mature plants in your garden will be an asset to a new design. They give a sense of establishment the first year, and may be divided to provide larger groups. Any you don't want to keep can be traded with friends, too.

Keeping Track: Maps and Labels

No one can keep track of everything that goes on in the garden in their head. It is very difficult to remember the name and location of every variety and the intended bloom sequences. Save the original planting plan. If it is done in pencil, it can be easily updated, or an updated plan can be drawn on one of the photocopies of the empty bed drawing. You can record how the bed looked at any given time in photographs. You can even mark the photo to show how to change and improve it when transplanting time arrives. Don't assume you will just be able to remember—few people can.

Many gardeners find labels that mark a plant's location with its name very helpful. Sometimes a label means the difference between digging into or stepping on a valued specimen and avoiding disaster. A label enables you to find the plant at the proper time for transplanting even though it may be dormant and give no hint of its location.

Labels have their problems. Plastic ones are subject to deterioration in the sun's ultraviolet rays, and eventually become brittle. In winter extreme cold makes them brittle and easily snapped off by passing wildlife. They are also heaved out by the frost and blown away in the March wind. Surprisingly, writing in pencil seems more durable than indelible marker, which tends to fade after a year or two. Labels can be raked out by accident and may complicate maintenance, but they are a means of identifying exact locations and keeping names straight.

Metal labels are more durable. They can be stepped on and won't break off. Long prongs can be pushed deep into the ground to prevent frost heaving. Zinc face plates hold markings well whether it be in graphite pencil, indelible marker or grease pencil. (I find an especially durable combination to be pencil overwritten with indelible marker.) They are more expensive, but last much longer.

However well designed a garden may be, it will never be a finished, static affair, but evolves over time. Surrounding trees grow and light changes. Certain plants crowd others. Disease strikes a variety, and something else must be substituted. Tastes change, and gardeners yearn to try something new. Gardening is learning. Changing situations create new opportunities. The result is that both gardens and gardeners usually improve with age.

Herbaceous Flower Border for Partial Shade

About the Plan:

This border along the edge of a woods is designed to provide bloom from early spring to early fall in colors of yellow, pink, purple and white. Foliage plays an important role as it supplements bloom for a continuously full effect. Spring color is provided by bulbs and *Viola × wittrockiana* (pansies). Since shade borders are less intensively maintained than those in sun, such bulbs as *Narcissus* (daffodils) and *Galanthus* (snowdrops) can have a more prominent role among certain perennials that need infrequent replanting, where they can be left undisturbed for many years. If more spaces were left between the varieties of perennials or if more low-growing groundcovers were used, bulbs could play an even more prominent role than they do in this plan. Shade-loving hybrids of *Lilium martagon* can be used among low-growing perennials.

In this plan, plant varieties are identified by numbers corresponding to the plant lists that follow. Perennials are depicted by a dot surrounded by a circle, which shows the spread of the plants. These circles are connected to show the exact location of plants of each variety. Patches of annuals are depicted in open spaces because annuals are less permanent and their spacing can be more flexible.

Numbers in squares in the gray-tinted areas indicate plantings for early spring such as bulbs, which may be interplanted between perennials, and cool-season annuals, which provide early-spring bloom before summer annuals are planted in those same areas. Summer-blooming lilies are also identified by boxed numbers because they are interplanted between perennials.

Tips on Care:

Keep a fine-textured mulch on the bed to suppress weeds and retain moisture. In late winter remove any coarse leaves such as those of hosta, which can inhibit the smaller bulbs. Cut down unsightly epimedium foliage (which will be at least partially winterkilled in most regions). During the growing season, transplant seedlings of *Digitalis purpurea* to desired locations to replace old plants.

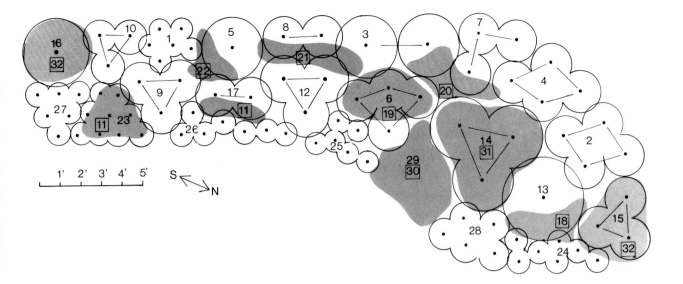

Note: Numbers in parentheses indicate foliage height.

Tall Perennials:
1 *Aconitum × bicolor* 'Spark's Variety', 48 × 12 in.
2 *Anemone × hybrida* 'Margarette', 60(30) × 24 in.
3 *Aruncus dioicus*, 6 × 3 ft.
4 *Cimicifuga racemosum*, 6(3) × 4 ft.
5 *Ligularia dentata* 'Desdemona', 4(3) × 3 ft.
6 *Polygonatum commutatum*, 3–7 × 2 ft.
7 *Thalictrum rochebrunianum*, 36–60 × 24 in.
8 *Thalictrum speciosissimum*, 36–60 × 24in.
9 *Tricyrtis* 'Sinonome', 3–5 × 2 ft.
  Tall Biennials:
10 *Digitalis purpurea* 'Excelsior', 60 × 18 in.
  Tall Bulbs:
[11] *Lilium martagon* hybrids, 72 × 15 in.
  Mid-sized Perennials:
12 *Astilbe × arendsii* 'Rheinland', 24–48 × 24-36 in.
13 *Clematis heracleifolia*, 36 × 48 in.
14 *Hosta* 'Krossa Regal', 60 (30) × 36 in.
15 *Hosta plantaginea*, 24–30 × 24 in.
16 *Hosta sieboldiana*, 24 × 36 in.
17 *Solidago caesia*, 24–36 × 24 in.
[18] *Endymion hispanicus*, 20 × 8 in.

[19] *Leucojum aestivum*, 15 × 6 in.
[20] *Narcissus* (trumpet), 15 × 4–8 in.
[21] *Narcissus* (small-cupped), 15 × 4–8 in.
[22] *Narcissus* (triandrus hybrid), 15 × 4–8 in.
  Low Perennials:
23 *Epimedium × versicolor* 'Sulphurea', 12–15 × 12 in.
24 *Lamium maculatum* 'Beacon Silver' 8 × 12 in.
25 *Liriope muscari* 'Silvery Sunproof', 12 × 12 in.
26 *Pulmonaria saccharata* 'Argentea', 12 × 18 in.
  Low Grasses:
27 *Hakonecloa macra* 'Aureola', 12 × 18 in.
  Low Ferns:
28 *Athyrium nipponicum* 'Pictum', 12–18 × 18 in.
  Low Annuals:
29 *Impatiens walleriana*, 8–15 × 12 in.
[30] *Viola × wittrockiana* (blue), 8 × 8 in.
  Other Suggestions:
Begonia × semperflorens-cultorum, 12 × 12 in.
Browalia americana, 12 × 12 in.
  Small Bulbs:
[31] *Galanthus nivalis*, 6 × 4 in.
[32] *Scilla sibirica*, 6 × 4 in.

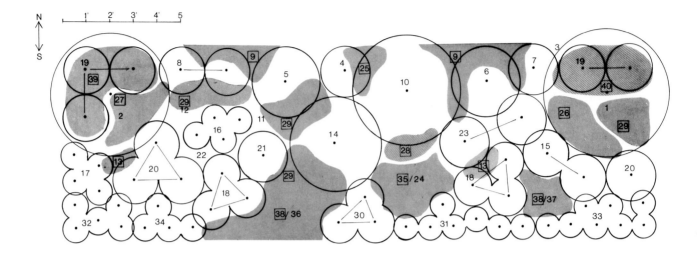

Mixed Flower Border for Sun

About the Plan (illustrated in color on page 84)

In contrast to the plan for shade (page 81), this design requires intensive management for maximum performance. The color scheme for this planting is blue, lavender, pink and pale yellow. Foliage colors of gray and purple highlighted by a bold variegated grass complement bloom throughout the season. The bloom season extends from April to October, with peak bloom through midsummer. Early bloom is primarily from bulbs and cool-season annuals. Cool-season annuals are replaced by warm-season annuals that will carry bloom into early fall, often up to frost. Late perennials add to this early fall display. While the selection of plants available for such a garden as this is practically endless, I have selected those that I have found to be most reliable for season-long performance. With time, changes should be made, adding varieties with superior performance under your climatic conditions.

Summer-blooming shrubs that are severely pruned in spring provide opportunities for spring bloom under them, as do large widely spaced perennials toward the back of the bed. Bulbs and cool-season annuals are used to fill these empty spaces before the area is covered with foliage. Such strongly perennial bulbs as daffodils and small bulbs as *Chionodoxa* and *Scilla* are more suited to planting under shrubs, where they are disturbed less than elsewhere in the bed. Such early-flowering perennials as *Dicentra spectabilis* that go dormant in early summer or can grow in substantial shade through the summer also thrive in these spaces. Tall annuals can be planted in gaps between perennials at the back of the bed. *Digitalis* thrive in shade and are planted between the largest perennials at the back of the bed where they will be properly situated for their tall spikes in late May and June.

Some plants, such as daylilies, tulips and daffodils, are available in such a multitude of hybrids that I have

avoided recommending a particular variety. Choose your own favorites from those currently available from catalogues and garden centers.

In this plan, plant varieties are identified by numbers corresponding to the plant lists that follow. Shrubs and perennials are depicted by a dot surrounded by a circle, which shows the spread of the plants. These circles are connected to show the exact location of plants of each variety. Patches of annuals are depicted in open spaces because annuals are less permanent and their spacing can be more flexible.

Numbers in squares in the gray-tinted areas indicate plantings for early spring such as bulbs, which may be interplanted between perennials or under shrubs, and cool-season annuals, which provide early spring bloom before summer annuals are planted in those same areas. Summer-blooming lilies are also identified by boxed numbers because they are interplanted between perennials. *Digitalis purpurea* is also depicted by a boxed number in gray-tinted areas because in a sunny location they can be planted in the shade of larger perennials.

Tips on Care:

Early spring should begin with severe pruning of the shrubs and removal of any perennial and grass stems left standing for winter effect. Then, plant frost-tolerant, cool-season annuals. When weeding, watch for seedlings of self-sown annuals and biennials, which should be saved either where they are or moved to another location. (The earlier they are moved, the better they will perform.)

The clematis is a variety that can be severely pruned in spring along with the buddleia. What remains of the clematis trunks should be tied to the fence or into the buddleia, into which it will grow.

Note: Numbers in parentheses indicate foliage height.

Tall Shrubs:
1 *Buddleia* 'Nanho Blue', 5 × 5 ft.
2 *Hibiscus syriacus* 'Helene', 5–6 × 5 ft.
   Vines:
3 *Clematis* 'Duchess of Albany', to 10 feet
   Tall Perennials:
4 *Aster tataricus*, 4–6 × 2 ft.
5 *Filipendula rubra* 'Venusta', 6–8 × 3 ft.
6 *Helianthus salicifolius*, 6–8 × 3 ft.
7 *Thalictrum rochebrunianum*, 3–5 × 2 ft.
8 *Thalictrum speciosissimum*, 3–5 × 2 ft.
   Other Suggestions:
   Aconitum carmichaelii 'Arendsii', 4 × 1 ft.
   Solidago sempervirens, 4–6 × 2–3 ft.
   Tall Biennials:
9 *Digitalis purpurea*, 24–60 × 18 in.
   Tall Grasses:
10 *Miscanthus sinensis* 'Variegatus', 6–8 × 4–5 ft.
11 *Abelmoschus manihot*, 4–8 × 1 ft.
12 *Cosmos bipinnatus* 'Sensation Mix', 6 × 1 ft.
    Tall Bulbs:
13 *Lilium* 'Pink Perfection' (Aurelian Hybrid), 72 × 15 in.
    Mid-sized Shrubs:
14 *Abelia* 'Edward Goucher', 4 × 4 ft.
15 *Berberis thunbergii* 'Crimson Pygmy', 2 × 2 ft.
    Mid-sized Perennials:
16 *Artemisia ludoviciana* 'Silver King', 24–36 × 12 in.
17 *Aster frikartii* 'Monch', 2–3 × 1 ft.
18 *Coreopsis verticillata* 'Moonbeam', 15 × 18 in.
19 *Dicentra spectabilis*, 30 × 24 in.
20 *Hemerocallis* (large flowered, pink), 3–4(1–2) × 2 ft.
21 *Iris sibirica* (tall, purple), 3 × 2 ft.
22 *Papaver orientale* (pink), 24–48 × 18 in.
23 *Phlox paniculata* 'Bright Eyes', 3–4 × 2 ft.

Other Suggestions:
Clematis heracleifolia, 3 × 4 ft.
Kniphofia 'Primrose Beauty', 30 × 30 in.
Monarda didyma 'Cambridge Scarlet', 36 × 18 ft.
Mid-sized Annuals:
24 *Salvia farinacea* 'Victoria', 18 × 12 in.
    Mid-sized Bulbs:
25 *Allium* 'Purple Sensation', 30(15) × 8 in.
26 *Narcissus* (trumpet), 15 × 4–8 in.
27 *Narcissus* (small-cupped), 15 × 4–8 in.
28 *Narcissus* (cyclamineus hybrid), 15 × 4–8 in.
29 *Tulipa* (April-May flowering), 6–30 × 8 in.
    Low Perennials:
30 *Achillea* × 'Moonshine', 24(12) × 18 in.
31 *Geranium sanguineum striatum*, 6 × 12 in.
32 *Heuchera sanguinea* (rose-pink), 12–24(8) × 12 in.
33 *Stachys* 'Helene von Stein', 15 × 12 in.
34 *Veronica* 'Goodness Grows', 10–12 × 12 in.
    Other Suggestions:
    Dianthus × *allwoodii*, 12 × 8–12 in.
    Low Annuals:
35 *Bellis perennis* (pink), 6–8 × 6 in.
36 *Catharanthus roseus* (rose-pink), 12–18 × 12 in.
37 *Nicotiana alata* 'Nicki Pink', 16–18 × 12 in.
38 *Viola* × *wittrockiana*, (blue), 8 × 8 in.
    Other Suggestions:
    Antirrhinum, dwarf, 8–12 × 8 in.
    Begonia semperflorens-cultorum, 12 × 12 in.
    Dahlia merckii, 18 × 12 in.
    Verbena × *hybrida*, 8–12 × 10 in.
    Small Bulbs:
39 *Chionodoxa luciliae*, 6 × 3 in.
40 *Scilla sibirica*, 6 × 4 in.
    Biennials (not shown)-which can be allowed to self sow among perennials:
    Lychnis coronaria, 36 × 8–12 in.
    Silene armeria, 12–24 × 6 in.
    Verbena bonariensis, 4 × 1 ft.

The Mixed Border for Sun in spring

The Mixed Border for Sun in summer

The Mixed Border for Sun in fall

PART II

The Green Thumb — The Keys to Success

The purple foliage of Perilla frutescens *'Crispa' intensifies the color of* Aster novae-angliae *'Alma Potschke' at Stonecrop, Coldspring, New York.*

FIVE

Nurturing the Display

As I begin this chapter, it is mid-May and excitement is mounting out in my garden. The tulips have just finished, although pansies and forget-me-nots continue to bloom exuberantly while the beds fill up with fresh, clean foliage. Iris, peonies, poppies, pyrethrum daisies, columbines and other perennials are showing their color. The pace is quickening, and by June an abundance of perennials will spill from these same beds, mingling with and backed by roses and clematises. It sounds like the perfect English garden, but it is in Pennsylvania, and we Americans have grown flower gardens like this for nearly a century too.

The success of such a display depends on proper training and nurturing of the plants, from the start and through the summer, to achieve succession of bloom. This chapter is about the everyday care of the plants themselves, how to make them look their best through training, staking and grooming.

Are you a perfectionist or not? Your garden will most likely reflect this. Some of the finest horticulturists have untidy but lovely gardens. Formal gardens require a higher standard of maintenance than informal woodland plantings, but the woodland garden still makes the best presentation when it is neat and the plants are healthy. All garden owners must decide for themselves just how perfectly maintained their garden is to be.

In the author's garden this bed, backed by a rose trellis, is shown in three seasons. Above left: In late April, the perennials are still short, allowing tulips less than 2 feet tall to dominate. Early-flowering Phlox subulata in the wall is visible because the Hybrid Tea roses in the bed below the wall have

been cut short. Above right: Five weeks later, in early June, the roses and perennials have grown up and the withering tulip foliage is hidden. All these plants were in the bed photographed in April. Below: In July a new set of flowers are in bloom, although nothing more has been planted.

Small gardens are more easily maintained to an immaculate standard. Of course, if the garden is a carefully planned work of art, demanding crisp lines and precisely balanced plantings, nothing will set it off more than a good manicure.

Don't overdo it. Just as neglect detracts from a garden, so does *over*maintenance. I know of a garden where the owners are so obsessive that every plant is rigidly staked and trimmed to within an inch of its life, and where most annuals and perennials are surrounded by wire cages, forcing them to conform to unyielding standards. The natural beauty of plants in this garden is suppressed, because nonconformity is strictly prohibited. When my friends refer to "the dictators' " garden, the meaning is understood. Make and care for your garden the way you want it to be, but I'd advise against being too much of a dictator. Encourage and train your plants—don't stifle them. Let each one show its own natural beauty or personality, adding to the romance of your garden.

Your garden will be more beautiful and easier to care for if you allow the plants to grow naturally in their own forms. Provide some training to improve appearances where necessary but not the sort that radically changes the plants' habit and form. For example, when staking is necessary, stake only enough to hold the plant up in its natural position.

Neatly clipped hedges are attractive, but don't clip every shrub in the garden into a round ball. Tightly clipped shrubs look untidy as soon as the first few straggly shoots appear. Choose shrubs that will grow to the desired size, or prune in such a way that the natural texture and appearance are maintained. You can either run hedge clippers over forsythia or remove the longest shoots from the base to control size. The second method gives a more graceful plant with much more bloom and provides better branches to cut and force indoors in early spring. Match vines with the proper type of support or trellis so they can take care of themselves, growing naturally without demanding too much attention. Clematis won't cling to a bare wall or hold on to most types of trellises. Ivy isn't satisfactory for trellises either. (See page 98 for advice on support for specific vines.)

What doesn't show counts a lot in the flower garden. Good planning, masterful training of plants, and absence of weeds do not attract attention in themselves, but they make the display outstanding. Poor garden practices detract from the display, just as stray or sloppy brushstrokes spoil a painting. Anticipate problems with preventive maintenance. Know which of your perennials can be pinched to avoid the need for staking later, and do it before they get leggy, or it will be too late. Keep an eye on dangerously tall

The climbing rose 'Tausenchön' in June at Old Westbury Garden.

stems that risk falling over with the next rain or hard wind. It's easier to support them before they fall and become misshapen.

TRAINING KNOW-HOW

Good training of plants is more than a last-minute remedy. It allows the gardener to direct the type of growth and behavior of the plants, and influence their appearance. Good training can have a marked effect on a plant's manners. Training of vines is a case in point. Untrimmed, they are messy. Cut them to the ground, and they will be likely to sprawl every which way. But trim them back to their trunks, still in place on the trellis, and they will grow up where you want them and oblige you with a well-placed display.

Training improves the behavior and performance of annuals and perennials too. Many can be pinched to improve their habits. Pinching takes only a few minutes, and you can do it with your fingers, without running for the pruners. But you need to know which plants and when. That in part is what this chapter is all about. Additional hints on training of specific plants can be found in the reference section at the back of this book.

ANNUALS

Most annuals grow into bushier plants if pinched when young. Pinch them when you transplant them to their final locations. If they are direct sown, pinch when they are a couple of inches tall to encourage branching. For dahlias grown from tubers rather than seed, pinch each shoot back to the first node as it emerges from the soil. Allow two nodes to grow on each branch and pinch out the tip again above these nodes. Of course, there are exceptions. Any annual that forms a spike or single head of flowers must not be pinched. This includes larkspur and crested cockscomb. I used to work in a public garden where all the seedling annuals were routinely pinched in the greenhouse. Somehow the grower could never remember to avoid pinching the cockscomb, so we never managed to grow any with big heads.

Midway through the season, many annuals get tired. They could be replaced, but many can be rejuvenated for a second wind with a stiff trimming and feeding. Cut them back to inner branches and buds, and be sure to remove all spent flowers and seeds. They will make fresh growth below the cuts and bloom for the rest of the summer. Petunias and wishbone flower respond well to this treatment. China asters (*Callistephus*) don't, however, as they bloom only once and then leave a bare spot. (For this reason, they are best grown in the cutting garden.) Such trimming isn't usually necessary for salvia and impatiens, because they tend to keep performing right up to frost and seldom need rejuvenation. (Of course, they may become damaged and need pruning to reshape them.) There is nothing wrong with cutting back annuals that have become too large. Rejuvenation often makes more sense than replanting and is usually less trouble.

PERENNIALS AND BIENNIALS

Nobody talks about it, but most perennials can be pinched to encourage a bushier habit with greater stability and to reduce the need for staking. In fact, some perennials can scarcely be controlled without pinching and pruning back to keep them neat. The most commonly pinched perennial is the chrysanthemum. Many gardeners know the rule about not pinching mums after mid-July. Many fewer people know that asters should be pinched in the same way to make bushy plants.

Sometimes you discover things quite by accident, as I did with balloonflower (*Platycodon*) a couple of summers ago. A self-sown seedling was leggy and lying around in an untidy manner. In my harried mood of the moment, I couldn't be bothered to try and tie it up but didn't want to pull it out either, so I cut it back halfway. To my surprise, it branched and flowered as a well-shaped but short plant. Mullein pink (*Lychnis coronaria*) and feverfew (*Chrysanthemum parthenium*) are biennials that always get pinched in my garden. Otherwise, just as they come into bloom, it seems that a rain shower knocks them over. If I take out the tips when they are about 6 inches tall, they usually stand on their own. Catchfly (*Silene armeria*) should be pinched at about 4 inches.

Some perennials shouldn't be pinched or trimmed. Any that form a single spike or a predominant large head will be spoiled by pinching. Obvious examples are delphinium, foxglove and lupine. If pinched, their single spikes or large heads won't be produced, although many will form smaller side clusters. If you pinch astilbe you are, quite simply, out of luck. Others such as coralbells, *Geum*, oriental poppy and daylilies form a basal rosette and send up long flower stems. There is no need to pinch the rosettes, and if you pinch the long stems, the flowers are gone. I've also found it useless to pinch *Thalictrum rochebrunianum*. It just forms another strong shoot from the top bud and continues skyward. *Phlox paniculata* is an "in-between" plant. Normally, I'd say don't pinch it because you will get a nice big flower head at the top. It's worth staking instead of pinching. If you want it to be shorter, plant a shorter variety. However, I have been in a situation where it seemed best to pinch the phlox in order to get shorter plants, and they still gave a fine floral display of smaller clusters.

Begin pinching early, especially with those such as chrysanthemums and asters that need several pinches. By early, I mean mid-spring, about the time the tulips have finished. Others, such as balloonflower, need only one pinch, so wait until they have made approximately half of their growth. This could be mid-spring or later, depending on rate of growth and bloom time. If you pinch too close to bloom time, then bloom will be delayed, which may or may not be a good thing.

As you pinch or cut, try to have the top bud pointing out and away from the center of the plant. This bud will grow most vigorously and you don't want it crowding the other stems and encouraging disease. Repeat pinchings should be made after the growth of two or three nodes. Pinch the front and sides shorter than the central stems. This keeps fresh foliage low down to hide the dead leaves that occur on the lower sections of the inner stems. It also encourages a better distribution of flowers over the plant.

Thinning

You will get better performance from some perennials if you thin out the stems when you do the first pinch. The main reason for this is disease prevention, especially with asters and phlox. It allows better air circulation, and if you spray for disease, it makes it easier to get the spray into the center. The weaker stems aren't needed, and removing them allows the stronger stems more space to grow and develop. Thinning also allows the remaining stems to branch more fully after pinching.

To thin perennials, simply cut the weaker stems out from among the stronger ones. (Often you can pull them out from a well-rooted plant; it's a lot faster.) The remaining stems should be about an inch apart and evenly spaced. A two-year-old aster might be left with only four stems, whereas an older plant may have about eight. The actual number is not critical because more widely spaced stems will branch more and make up the difference, but I feel it is better to err on the side of fewer shoots or thinning won't count for much.

Pinching and Bloom Time

The rule about not pinching chrysanthemums after mid-July is not set in stone. I use the effect of later pinches to advantage. The later you continue to pinch, the later your mums will bloom. In the North, it is good advice to stop pinching in mid-July, or they won't bloom before frost. Here, near Philadelphia, I don't want mums in September when it still seems like summer. (I wish garden centers wouldn't start selling them here right after Labor Day.) I want mums in early October, so I pinch them a couple of weeks longer, into late July. Similarly, by pinching a little longer, I can have New England asters later in the fall when bloom is a bit more scarce. There

Perennials and Biennials That Should Not Be Pinched

Achillea species (Yarrow)
Aconitum species (Monkshood)
Alcea rosea (Hollyhock)
Anemone × *hybrida* (Japanese anemone)
Aruncus species (Goatsbeard)
Astilbe species and hybrids (Astilbe)
Campanula species (Bellflower)
Chrysanthemum coccineum (Painted daisy)
Crambe cordifolia (Colewort)
Delphinium species and hybrids (Larkspur)
Dianthus species and hybrids (Pinks)
Dictamnus albus (Gas plant)
Digitalis species (Foxglove)
Filipendula species (Meadowsweet)
Geranium species and hybrids (Hardy geranium)
Geum species (Avens)
Hemerocallis species (Daylily)
Hosta species and hybrids (Hosta or plantain lily)
Iris species and hybrids (Iris)
Kniphofia species and hybrids (Red-hot poker)
Liatris species (Gayfeather)
Ligularia species (Ligularia)
Lupinus Russell Hybrids (Lupine)
Paeonia species (Peony)
Papaver species (Poppy)
Polygonatum species (Solomon's seal)
Rodgersia species (Rodgersia)
Smilacina racemosa (False Solomon's seal)
Verbascum species (Mullein)
Veronica species and hybrids (Speedwell)

Perennials and Biennials That Respond Well to Pinching

Aster species and hybrids (Michaelmas daisy)
Artemisia lactiflora (White mugwort)
Chrysanthemum × *morifolium* (Garden mum)
Chrysanthemum parthenium (Feverfew)
Lychnis coronaria (Mullein pink)
Platycodon grandiflorus (Balloon flower)
Salvia guaranitica (Salvia)
Silene armeria (Catchfly)

Rejuvenating Perennials

Certain perennials can be pressed into service for a second, if somewhat reduced, round of bloom if the old stalks are cut down to the ground immediately after the first flowering. Delphinium and the perennial cornflower (*Centaurea montana*) both give a second bloom from this treatment. Some other perennials will not respond with more flowers, but they will provide a crop of fresh foliage to fill the space for the rest of the summer. Shasta daisy and *Filipendula* will reward you with foliage. This second growth of foliage on *Filipendula ulmaria* 'Aurea' remains a beautiful golden color into the autumn to complement asters planted behind.

SHRUBS

Among herbaceous plants, flower garden shrubs require firm treatment to keep them tidy and in scale and to prevent them from overrunning their perennial neighbors. Most of the shrubs that I prefer to include in the flower garden (page 33) bloom in summer on new growth and are weak wooded in that they tend to have a lot of dieback during the winter among the smaller twigs. (In cold climates, they often die to the ground.) You

are early- and late-blooming varieties of asters and mums. If you don't happen to have the late ones, late pinching gives you another option. Besides, the mums you do buy at garden centers will almost certainly be the early-blooming varieties, and if you are like me, you'll want to pinch them longer.

could spend an inordinate amount of time cutting out this dead wood, but it would be pointless because what remains would not be of good vigor. A better solution is to get out the loppers and get rid of the whole mess. Cut back to heavy stems, leaving as little as 6 to 12 inches for some shrubs, more trunk for others.

Butterfly bush (*Buddleia davidii*) is a good example of a shrub to cut back to 6 to 12 inches before growth starts. Don't be afraid to use a saw for the heavy trunks. Remove all smaller side branches at the same time. You don't have to be as careful as you do with roses because any strong branch will sprout vigorous flowering shoots. By midsummer they will have regained their former height and be in flower. Most summer-blooming flower garden shrubs respond to similar treatment. The actual severity and height of pruning depends on the variety, desired height and amount of winter kill.

Approximate Pruning Heights for Flower Garden Shrubs

Abelia ×*grandiflora* (Glossy abelia), moderate (3 to 5 feet), only enough to control size

Buddleia davidii (Butterfly bush), 6 to 12 inches

Caryopteris ×*clandonensis* (Bluebeard), 4 to 6 inches

Cotinus coggygria (Smoke bush; purple foliage forms), 6 to 12 inches

Hibiscus syriacus (Rose of Sharon), 2 to 4 feet or higher

Hydrangea paniculata (Panicle hydrangea), 2 to 4 feet or higher

Lagerstroemia indica (Crape myrtle), to ground or higher

Potentilla fruticosa (Bush cinquefoil), moderate, also remove oldest canes

Sambucus nigra 'Aurea' (Golden European elder), 2 feet or higher

Sorbaria aitchisonii (Kashmir false spirea), 2 feet or higher

Vitex agnus-castus (Chaste tree), 1 foot or higher

Remember that you can't cut spring-flowering shrubs back until after they bloom or you will cut off all the flower buds. Only summer-blooming shrubs that bloom on the current season's shoots can be pruned in early spring.

ROSES

Success of roses in the scheme of a flower garden depends on how they are pruned. Fortunately, major pruning for most roses can and should be done in early spring when there is less to do elsewhere. Specialist rose books cover the subject in great detail; here is my simplified version.

Pruning

All roses can be pruned in early spring. In my climate, I prefer to do it in late March, and figure it should be done by the time the forsythias bloom. Climbing roses that flower only once can be pruned then too, but respond better if their major pruning is done immediately after flowering in early summer.

If you live in a climate typically plagued by late spring frosts that threaten to kill back the new shoots, delay pruning for a couple of weeks. The more developed the buds and young shoots are, the more susceptible to frost they are. The first buds to grow will be at the ends of the canes. You will be cutting most of these away and the lower buds will have to start growing anew. With this two-week delay, severe frosts should be past by the time the new shoots reach the more vulnerable stage. The same number of buds should develop, so the total amount of bloom will not be affected.

Don't worry unduly about light frosts. There will almost certainly be some frost after the buds on your roses have begun to expand. Nature has equipped these buds with a remarkable ability to withstand light frost, to about 25°F. If the temperature drops to 15° after the new shoots have extended to 1 or 2 inches, there will almost certainly be damage.

An important difference between roses and trees is that in roses, the strongest shoots come from the base of the plant, rather than from the top. The higher up on a rose plant a shoot starts, the smaller and less vigorous it will be. With each successive year, a cane will branch into even smaller twigs. These bear progressively smaller flowers until they become barren.

Generally, when roses are pruned, the oldest canes are removed to the base of the plants and these are replaced by vigorous young ones. Old canes can also be cut back to vigorous offshoots closer to the base. A good clue to the age of a cane is the color and roughness of the bark. Young canes are normally smooth and green. Old ones have rough corky bark. There are few rose varieties where a cane should be left for more than three or four years. The canes of Hybrid Teas and Floribundas should be removed after a year or two as indicated by their decline in vigor.

Rose pruning begins with the "three Ds": First remove the Dead, Dying and Diseased wood. In other words, remove anything that is unhealthy or damaged. Where branches cross or rub, prune out the weaker or older ones.

Hybrid Teas, Floribundas and Grandifloras

These three groups of modern hybrid roses, often termed bush roses, are very similar and have the same cultural requirements. In effect, they almost behave (or can be made to behave) like herbaceous plants. The canes are not long lived, and even if killed to the ground by a cold winter, the new canes will flower normally, provided the graft union was protected below the soil. What this means is that you can cut them back severely in the spring, and you should! (Gawky rose branches aren't very attractive, so why leave any more than you have to?) Most people don't prune their roses hard enough. Rose fanciers who grow prize-winning exhibition blooms cut their Hybrid Teas back to just a few inches to encourage the most vigorous stems with the largest flowers, but they don't get as many blossoms. For garden effect, the same plants are best

cut to 1 or 2 feet, leaving more buds to give more flowers. In warmer climates, roses are more vigorous and are pruned higher. Whatever height

How to prune a bush rose, such as hybrid tea, floribunda and grandiflora types

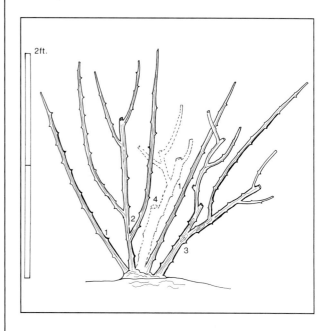

1) Unpruned bush rose

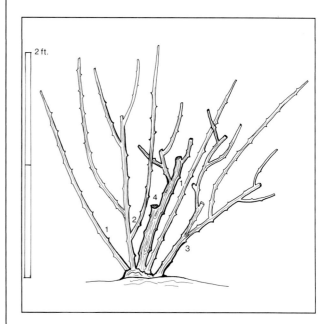

2) Remove dead, dying and diseased wood. Remove stems more than 2 or 3 years old, and shorten others back to young branches, preferably one-year canes.

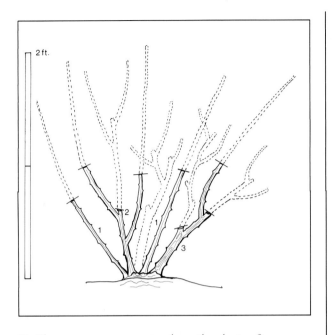

3) Shorten one-year canes to shape the plant and encourage growth from lower buds for compactness.

your roses are cut to, each trunk should end with a smooth green cane of the previous summer's growth, because only these are capable of producing strong blooming shoots.

I like to keep the Hybrid Tea roses in my garden extra low because they are in front of a low wall. So I cut them back especially hard, to about 4 inches every spring. It seems drastic, but it works and they bloom beautifully on neat plants. To prune your bush roses, first remove the three Ds. Next remove the oldest canes or cut them back down to the lowest one or two young side branches. The object is to shorten the old wood as much as possible, and still have at least three or four well-distributed, year-old canes. Last, trim these year-old canes to the desired height with the top bud pointing away from the center of the plant.

Shrub Roses

Shrub roses are so called because their stems are more strongly woody and they are indeed shrubs. They vary considerably, so what follows is a very general discussion. Many of the older types

bloom only once, in early summer. Some are repeat blooming through the summer, which is nice, but the show never equals the first big flush.

The pruning strategy with shrub roses in early spring is to clean them up for the growing

How to prune a shrub rose, such as old-fashioned and rugosa types

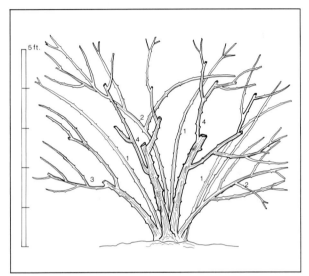

1) Unpruned shrub rose

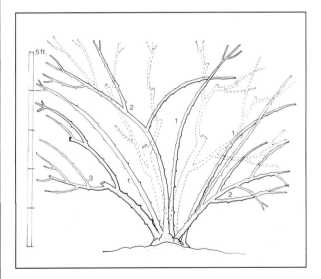

2) Remove dead, dying and diseased wood. Remove the oldest, most woody stems, usually those more than 3 years old. Less vigorous plants may require keeping more of their older wood. Shorten other stems back to young offshoots to remove congested, least vigorous twiggy branches.

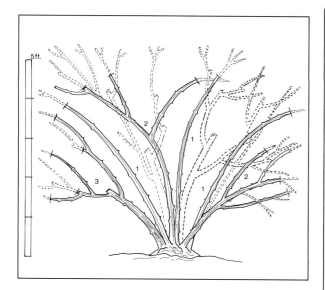

3) Shorten remaining one-year growth by as much as a third to shape the plant and make it more compact. Twiggy side growth can be shortened to two or three buds to increase their vigor. If shoots are not shortened, the shrub will have a leggy appearance. The fewer buds there are per branch, the larger the flowers, but there will be fewer of them.

season but not to do much more trimming than necessary, as the flowers are borne on last year's growth. Try to maintain their graceful natural shape. First, prune out the three Ds. Next, completely remove a few of the oldest stems, particularly where they are crowding younger growth. Congested twiggy growth can also be cut back to stronger shoots. Twiggy side shoots can be shortened to two or three buds to improve vigor. Finally, shorten long straggly canes by as much as a third to shape the plant.

During the summer watch to see the effect of your pruning. Where do the blooms occur and how did your pruning affect growth? If the plant is too floppy, perhaps the canes should have been shortened more. If bloom is sparse, perhaps too many old branches were removed. You need to develop a feel for the response of each variety.

Many shrub roses develop attractive hips in fall. These varieties should not be pruned or deadheaded after bloom. Varieties that flower only once, without producing hips, may be pruned after they flower, much as they would be in early spring. This summer pruning will en-

courage vigorous young shoots that will flower profusely the next year. Only a moderate trimming is then required in early spring.

Climbing Roses

Climbing roses are pruned in much the same way as the shrub roses. The main difference is that with much more vigorous shoots, they require the support of a fence, trellis or wall. Once-blooming climbers flower on the previous year's growth. Everblooming climbers continue to flower on the current season's growth.

Begin pruning, as for all other roses, by trimming out the three Ds. Then, cut out the oldest stems, those that show lack of vigor. Shorten lengthy side branches. The object is to end up with a good distribution of young canes. The final step is to shorten the long canes to bring them into proportion. With climbing roses, you can move the canes around and tie them into the spaces where you need them.

Rose growers know that the position of a cane will influence its flowering. Upright canes flower from the buds near the end. If the cane is shortened, the same number of buds closest to

How to prune a climbing rose

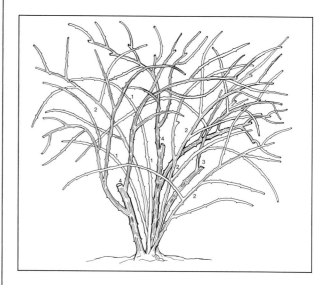

1) Unpruned climbing rose

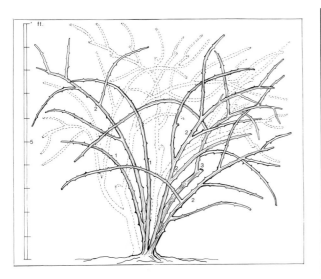

2) Remove dead, dying and diseased wood. Remove the oldest, most woody stems, usually those more than 3 years old. Less vigorous plants many require older wood to remain. Shorten others back to young offshoots to remove congested, least vigorous twiggy branches. The stems may become detached during pruning, but will probably need to be rearranged to fill in gaps. Tie all branches to support them, using soft string; move them to fill spaces as necessary.

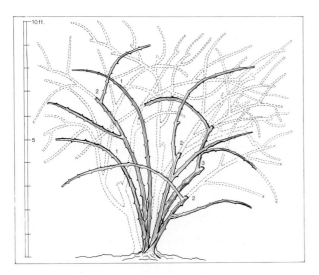

3) Shorten one-year canes to achieve a good distribution of buds over the plant. Shorten side branches, depending upon their vigor, leaving only one or two buds on the weaker ones. Young vigorous canes can be left quite long. The fewer buds per branch, the larger the flowers, but there will be fewer of them.

the end will flower, giving a more compact plant. But if the same cane is trained horizontally, it will flower from many more buds all along the cane. When training climbing roses, try to train as many canes horizontally, or as close to horizontal, as possible. You can even train them to loop down to cover the base of the plant if it is bare.

As for shrub roses, varieties that flower only once are best pruned in summer after flowering. Few produce worthwhile hips. However, in a situation where climbers are grown with other vines (see page 104), this may be difficult to accomplish and the whole job can be done at once in the spring, although the rose may not develop as much flowering wood. A compromise is to remove a few of the oldest canes in the summer, leaving the major part of the pruning until early spring, when vines and roses are dormant.

Summer Maintenance Pruning

Whether to deadhead once-blooming roses is your choice. If no hips are to follow, the only advantage is to clean up the plants. In the case of repeat-blooming and everblooming roses, bloom will definitely be more prolific if they are deadheaded.

For best results when deadheading, be sure to cut back to a strong bud. This usually means a node with a leaf of normal size, rather than the smaller leaves that normally occur just below a flower. Often there will already be a bud beginning to expand at this point. On floribunda roses and hybrid teas this will usually be a leaf with five leaflets.

Climbing and shrub roses make excellent companions for vines, as explained in the discussion of vines that follows.

VINES

My experience with vines began when I was a student at England's Wisley Garden where I found myself one day at the top of a ladder nearly two stories tall. With my head in a jungle of tangled stems, my task was to tame that jungle without going so far as to impart a manicured appearance. The experience was a lesson in understanding vines and how to deal with them on their own terms. After tackling that tangle, I realized that I could cope with vines in any situation.

While vines are assets to any garden, they can be frustrating until you begin to understand them. The first rule is, *don't* cut them down to the ground. Instead, when drastic treatment is required, cut them back to their trunks. Vines are lax by nature and need support. They sprawl until they find it. If you cut them down, then you've got to go to the extra trouble to train them back up onto the support. If you keep the trunk already in place, half the battle is won.

In fact, a vine's trunk can be one of its biggest assets. Ropy lianas spread across a wall or draped over a trellis have a sculptural, almost macrame quality, full of romance. Their pliable stems can be spread, twisted, tangled and draped for the desired effect. The best time to train vine trunks is in the dormant season, when much of the smaller growth can be trimmed away and you have the freedom to rearrange the stems as you wish.

The second rule for vines is to match them with the proper support and location. A discussion of where to place annual, perennial and woody vines is found on page 55. Mismatching vines with the wrong support causes extra work

with poor results. Vines fall into four categories, depending on the means by which they climb.

Clingers attach themselves directly to any surface. Examples are English ivy, Boston ivy, Virginia creeper and climbing hydrangea.

Twiners climb by twining their stems around their supports. Examples include honeysuckle, actinidia and wisteria.

Grabbers grab their supports. Grapes have tendrils that wrap around whatever they touch. Clematis grab with their petioles (leaf stems).

Sprawlers lie on their supports, which in nature are shrubs and trees, sending up progressively taller shoots to arch over higher branches. Examples are jasmine and roses. Sprawlers need to be tied to their supports in the garden to stay tidy.

A classic mismatch is the climbing hydrangea that is planted at the base of a wall trellis. A clinging vine has no use for a trellis, and won't pay any attention to it as it makes its way up a wall.

An equally unsuccessful match is the clematis planted to grow on a trellis. Clematis petioles can't grab onto the thick cross pieces. Clematis are adapted to grab small twigs as they grow over a shrub. If a trellis is to be used, they need the addition of wire to grab onto. Otherwise, you

Clematis ×jackmanii *climbs into the climbing rose 'American Pillar'. Both bloom in June.*

Clematis *'Duchess of Albany' grows into an azalea and provides a second season of bloom in June. Like other* C. texensis *hybrids, this cultivar has bell-like flowers.*

will need to tie it constantly in place and the poor vine will still have the look of being hung from a gallows.

The twiners and the grabbers originally adapted themselves to climbing over shrubs, an imaginative and beautiful sight in many garden situations. Clematis are among the best subjects for this treatment and will find their own way up low-branching shrubs, where they make themselves right at home. I grow clematis up on azaleas, mountain laurel, shrub roses and climbing roses. *Clematis montana* is extremely vigorous and drapes itself on the limbs of a large conifer in my garden, a magnificent sight in May. I even grow coral honeysuckle in a holly where it peeks out from among the branches. These vines aren't intended to engulf their hosts, but rather to provide a highlight and additional season of bloom.

A yearly vine pruning is usually enough to prevent the shrub beneath from being shaded out. I prune summer-flowering clematis and honeysuckle in very early spring, removing the mass of stems on the outside and top, while leaving most of those stems that are inside among the shrub's branches. This leaves plenty of buds to grow and provide the coming season's bloom. Early-blooming *Clematis montana* is pruned after flowering. Every few years large portions of it

The white flowers of the viticella hybrid Clematis *'Alba Luxurians' are effectively displayed against the dark green foliage of its host* Cotoneaster horizontalis.

Clematis *'Betty Corning', a viticella hybrid, reaches from a nearby shrub to grab the stems of a martagon hybrid lily (*Lilium ×dalhansonii*).*

need to be pulled down and removed to prevent it from becoming too dense and causing permanent damage to the tree. Reconsider using trees and shrubs as supports if you feel that you can't keep up with the pruning to protect them from damage. Be sure that vigorous vines are used in large trees only, or not in trees at all.

Trellises are well suited to twining vines, but less so for grabbers. The twiners climb up and then branch. You can pinch them or push them around to get a good distribution or framework. For a trellis too coarse for clematis to grab (as most are), a few strands of wire between the cross pieces will usually solve the problem.

Clematis 'Nelly Moser' climbs effortlessly on a trellis to which a discreet wire grid has been added. Clematis should always be planted about 4 inches deeper in the soil than they were growing in their pots. This allows more roots to grow along the stem and shelters extra buds below the soil in case of mishaps.

Always use nonrusting wire, galvanized or plastic coated. Heavy-gauge stainless steel is too stiff. Plastic-coated wire must be an earth color or one that blends with its surroundings. Green never matches the green of foliage and looks odd in winter. White only looks right on a white trellis. Black tends to disappear visually, which is just what you want. String works fine until it rots and you find you haven't got time to replace it yearly.

The two-story wall at Wisley didn't have any trellises, yet grabbers and twiners climbed it with ease, supported by a discreet wire grid. The gardener can allow grabbers and twiners to climb where they wish or train them to grow in any position desired. Wall shrubs are easily tied to wires as well.

I prefer to set up my own wire network rather than use a prefabricated wire mesh; I have more control, and I find it looks much better. The spaces between the criss-crossing wires should be about 8 inches and the wires should be held about 1 inch out from the wall, which helps the climbers get a good grip. This inch is essential for clematis that need to pass the leaf at the end of their prehensile petioles behind the wire. If they don't have it, they won't do their own climbing.

Installing the wire network is simple. The ideal means of attaching the wires to the wall would be with galvanized screw eyes that have a 1-inch shank between the eye and the threads, but you can't get them. So, I use number-12 screw hooks that I bend closed with pliers. Screw the hooks into the fence or wall at approximately 8-inch intervals. In masonry walls, make a hole with an electric drill fitted with a masonry bit. It is easiest to drill into the mortar rather than the blocks or bricks, so plan the pattern accordingly. Insert a lead or plastic screw anchor or rawl plug into the hole and screw the hook into it. There must be a hook at each point around the inside of the grid—top, bottom and sides—and at just enough intervals in the middle to prevent sagging. String the wire between the hooks, pulling it tight and securing it thoroughly at each point. I use number-18 galvanized wire. Number-20 is easier to work, but is weaker and

Clematis alpina *blooms in April and climbs among vines and roses supported by a wire grid attached to the wall.*

Once a wire grid has been established on a wall, vines and shrubs can be trained across the surface to intermingle for an exuberant display. The honeysuckle at left twines around the wires and even reaches over to twine on the rose in the middle. The rose has no means of holding onto the wires itself and needs to be tied in, but this allows the gardener to move stems into new positions to fill gaps. The clematis at right grabs the wire with its prehensile petioles, and it grabs the rose also.

doesn't last as long. Be sure the wire is straight and tight. Messy wire shows; straight wire vanishes from sight.

Discreet is the idea here. Choose an appropriate color of rust-proof wire. Galvanized wire blends in well against gray stone, cinder blocks and earth colors. Obvious hooks can be painted to tone them down. Even before the vines reach the top to cover the grid entirely, the wire should be scarcely visible.

Vines are great for fences. The clingers will climb almost any fence, particularly a stockade fence. Use the wire grid, described above for walls, to support twiners and grabbers on a stockade fence. Twiners and grabbers can really get a good grip on a wire or chain-link fence, and clingers will readily make their way up through the mesh as well. Vines are an effective way to enhance or hide a fence, but remember that covering it may hold in moisture longer and encourage rot or rust, which can shorten the life of the fence.

If you need a vertical accent in your garden or simply haven't any other place for that favorite vine, try a post. A rot-resistant wood such as treated lumber is advisable. An old cedar trunk or log, with inherent rot resistance, has more character and will last for years. The clingers will climb right up to the top on their own. So will the twiners, unless the post is too fat. Wisteria can go around large tree trunks, but this may lead to eventual strangulation of live trunks.

The grabbers need more help. A loose spiral of a fairly stiff wire, stapled at intervals up a post, does the trick and virtually disappears visually. (The best wire of all has proved to be a coil of old copper wire that had been in my garage when it burned some years ago. The patina on the burned wire blends with the clematis stems and old post it's wrapped around.) There is no need to surround the post with wire mesh, such as chicken wire, unless you are trying to create a permanent garden eyesore.

A dormant-season pruning and cleanup is the key to maintaining order with most vines. Summer-flowering vines should be pruned severely at this time to remove long, excess growth. This usually means spurring back last year's growth to the trunks and main branches. "Spurring back" means leaving short spurs consisting of only the lowest two or three buds from each shoot of last year's growth. I cut the summer-blooming clematis even harder, since they make so much growth before they bloom. Of course, there aren't any rules that say you can't leave longer shoots if you need a longer branch to fill a space, or want to let the vine get a bit larger.

Spring-flowering vines won't bloom if given such heavy-handed treatment when dormant, because the flower buds will be cut away. But even they can be neatened by removing dead wood and any misplaced branches that you wouldn't want anyway. Also trim away overly vigorous shoots (which usually don't flower well). Stems can be repositioned as needed. It is always easier to see these things when the branches are devoid

A post with a loose spiral of wire supports Clematis *'Mme Eduard Andre'.*

of leaves, exposing the plant structure. If needed, spring-blooming vines can be given their hard pruning just after they finish blooming, before they have a chance to make much growth.

Vines will do what you want them to do if you give them a little attention while they are growing. I push the growing tips around to point them in the direction in which I want them to grow. (If the vines are properly matched to their support, they will take the hint and attach themselves without the need for tying.) The gardeners at Sissinghurst Castle Garden, in England, call this process twiddling. The most intensive twiddling season is spring, when growth is most rapid. Clematis in particular should be twiddled to separate the young stems, which tend to bunch.

Summer-blooming Vines to Prune Hard in Early Spring

Campsis species and hybrids (Trumpet vine)
Clematis (late spring and summer flowering)
Clematis texensis and hybrids
Clematis viticella and hybrids
Jasminum officinale (Poet's jasmine)
Lonicera × *heckrottii* (Goldflame honeysuckle)
Lonicera sempervirens (Trumpet honeysuckle)
Vitis species (Grape)

Summer pruning helps to maintain order. Long growths on honeysuckle vines can be shortened, and they will bloom from the side buds. Wisterias bloom in spring from the congested buds at the base of the previous season's growth. The stringy growth can be trimmed back repeatedly during the summer, and this tends to stimulate secondary summer bloom. Actinidia looks neater if trimmed during summer too. Just don't use hedge shears, ever, because they indiscriminately cut good and bad shoots, hacking and tearing leaves. Proper pruning guides vine growth.

Even experienced gardeners can be brought to their knees by a vine that has gotten out of

Vines to Prune Only Lightly in Early Spring

Actinidia species
Celastrus species (Bittersweet)
Clematis alpina
Clematis armandii
Clematis macropetala
Clematis montana
Clematis spooneri
Hydrangea anomala petiolaris (Climbing hydrangea)
Schizophragma hydrangeoides (Japanese hydrangea vine)
Wisteria species

hand. Drastic action is best taken during the dormant season, preferably very early spring. Follow these steps:

1. Lift the mass of foliage or twigs and peer underneath. Examine the trunks, the way in which they hang and twist together, and where they branch. Try to follow these branches out to the foliage. This should give a pretty good idea of the hidden personality of the vine and how to improve it. If it is still difficult to make sense of the confusion, try pulling out some of the dead wood. Dead wood is brittle and will usually break off in your hand. (Be cautious with clematis, however, since the live stems of many varieties are brittle too.)

2. Cut away the majority of the mass of smaller branches. Lift the mass and cut back every stem underneath to a length of about a foot from the main trunks. Once the main trunks are exposed, the worst is over.

3. Trim off all the dead wood to reveal the living trunks and branches. If you can't tell the living from the dead, scratch the bark. Living branches have green tissue (cambium) under the bark; dead ones have brown.

4. Select the strongest and most interesting trunks as the mainstay for the future. In small spaces, one trunk may suffice, but large vines may have several trunks. Side branches are helpful, but not essential, because most vines will branch freely along the trunks. Remove the small growth and extra trunks at the bottom. Cut them out as close as possible to the remaining trunks to minimize extraneous sprouts. Stumps sprout very readily and the idea is to force the vine's strength up into the remaining trunks.

5. The final pruning involves cleaning up what is left. Position the trunks where you want them. They will be flexible and probably detached from their support by this stage, so they can be arranged as desired. Trunks of clingers can't be detached as there isn't an easy way to reattach them to a blank wall, but unwanted trunks can be removed. Shorten trunks to be a little shorter than the intended maximum height or the top of the support or trellis. Lastly, shorten all branches back to a couple of nodes (buds), unless a longer one is needed to fill in an empty space. Be sure that everything is tied in securely using loose loops to allow the stems to expand as they grow (see about twine and jute, page 107).

During the following growing season, keep the base clean of unwanted suckers and shoots and keep the top trimmed lightly to keep it neat. The transformation will be miraculous!

TRAINING VINES, ROSES AND WALL SHRUBS TOGETHER

If you have roses on a trellis or have wall shrubs, certain vines of moderate vigor, such as clematis and honeysuckles, make excellent companions. The roses and shrubs are easily grasped by the vines. It is imperative, however, that order be maintained in such a mixed planting.

One of the most successful spots in my garden is a wall covered with honeysuckles, several clematises, hardy passionflower (*Passiflora incarnata*), a climbing rose and a winter jasmine. Bloom begins in late February or March with the yellow flowers of winter jasmine (*Jasminum nudiflorum*). In April and May the tubular orange flowers of trumpet honeysuckle (*Lonicera sempervirens*) begin their display, which will continue into October. During late May and June, the rose blooms among the honeysuckle. By July, the passionflower has scrambled up on the other inhabitants of the wall, shading them lightly, and bears its striking lavender-blue flowers through September. In addition to the continuous floral display, this wall planting is a medley of textures

*The old-fashioned climbing rose 'Zephirine Drouhin' mingles with coral honeysuckles (*Lonicera sempervirens *and* L. s. *'Sulphurea') on an otherwise mundane wall fitted with a wire grid.*

*Trumpet honeysuckle (*Lonicera sempervirens*) flowers all summer long but is most profuse and lovely when it coincides with rose 'Zephirine Drouhin' in late May.*

and shapes. For autumn interest, I think I should add a willow-leafed cotoneaster (*Cotoneaster salicifolius*) for its red berries and evergreen foliage. More than a garden on a wall, this is a floral arrangement that unfolds throughout the season and is the equal of any flower border.

All of the plants on this wall grow together on a wire grid with seemingly reckless abandon, either as neighbors or as intimate companions sharing the same space. But while the look is natural and somewhat wild, feigning romantic neglect, there is a strong underlying measure of control. Although some tidying up is done throughout the year, the most important pruning is done in late winter or early spring, when each variety is brought back into bounds. All extra stems and wood are removed, and a bit of rearranging takes place. Here is how to go about it.

1. Remove all herbaceous vines. The hardy passionflower, or maypop (*Passiflora incarnata*), dies back to the ground each winter and so fits into this category. So do annual vines such as morning glory, moon vine and the cup-and-saucer vine.

2. Trim the woody twiners. Because they twine around the wires, they are the least mobile and often can't be moved. Spur back the honeysuckles, leaving only about two nodes of last year's growth per branch, unless you need a longer branch to fill in an empty space. These first two steps remove a lot of the clutter so you can see what needs to be done next.

3. Trim the grabbers, such as clematis. They are more detachable as the stems don't actually encircle the wires. Early-blooming clematises that bloom from last year's growth don't get trimmed—just work around them carefully (they are brittle). Summer-blooming clematis can be cut severely, because they will quickly reclaim old territory before they bloom. Cut them to about 2 feet high and fan out the stems.

4. Now that you can see where the twiners and grabbers are going to be, trim the rose, removing the oldest wood and tying in the remaining stems where they are needed. Don't tuck the rose canes behind the wires. Tie them instead, which makes it easy to move them around in the future. Climbing roses can also be pruned in midsummer after they have finished blooming, if not too entwined in the other vines.

5. Early-blooming Clematis alpina *and winter jasmine, which can't be touched in early spring, are pruned later, after they've finished blooming.*

6. Pruning of wall shrubs depends on their bloom season and their association with other inhabitants of the wall. While these shrubs may support some vines, they should be less entwined with the vines than the roses, so they are usually easier to prune separately. Throughout the growing season, keep an eye on new growth and shorten it or tie it in.

Policing Plants

In chapter three we discussed how to manage annuals and biennials. Some of these short-lived plants won't stay in your garden in their next generation. I call these "transients" because they leave quickly, rarely propagating themselves. Exactly which varieties behave as transients depends on your climate and your garden, but the result is the same: They must be replanted yearly if you want to have them. You will grow transients because they are worth the extra trouble. Fortunately, many are available from garden centers.

"Nomads" are the ones that need policing. Though short-lived, they stay in the garden by providing numerous offspring. The problem is that they tend to move around, showing up everywhere. Foxglove, a biennial, and spider flower (*Cleome*), an annual, are perfect examples. Fortunately, they are easy to transplant to where you want them when small, and the extra seedlings are easy enough to annihilate. Select spider flower seedlings in spring, foxglove seedlings in early to midsummer. I find nomads more convenient than the expense and effort of planting lots of transients each year. With nomads the danger is that they often seed into less vigorous neighbors and can crowd them out if you are not on the ball policing them.

One strategy of minimizing work in the flower garden is to avoid perennials that spread or need frequent dividing. Make your first choices from the clumpers, those that stay put (see page 39). This strategy is a little restrictive from the creative standpoint, and sooner or later you will find you need to include one of the spreaders. Spreaders need policing, and it should be a part of your yearly schedule to review their progress and curb them where necessary.

I prefer to do as much work on my perennials in the fall as I can, because that's when I have the time. In the case of all but a few fall-blooming perennials, you can dig and divide them as long as you don't bareroot them, which would make them subject to frost-heaving during winter. (It is more difficult to move and divide perennials without barerooting them in sandy soils than clay soils.) When growth slows and the first frosts are near, I begin fall perennial renovations. The spreaders may have enlarged their size and territories considerably. Decide just how large you want each to be. Drive a spade into the ground at this point all around the clump. This severs all the rhizomes from the rest of the clump so they can be forked out without disturbing the part you intend to leave behind. (Really fast spreaders can be slowed down by driving a spade in around the clump in midsummer, too.) After a few years' growth, the center will probably become too congested and should be replaced. Save vigorous sections from the outer edge and replace the old center with these.

Another way to slow underground spreaders is with a barrier surrounding the clump. A bottomless plastic tub, sunk 1 foot deep in the soil, usually does the trick. Such tubs are cheap, and it is easy to cut out the bottom. Use the largest tub you can buy, and sink it in the ground before planting the perennial. Leave ½ inch of the rim exposed to foil shallow rhizomes; the tub should be brown so it won't show.

Some spreaders can be controlled in midsummer. Cottage and Cheddar pinks bloom in

To reduce the size of mat-forming perennials and annuals without leaving an unsightly trimmed edge, lift the foliage and trim underneath.

early summer, and then exist as a mat of glaucous foliage for the rest of the summer. They spread by surface stems, rather than underground rhizomes. Each year these stems spread to become a wider mat. If you trim the pinks back after they have bloomed, next year's flowers will not be affected, but the size of the plant is easily controlled. Here's a tip to avoid the trimmed look: Lift the foliage along the edge of what you want to keep. Cut away the extra stems underneath. Drop down the foliage again and no cut edges will show. (Use this method to control sprawling annuals in summer too.) With only a few spreaders in your garden, you can keep order year after year.

Policing duties are not confined to the spreaders and the nomads. One plant or another is always getting out of line and bullying a neighbor. In spring, daffodil foliage falls over onto any adjacent coralbells and can cause one side of the clump to die off, leaving a gap. You need to take notice and push the daffodil leaves to the side. In late summer, a marigold gets too large and sprawls over a neighboring dianthus. That part of the dianthus will die out and won't be there to bloom the following spring. Be there to cut back the marigold a bit and save the dianthus. The marigold will quickly recover and may even bloom the better for it. With experience, you will develop an eye to spot these conflicts and resolve them in minutes.

STRATEGIC STAKING

The need for staking can be greatly reduced through selection of varieties that don't require artificial support, and through a bit of timely pinching. Still, staking can't be avoided entirely. Even the most compact or strong-stemmed varieties will come through a summer thunderstorm in better condition if given some extra support. A little shade may render some normally strong-stemmed varieties leggy enough to benefit from some form of staking.

With experience, you will learn which plants must have support, and at what stage they are likely to fall over without it. Don't put staking off beyond the fall-over point because once a plant has gone over, the tips of the stems will turn up toward the light; these crooks will never totally disappear, even after you stand the stems up again. Learn which method is best suited to each plant variety.

Many materials lend themselves for use as stakes. Peasticks, discussed below, are free. I often use bamboo stakes, purchased at local garden centers, nurseries or hardware stores. They are strong and relatively rot resistant. I find they can be reused for several years, although they gradually become shorter as the bottoms rot off. Plastic stakes are also available and last almost indefinitely. Some manufacturers choose a green that is too bright to blend in well with foliage. A light dusting of brown spray paint will tone it down and allow it to get lost in the shadows. (When will they learn that a dark brown would blend in best?)

Scavenge old broom sticks and metal rods too. Bend the tips of metal rods into a loop as a safety measure for people who don't wear glasses; it is hard to see a thin stake from above when bending over. For the tallest stakes, I scavenge old pipes. The rustier the better, and again, a little brown spray paint will darken an overly clean metallic surface.

Plenty of convenient flower supports are available, including linking stakes, rings, grids and stakes with a terminal loop. These are easy to use, as in the case of grids or link stakes to corral peonies. For some uses, though, they may be too visible for too long. It's your choice.

The indisputably most useful material for tying up flowers is a thin green twine that comes in balls of a size that fits in the palm of my hand. It also comes in large spools, which aren't very useful for pushing through a dense clump of perennials as described below for the internal support method. If your local garden center doesn't have the balled twine, tell them that it can be ordered from a good greenhouse supply company. It is fine enough not to be noticed, but strong enough to hold up most flowers and last a season in the garden (although constant rain rots it). It is weak enough to be broken with the hands rather than cut, which is convenient.

For heavier jobs, green jute is available. It is thick enough that it doesn't cut into soft stems. It fades to brown, but all the better! Tarred jute lasts the longest, up to two years out in the weather, so it is good for things like climbing roses that don't need to be retied annually. Unfortunately, it is hard to get. Clothesline is another long-term alternative, but unless you have a white trellis, it won't look right. (When old and dirty, it looks okay against a gray wall.)

Wire twist-ties coated with either paper or plastic are useful for some jobs where a lot of individual stems need tying and tying twine would be cumbersome. Garden centers sell it in green. For larger jobs, the twist ties are too stiff and heavy looking to be discreet. I don't use the plastic-coated kind because they aren't biodegradable and will be in the soil forever. Most gardeners are justifiably concerned about such things.

In a pinch, when you must use white string, soak it in a mud puddle first, or rub it with mud. This will darken it and save your reputation among your gardening friends. While we are on the subject of aesthetics, remember that strips of old sheets make great ties too—but only in the vegetable garden.

Single-Stake Method

Tall, single-stemmed plants should be staked with a single stake, particularly if they are sparsely foliaged. Often, several stems in a group can be tied individually to one centrally located stake.

First loop or tie the twine around the stake, then loop it around the plant stem. Tie the stems in their natural positions, not so tightly that they bend in toward each other. Breakage is reduced if the stems have latitude to move with the elements and if they are supported as high up as possible. Stake stems to at least two-thirds of their mature height, higher for those that are weak. Tall spikes of *Delphinium*, for example, should be supported high into the flower spike, even to the tip; otherwise the weight of the flowers may topple the stem over at the point of the highest attachment tie. The tallest *Delphinium* I ever grew reached 7 feet, but at their peak of bloom, they were reduced by a thunderstorm to 4-foot hunchbacks, the height of my tallest stake. It was heartbreaking.

If a stem falls over or breaks, it can often be splinted back into shape by tying it tightly to a stake. A bent stem often retains enough functional vascular tissue to continue to supply the

The single stake method is used to support single stems or a limited number of stems where there is insufficient foliage to conceal other staking methods. First tie the twine around the stake and then loop it around the stem.

Left: Such tall single stems as delphinium need firm support. The tall flower spike should be tied to the stake too, to prevent breakage in storms.

Right: Even with four stems, this delphinium is most discreetly supported by a single stake. Each stem is held in its natural position, not too tightly.

flowers as long as you don't work it back and forth too many times in the process of bringing it back up again. Straightening crooked (as opposed to broken or bent) stems, once a plant has fallen, is important because crooked stems often destroy the visual lines of the plant.

Internal-Support Method

Large clumps of perennials with many stems require internal support as well as support around the outside. Internal stems tend to lean toward the outside of the plant, leaving an open center. Surround the clump with stakes and connect the stakes with twine passed through the middle of the clump as shown in the drawings on this page. Five or more stakes hold the central stems of the clump upright. Connect the stakes around the outside. If some stems are pulled in too tightly by this outer string, release them from their tight corral and loop an additional looser string to sup-

port them in a more natural position. I must stress the importance of not tying in the stems too tightly. They will make it look as though the poor plant is wearing a girdle. Most perennials flare out as they rise, and this should be preserved when staking. Even highly trained professionals make this mistake repeatedly; if only they would loosen up.

Groups of the same variety are staked together as one mass. Insert stakes in among the mass (between the clumps), as well as around the edge. Use the tallest possible stakes, connecting them with the twine as high up as the plants can hide it, to provide maximum support and minimize breakage, even in the worst storms. The advantage of this method, as opposed to the peastaking method described on page 110 , is that it can be done when the perennial is well developed, rather than earlier in the season when it is shorter and incapable of disguising the stakes.

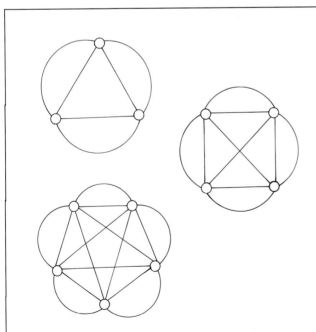

Three or more stakes are required for the internal support method. The examples above show the configuration of twine from above and how more stakes provide better support with more twine passing through the mass of stems. The drawing at right shows how the flowers and foliage conceal the stakes and the twine.

Reconstructive Staking

What do you do when you discover that an unstaked perennial has fallen apart and lost its shape? Use the internal-support method described above to reconstruct the plant. It is remarkably effective in restoring the display.

First, visualize the size and spread that the plant should have. Surround the clump with stakes to support the outermost stems. Tie twine to one stake and pass it to the opposite stake; in the process, lift all the stems that have fallen under the twine so that they will lean against it. As the twine is passed to another opposite stake, again lift the stems that have fallen under it, and continue the process until all stakes are connected. Last, loosely connect the stakes around the outside, supporting the outer stems and taking care to tighten the twine enough to hold the stems in the desired position. This should result in the stems being held near to their original upright positions with a natural spread.

The final step is to correct the crooked shoot tips. They will attempt to straighten themselves, and if they have not lain down for long, the crook will be small and might be disguised by the leaves.

Bamboo peasticks support Coreopsis verticillata. *Ideally, the sticks should be slightly lower to be less visible.*

Another measure can be taken if the plant is not close to its bloom season or if the flowers are not a decorative feature, as in the case of *Artemisia ludoviciana* 'Silver King': Simply pinch off the bent tips. The stems will quickly branch for an even fuller effect. Late-blooming perennials will bloom from the branches.

Peastick Method

The peastick (or peastake) is the backbone of many a grand English perennial border. Peasticks are twiggy branches cut from trees and shrubs and stuck in the ground to support other plants. They were first used in vegetable gardens for peas to climb on, hence the name. In the flower garden, peasticks can be placed right in the middle of a group of plants to support the plants evenly from within, all through the clumps from top to bottom. This network of branches and twigs, hidden by the foliage, holds the stems in the exact position where they have grown. The result is similar to the internal-support method, but more natural.

You can't buy peasticks, but have to gather them yourself. They are usually a by-product of work around the garden and cost nothing. In England, hazel twigs are the sticks of choice. Many other woody plants will do. The best are finely twiggy and three-dimensionally branched and strong enough not to be too brittle when dead. I find the prunings of such flower garden shrubs as buddleia and *Vitex* to be ideal, and I cut them down each spring anyway. I've also used birch, pin oak, *Sorbaria* and mock orange. (Nothing is pruned without thought as to its possibilities as a peastick.) I even watch the activities of neighbors for suitable prunings and offer to take them off their hands. By spring, I have accumulated a pile more than sufficient for the season. Some bamboos make excellent peasticks (*Phyllostachys* is one of the best). The strongest sticks can be used again the next year.

Peasticking is best done in early to midspring when the plants are still relatively short. At first it will show, and this is objectionable to some people, especially in a small garden.

The advantage is that with a bit of practice it can be done more rapidly than the internal-support method. Insert three or more sticks around each clump so the branches cross through and support the middle shoots. Large clumps or groupings require sticks in the middle too. The perennials will grow up between the sticks and cover them with foliage. In a group of several clumps of the same variety, arrange the sticks so that the whole group grows together into a single mass. To provide good support, and still be hidden, the sticks should be about 6 inches shorter than the ultimate height of the foliage. You can bend the tips over horizontally to provide additional support. The flexible tips of bamboo can even be twisted together. Envision the final appearance of the plant around the sticks as you work.

At England's Wisley Garden, where I learned this technique, we had a little red book for the grand flower borders along the Broad Walk. It was like an encyclopedia, giving the proper height of peasticks for each variety. In your garden you can estimate the proper height by taking the foliage height of a variety and mak-

Neatly done, peastaking can be a work of art. At Wisley Garden, England, Artemisia 'Silver Queen' *has been staked and mulched in May, in preparation for summer. These hazel twigs are the peasticks of choice. Note that each has been cut to the proper height. Before long, this will become a solid mass of silver foliage, obscuring the sticks entirely.*

Bamboo peasticks are placed over Artemisia 'Silver King' *so that it will grow through them and be supported later in the season. The flexibility of bamboo allows the tips to be arched over and twisted together, creating a basketlike network. Although perhaps less attractive, fewer sticks are required.*

ing the sticks a bit shorter. New plants are usually shorter the first year, so take this into account. The sticks can always be trimmed down later if you overdo it. Ideally, no further support should be needed, but for good measure, I cheat a bit and run a piece of green twine around each group to catch renegade shoots before they slip out of place. Purists would not approve.

To the educated eye, a well-peastaked border can be a work of art. The ultimate height and spread of each variety is depicted by neatly placed sticks. It is not long, however, before the rapid growth of the perennials in late spring covers the sticks. Peasticks are not the solution for every plant. In the local garden of a friend, sticks were used to support some lilies. To me, the sight of these lilies growing through a thicket of dead wood was an eyesore. Peasticks shouldn't be used for any plant that doesn't develop adequate foliage to cover them.

Having made the above statement, I must point out an exception, illustrated by coralbells

(*Heuchera*). They have low foliage with the flowers borne on long wiry stems. I use birch twigs to hold these stems in a more prominent upright position. The birch twigs are the same thickness as the coralbells' stems and blend in so well that they go unnoticed. Keep a few sticks around as a reserve throughout the summer. When something falls over unexpectedly, often it can be discreetly supported with a peastick or two. The unevenness of the peasticks maintains an airy, uncrowded look while providing well-distributed support. Good staking is insurance you will collect on many times throughout the season. Sudden storms wreak havoc in a flower garden, destroying a season's growth and anticipation in a few moments. In my garden few stakes are seen—they work behind the scenes. I can rest assured that no mere storm will knock my perennials over.

Very fine birch twigs blend discreetly with the delicate stems of coralbells as they hold them upright at the front of this border.

MAINTAINING AND GROOMING THE DISPLAY

In much of North America, the hot muggy weather of midsummer takes its toll in the flower garden. Spent flowers and weather-beaten, withered foliage make the display look tired. On the West Coast, a strong dry wind will parch foliage. This needn't be. Good care will keep the garden looking fresh all season long, and good grooming can restore the scene. Grooming is the final, gratifying step toward perfection.

Deadheading is the removal of old or spent flowers from your plants. It is usually the correct thing to do, but not always. There are two main reasons for deadheading: to improve appearance and flowering. In either case there may be a good reason not to deadhead a particular plant. Faded flower clusters and seed heads can be decorative. One of the most desirable attributes of ornamental grasses is the plumy inflorescences that change with the seasons and last well into winter. You wouldn't want to deadhead these. By the same token, faded astilbe spikes will provide fall and winter interest if you don't mind leaving them there for the summer; this is more appropriate in an informal setting. I find the spent flower heads of *Filipendula purpurea* especially attractive throughout the summer as they take on a reddish tint. *Rodgersia sambucifolia* is even better, leading the casual observer to believe that it has not yet finished blooming. In the shade garden, false Solomon's seal (*Smilacina racemosa*) gives a fine display of red berries in the fall. You wouldn't want to cut these off. Also in the shade among heavy rhododendron foliage, the airy flower heads of lacecap hydrangeas engage in a gradual transformation through shades of garnet before assuming a papery brown in autumn that persists through the winter.

Short-lived perennials, biennials and annuals must be allowed to reseed themselves if they are to persist in your garden. They can't do this if you deadhead them completely, but perhaps the inflorescence could be reduced or shortened, if it is unsightly, and still produce sufficient seed from the lowest flowers. This is how I handle foxgloves. In other cases, prompt deadheading will

stimulate a second flush of bloom and this can be allowed to go to seed instead; it will be smaller and less noticeable.

Improved flowering is not guaranteed by deadheading, but it is always more effective when done soon after the flowers fade. Astilbe blooms just once per year and the display will be every bit as good the next year whether you deadhead or not. Don't bother with *Cimicifuga* either. Generally, plants that bloom better as a result of deadheading are those that have the capability to reflower again during the same growing season. Examples include many annuals (unless, like impatiens and marigolds, they produce so many flowers that it just doesn't matter). *Nicotiana* will reflower better if given a good trimming after the first flush. Balloonflower and *Campanula persicifolia* will flower longer if the young seedpods are picked off of the spikes regularly. They form new buds from the same nodes along the spike. Deadhead veronica by removing the entire spike for a second flush of smaller spikes. Other perennials, such as *Centaurea mon-*

tana, delphinium and globe thistle require more drastic treatment. The old stalks should be cut to the ground immediately after flowering to stimulate a second, although shorter, flush of flowering growth. Deadheading bulbs that flower only once, such as tulips, daffodils, lilies and gladiolas, directs all the plant's strength back to the bulb. The result is a more impressive bloom next year.

The effect of deadheading shrubs that bloom only once is harder to determine. A neighbor once told me that she definitely felt that deadheading her lilacs made them bloom better. In his book *The Well Tempered Garden*, Christopher Lloyd states that deadheading lilacs doesn't increase bloom. He's tried it. I'm more inclined to believe him. However, I do believe that pruning certain shrubs will improve flowering, if for no

In October, Gaura lindheimeri *assumes red autumn tints. It is backed by* Sedum *'Autumn Joy' and surrounded by gray foliage at the Scott Arboretum of Swarthmore College, near Philadelphia.*

other reason than when properly done it encourages the right kind of vigorous flowering wood. Technically though, this is more than just deadheading. One shrub definitely worth deadheading is butterfly bush. You don't need it to reseed (although it will), the old heads are unsightly, and deadheading will definitely encourage stronger growth and better flowers as summer goes on.

There is no doubt that your garden will benefit greatly from selective deadheading. It is up to you to decide when it is aesthetically appropriate, as in the case of astilbe, and when it is worth the effort. If you are not sure, experiment. That is how all gardeners learn.

Deadleafing

The purpose of deadleafing is to get rid of tired, weather-beaten foliage. A planting may look dishearteningly bad due to the condition of the foliage. Often there is another crop of fresher foliage lurking just underneath, out of sight. You just need to expose it.

The process of deadleafing can take a bit of time and care, but the result is entirely worth it.

It's like having a new garden. Most of the time deadleafing simply involves removing dead or withered foliage. Daylilies are a perfect example. It seems they have a propensity for mixing fresh leaves in with the dead ones. Grab as many dead leaves at a time as you can and pull them out. They aren't held in by much, but it can take a while to get them all out. Taller perennials, such as asters, phlox and veronica, often have dead leaves on the lower part of the stem. These can be stripped off easily. Bulb foliage must be left until it is dead (or at least yellowing) to nourish the bulbs for the next year. Often it can be pushed aside behind other plants when it becomes unsightly.

The other aspect of deadleafing is rejuvenation. This works only for certain kinds of perennials, and many of these plants give a clue by showing the beginnings of secondary growth along the stems or at the base of the plant. Although cutting back hard may not stimulate a second flowering, it will often result in a new crop of fresh foliage. *Filipendula* (except *F. purpurea*) will generate a nice rosette of foliage after the flower stalks are cut back to the ground. It looks bare for only a little while. The golden regrowth on *Filipendula ulmaria* 'Aurea' is especially nice. Shasta daisy will regenerate a low groundcover of deep green leaves for the rest of the year. This also works well for the hardy geraniums. Normally I cut out the flower stems and leave any basal leaves, but this takes a good hour on a big mass of *Geranium maculatum*, so I cut the whole thing down to the ground right after the last bloom fades. In a couple of weeks, new foliage forms a nice groundcover. Cut back *Thalictrum speciosissium* only halfway. Fresh foliage will be stimulated from the remaining stems.

Oriental poppies present a unique situation. Normally, they die down for the summer after flowering, then sprout new leaves in the fall. If cut back to the ground immediately after flowering, new (although smaller) foliage will appear immediately and remain to fill the space through the summer. This many not be needed in many garden designs where surrounding plants expand to cover the space. It's nice, however, to know the tricks and have the options.

INTO THE FALL AND WINTER

The flower garden should be an integral part of the autumn and winter scene in your garden, just as a field or meadow is a feature in the winter landscape of the countryside. With the closing of summer, the colors of the landscape change and the flower garden undergoes its own transformation in harmony with the season. Withering stalks and straw-colored stems are no longer out of place among the fallen leaves and autumn colors. Late-blooming perennials and annuals catch the autumn light with a softness unique to the season. Some perennials assume autumn tints of their own. Balloonflower, amsonia and Solomon's seal (*Polygonatum commutatum*) turn striking shades of yellow. *Geranium macrorrhizum* and leadwort (*Ceratostigma plumbaginoides*) develop reddish pigments in their foliage that, in the case of leadwort, is especially attractive combined with the blue flowers. False Solomon's seal (*Smilacina racemosa*) ripens clusters of red berries, while the fruit of liriope is black. Others, including bergenia, liriope, many epimediums, and the Lenten and Christmas roses (*Helleborus orientalis* and *H. nigra*) are evergreen and often continue to display a refreshing touch of green throughout the winter.

Any discordant or messy elements such as collapsed perennials can be cleared away, but use discretion. Many perennials, grasses and flower garden shrubs display attractive forms that persist through the winter, assuming even greater beauty when they catch the snow. Grasses in particular rustle as they catch the wind, adding the dimension of sound to the winter garden.

This mixed border captures the spirit of the season on a misty October morning in the author's garden. Tall Aster tatarica, *backed by Japanese red maple, is a special favorite in the autumn light.*

This October combination of Anemone ×hybrida *'Queen Charlotte' and* Cimicifuga simplex *'White Pearl' has a freshness reminiscent of an earlier season.*

The garden at Wavehill becomes a medley of flowers, foliage and rose hips in early autumn. Plumy Amaranthus hybridus erythrostachys *(left),* Dahlia *'Japanese Bishop' (back) and* Perilla frutescens *'Crispa' (bottom) all have reddish foliage.* Rosa glauca *bears plum-colored foliage earlier but displays colored hips from August.*

The native perennial sunflower (Helianthus salicifolius) *waits until October for its big show. The scene is made complete with a red dahlia.*

Above: *Ornamental cabbage* (Brassica oleracea) *develops colored foliage in autumn and is remarkably frost tolerant on a November morning.*

Below: *The yellow fall color of Solomon's seal* (Polygonatum commutatum) *becomes an accent in a groundcover of English ivy at Brookside Gardens, Wheaton, MD.*

WATERING

West Coast gardeners find that summer rain is a rarity; watering is necessary in most gardens and automatic watering systems are common. In the East, where rain routinely occurs throughout the summer, this natural watering is relied on and less thought is given to supplemental irrigation. When there is a drought, eastern gardeners are caught by surprise, and the plants may suffer before anyone has taken notice.

The conventional advice is that the garden should get 1 inch of rain (or watering) per week in the East. In the West where humidity is lower, more water is required. An inch refers to the depth of water that is collected in a straight-sided pan or bucket when set out in the rain or under a sprinkler. This is fine for a flower bed with bare soil. Under trees, less of the rain will actually reach the ground. If there is a heavy mulch, it is likely that none of that inch of water will reach the soil and plant roots underneath. (Mulches conserve water only once it is actually in the soil.)

The best way to determine your water needs is to take a small trowel, push the mulch aside, and dig down to examine the moisture content of the soil. How moist is the soil 6 inches down? How does it differ from the exposed flower bed under the trees? Keep an eye on the areas that dry out first as an indication of the soils water content. Look to the higher areas, tops of slopes, and under trees where voracious roots rob the soil of moisture (some trees are worse than others—see page 18). In all cases, water as deeply and as infrequently as possible. Deep watering encourages deep roots that can tap into a larger volume of soil as well as deeper moisture reserves.

Most established plants have adapted to survive some drought. They have the ability to conserve water in times of stress by closing their stomata (leaf pores), and they have the ability to extract water from soil that appears dry and hard. Even dry soil contains water, tightly bonded to the soil particles. Some of this water is available to plants, but it takes extra effort and they can't get enough to stay in tip-top form and grow well. Light drought won't kill most estab-

lished plants, but it will inhibit their best performance.

As drought stress increases, plants take some measures to ensure survival. They may shed leaves, die back or even go into forced dormancy. Even so, many plants can survive. The gardener's concern is that their decorative value is diminished. What with water restrictions and busy life-styles, when is the right time to start watering? Watering in the early stages is essentially for aesthetic reasons when, by keeping plants in prime condition, you keep them looking their best. During severe drought it is painful for us to look at a garden full of wilted plants. At this stage, some will die if they don't get water. However, it is always a revelation to see what will come back and grow the year after a drought.

Deciding Which Plants Need Water Most

Gardeners from moist climates have difficulty understanding the drought tolerance of plants from drier regions, even though they may have some of these plants in their gardens. Many species from eastern North America have related western species that can survive long, dry summers. Assuming that these do not grow only in moist pockets in their western habitats, they are probably adapted to any droughts the eastern climate can dish out. Even eastern natives have had to adapt to survive periodic droughts. Still, they don't look as nice while they are occupied with the rigors of merely surviving.

All too often, garden books say that a plant requires a rich moist soil. Not necessarily so. Often books are written by armchair gardeners or authors who spend most of their time in the library. They perpetuate as fact the published opinions of authors who've preceded them. For a more realistic picture, look further into books about native flora, which describe a plant's native habitat, or better still, get out and see those habitats. I consider flora of states or counties when researching the cultural needs of an American native plant, or books such as *The Flora of Japan* for exotic species because they explain where plants grow naturally.

Watering priorities in your garden should be as follows:

1. The most important decorative areas, such as summer flower borders, that need to maintain their fresh appearance.
2. Areas that dry out first, such as under trees and tops of slopes.
3. Plants with higher water requirements

Water Conservation

1. Avoid overhead sprinklers whenever possible. Instead, use soaker hoses and drip systems.
2. If you do use sprinklers, water only in the morning or evening, when less water is lost to evaporation. (To avoid disease, be sure all foliage is dry before sunset.)
3. Measure water use. Place a pan under sprinklers. After water has been fully absorbed by the soil (this won't be until the next day for clay soils), dig down to determine the effectiveness of the watering.
4. Water deeply to encourage deep, drought-resistant roots. Wait until soil has dried again before watering.
5. Mulch to reduce evaporation of soil moisture.
6. Remove weeds because they compete with other plants for water.

PESTS, DISEASES AND AESTHETICS

A few aphids or caterpillars and a few leaf spots from a fungus are not going to be enough to destroy the display in your garden. In fact, there need to be a few pests to support a population of predators that maintain the natural balance. This natural balance works in the gardener's favor. You must decide how much damage is acceptable, and at what point you will intervene. In the future you can also eliminate those plants that are the most troubled. Some people don't

grow phlox, for example, because it is so prone to mildew.

As in any other aspect of garden maintenance, try to work with nature rather than against it. Many problems will solve themselves if left alone. Others are best taken care of before they go too far. When measures are warranted to control a problem, use the least toxic method available, and limit its use to the specific area of trouble. Aphids, for example, can be crushed or washed off with a strong spray of water. Slugs can be found at night with a flashlight, or trapped in a pan of stale beer. Both aphids and mites are effectively and safely controlled with nontoxic insecticidal soap. While it is true that even beneficial insects will be killed if they get sprayed with soap, others replace them much sooner because it doesn't leave a toxic residue. The old advice that any extra spray will do good wherever it falls is not necessarily true. It might do harm.

Integrated pest management is the best strategy. This combines the disciplines of cultural, biological and chemical controls. Fortunately, the garden style advocated in this book—incorporating a diversity of plants chosen to suit the location—establishes a firm base for cultural controls. A diversity of plants discourages epidemics that can develop in monocultures, as each plant has different pest resistances and susceptibilities. Plants suited to their sites are healthy plants, and they are most able to ward off infections and infestations on their own. Biological controls are also encouraged by a diversity of plants, which encourages a diversity of beneficial insects and predators. You can also introduce beneficial organisms such as ladybugs and predatory mites, which are available from mail-order sources. Use chemical controls only as a last resort and where specifically needed.

This is a simple approach to the complex subject of pest and disease control, in a book that is not intended to cover the subject, but the philosophy is a sound and responsible one. For more information consult the references listed at the back of this book and those available at local public gardens and your local agricultural extension service.

The Experiences of Gardening

Take the time to step back from the routine and familiarity of your garden and experience it as an observer. Try to look through the eyes of a visitor. You will be able to focus on your successes, and the garden's shortcomings will fade in importance. Your garden is part of a year-'round landscape that should enrich the quality of your life during every season. With good management it can be kept attractive all year long.

The plantings, designed by the author, in the flower garden at Meadowbrook Farm near Jenkintown, Pennsylvania, change character with the seasons. Below: *Summer.* Opposite top: *November.* Opposite bottom: *January.*

The cooler weather of late summer and autumn revitalizes nasturtiums and brings such late perennials as Aster *'Our Latest One'*
and Solidago sempervirens *into bloom in October.*

Dynamic Flower Garden Management

You want the most beautiful garden possible, but there is a limit to the time and effort you can devote to it, no matter how much you enjoy caring for your flowers. The key is efficiency through understanding the why, how and when of the techniques you use and doing it right the first time. No more spinning your wheels out there!

Flower gardens are not static landscape features. They change through the seasons and from year to year. The care and maintenance they need changes with the seasons too. Some tasks actually affect the appearance of the garden the next year by rejuvenating a plant or keeping it from overgrowing its space. Plan to provide some care for the garden all through the year and perform tasks when they are most effective. This takes some of the pressure off the busier seasons. Gardening isn't a big chore to be "taken care of" and completed in one fell swoop on the first nice spring day. You'll need a good understanding of some nitty-gritty techniques, and in this chapter I'll tell you what you need to know about mulching, weeding and seasonal maintenance, as I've found to work best.

THE ROLE OF MULCH

Mulch is good for the garden and the gardener. Mulches have so many benefits that there is scarcely a situation in which they should not be used. Most of these benefits contribute to a greater return for the efforts of the gardener. Mulch is a covering. It is not a soil conditioner or amendment. By definition, it is a layer on top of the soil. It is not incorporated into the soil, at least not until it has served its purpose as a mulch.

The most widely recognized benefit of mulch is weed control. There seems to be great misunderstanding as to why mulches control weeds. I once read that mulches are too acidic for weeds, but as you've probably noticed, weeds will grow anywhere, even where your flowers won't. The simple truth is that most weed seeds require light to germinate. When they come to the soil surface, they grow. Mulch serves as a weed free layer that keeps weed seeds in the dark. The key is to be sure the mulch itself is weed free. Mulch is a very effective means of controlling annual weeds, but does little to control perennial weeds when the roots are already in the soil. (For more about weed control, see page 127.)

Another widely acknowledged advantage of mulch is that it helps to conserve moisture in the soil. Remember, however, that mulch only reduces evaporation from the surface. It does nothing to prevent roots of neighboring trees and shrubs from robbing the soil of water. Mulch can even complicate overhead watering because it must be moistened before the water can reach the soil, and some mulches can even repel water. For this reason, drip irrigation is a very efficient method of watering under mulch.

Mulches also protect the soil from water damage. Yes, I said water damage. There are two ways water can damage your soil. Most people know about erosion. Raindrops falling on the soil dislodge soil particles and carry them away. You lose your soil, which is carried to streams and rivers as silt, harmful to aquatic life.

The other type of damage is called puddling. Normally, fine soil particles are bonded together into larger aggregates that make the soil looser and easy to work, and improve aeration through larger pores between the larger aggregates. These aggregates are referred to as the structure of the soil. Adding organic matter is one way to improve the formation of aggregates and therefore structure. When rain falls on exposed soil, the impact breaks down the structure of the aggregates and closes up the pores on the surface; water can't seep into the soil as efficiently, and puddles are formed. A light mulch is enough to prevent puddling and increase water absorption by the soil.

Some mulches are very nutritious and all organic mulches contribute valuable organic matter to the soil when they decompose. Organic matter is an excellent soil conditioner, but not necessarily nutritious by itself. Peat and bark contain few nutrients, whereas shredded leaves and spent mushroom soil are especially high in nutrients, although even they are not a complete diet. Mulches feed slowly and evenly, something plants like.

The final benefits of mulches involve winter protection of your plants. Even light mulches insulate the soil remarkably effectively. Although bare soil is frozen hard, mulched soil is often unfrozen. Winter mulch protects your plants in two ways.

Warmer soils mean the roots of plants are less subject to cold damage. Herbaceous perennials can be grown farther north than their normal hardiness range with a heavy winter mulch. Warmer, mulched soil around trees and shrubs keeps the roots more active through the winter so they supply branches and leaves with water lost from drying winter winds. (This is a particular benefit for evergreens.) Winter mulches also promote more consistent soil temperatures. Once frozen, soil tends to stay frozen until a long spell of warm weather returns. Rapid freezing and thawing can damage plant roots and heave them out of the ground, subjecting them to dehydration. If bare-root perennials must be planted in the fall, their best chance of survival is under a heavy mulch.

Generally, I apply mulch in the spring and the fall. Thin spots can be supplemented at any time, and new plants should be mulched right away. Don't mulch in spring if the soil is wet and you want it to dry out, or if the soil is cold and you want it to warm up. Some plants need the soil to warm before planting or they are subject to rotting. In the heat of summer, however, most plants prefer a mulch to keep their roots cool. If you remove it, don't forget to put it back.

Don't mulch until late fall if you have a problem with rodents eating perennial roots and bulbs. In autumn rodents search for cozy places to spend the winter. They will enthusiastically move into your mulch and spend the rest of the winter feasting on your plants. If you wait until late fall when the ground has begun to freeze, the little rascals won't be house hunting any longer. I'd suggest putting out some rodent bait in troublesome areas, just to be sure. Rodent bait should be placed in appropriate containers to keep it from other wildlife.

My favorite mulch is shredded leaves. Leaves are very nutritious, usually free, and seem to work on almost everything except rock-garden plants. Shredded leaves usually don't blow away and aren't so coarse that they inhibit the growth of smaller plants. They work very well in flower borders. Shredded leaves have all the advantages of a good mulch and lack the problems associated with some others. They can be applied as much as 3 to 4 inches deep as they decompose rapidly. Of course, shredding leaves can be a bit of work, so I only use the shredded ones where I really need them. Whole leaves are perfectly all right in naturalistic areas.

The best leaves are those that have some stiffness to them and do not pack down. Oak leaves are perfect. Maple leaves are less satisfactory because they tend to mat down flat and can reduce aeration to the roots as well as smother smaller plants. They do make great compost or leaf mold. Avoid walnut leaves for compost and mulch due to their toxicity.

Leaf mold is not recommended as a mulch as it is already too broken down. Use it as a soil conditioner. Many municipalities sell leaf mold full of weed seeds and, worse still, perennial weed roots. When you spread this on your garden, you are spreading trouble. Check into the weed content before you buy, or make your own.

Pine needles (or pine straw) make an excellent mulch because they don't pack down and are effective insulators in winter, allowing good air circulation even when piled high around tender plants. Pine needles don't blow away. Mix them with leaves to stabilize and lighten them. If you have pine trees, you're lucky. If not, pine needles are available from some garden centers, particularly in the South. For weed control, apply a 2- to 3-inch layer. Note that continuous use of pine needles as mulch over a period of years tends to acidify the soil, and this might be of concern, depending on the plants you wish to grow.

If you are fortunate enough to live near a mushroom grower, you have access to the spent compost in which mushrooms have been grown. This makes a nutritious and good-looking mulch for the flower garden. (It's also a good soil conditioner when mixed in.) Although it can have a high salt content, this is not usually a problem as long as you do not plant in pure mushroom soil, or pile it up against plant stems. Don't use mushroom soil on acid-loving plants such as rhododendron and azaleas, because it contains lime and can be quite alkaline. Use it about 2 inches deep between plants. Be sure the mushroom soil is weed free. Sometimes it is allowed to sit outdoors in piles, and weed seeds blow onto it (especially in the fall). I always insist on having what has just come out of the mushroom houses. The "aged" kind is a prescription for weeds, and probably costs more besides.

Another good mulch for annuals and perennials is licorice root. It has a fine texture and doesn't harm soft herbaceous stems. It should be used about 2 inches deep.

Wood chips are often cheap, and may come for free. They are too coarse for all but the larger perennials, but are suitable for shrubs. I use them at the back of large beds. Don't mix them into the soil until they are fully decomposed into humus, because rotting wood has a tremendous appetite for nitrogen and will get it before your plants do. Nitrogen deficiency symptoms will show up, guaranteed. Wood chips are fine on top of the soil. Around large plants at the back, use them about 3 inches deep.

Stone or gravel mulches have their place, but not in most flower gardens. They reflect heat and contribute nothing to your plants. Stone is heavy to apply, and these mulches eventually fill up with dirt and debris and need to be added to or replaced. The benefit may not be permanent but the stone itself is because, once added to your soil, it is difficult to remove and can make digging harder in the future.

Stone mulches have a place in rock gardens. Delicate plants subject to rotting in damp, humid weather have a far better chance with a gravel mulch. It allows perfect drainage around the base of the plant and underneath the leaves. The heat it reflects drives away extra moisture rapidly. In the flower garden, Mediterranean species and many gray-foliaged plants benefit from a gravel mulch, in conjunction with good air circulation and full sun. Stone mulches should cover the soil; 1 inch or more deep is appropriate, but this depends on the size of the gravel and the size of the plants.

Landscape fabric and plastic mulches have little place in the flower gardens of serious gardeners. (If you've read this far, you must be pretty serious.) Organic, biodegradable mulches accomplish everything that the synthetic ones do, and help build your soil as well. Synthetic mulches must eventually be replaced (which isn't easy) as they prevent weeds only until covered with enough debris on top to grow weeds there. You still have to add mulch or the synthetic material will show through. It's impossible to manage a dynamic flower bed with all that plastic in the way. Leave the landscape fabric and plastic to the industrial sites.

The mulch you use can affect your soil. Pine needles and oak leaves are acidic. If used on plants that prefer a neutral soil, you may need to apply some lime to balance things out. Beech leaves also are acidic, unless the trees are growing on a limy subsoil where they will absorb lime and deposit it in their leaves. If you live in an area where the subsoil is limy, don't put beech leaves on acid-loving plants.

Some mulches cause problems if used in the wrong situations. Certain bark mulches appear to cause toxicity problems when used on annuals and perennials. Peat repels water when it dries out. If it doesn't blow away, it is so buoyant that it floats away in a good rain. Mushroom soil tends to have a high salt content and should not be applied close to soft herbaceous stems. Stone mulches don't float away, but because they are not degradable, they will be in your soil for good once you apply them. Choose the mulch that is right for your needs and you won't have problems.

How to Mulch

If soil shows through the mulch, weeds will be likely to grow there. Take some time to smooth out the bed and level the soil. The garden will look instantly better for this. Remove all weeds, even inside clumps of perennials and underneath the foliage, where you can't see them unless you're looking for them. Unseen weeds are a source of more weeds. Apply mulch most heavily between plants and try not to cover the crowns of perennials, as some mulches may cause crown rot. Begin at the back of the bed, or the middle in the case of island beds. Spread the mulch to the back and sides in an even layer, then bring it right up to the front edge. Mulch under adjacent shrubs. A coarser mulch may be used at the back between the larger perennials and under shrubs. Remulch any bare spots resulting from transplanting and maintenance. You will still need to check periodically for weeds, but those you find can be easily and quickly picked out.

Organic mulches disappear in two ways: They decompose, and they get blown or washed away. Each mulch has a different rate of decomposition, and this is further affected by temperature and moisture. None should be expected to be fully effective in the second year, and most last through only one growing season. Replacing mulch is part of garden maintenance.

Keeping mulch in place is a matter of common sense and strategy. In my garden I have lots of trees, and mulch extensively with fresh, unshredded leaves in natural areas and under shrubs. We learned the hard way that whole leaves are likely to blow away or back onto the lawn on the next gusty day. Once we mulched some flower beds with peat moss. The next hard rain, the peat floated out onto the lawn. A fine mulch on a slope will wash off to the bottom in a heavy rain, or do so gradually over time with lighter rains.

Now when I mulch with leaves I do something to hold them in place and prevent them from blowing away. A scattering of wood chips on top works wonders. Sticks and twigs in less visible areas are effective, and look convincingly natural. Alternatively, when planning to mulch an area with leaves, lay down a layer of sticks first, then add the leaves. The leaves get caught in the sticks and stay in place. You can also use older, wet leaves, which are generally less prone to catch the wind and move around.

All organic mulches will float, so there isn't much that can be done to protect against floods. (Even stones are not the solution because flood waters will wash all sorts of debris and soil on top of them.) Peat will float on a thin film of water, but wood chips require 1 or 2 inches of depth to start moving. On a slope, use coarsely shredded hardwood bark. The pieces tend to get tangled and hold each other in place. Coarser pieces are more likely to stay in place.

Of course, you would not incorporate all of the above suggestions into your finely manicured flower garden, but a garden consists of many types of plantings that contribute to the effect of the property. A well-mulched garden is a healthier garden, a more thoroughly enjoyed garden, and a more easily managed, more ecologically sound garden. A final thought: Mulches won't solve bad soil problems. Amending problem soils before planting is essential.

STRATEGIC WEEDING

There's no doubt about it: Unorganized weeding is an arduous, never-ending task. But, armed with a basic understanding of the different types of weeds and how they grow, you will be provided with the commonsense strategies to beat them. Annual weeds, like annual flowers, are short lived. The roots are small and rarely have the potential to resprout if the tops are destroyed. Annual weeds can, however, be hardy, cool-season plants, living and growing through the winter. Like hardy annual flowers, they are generally intolerant of heat and disappear during summer (although, with shade and adequate water, they can grow all year long). Chickweed is a good example. Others, like purslane, are tender, warm-season weeds and don't even appear until it gets warm.

Annuals rely on a profusion of seed to perpetuate themselves. A vigorous chickweed plant may produce as many as 15,000 seeds and a shepherd's purse plant up to 40,000 seeds. In addition, the seed may have tremendous longevity, depending on the species. Some seeds live for many years buried in the soil, waiting to be brought to the surface. Others have a relatively short life of two or three years during which they must germinate or die. Seeds are often light sensitive; when brought to the surface by cultivation, they germinate.

Perennial weeds are longer lived and have underground roots, rhizomes or bulbs that persist year to year. Often they are highly invasive and difficult to remove, particularly as any piece left in the ground has the ability to resprout and grow. Hoeing perennial weeds is an exercise in futility and may even serve to propagate them by breaking the roots into more pieces. Some of the worst perennial weeds are mugwort, goutweed, Canadian thistle and bindweed.

Controlling Annual Weeds

The key to getting the upper hand with annual weeds is population control. Don't let them produce seed. If they do, get it out of the garden and keep it out of your compost and mulch. This also means controlling weeds in areas surrounding the garden. Preventing seed production means eliminating weeds when they are young, early in their life cycle. This won't necessarily prevent weeds the following year, because there will still be a seed population in the soil, but it will prevent any addition to that seed population and the benefit will become apparent.

Given a quantity of seed of a certain weed species in the soil, each year a percentage of that seed will die. Not every seed is created equal, and some will be programmed for shorter lives than others. Each succeeding year, however, a larger percentage of the remaining seeds will die—if you don't add to the population. In the case of chickweed, I've noticed that after two or three years of total control, scarcely a single plant appears. Purslane, on the other hand, has a long seed life and it will be many years before you start to notice its decline.

Solarization is an effective means of eliminating weed seeds from an empty bed, if the bed is situated to receive the hot sun during the heat of summer. Loosen the soil about a foot deep. Water it until it is soaking wet. The next day, cover the bed with clear plastic and seal the edges tight with soil. Leave the plastic in place for 6 to 8 weeks. During this time, soil temperatures will soar as high as 140°F at the surface, and up to 100° deeper down. The heat and humidity in the soil will kill weed seeds in the top 4 inches, and many plant diseases deeper down as well. To be effective the soil must receive the maximum amount of sun possible, and this procedure is best done during July and August.

A technique for reducing weeds in annual plantings is to encourage an early weed germination that can then be destroyed before planting the flowers. It works this way: Prepare the bed by tilling, incorporating compost, and whatever else you plan to do. Level the soil and prepare the surface. Now wait a week or so for the weeds to germinate. If the weather is dry, speed the process by watering. Once the weeds have appeared, control them by *shallow* hoeing or cultivation (so as not to dredge up more seeds), or with a rapidly biodegradable herbicide, such as glyphosate (see page 129), which won't persist in the soil (read the label thoroughly and follow directions carefully). Then, sow your flower seed using the direct sowing method or plant your transplants.

Hoeing is an ancient method of killing annual weeds. Wait for a hot, sunny, dry day for maximum effectiveness. Skillful hoeing cuts weeds from their roots, just below the point at which they can resprout, usually just below the surface of the soil. The sun does the rest. In cloudy, damp weather, the weeds may reroot, particularly if you push too much soil around, thereby burying and, in effect, replanting them. Succulent weeds such as purslane reroot even in the sun and need to be physically removed.

My favorite type of hoe is unquestionably a scuffle hoe, or Dutch hoe, as it is better known in England. Scuffle hoes are pushed away from, instead of pulled toward, the operator. The blade is mounted on an angle so that it cuts under a thin layer of soil. The weeds stay on top, facing the sun and drying up. Scuffle hoes also allow amazing dexterity so that you can reach around and between plants and under overhanging foliage to really get at weeds. Hoes work best on bare soil, but I've even used a scuffle hoe in beds with a mulch. It is so easy to use that you can even hoe with one hand if you have a strong wrist, and keep your back straight.

Preemergent herbicides are recommended by some authorities for use in the garden. They kill germinating seeds, but not older, established plants—usually. This would seem perfect for a perennial garden where you want to prevent weeds. These herbicides are designed to stay in the top layer of soil, and are very slow to wash down more deeply. They usually last about half the summer. Certain plants have a sensitivity to certain preemergent herbicides, however, and if they are used will be damaged or deformed. The label on the package doesn't list all these sensitive plants. In fact, it is illegal to use these herbicides on plants not specifically listed on the label. In all probability, there are many more kinds of plants in your garden than the label includes. What then? These herbicides also prevent the regeneration from seed of short-lived plants like annuals and biennials. I prefer to save myself and my plants from these risks whenever possible, and use mulches, with their numerous other benefits, instead of chemicals for weed control.

Common Annual Weeds

Capsella bursa-pastoris (Shepherd's purse; cool season)
Digitaria species (Crabgrass; warm season)
Lamium amplexicaule (Henbit: cool season)
Poa annua (Annual bluegrass; cool season)
Portulacca oleracea (Purslane; warm season)
Stellaria media (Chickweed; cool season)

Controlling Perennial Weeds

Ideally, all perennial weeds should be eliminated from the soil before a garden is planted. They are far more difficult to control when growing between plants and when they have grown in among the roots of your valued perennials. Watch for perennial weed infestations in newly purchased potted perennials. If you plan to start a garden and there are perennial weeds in the plot, treat it with a systemic herbicide before you even start to dig. For the herbicide to be effective, all the roots must be attached to the leaves that absorb the herbicide. If you dig, the severed roots won't be killed. During warm weather, a couple of weeks is enough for the herbicide to do its work, then soil preparation may be started. Herbicides work more slowly in cool weather. If there is more time, perennial weeds can be starved out by covering the bed with black plastic or overlapping pieces of newspaper to exclude all light. This takes about a year. Of course, you also need to control the same weeds in the surrounding lawns or beds or the weed roots will run back into your bed. For the surrounding areas, you can spot treat, or use selective herbicides.

The worst thing you can do is chop up the roots of perennial weeds with a hoe, spade or tiller. You won't kill a single one, but will create hundreds more plants. I find the best strategy is not to disturb them until I can get around to treating them with a systemic herbicide that will be absorbed and translocated all the way down to the roots. Only attempt to dig them when you can get out every last piece of root.

If you still have perennial weeds in an established planting, don't despair. With a bit of care you can eliminate most of them in the first attempt. Perhaps the bed is infested with bindweed, climbing all over your plants. As it grows, carefully unwind it and coil it on the ground between the plants. Carefully treat these coiled stems with a systemic herbicide, such as glyphosate, but avoid getting even a little on adjacent plants. In a couple of weeks you will see the foliage yellow and die. (There's a vengeful fun to watching this!) With other types of perennial weeds, lean them out away from your plants or peg them down to the ground where you can safely treat them. Some regrowth will occur but it will be minimal and can be quickly dealt with if your first attack has been thorough.

HERBICIDES

The trend today is beginning to move away from the use of chemicals, including those in the garden. With all the concern about introducing chemicals into the environment and how they affect the user, this is an important consideration. I prefer the organic approach and avoid using chemicals more than I have to. I'm always handling the plants, and having my hands in the soil. I just don't want to be exposed to all these chemicals all of the time. In most cases, there are alternatives to using chemicals; the organic methods discussed above are perfectly satisfactory. In fact, chemicals can't be substituted for good cultural practices.

The only instance where a herbicide is difficult to replace is where a systemic is needed to control the deep roots of perennial weeds that will keep coming up in your flower bed. Current research indicates that glyphosate (sold as Round-up and Kleen-up) is safer for people and the environment than most other herbicides. It is extremely effective, but does not persist in the soil. Once sprayed on the foliage, it is circulated throughout the plant so that even the deepest roots are killed. Remember, glyphosate will kill any vegetation that it touches including flowers, lawn and shrubs, so use it with care and prevent the mist from the spray from drifting onto other plants, and damaging or killing them.

If you do use chemicals in your garden, be sure to read the labels carefully, follow directions, and take recommended safety precautions, including wearing rubber gloves on your hands. For specific recommendations and advice, consult your local agricultural extension service.

Weeds and the Plant Community

Some years ago, while working in a very fine private garden, I spotted a patch of "weeds" that, while not ugly or invasive, were not as nice as most of the other plants in the garden. I asked the owner why they had not been removed. She replied that if they were taken out something that she wanted less would be likely to take their place. In other words, they held a space and kept it under control. Later, the "weeds" were removed and the spot was promptly replanted with a more desirable plant. It did not sit empty. That was a valuable lesson.

In Chapter 4, proper spacing is discussed as a part of the design process. For aesthetic reasons, plants should be spaced tightly for a full appearance, but this also serves to crowd out weeds and make maintenance easier. Weeds are opportunists. Bare soil is their invitation. Weeds find it difficult to invade an established community of plants adapted to the site. The best weed control is to shade them out with dense (but not overcrowded) plantings. Use the spacing distances given for each plant in Part III to avoid empty spaces between plants.

SEASONAL PLANTING AND TRANSPLANTING

The success and the health of the plants in your garden begin with a good start. Why handicap them by planting and transplanting at the wrong time? A glaring example is the person who plants leggy pansies at the beginning of the hot season,

when they are already worn out and readily succumb to the heat. Had they been planted a couple of months earlier, these same pansies would have given a command performance. By the same token, don't buy tulips in bloom in spring as an addition to your garden. They will never be as strong again and you can't plant them deeply enough from shallow pots. Reputable garden centers won't sell you such plants for garden planting.

A more subtle but nonetheless significant factor is bad timing, which can drastically reduce performance for an entire season. Perennials planted at the beginning of the hot season will not attain the vigor and flowering of those planted earlier, whose roots have had adequate time to become established and spread. It's best to plant and transplant at the beginning of a growth cycle. When entering into a period of active growth, plants show a remarkable ability to regenerate lost roots and make a rapid recovery.

One of the great boons to modern gardeners is the availability of container-grown plants at nurseries throughout the growing season. Container-grown plants can be planted at almost any time because minimal root disturbance occurs when they are transplanted. Still, good transplanting practices and aftercare can spell the difference between success and failure.

It is better to plant container-grown plants at the beginning of a growth cycle, as described above. In order to survive dry spells, plants need to have established, far-reaching roots, and these develop mostly in spring and fall. If you plant in late spring and summer, regular watering will probably be required through the summer because the roots won't make much extra growth.

It's also essential to loosen the roots against the side of the pot. Roots growing in rich, well-aerated container soils have become spoiled and are often hesitant to leave their comfort. Force them to do so by spreading them into the surrounding soil. Woody plants also require that coiled, potentially strangling roots be spread out. It is safer to do this in spring and fall when roots are actively growing and can recover more quickly.

Late-Summer Division and Planting

Experienced gardeners acquainted with the growth cycles of individual plants can spot opportunities to plant and rejuvenate. For example, perennials that bloom in early summer often have a second flush of growth (mostly foliage) in late summer. A case in point is the Shasta daisy (*Chrysanthemum* ×*superbum*). If not divided every two or three years, it will crowd itself out. If rejuvenated, however, it can be perpetuated indefinitely. The usual time to divide is in early spring. Plants will then take the first summer to recover with a reduced show the first year. A window for division also exists in late summer, just as they begin their fall growth. Warm soils and the impending winter encourage a rapid recovery, with firmly rooted plants and better bloom the following summer. By dividing in late summer you won't lose a season's top performance.

Late summer and early fall are also good times to plant seedling perennials and biennials. It must be done early enough that they have plenty of time to develop deep roots and grow into strong plants. The benefit of these strong plants the following spring is obvious. Set out seedling delphinium just after the heat of summer breaks. They dislike hot summers, but make good use of a long, cool fall to get ready for a striking show the following summer.

Fall-planted Perennials

Planting and dividing perennials in the fall can be tricky, because they might not survive the winter. If disturbed too much, the roots will not be able to hold the crowns in the ground through the winter's freezing and thawing. This is called frost heaving. When the roots are heaved out on top of the soil, they are exposed to temperature changes and dehydration.

Don't plant bareroot perennials in the fall unless they are deeply planted types, such as oriental poppy or peony. Don't buy bareroot perennials in the fall, either. It is perfectly all right to transplant firmly rooted perennials, if the root ball is not broken up. You can even divide the root ball into halves or quarters as long as it holds together and is not too small. A firm root ball will not frost heave out of the ground.

Frost heaving is a gradual process as freezing recurs through the winter. It can be prevented by allowing the soil to freeze thoroughly before applying a winter mulch. The mulch will then keep the ground frozen and prevent heaving. (Don't use this technique with marginally hardy plants, as they tend to be less hardy when not fully established.)

Certain perennials should not be divided in the fall. Fall-blooming perennials are often said to belong to this group. It seems that when they are in the flowering mode, they cannot reestablish to survive the winter. I haven't found this to be a problem with New England aster, but I leave most other fall bloomers alone until spring. Ornamental grasses native to Asia, as a rule, fall into this temperamental group too. Don't disturb the roots of *Miscanthus* until spring. (European fescues, which are somewhat evergreen, can be divided in fall if not done too late.) I also leave half-hardy plants alone until spring because their survival rate is likely to be decreased.

Fall-planted Annuals

From Zone 6 south some annuals can be planted in the fall, if you can get them. The hardiest are the pansies, violas and forget-me-nots. In Zone 6, they will just grow and strengthen until cold brings on dormancy. In early winter, apply a light, fluffy mulch of salt hay or pine needles until spring for protection. If planted early enough, they will make a few blooms before winter. Farther south, bloom will continue through the winter. The greatest benefit of fall-planted annuals is gained in the Deep South and on the Pacific Coast, where a wide range of cool-season annuals, such as calendulas and iceland poppies, can be depended on for winter bloom.

TRANSPLANTING SPRING BULBS

The ideal time to dig and move bulbs is just as the foliage is turning yellow, when you can still find them. If done before the foliage fully dries, it will stay attached to the bulbs and help you find them in the soil. Once the bulbs are out of the ground, either they can be replanted immediately where you want them or they can be cleaned and saved for planting at the proper time in fall. It is best to save tulips in a dry state until fall, since they prefer dry summers. Daffodils are also best saved unless they will be planted back in a cool soil in shade; warm soils in sun encourage basal rot. Other small bulbs are often safest back in the soil where they are protected from dehydration.

Proper cleaning and drying are critical for storing bulbs. After digging, carefully wash bulbs to remove soil. Spread them out on burlap or newspaper to dry in a shaded location with good air circulation. A screened porch is ideal. Drying will take about a week. Guard against animals, remembering that crocus and tulip bulbs are especially delectable.

To store bulbs, place one or two dozen in an old stocking, net bag or paper bag. Hang or spread them out on shelves in a dry location with good air circulation and temperatures around 70°F. Don't store bulbs in a hot attic or damp cellar. Never place bulbs in a plastic bag—it traps moisture and leads to rotting. Check regularly to remove any bad bulbs before others are infected.

Plant daffodils as soon as the summer heat begins to subside. Tulips may be planted up until the ground freezes, or a month or two after daffodils are planted.

Transplanting bulbs and getting the colors and placement right can be a problem. The ideal time to dig them is when they are dormant. The problem is that if you didn't label them or the label gets lost, you won't know which varieties are which. Besides, you can't compare colors and bloom times when they are out of flower.

Some bulbs can be transplanted "in the green," which means while they have green foliage. It is not the best time, but it works and serves the gardener's needs. I have a large area of naturalized daffodils. The only time I can see where I need more, and what colors I want there, is when they are in bloom. So, I move them then and it works.

The best bulbs to transplant in the green are the really tough varieties that are easy to grow in your climate. (If you damage them, they grow strong enough to recover.) Bloom the following year might not be as profuse as before, but recovery should be complete by the year after. Transplanting in the green is less successful with tulips, which tend to run out and weaken with time anyway.

The bulbs most frequently recommended for transplanting at this time are snowdrops, but I've found it works well enough with daffodils, *Chionodoxa*, grape hyacinths and others. Move them just as the flowers are fading so you can see what colors you are putting where. As with any other transplants, treat the roots with care. Carefully separate the bulbs and roots into small bunches or even single bulbs. Don't forget to water them in, after replanting.

SEASONAL MANAGEMENT

The garden offers something to be enjoyed at every season, and each season has its own tasks to justify time spent there. In southern regions, winter activities are more numerous than in the North, but winter can be a beautiful season in any climate.

Spreading the care of your garden out over as many months as possible allows a much higher standard of maintenance with seemingly less effort. Many jobs are simply best done during the off-seasons—best for the plants, and in the case of heavier work, best for the gardener as well, because the weather is cooler. Jobs taken care of during the less busy seasons are out of the way when time is at a premium. I try to do everything that I can when life is less busy. This leaves more time to do the necessities and enjoy the garden at its peak of growth and bloom. It also keeps me more in touch with the rhythms of the garden and plants through the four seasons.

Admittedly, it is often difficult to remember what was planned from one season to the next. Try keeping a calendar or simply a list of jobs intended for each season. In July, when you see a perennial or shrub you want to move, put it down on the list for fall or spring, or more specifically for October, or March (or whatever month is best in your climate). Keep a garden planning clipboard or binder for these notes and lists. With just a bit of planning, it is easy to keep in step with your garden and enjoy the rewards. The following seasonal overview is based on the average climate of Zone 6. The entire schedule is meant as a guide and will need to be adjusted according to local climatic conditions. In colder climates, fewer jobs can be done in late fall, and the spring schedule begins later; in the South the reverse is true.

SEASONAL MAINTENANCE OVERVIEW

Fall

Wherever you live, think of fall as the beginning of the yearly cycle and planting season. Cooler weather is revitalizing to both plants and people. It is also a less busy time than spring, and there is time to catch up and get ahead on things while implementing some new ideas.

Fall is the best time to do much of the preparation for planting and begin new gardens, whether you will be planting in the fall or the spring. You'll have clearer ideas and stronger inspiration at this season, while the new ideas of the closing summer are still fresh in mind. The soil is also easier to work since it is seldom as wet in fall.

Many plants can be transplanted in fall, which gives them an extra season to get established before the heat and possible droughts of summer. Those that can't be moved in fall can be moved first thing in spring if the site was prepared the previous autumn. They will then have the maximum possible time to get settled.

Do:
- Reposition established perennials
- Transplant fully hardy shrubs
- Transplant hardy seedling annuals and biennials: pansy, viola, Johnny-jump-up, forget-me-not, English daisy, wallflower
- Direct sow hardy annuals: forget-me-not, Chinese forget-me-not, larkspur
- Seedlings to be planted in early fall: delphinium, foxglove, lupine, shasta daisy
- Bulbs best planted in early fall: daffodil, snowdrops, crocus, other early small bulbs
- Bulbs best planted in late fall: tulip
- Perennials best planted in fall: oriental poppy, bearded iris (by mid-September, if you can get them) and peony
- Keep winter-growing weeds cleaned up: chickweed, shepherd's purse, etc.
- Mulch to prevent weed growth and winter heaving
- Neaten garden for winter, selectively removing messy stems and stalks but leaving others for winter interest.

Don't:
- Plant bareroot perennials
- Plant or transplant tender or marginally hardy plants
- Transplant most fall-blooming perennials and grasses

Summary of Steps to Improve the Flower Garden:
- Consult notes from growing season
- Adjust largest plants first (shrubs, perennials)
- Move seedling biennials and hardy annuals into empty spaces
- Last, plant bulbs

Winter

In all but the warmest climates, there is little to be done in the flower garden in winter. It is a good season to catch up in other parts of the landscape. Winter is a great time to prune hardy deciduous trees and shrubs in preparation for spring. Evergreens must be trimmed with a bit more caution, because newly exposed foliage and bark may sunburn on sunny days in late winter and early spring, when it is still quite cold.

Winter is also a great time to generate ideas and inspiration through books and catalogs. Make plans to solve problems and improve plantings that didn't quite work as you had hoped.

Spring

As soon as the frost is out of the ground, planting of dormant plants such as bareroot perennials and shrubs can begin. If preparation of the site was done the previous fall, this is quickly and easily done as the plants arrive from mail-order sources, or become available in garden centers.

Soils may be too wet for planting, particularly heavy soils with less-than-ideal drainage. Usually, if the soil has been prepared, planting can be accomplished with minimal disturbance, even when it is too wet to till or otherwise mix in amendments. Use special care not to overwork clay soils when wet to avoid puddling and loss of structure. (For more about puddling and soil structure, see page 20.)

Light frosts and surface freezing of the soil should not be harmful to hardy plants when planted in a dormant state at this season. Don't apply a mulch immediately, so that the spring sun can warm the soil more quickly, encouraging more rapid root establishment. If severe late frosts should occur (below 20°F), cover crowns with mulch for protection, and watch for frost heaving.

Do in Early Spring:
- Planting and transplanting of dormant shrubs and perennials
- Check under mulch to see that bulbs are not being trapped underneath or smothered

Do in Early–Mid Spring:
- Remove winter mulch on beds to be remulched for summer
- Finish off beds and fork soil to reduce compaction and to smooth surface

- Mulch (mulching can be delayed if soils are cold)
- Begin staking
- Sow half-hardy annuals
- Plant frost-tolerant annuals: pansy, viola, forget-me-not, stock
- Transplant some bulbs "in the green"
- Prune roses
- Prune summer-blooming shrubs, such as buddleia and *Caryopteris*
- Prune summer-flowering vines, such as honeysuckle and many clematises

Do in Late Spring:
- Begin training, pinching annuals and perennials
- Staking
- Deadheading
- Transplant self-sown annual seedlings
- Replace spring annuals and bulbs with summer annuals
- Dig spring bulbs if necessary
- Twiddle vines
- Begin planting summer bulbs when soil is warm
- Control pests and diseases
- Weed control while young
- Prune spring-flowering shrubs and vines after they finish blooming

Summer

The main activities of summer are grooming, maintenance and enjoying the flower garden. The better your grooming techniques, the more it will be enjoyed.

Do throughout Summer:
- Grooming—deadheading and deadleafing—at least monthly
- Replace mulch as needed to suppress weeds and conserve moisture
- Staking as needed
- Control pests and diseases
- Weed control while young
- Note changes and improvements for next year

Do in Early Summer:
- Prune spring-flowering shrubs and vines after they finish blooming
- Prune noneverblooming climbing and shrub roses after they finish blooming, unless hips are desired for fall display

Do in Midsummer:
- Sow annuals for fall bloom
- Transplant self-sown biennials
- Lightly trim vines to neaten and maintain order

Do in Late Summer:
- Plant fall blooming bulbs
- Divide and transplant early-summer-blooming perennials
- Divide and replant bearded iris, if needed.

Following pages: A rich medley of bloom, foliage and autumn tints is displayed in this border in late October. The Terry Shane Teaching Garden at the Scott Arboretum of Swarthmore College, near Philadelphia.

PART III
The Gardener's and Designer's Resource Guide

The success of a flower garden depends on well-designed plantings. Successful plantings require planning and the selection of the right plants to fill design needs. Finding the plant with the right appearance is often one of the most mind-racking tasks.

The purpose of this reference section is to support the ideas discussed earlier in the text and give options for filling specific design needs. This is not meant to be a complete listing, but rather suggested plants and information on using them well. Many of those plants are dependable performers and easy to grow. Some are more challenging or restricted in their use but fill a particular need, and so have been included with a note concerning their drawbacks. Most of the plants included are commonly available at better garden centers or from mail-order nurseries. A few are not commonly available but must be searched for through specialist nurseries or plant societies; they are well worth the effort. Scientific names are used as the primary listing for clarity, but plants can be located by common name by using the index.

The Gardener's and Designer's Resource Guide includes the following:

Encyclopedia of Bulbs. Winter hardy or tender (annual), for spring, summer or fall, listed alphabetically. For discussion, see pages 141–148.

Encyclopedia of Annuals and Biennials. Hardy, half-hardy and tender, listed alphabetically. (Annual vines are included in the Encyclopedia of Vines.) For discussion, see pages 149–163.

Encyclopedia of Perennials. Listed alphabetically. For discussion, see pages 164–195.

Encyclopedia of Ferns. Listed alphabetically. For discussion, see pages 196–197.

Encyclopedia of Grasses. Listed alphabetically. For discussion, see pages 198–199.

Encyclopedia of Vines and Climbers. Hardy and nonhardy woody, perennial and annual vines, listed alphabetically. For discussion, see pages 200–207.

Encyclopedia of Flower Garden Shrubs. Shrubs I particularly recommend for flower gardens. For discussion, see pages 208–211.

Bloom Seasons: Perennials, Biennials, Hardy Bulbs, Flower Garden Shrubs and Vines by Month and Color. Hardy plants with typically limited bloom seasons, listed by month of bloom and flower color. For discussion, see pages 212–222.

Bloom Seasons: Annuals and Tender (Annual) Bulbs by Cool or Warm Season and Color. Plants that require replanting each year and typically have a long or continuous bloom season, listed by season and color. For discussion, see pages 223–225.

Notable Foliage Colors: Perennials, Annuals, Bulbs, Shrubs and Vines. For discussion, see pages 226–227.

Notable Flower Forms and Foilage Types (Textures): Perennials, Annuals, Bulbs, Shrubs and Vines. For discussion, see pages 228–230.

About the Encyclopedias

Hardiness Zones: Ratings are based on the USDA Plant Hardiness Zone Map. The first number indicates the northernmost or coldest zone in which the plant can normally be expected to survive. Such factors as duration of cold spells, exposure to sun and wind, and the insulating effect of snow or mulch can radically affect survival. A second number in parentheses indicates that, under favorable circumstances, such as with a mulch or in a sheltered spot, the plant will survive in this hardiness zone. The second number indicates the southernmost zone in which the plant can normally be expected to perform. This is limited not only by a lack of winter cold but also by an excess of summer heat. A "?" after a number indicates that the northern or southern limit is uncertain. Many plants will grow in a warmer zone along the Pacific Coast where summers are cooler as opposed to the hot humid southeastern states. For example, minimum winter temperatures along the coasts of both Washington State and Louisiana fall to about 20°F, as defined for Zone 9, but summer temperatures in Louisiana soar into the upper '90s with high humidity, while in Washington, they usually remain in the '80s with lower humidity.

When hardiness ratings are given for annuals and tender bulbs they can perform as perennials in those southern regions, although readers from northern regions will find it necessary to treat them as annuals, either by cuttings or seeds. Most annuals receive no hardiness rating because they are short lived.

Plant Type: Plant types provide an indication of the culture and use of that plant in the garden. Types are fully explained in the text of this book.

Hardy Bulb, page 48
Tender Bulb, page 48
Hardy Annual, page 43
Half-hardy Annual, page 43
Tender Annual, page 43
Hardy Biennial, page 40
Tender Biennial, page 40
Perennial, page 38
Twiners (Vines), page 55
Grabbers (Vines), page 56
Clingers (Vines), page 56

Light Requirements: The distinction between "full sun" and "part sun" is made for the benefit of gardeners with tall trees that cut out the early- or late-day sun, leaving only partial sun. Plants designated for "full sun" only will not perform well under these conditions.

In hot climates in the South, many plants that will tolerate full sun in the North require afternoon shade to shelter them from extreme heat. When using plants in the South that have a hardiness rating that also extends into northern zones, consider them to prefer the lower light intensities given.

The preferred light intensity is given first. For instance, if a plant will tolerate part sun, but grows better with partial shade, it will be designated as "part shade; part sun." (See page 15 for a discussion of light.)

○ Full Sun—More than 6 hours of direct sun, preferably all day.

◑ Part Sun—A total of 4 to 6 hours of direct sun.

◐ Part Shade—Less than 4 hours of direct sun, or bright high shade with dappled light all day.

● Full Shade—No direct sun or bright shade

◫ Deciduous Shade—Under trees and shrubs that lose their leaves in winter, allowing sun to shine through. (See page 16.)

Height: Both height and spread are given for the purpose of planting plans. Foliage height is also provided, in parentheses, when significantly lower than flower height. When two numbers are given, the first measurement is the height, and the second is the spread. See page 139 for a discussion of how to use height and spread.

Flower Garden Size: This is provided only for shrubs. As they should be pruned (as described on page 93), they will not attain their maximum size.

Maximum Height: This is given only for shrubs and vines as an indication of relative vigor. It is assumed that the size of shrubs and vines will be controlled by pruning to fit the space available in the flower garden. Vines are also controlled by the size of the support provided, and they can be successfully grown on supports considerably shorter than their maximum possible height.

Appearance: Descriptions of the plant's appearance are based on design characteristics such as the relative size and shape of the leaves and flowers, as described in Chapter 4. The most important or common colors are given for each plant type. Colors given in parentheses are less frequently seen, but are included as the discriminating designer may feel they are worth searching for.

Bloom Period: The time of bloom is given as it occurs in the region of Philadelphia, which is a rough average of that across the country. This was done because it gives more specific information to help coordinate the bloom of different plants when planning combinations. In the South, a gardener can estimate how many weeks earlier most plants bloom in their specific region. Northern gardeners can estimate how many weeks later bloom will occur for them. Although this is by no means a perfect system, I believe it is more useful than such generalizations as "early summer" or "spring."

Perennials bloom for two or three weeks on

the average. Some bloom for longer, and a few have a bloom period extending over a couple of months. The most prolific bloom usually occurs near the beginning of these extended seasons. Toward the end, flowers are likely to be sparsely produced, though we still value their enduring, although often half-hearted, contributions. The strongest marriages combine flowers that begin to bloom at about the same time.

Propagation: The most important means of propagation for the home gardener are given. Although it might be noted that most perennials can be grown from seed, this method may not be listed because it is less commonly used and many perennial, bulb and woody plant varieties do not come true from seed.

Uses: A brief summary of use in combination with other plants in the garden, and which are useful for cutting and drying.

Notes: This section contains special tips about disease resistance and susceptibility, cultural techniques and general plant behavior, as well as the soil conditions required for each plant. Assume that all plants will grow in a normal loam soil with good drainage, unless specified.

Varieties: It is impossible to list the many varieties and cultivars available in catalogs and nurseries, particularly as the selection of currently popular and available varieties is constantly changing. Varieties and cultivars are listed only when I believe that they have special merit or would be of particular use to the reader. These varieties are described only as to how they differ from the main entry.

Related Species: Recommended species, hybrids and cultivars that can't be classified under the primary entry are listed here.

Colchicums bloom in autumn without any leaves of their own, so they are best grown where the naked flowers can be clothed by other foliage. In September, Colchicum bivonae *blooms among* Bergenia. *It is the parent of such large-flowered, checkered hybrids as* 'Princess Astrid' *and* 'The Giant'.

Encyclopedia of Bulbs

ALLIUM AFLATUNENSE
Flowering Onion

Hardy Bulb ○ ◑ ◫
Zones: 4 to 8
Height: 30 (15) inches tall; 8-inch spread
Appearance: Lavender ball-shaped flower head; straplike green foliage
Bloom Period: May
Propagation: Division or seed; plant 6 inches deep
Uses: Middle of bed; good fresh-cut flower
Notes: One of the easiest flowering onions to grow. Requires a well-drained soil. Leaves die down promptly after flowering, before the end of May.
Related Species: 'Purple Sensation', deep reddish purple, a hybrid considered better than the species in every respect.

ALLIUM CHRISTOPHII
Flowering Onion

Hardy Bulb ○ ◑
Zones: 4 to 8
Height: 24 (18) inches tall; 8-inch spread
Appearance: Silvery lilac, ball-shaped flowers; straplike green foliage
Bloom Period: June
Propagation: Division; plant 6 inches deep
Uses: Middle or foreground of bed; good for fresh-cut or dried flower
Notes: Also called *A. albopilosum*. Requires a well-drained soil. Flower heads are unusually large for their height.

ALLIUM CAERULEUM

Hardy Bulb ○ ◑
Zones: 4 to 8
Height: 2 to 3 (1) feet tall; 8-inch spread
Appearance: Small balls of deep blue flowers on a slender stem, low narrow leaves
Bloom Period: June

Propagation: Division; plant 4 to 6 inches deep
Uses: Middle of border; good fresh-cut flower
Notes: Also called *A. azureum*. Flowers are a particularly good blue. Best planted in masses for maximum effect. Requires a well-drained soil and prefers a dry site in summer.

ALLIUM GIGANTEUM
Giant Flowering Onion

Hardy Bulb ○
Zones: 4 to 8
Height: 36 to 60 (12) inches tall; 15-inch spread
Appearance: Purple flowers in dense ball; straplike green foliage
Bloom Period: June to July
Propagation: Division; plant 8 inches deep
Uses: Background or middle of bed; good for fresh-cut or dried flower
Notes: The most dramatic onion and useful for its late bloom season. Often difficult to grow; susceptible to black rot. Requires rich, very well drained soil. Good drainage should help.

ANEMONE BLANDA
Greek Anemone (Greek Windflower)

Hardy Bulb ○ ◑ ◫
Zones: 4 to 8
Height: 4 inches tall; 3-inch spread
Appearance: Blue, white or pink flowers; green foliage
Bloom Period: March to April
Propagation: Division or seed; plant 4 inches deep
Uses: Foreground of bed
Notes: Flowers must have the sun shining on them to open. Soak corms in water overnight before planting to improve results. Requires well-drained limy soil, kept dry in summer.
Varieties: 'Radar', pink with white center, and 'White Splendour', large white flowers, are considered the most perennial cultivars.

ANEMONE CORONARIA
Poppy-flowered Anemone

Moderately Hardy Bulb ○ ◑

Zones: 7 to 9

Height: 12 to 18 inches tall; 8-inch spread

Appearance: Blue, red, pink or white flowers; deeply cut green foliage

Bloom Period: April to May

Propagation: Division; plant 3 inches deep

Uses: Foreground of bed; good fresh-cut flower

Notes: Large-flowered but unfortunately not hardy in the North. Requires rich, well-drained soil containing lime with neutral to alkaline pH; prefers dry soil in summer.

Varieties: Commonly offered hybrids 'DeCaen' (single) and 'St. Bridgit' (semidouble double)

Related Species: A. ×*fulgens* (flame anemone) is scarlet and is the hardiest, to Zone 5.

BEGONIA ×TUBERHYBRIDA
Tuberous Begonia

Tender Bulb ◑ ◑ ●

Zones: —

Height: 12 to 18 inches tall; 12-inch spread

Appearance: Large red, orange, yellow, salmon, white or bicolored flowers; large foliage

Bloom Period: May to October

Propagation: Start tubers indoors in April or outdoors when soil is warm; also by seed or cuttings; plant 1 to 2 inches deep

Uses: Middle or foreground of bed; edging

Notes: In hot climates shade from afternoon sun, but they grow best where nights are cool; best to stake brittle stems. Requires rich, moist, well-drained soil. Avoid stem rot by using mulch to prevent splash of soil and mud on stems and leaves.

CALADIUM ×HORTULANUM
Fancy-leafed Caladium

Tender Bulb ◑ ◑ ●

Zones: —

Height: 12 inches tall; 12-inch spread

Appearance: Insignificant flowers; large, heart-shaped leaves colored with pink, red, green and white

Bloom Period: —

Propagation: Division of tubers; start indoors in March in warm place, set out in May when soil is warm or set out as dormant tubers in May when soil is warm; plant 1 inch deep

Uses: Middle or foreground of bed; edging

Notes: Don't set out too early, as cold will set back plants. Store dormant tubers in warm dry place. Requires rich, moist soil. Remove flowers for better leaf display, foliage lasts all summer.

CAMASSIA LEICHTLINII
Camassia

Hardy Bulb ○ ◑ ◐

Zones: 5 to 9

Height: 24 to 36 inches tall; 10-inch spread

Appearance: Blue, cream or white flowers; straplike green foliage

Bloom Period: May

Propagation: Division or seed; plant 6 inches deep

Uses: Middle of bed; good fresh-cut flower

Notes: Native bulb that blooms after most spring bulbs; plant with daffodils to extend seasonal color. Requires rich, moist soil. Noteworthy for its ability to grow in wet, poorly drained, clayey soils.

Varieties: 'Blue Danube'—deep blue flowers, neat foliage is more compact than some other varieties.

CANNA ×GENERALIS
Canna

Tender Bulb ○ ◑

Zones: 8 to 11

Height: 36 to 60 inches tall; 36-inch spread

Appearance: Red, pink, orange or yellow flowers above large, wide, dark green or purple leaves

Bloom Period: June to October

Propagation: Division; plant tuberous rhizomes about 4 inches deep when soil has warmed in spring

Uses: Background or middle of bed

Notes: Roots are dug in fall and stored dormant indoors over winter; divide in spring. Requires rich soil. Japanese beetles may be a problem.

CHIONODOXA LUCILIAE
Glory-of-the-Snow

Hardy Bulb ◐ ◑ ○
Zones: 3 to 9
Height: 6 inches tall; 3-inch spread
Appearance: Blue flowers with white center; straplike green foliage
Bloom Period: April
Propagation: Division or may reseed in garden; plant 4 inches deep
Uses: Foreground of bed; under deciduous shrubs; good fresh-cut flower
Notes: One of the easiest small bulbs to grow. Generally adaptable and will easily reseed in favorable locations.
Varities: The variety *alba* has white flowers; 'Pink Giant' has pink flowers

COLCHICUM species and hybrids
Colchicum (Meadow Saffron)

Hardy Bulb ○ ◑ ◐
Zones: 4 to 9
Height: 8 inches tall; 8-inch spread
Appearance: Large, pink or white, crocuslike flowers; coarse green foliage
Bloom Period: September
Propagation: Division; plant 6 inches deep
Uses: Foreground of bed; in groundcovers; good fresh-cut flower
Notes: Leaves appear in spring, die away by summer, and flowers (but no leaves) appear in September. Requires well-drained soil; tolerates clay. Very effective planted among pachysandra. Cut flowers stay fresh without water!
Varieties: Best hybrids (all pink) 'Lilac Wonder' (late), 'Princess Astrid' (early), 'The Giant' (midseason), 'Violet Queen' (midseason) and 'Waterlily' (double, midseason)
Related Species: Best species *C. autumnale* and *C. autumnale album* (white, midseason), *C. byzantinum* (early), *C. speciosum* (midseason)

CRINUM × POWELLII
Crinum lily

Moderately Hardy Bulb ○ ◑ ◐
Zones: 7 (6) to 10
Height: 3 to 4 (2 to 3) feet tall; 3- to 4-foot spread

Appearance: Clusters of pink or white trumpet-shaped flowers on tall stems above long, straplike leaves
Bloom Period: July to September; fragrant
Propagation: Division or seed; plant 6 to 8 inches deep in Deep South, 8 to 12 inches deep North
Uses: Middle of border
Notes: *C. bulbispermum* × *C. moorei*; hardy to Zones 6 or 7 if planted with base of bulb deep; provide with heavy winter mulch. Requires well-drained soil.
Varieties: 'Album', white flowers; 'Ellen Bosanquet', deep rose pink flowers

CROCOSMIA species and hybrids
Crocosmia, Montbretia

Hardy Bulb ○ ◑
Zones: 6 (5) to 10
Height: 24 to 36 inches tall; 8- to 12-inch spread
Appearance: Small red, orange or yellow flowers in a spike above grassy or straplike leaves. Like graceful, miniature gladiolus
Bloom Period: July to August
Propagation: Division, but do not separate "strings" of corms, which continue to support each other. Plant 6 to 8 inches deep in North, 4 inches deep in South; 3 inches apart in groups.
Uses: Middle of border, fresh-cut flower
Notes: Long regarded as a tender bulb, many varieties are proving hardier than previously believed. Eventually forms tight clumps. Requires well-drained soil. Provide winter mulch north of Zone 7. Dig where not hardy and store in dry peat, sand or sawdust in cool frost-free location.
Varieties: 'Citronella', yellow; 'Emily Mckenzie', wide orange flowers with striking reddish purple center; 'Lucifer', tall plant to 4 or 5 feet in rich soil, scarlet red.

CROCUS CHRYSANTHUS
Snow Crocus

Hardy Bulb ◐ ◑ ○
Zones: 4 to 9
Height: 4 to 6 inches tall; 4- to 6-inch spread
Appearance: Small, brightly colored and patterned yellow, white or blue flowers with grassy foliage.
Bloom Period: February to April
Propagation: Division or seed; plant 3 to 4 inches deep

Uses: Foreground of bed; in low groundcovers; under deciduous shrubs

Notes: Early bloom and bright, clear colors make these among the most striking late-winter flowers. Requires rich soil. Birds sometimes tear up early flowers (temporarily cover with wire mesh).

Varieties: 'Cream Beauty', lovely creamy white with golden center, very vigorous; 'Fusco-tinctus', very old variety, bright yellow with brown feathering on outside of flowers, attractive in bud too; 'Lady Killer', white with purple blotch on outside of petals; 'Princess Beatrix', light blue.

CROCUS SPECIOSUS
Autumn Crocus

Hardy Bulb ◐ ○ ◑
Zones: 5 to 9
Height: 4 to 6 inches tall; 4-inch spread
Appearance: Lavender-blue flowers with darker veins and striking orange stigmas; grassy green foliage
Bloom Period: October
Propagation: Division; plant 4 inches deep
Uses: Foreground of bed; good fresh-cut flower
Notes: Leaves appear in spring, die away by summer, and flowers (but no leaves) appear in October. Plant under low groundcover so that flowers will not be hidden by taller foliage. Requires average soil.
Varieties: 'Albus', white flowers
Related species: *C. kotschyanus* (used to be called *C. zonatus*), smaller lavender flowers with darker veins and a golden center

CROCUS TOMASINIANUS
Snow Crocus

Hardy Bulb ◐ ◑ ○
Zones: 5 to 9
Height: 4 to 6 inches tall; 4-inch spread
Appearance: Small lavender flowers with grassy foliage
Bloom Period: February to April
Propagation: Division or seed; plant 3 to 4 inches deep
Uses: Foreground of bed; in low groundcovers; under deciduous shrubs; in grass or lawns

Notes: Perhaps the most adaptable and perennial crocus for the eastern United States where it is found colonizing neglected gardens. Requires average soil.
Varieties: 'Barr's Purple', deep purple buds with flowers fading to lavender as they age; 'Taplow Ruby', reddish purple; 'Whitewell Purple', deep purple, very vigorous.

CROCUS VERNUS hybrids
Dutch Crocus

Hardy Bulb ◐ ○ ◑
Zones: 3 to 9
Height: 4 inches tall; 4-inch spread
Appearance: Purple or white flowers; grassy green foliage
Bloom Period: March to April
Propagation: Division or seed; plant 4 inches deep
Uses: Foreground of bed; under deciduous shrubs; good fresh-cut flower
Notes: Many hybrids available in varying shades of purple and white, often with stripes. Largest-flowered crocus and latest to bloom. Requires rich soil.
Related Species: 'Yellow Mammoth', bright yellow, begins blooming about a week earlier, probably a sterile hybrid

CYCLAMEN HEDERIFOLIUM
Hardy Cyclamen

Moderately Hardy Bulb ◐ ◑
Zones: 6 to 9
Height: 4 inches tall; 12-inch spread
Appearance: Pink or white flowers on bare stems, followed by dark-green ivylike leaves that last through the winter
Bloom Period: August to September
Propagation: By seed; plant with concave top of bulb level with soil surface
Uses: Shade garden, under shrubs and around tree trunks, in low groundcovers
Notes: Dormant in summer. Needs evergreen shade to protect from winter sun in the North. Requires good drainage. It's drought tolerant; mulch lightly. Small nursery-propagated plants grow better, with greater vigor, than wild-collected corms.
Varieties: 'Album', white flowers
Related Species: *C. coum*, blooms in spring with pink or white flowers; Zones 7 to 9.

DAHLIA HYBRIDS
Dahlia

Tender Bulb ○ ◕

Zones: 8 to 9
Height: 24 to 72 inches tall; 24-inch spread
Appearance: Red, orange, yellow, lavender or white flowers; husky plants with dark green foliage
Bloom Period: June to October
Propagation: Divide tubers in spring and replant; be sure piece of central stem with bud is attached to each tuber. Plant 5 inches deep.
Uses: Background or middle of bed; good fresh-cut flower
Notes: Most valuable in fall garden. Hybrids available with different flower types including peony flowered, cactus and pompon; most need staking. Requires rich, moist soil.
Varieties: 'Japanese Bishop', deep purple foliage, red flowers.

ENDYMION HISPANICUS
Wood Hyacinth (Spanish Bluebell)

Hardy Bulb ○ ◕ ◫

Zones: 4 to 8
Height: 20 (10) inches tall; 8-inch spread
Appearance: Blue, pink or white flower spikes; straplike green foliage
Bloom Period: May
Propagation: Division; plant 6 inches deep
Uses: Middle or foreground of bed; good fresh-cut flower
Notes: Usually sold as *Scilla campanulata* or *S. hispanica*. Very easy to grow and good for naturalizing. Blooms after most spring bulbs.

ERANTHIS HYEMALIS
Winter Aconite

Hardy Bulb ◫ ◑

Zones: 4 to 8
Height: 3 inches tall; 3-inch spread
Appearance: Yellow buttercuplike flowers; deeply cut green foliage
Bloom Period: February to March
Propagation: Division or seed; plant 4 inches deep
Uses: Under deciduous shrubs and trees; foreground of bed

Notes: Needs a cool, shady location in summer. Soak corms in water overnight before planting for better results. Requires rich, moist soil; prefers acid pH. Can reseed.

FRITILLARIA IMPERIALIS
Crown Imperial

Hardy Bulb ○ ◕ ◑

Zones: 5 to 8
Height: 30 to 48 inches tall; 12-inch spread
Appearance: Red, orange or yellow flowers; narrow green foliage along stem
Bloom Period: April
Propagation: Division; plant 8 inches deep
Uses: Middle of bed; good fresh-cut flower
Notes: Popular, expensive, and not the easiest to grow; it will thrive in just the right spot. Requires rich, well-drained soil. Plant has a skunky odor.

FRITILLARIA MELEAGRIS
Guinea Flower

Hardy Bulb ◕ ◑

Zones: 3 to 8
Height: 12 inches tall; 4-inch spread
Appearance: Checkered purple and white flowers; grasslike green foliage
Bloom Period: April
Propagation: Division or may reseed in garden; plant 4 inches deep
Uses: Foreground of bed
Notes: Naturalizes in moist locations. Requires rich, moist soil.

GALANTHUS NIVALIS
Snowdrop

Hardy Bulb ◫ ◕ ◑

Zones: 3 to 9
Height: 6 inches tall; 4-inch spread
Appearance: Hanging white flowers: straplike green foliage
Bloom Period: February to March
Propagation: Division; may reseed in garden; plant 4 inches deep.
Uses: Shade garden; under deciduous shrubs; good fresh-cut flower

Notes: Transplant and divide when in bloom or just after blooming. Requires rich, moist soil.

Related Species: 'Atkinsii' and 'S. Arnott' are the largest-flowered hybrids, up to 8 inches tall; very vigorous, earlier flowering and well worth the price

GALTONIA CANDICANS
Summer Hyacinth

Moderately Hardy Bulb ◯ ◑

Zones: 6 to 9

Height: 24 to 48 (18 to 24) inches tall; 24-inch spread

Appearance: Tall spikes of nodding white flowers above straplike leaves

Bloom Period: July

Propagation: Division; plant 6 inches deep

Uses: Middle or background of border

Notes: Hardy if mulched for winter protection in Zone 6 and possibly Zone 5. Requires rich, moist, soil.

GLADIOLUS HYBRIDS
Gladiolus

Moderately Bulb ◯ ◑

Zone: 7 (6) to 11

Height: 36 to 48 inches tall; 8-inch spread

Appearance: Red, pink, yellow, apricot, lavender or green flowers on stiff spike; straplike green leaves

Bloom Period: June to October

Propagation: Plant corms outdoors when soil has warmed; plant 6 inches deep

Uses: Background or middle of bed; good fresh-cut flower

Notes: For succession of flowers, plant every 3 weeks until July. Good for accent in middle of bed among other flowers to fill empty spaces in summer. Requires rich, well-drained soil.

Varieties: Miniature (Tiny Tot) and Butterfly (multicolored) types are smaller and fit better into most flower garden situations.

Related Species: Fragrant gladiolus (*Acidanthera bicolor*), white with a purple blotch; not winter hardy north of Zone 8

HYACINTHUS ORIENTALIS
Hyacinth

Hardy Bulb ◯ ◑

Zones: 3 to 7

Height: 12 inches tall; 6-inch spread

Appearance: Blue, pink, purple or white flowers; straplike green foliage

Bloom Period: April; very sweetly scented

Propagation: Division; plant 6 inches deep

Uses: Foreground of bed; good fresh-cut flower

Notes: Jumbo-size bulbs (more than 18 centimeters) have huge flower heads that tend to fall over; smaller flower heads of midsize bulbs (16 to 17 centimeters) stand better in garden. Size of flower head tends to decrease after first year, giving plant more natural appearance. Requires rich soil.

IRIS XIPHIUM HYBRIDS
Dutch Iris

Hardy Bulb ◯ ◑

Zones: 6 (5) to 9

Height: 18 to 24 inches tall; 8- to 12-inch spread

Appearance: Purple, blue, yellow or white flowers above grassy foliage

Bloom Period: May to June

Propagation: Division; plant 6 inches deep

Uses: Accent in low annuals and perennials; fresh-cut flower

Notes: In many situations, not long lived and needs to be replaced periodically. Requires rich well-drained soil that dries in summer.

Varieties: Beauty Series includes a wide range of spectacular, color forms such as 'Amber Beauty' (golden yellow and cream), 'Oriental Beauty' (lavender-blue, creamy yellow and gold) and 'Rust Beauty' (golden bronze with darker veins)

Related Species: *I. xiphioides* (English Iris) is similar but does not require summer dryness.

LEUCOJUM AESTIVUM
Summer Snowflake

Hardy Bulb ◯ ◑ ◫

Zones: 4 to 9

Height: 15 inches tall; 6-inch spread

Appearance: Hanging white flowers; straplike green foliage

Bloom Period: April to May

Propagation: Division; may reseed in garden; plant 6 inches deep

Uses: Middle or foreground of bed; good fresh-cut flower

Notes: Good for wet, poorly draining soils. Called summer snowflake because it blooms after the spring snowflake (*L. vernum*). Requires rich, moist soil.

Varieties: 'Gravetye Giant', a large-flowered form from Gravetye Manor, William Robinson's estate

Related Species: *L. vernum* (Spring snowflake), 12 inches tall; blooms March to April, with *Chionodoxa*, just after snowdrops

LILIUM species and hybrids
Lily

Hardy Bulb ○ ◑ ◐ (for Martagon hybrids)

Zones: 3 to 9

Height: 24 to 72 inches tall; 8- to 24-inch spread

Appearance: Yellow, orange, pink, lavender, red or white flowers on tall stems; narrow green foliage along stem

Bloom Period: June to September

Propagation: Division; plant 3 to 6 inches deep

Uses: Background or middle of bed, depending on height; good fresh-cut flower

Notes: Many types of species and hybrids available. Requires rich, deep, well-drained soil.

Varieties: Hybrid groups include Asiatic, 24 to 60 by 8 inches, flowers face up, blooms May, June (most) and July; Aurelian, Chinese trumpet, Sunburst, 48 to 72 by 15 inches, fragrant, trumpet-shaped flowers, blooms June to July; Oriental, 24 to 72 by 15 inches, fragrant, blooms July (few varieties), August and September; Martagon hybrids, 36 to 60 by 8 inches, for shade garden, blooms June to July; *L. candidum* (Madonna lily), white, blooms May to June; *L. tigrinum* (Tiger lily), orange, blooms July, one of the last to bloom. See the Appendix for further explanation (pages 236–237).

LYCORIS SQUAMIGERA
Hardy Amaryllis (Resurrection Lily)

Hardy Bulb ○ ◑ ◗

Zones: 5 to 9

Height: 24 inches tall; 8-inch spread

Appearance: Pink flowers on tall stems; straplike green foliage

Bloom Period: August

Propagation: Division; plant 6 inches deep.

Uses: Middle or foreground of bed; in groundcovers; good fresh-cut flower

Notes: Leaves grow in spring and die down in June; flower stalk appears without leaves in August. Best grown among a low groundcover. Requires deep, rich soil.

Related Species: *L. radiata*, spidery red flowers on 15-inch stems, blooms September, Zones 8 (7) to 9

MUSCARI ARMENIACUM
Grape Hyacinth

Hardy Bulb ○ ◖ ◗

Zones: 4 to 8

Height: 12 inches tall; 3-inch spread

Appearance: Blue flowers; grasslike green foliage

Bloom Period: April to May

Propagation: Division or may reseed in garden; plant 4 inches deep

Uses: Foreground of bed; edging; under taller spring bulbs; good fresh-cut flower

Notes: One of the easiest bulbs to grow; often naturalizes. A long bloom season allows it to overlap with many other spring bulbs.

Related Species: *M. botryoides* 'Album', white flowers

NARCISSUS species and hybrids
Daffodil, Narcissus

Hardy Bulb ◗ ◖ ○

Zones: 4 to 9

Height: 4 to 15 inches tall; 4- to 8-inch spread

Appearance: Yellow, orange, pink and/or white flowers; straplike green foliage

Bloom Period: March to April

Propagation: Division; plant 4 to 8 inches deep

Uses: Middle or foreground of bed; good fresh-cut flower

Notes: Hot locations in the South promote end rot during summer; mulch and shade help to keep soil cool. Among the easiest and showiest of garden bulbs. Requires rich soil.

Varieties: Many hybrids with different heights, flower shapes and bloom seasons. See the Appendix for further explanation (pages 232–237).

POLIANTHES TUBEROSA
Tuberose

Tender Bulb ○
Zones: 8 to 11
Height: 36 to 48 (18 to 24) inches tall; 24- to 36-inch spread
Appearance: Spikes of white flowers above a rosette of grassy foliage
Bloom Period: August to October; very fragrant
Propagation: Division; plant 3 inches deep
Uses: Late summer accent; good fresh-cut flower
Notes: In the North, best to replace bulbs each year, because season is too short to promote good bloom second year. Save bulbs in Zones 6 to 7, dig and store dry, above 60°F, and don't divide unless very crowded. Requires rich, well-drained soil.
Varieties: 'Mexican Single', blooms about a month earlier and is more fragrant; 'The Pearl' ('Excelsior'), double white

SCILLA SIBIRICA
Siberian Squill

Hardy Bulb ○ ◑ ◫
Zones: 2 to 8
Height: 6 inches tall; 4-inch spread
Appearance: Blue or white nodding flowers; straplike green foliage
Bloom Period: March to April
Propagation: Division; may reseed in garden; plant 4 inches deep.
Uses: Under deciduous shrubs; edging; good fresh-cut flower
Notes: Very easy spring bulb. Doesn't like very hot climates.
Varieties: 'Alba', white; 'Spring Beauty' ('Atrocaerulea'), larger blue flowers, most common variety sold

STERNBERGIA LUTEA
Sternbergia

Moderately Hardy Bulb ○ ◑ ◫
Zones: 7(6) to 9
Height: 6 inches tall; 4-inch spread

Appearance: Yellow, crocuslike flowers; straplike green foliage
Bloom Period: September to October
Propagation: Division; plant 6 inches deep.
Uses: Foreground of bed; in low groundcovers; good fresh-cut flower
Notes: Leaves appear in fall and last all winter. In the North, choose a south-facing location and cover with salt hay or evergreen branches for winter. Requires rich, well-drained soil, kept dry in summer.
Related Species: S. clusiana, larger, goblet-shaped flowers, foliage appears in spring, less hardy, Zones 7 to 9

TULIPA HYBRIDS
Tulip

Hardy Bulb ○ ◑
Zones: 3 to 8
Height: 6 to 30 inches tall; 8-inch spread
Appearance: Flowers come in all colors; green foliage, sometimes mottled with purple
Bloom Period: March to May. Some varieties sweetly scented
Propagation: Division; plant 6 to 10 inches deep.
Uses: Background, middle or foreground of bed; good fresh-cut flower
Notes: Many hybrids provide range of bloom season, color, size and form. In Deep South, bulbs must be precooled before planting. Rich, well-drained soil; prefers neutral pH.
Varieties: Darwin hybrids, 20 to 26 inches tall, large flowers, blooms late April; Darwin and Cottage, 20 to 26 inches, some fragrant, blooms early to mid-May; Fosteriana hybrids, 10 to 20 inches, large flowers, blooms late April; Greigii hybrids, 8 to 12 inches tall, mottled leaves, blooms late April; Kaufmanniana hybrids, 5 to 8 inches tall, blooms early April; Single and Double Earlies, 12 to 14 inches tall, usually fragrant, blooms early April. See the Appendix for further explanation (pages 232–233).

Encyclopedia of Annuals and Biennials

ABELMOSCHUS MANIHOT
Sunset Hibiscus

Half-hardy Annual/Tender Perennial ○ ◐
Zones: 8 to 11
Height: 48 to 96 inches tall; 12-inch spread
Appearance: Large pale-yellow flowers with purple centers on tall plants with palmate leaves
Bloom Period: July to September
Propagation: Sow seed indoors 6 to 8 weeks before setting out, germinates in a week, or sow seed outdoors after danger of frost. Self-sows readily.
Uses: Middle or background of border
Notes: Also called *Hibiscus manihot*. Blooms mid- to late summer on tall plants if started early indoors; blooms late summer to fall on shorter plants that don't need staking if sown after frost outdoors. Color goes well with asters in late summer. Requires rich soil; likes hot locations.

AGERATUM HOUSTONIANUM
Ageratum, Flossflower

Tender Annual ○ ◐ ◑
Zones: —
Height: 15 inches tall; 15-inch spread
Appearance: Blue or purple (white) flowers; oval, bright-green foliage
Bloom Period: June to October; faintly scented
Propagation: Sow seed indoors in March, germinates in 5 days; also by cuttings
Uses: Middle or foreground of bed; edging; good fresh-cut flower
Notes: Avoid hot, dry sites; remove old flowers to prolong bloom; watch for mites. Requires rich, moist soil.

ALTHAEA ROSEA
Hollyhock

Hardy Biennial/Annual ○ ◐
Zone: 3 to 8
Height: 60 to 84 inches tall; 24-inch spread
Appearance: Tall spikes of single or double pink, red, yellow or white flowers with palmate leaves along the stem
Bloom Period: July to August
Propagation: Sow annual strains indoors 2 to 3 months before planting out; as biennials, sow outdoors midsummer for bloom the following year; germination takes up to 2 weeks; frequently self-sows.
Uses: Background of the border or accent in middle of the border
Notes: Faster-maturing strains can be grown as annuals and bloom later in summer than those grown as biennials. Watch for rust and mites. Tolerant of soil types, but best on rich moist soil.

AMARANTHUS HYBRIDUS ERYTHROSTACHYS
Prince's-feather

Tender Annual ○
Zones: —
Height: 36 to 48 inches tall; 18- to 24-inch spread
Appearance: Red or brownish red plumes above reddish or green foliage
Bloom Period: August to September
Propagation: Self-sows readily in the garden or sow seeds after soil is well warmed; transplant seedlings when small, before they bloom; in cool climates sow indoors in March at 75°F.
Uses: Late summer and fall bloom in background of border

Notes: Heat, sun and a sparse diet will ensure success. Prefers warm climates; avoid rich soil.
Related Species: A. caudatus (Love-lies-bleeding), slender, pendant flower clusters. *A. tricolor* (Joseph's coat), leaves variegated red and yellow.

ANTIRRHINUM MAJUS
Snapdragon

Half-hardy Annual ◯ ◗ ◐
Zones: 8 to 9
Height: 8 to 36 inches tall; 8- to 12-inch spread
Appearance: Spikes of flowers in all colors except blue; green foliage
Bloom Period: June to October; faint sweet scent
Propagation: Sow seed indoors in early March, germinates in 2 weeks.
Uses: Middle of bed; good fresh-cut flower
Notes: May overwinter with mulch in South. To rejuvenate in summer, cut back, feed and water. Select rust-resistant varieties. Stake taller varieties. Requires well-drained soil.
Varieties: Many varieties, vary from dwarf, bushy plants to tall spikes; in addition to typical flower types that "snap," some varieties have flared, trumpet-shaped flowers.

ASCLEPIAS CURASSAVICA
Bloodflower

Tender Annual/Tender Perennial ◯ ◗
Zones: 8 to 11
Height: 42 inches tall; 18-inch spread
Appearance: Loose clusters of orange flowers atop stems with narrow leaves
Bloom Period: July to October
Propagation: Sow seed in February; set outdoors after last frost.
Uses: Middle to background of border
Notes: An annual with a perennial look. Requires average soil.

BEGONIA ×SEMPERFLORENS-CULTORUM
Bedding Begonia

Tender Annual ◯ ◗ ◐
Zones: —
Height: 12 inches tall; 12-inch spread

Appearance: Small pink, red or white flowers; rounded green or bronze foliage
Bloom Period: Continuous
Propagation: Sow seed indoors January to February and set out plants when all danger of frost is past; also by cuttings.
Uses: Foreground of bed; edging
Notes: Very heat resistant. Wide selection of varieties combine all flower colors with green or bronze foliage. Very adaptable but prefers rich, moist soil.

BELLIS PERENNIS
English Daisy

Biennial/Hardy Annual ◯ ◗ ◐
Zones: 4? to 8
Height: 6 to 8 inches tall; 6-inch spread
Appearance: White, pink or red, single or double daisies above rosettes of green leaves
Bloom Period: April to June, or until hot weather
Propagation: Sow seed outdoors in fall, or indoors 6 to 8 weeks before planting out, after danger of hard frost; seeds germinate in about 7 days.
Uses: Foreground of border; edging; under spring bulbs; good fresh-cut flower
Notes: Really a perennial but usually grown as an annual or perennial as it blooms rapidly from seed. Quickly dies out in hot weather. Requires moist, rich soil.

BRASSICA OLERACEA
Ornamental Cabbage and Kale

Half-hardy Annual ◯ ◗
Zones: 8 to 9
Height: 8 to 12 inches tall; 8- to 12-inch spread
Appearance: Rosettes of green leaves, often frilled, with white, rose or purple centers
Bloom Period: Foliage colored October to December
Propagation: Sow seed in early summer to midsummer, transplant to space 8 to 12 inches apart or grow in pots for setting out in fall.
Uses: Foreground of border, edging
Notes: Very frost tolerant and will last into early winter in many regions, even through winter in south; color only developes in cool weather; not a flower, but colored foliage. Watch for cabbage worms. Requires rich, well-drained soil, likes lime.

BROWALLIA AMERICANA
Browallia

Half-hardy Annual ◑ ◐

Zones: —
Height: 12 inches tall; 12-inch spread
Appearance: Blue (or white) flowers; green foliage
Bloom Period: July to October
Propagation: Sow seed indoors in March, germinates in 2 weeks; also by cuttings
Uses: Middle or foreground of bed; edging; good fresh-cut flower
Notes: Shade from hot afternoon sun for best blooming. Requires average to poor soil.

CALENDULA OFFICINALIS
Calendula, Pot Marigold

Half-hardy Annual ◯ ◑ ◐

Zones: 9 to 10
Height: 18 to 24 inches tall; 12-inch spread
Appearance: Yellow or orange flowers; green foliage
Bloom Period: July to October
Propagation: Sow seed indoors and set out as soon as soil can be worked; sow early to midsummer for fall bloom
Uses: Middle or foreground of bed; good for fresh-cut or dried flower
Notes: Select heat-resistant varieties in hot climates; makes a good showing well into fall; good winter annual in Deep South; deadhead to continue bloom. Requires rich; moist soil.

CATHARANTHUS ROSEUS
Rose Periwinkle, Madagascar Periwinkle

Tender Annual ◯ ◑ ◐

Zones: —
Height: 12 to 18 inches tall; 12-inch spread
Appearance: Pink, white or rose flowers; dark green foliage
Bloom Period: June to October
Propagation: Sow seed indoors early March, germinates in 10 days; also by cuttings
Uses: Middle or foreground of bed; edging
Notes: Also called *Vinca roseus.* Very pest and disease resistant. Adaptable to most soils.

CELOSIA CRISTATA PLUMOSA
Plumed Cockscomb

Half-hardy Annual ◯

Zones: —
Height: 12 to 36 inches tall; 8- to 12-inch spread
Appearance: Red, yellow, orange or pink flowers; green or reddish foliage
Bloom Period: June to frost
Propagation: Sow seed indoors in May or sow outdoors when soil temperatures reach 65°F; plant out seedlings after night temperatures reach 70°F.
Uses: Background to foreground of bed or edging, depending on variety; good for fresh-cut or dried flower
Notes: Pest free and dependable for a long season of color in hot summers and dislike cool weather in spring; perhaps difficult to blend with perennials, but more suited to mixed gardens than the crested cockscombs.
Varieties: Var. *cristata* (crested cockscomb), shape resembles rooster's comb, most useful for drying, available in short and tall strains.

CENTAUREA CYANUS
Bachelor's Button, Cornflower

Hardy Annual ◯ ◑ ◐

Zones: —
Height: 24 inches tall; 8-inch spread
Appearance: Blue (pink or white) flowers; green foliage
Bloom Period: April to June
Propagation: Direct sow outdoors fall to early spring; germinates in 5 to 20 days; mulch lightly for winter; dislikes transplanting
Uses: Background or middle of bed; good for fresh-cut or dried flower
Notes: A cool-season annual that fades with summer heat. For best results sow very early. Good source of early cut flowers. Tolerates poor, dry soil.

CHEIRANTHUS CHEIRI
English Wallflower

Half-hardy Biennial ◯ ◑
Zones: 8 to 9
Height: 24 inches tall; 8- to 12-inch spread

Appearance: Bushy plants with narrow leaves bearing several spikes of orange, yellow, pink, cream or ruby-red flowers
Bloom Period: April to May; sweetly fragrant
Propagation: Sow seed by midsummer for largest plants; transplant twice, as root disturbance encourages bushy plants; set plants out in fall; where not hardy outdoors, overwinter in 4-inch pots in cold frame, vented regularly to reduce gray mold.
Uses: Foreground of border, under spring bulbs; in pots and urns as tall accent with other spring annuals
Notes: Worth the extra effort in cold climates as a spring accent. Requires rich, moist soil.
Related Species: C. allionii (Siberian wallflower), to 15 inches, yellow or orange, hardier

CHRYSANTHEMUM PARTHENIUM
Feverfew

Hardy Biennial/Annual ◯ ◑
Zones: 4 to 9
Height: 18 to 30 inches tall; 8- to 12-inch spread
Appearance: Clusters of small single or double white daisylike flowers atop stems with light-green lacy leaves
Bloom Period: June to August
Propagation: Self-sows freely; as biennial, blooms June to July; seed sown outdoors in spring will flower as annual mid- to late summer.
Uses: Middle to foreground of border, depending on variety; filler between late-flowering perennials
Notes: Also called *Matricaria capensis*. Pinch when 4 to 6 inches tall. Requires average soil.
Varieties: Many varieties with various flower forms and heights. 'Aureum', golden foliage, comes true from seed.

CLEOME HASSLERIANA
Spider Flower

Half-hardy Annual ◯ ◑ ◐
Zones: —
Height: 36 to 60 inches tall; 15-inch spread
Appearance: Purple, pink or white flowers; palmately divided green foliage
Bloom Period: June to October

Propagation: Sow seed indoors 8 to 10 weeks before setting out; sow outdoors in early spring in areas with long summer.
Uses: Background or middle of bed
Notes: Easy to grow; self-sows vigorously, useful in semishade.

COLEUS ×HYBRIDUS
Coleus, Flame Nettle

Tender Annual ◯ ◑ ◐
Zones: —
Height: 24 inches tall; 18-inch spread
Appearance: Leaves variegated with green, red, pink and yellow; insignificant blue flowers
Bloom Period: —
Propagation: Sow seed indoors in March; also by cuttings
Uses: Middle or foreground of bed; edging; good fresh-cut foliage
Notes: Pinch for compact plants; remove flowers for better foliage display. Actually a tropical perennial that can be trained several feet tall if kept indoors. Requires rich, moist soil.
Varieties: 'Golden Bedder', one of the most sunproof of all golden-foliaged plants; propagate from cuttings only.

CONSOLIDA ORIENTALIS
Larkspur

Hardy Annual ◯ ◑ ◐
Zones: —
Height: 24 to 48 inches tall; 10-inch spread
Appearance: Spikes of blue, violet, scarlet, rose, pink or white flowers; fine-textured green foliage
Bloom Period: May to July
Propagation: Sow seed outdoors in fall or early spring; dislikes transplanting. Once established, self-sown plants appear the following year.
Uses: Background or middle of bed; good for fresh-cut or dried flower
Notes: An old-fashioned, spiky accent for the early summer garden. Also called annual delphinium or listed as *Delphinium ajacis*. Requires rich soil, kept on the dry side.

COREOPSIS GRANDIFLORA, see Perennials

COSMOS BIPINNATUS
Cosmos

Half-hardy Annual ○ ◑

Zones: —

Height: 72 inches tall; 12-inch spread

Appearance: Crimson, pink or white flowers; feathery green foliage

Bloom Period: June to October

Propagation: Sow seed indoors 6 weeks before setting out; sow outdoors after last frost; sow early summer for fall bloom.

Uses: Background of bed; filler between perennials; good fresh-cut flower

Notes: Rich soil encourages excessive height, delays bloom; pinch out terminal bud at 18 inches for bushiness; remove old flowers to prolong bloom. Requires poor, sandy or ordinary soil, kept on the dry side.

Varieties: 'Sensation Mix', earlier flowering and can be direct-sown outdoors.

COSMOS SULPHUREUS
Klondyke Cosmos

Half-hardy Annual ○

Zones: —

Height: 30 inches tall; 12-inch spread

Appearance: Yellow, orange or red flowers; fine-textured green foliage

Bloom Period: June to October

Propagation: Sow seed indoors 6 weeks before setting out; sow outdoors after last frost; sow early summer for fall bloom.

Uses: Middle or foreground of bed; good fresh-cut flower

Notes: Requires careful transplanting or grow in individual pots. Requires poor, sandy or ordinary soil kept on the dry side.

Varieties: 'Sunny Red', AAS award winner, scarlet, long flowering and tolerant of neglect, 12 to 14 inches tall; 'Sunny Yellow', yellow, 12 to 14 inches tall; 'Bright Lights', mixed colors, 36 to 48 inches tall.

DAHLIA MERCKII hybrids
Bedding Dahlia

Half-hardy Annual ○

Zones: —

Height: 18 inches tall; 12-inch spread

Appearance: Red, orange, yellow, pink, white or lavender flowers; green foliage

Bloom Period: June to October

Propagation: Sow seed indoors in March; division

Uses: Middle or foreground of bed; edging; good fresh-cut flower

Notes: Roots may be stored for winter, divided and replanted in spring. Requires rich, moist soil.

Varieties: 'Rigoletto Mix', 12 inches tall; 'Redskin Mixed', reddish foliage, 12 to 15 inches tall, AAS, Fleuroselect and All-Britain award winner.

DIANTHUS BARBATUS
Sweet William

Hardy Biennial/Annual ○ ◑

Zones: 3 to 9

Height: 12 to 18 inches tall; 10-inch spread

Appearance: Rounded heads of red, pink, white or rose flowers; narrow green foliage

Bloom Period: June to August; sweetly scented

Propagation: As annual, sow seed indoors 6 to 8 weeks before planting out for August bloom; as biennial, sow May to July, will bloom June of the next year.

Uses: Foreground of bed; edging; good fresh-cut flower

Notes: Self-sows in garden. Requires rich soil.

DIANTHUS CHINENSIS HYBRIDS
Annual Pink, China Pink

Tender Annual ○ ◑

Zones: 6 to 9

Height: 12 inches tall; 8-inch spread

Appearance: Mounded plants with pink, red and white flowers

Bloom Period: May to September

Propagation: Sow indoors in March for early bloom or sow outdoors after frost; germinates in about a week.

Uses: Foreground of border; edging

Notes: Often survives winter for early bloom in May to June; rejuvenate by cutting back for repeat bloom. Requires rich, moist, sweet soil.

Varieties: 'Telstar Mix', heat and drought tolerant

DIGITALIS PURPUREA
Foxglove

Hardy Biennial/Annual ○ ◖ ◑
Zones: 4 to 9
Height: 24 to 60 inches tall; 18-inch spread
Appearance: Spike of purple, lavender, pink or white flowers; coarse green foliage
Bloom Period: June to July
Propagation: As annual sow seed indoors 8 to 10 weeks before last frost; as biennial sow seed outdoors midsummer.
Uses: Background or middle of bed; fresh-cut flower
Notes: Replace old plants after they bloom in July or flowers will be small next year. Successfully grows in shade of tall perennials at back of bed. Requires rich soil; moderately drought tolerant.
Varieties: 'Excelsior', good biennial strain; 'Foxy', can be grown as an annual.

ERYNGIUM GIGANTEUM
Sea Holly, Miss Wilmott's Ghost

Biennial ○ ◖
Zones: 5 to 8
Height: 30 (12) inches tall; 12-inch spread
Appearance: Stiff, prickly, green, silvery-veined flowers; low, green heart-shaped foliage
Bloom Period: July
Propagation: By seed; self-sows; transplant only when very young.
Uses: Middle of bed; good for fresh-cut or dried flower
Notes: Flowers stately and sculptural. Requires poor, sandy, well-drained, dry soil.

ESCHSCHOLZIA CALIFORNICA
California Poppy

Tender Annual ○ ◖
Zones: 9 to 10
Height: 12 to 15 inches tall; 8-inch spread
Appearance: Orange or yellow flowers on mounded plants with lacy, finely cut foliage
Bloom Period: June to October; during winter in warm climates
Propagation: Sow seed outdoors in fall or early spring; does not like transplanting.
Uses: Foreground of border; edging
Notes: Suffers from intense heat and humidity. Requires average to poor, dry soil.

EUPHORBIA CYATHOPHORA
Annual Poinsettia, Mexican Fire Plant

Half-hardy Annual ○ ◖
Zones: —
Height: 2 to 3 feet tall; 18-inch spread
Appearance: Well-branched rounded plant with red leaves at top, resembling the familiar poinsettia
Bloom Period: July to frost
Propagation: Sow seed outdoors in spring when soil is warm
Uses: Middle or foreground of border; edging
Notes: Self-sown seed will overwinter outdoors. Thrives in hot locations. Sometimes wrongly called *E. heterophylla.* Requires average to poor soil.

GAZANIA RIGENS
Gazania

Tender Annual ○
Zones: —
Height: 8 to 10 inches tall; 8-inch spread
Appearance: Yellow, cream, orange, pink and bronze flowers; green foliage
Bloom Period: May to October
Propagation: Sow seed indoors in late March.
Uses: Foreground of bed; edging; good fresh-cut flower
Notes: Seems to be preferred food of rabbits. Thrives on heat but resents poor drainage and humidity. Requires sandy, well-drained soil; drought tolerant.

GOMPHRENA GLOBOSA
Globe Amaranth

Half-hardy Annual ○
Zones: —
Height: 6 to 18 inches tall; 6- to 12-inch spread
Appearance: Spherical purple (white or rose) flowers; green foliage
Bloom Period: June to October
Propagation: Sow seed 6 to 8 weeks before planting out, germinates in 20 to 25 days; soak seeds in hot water to speed germination.
Uses: Middle or foreground of bed; edging; good for fresh-cut or dried flower
Notes: Very easy to grow; prolific bloomer. Adaptable to most soils, but avoid rich soils; drought tolerant.

Varieties: 'Buddy', an excellent plant with glowing purple flowers, 6 to 8 inches tall
Related Species: *G. haageana*, orange flowers

HELIANTHUS HYBRIDS
Sunflower

Hardy Annual ◯ ◑
Zones: —
Height: 2 to 10 feet tall; 2- to 4-foot spread
Appearance: Large yellow, orange (or white) daisylike flowers on tall plants with large wide leaves
Bloom Period: July to September
Propagation: Sow outdoors after hard frost is past.
Uses: Background or middle of border, depending on variety
Notes: Dwarf multiflowered types are more suited to borders. Many varieties of various heights and colors. Requires average moist soil.
Varieties: 'Color Fashion', mixed colors, 5 feet tall; 'Italian White', cream with dark center, 6 feet tall; 'Teddy Bear', double golden yellow, 2 feet tall.

HIBISCUS ACETOSELLA

Tender Annual ◯ ◑
Zones: —
Height: 5 feet tall; 2-foot spread
Appearance: Tall, straight stems with reddish palmate leaves; insignificant flowers not produced except in long southern summers
Bloom Period: —
Propagation: Seed and cuttings
Uses: Background of border
Notes: One of the few tall purple foliage plants. Requires average soil.
Varieties: 'Red Sheild', beet-red foliage; the form usually grown.

IMPATIENS BALFOURII
Impatiens

Hardy Annual ◑ ◑ ◯
Zones: —
Height: 24 to 30 inches tall; 18- to 24-inch spread
Appearance: Bicolor white and rose flowers, green leaves

Bloom Period: July to frost
Propagation: Sow seed outdoors where it is to grow in early spring, easily transplanted when young, will self-sow in future years.
Uses: Middle of border, naturalize among perennials.
Notes: Lovely with golden foliage. Requires moist rich soil.

IMPATIENS BALSAMINA
Balsam

Tender Annual ◯ ◑
Zones: —
Height: 8 to 24 inches tall; 10-inch spread
Appearance: Pink, salmon, red, lavender or white flowers; green foliage
Bloom Period: May to October
Propagation: Sow indoors in March, germinates in 4 to 5 days; sow outdoors in May when soil is thoroughly warm; may reseed
Uses: Middle or foreground of bed; good fresh-cut flower
Notes: Dwarf varieties suited for edging. Prefers full sun, except in areas with hot summers where afternoon shade is beneficial. Very adaptable; prefers moist soil.

IMPATIENS NEW GUINEA HYBRIDS
New Guinea Impatiens

Tender Annual ◯ ◑
Zones: —
Height: 12 inches tall; 12-inch spread
Appearance: Red, pink, salmon or white flowers; green or bronze leaves, often variegated with pink and yellow
Bloom Period: Continuous
Propagation: Cuttings
Uses: Foreground of bed, edging
Notes: Will take more sun than common impatiens. Most varieties are only grown from cuttings. Require rich, moist soil.
Varieties: 'Tango', orange flowers; available as seed; AAS award winner.

IMPATIENS WALLERIANA
Impatiens

Tender Annual ◐ ◑ ●

Zones: —

Height: 8 to 15 inches tall; 12-inch spread

Appearance: Red, pink, purple, lavender or white flowers; green foliage

Bloom Period: Continuous

Propagation: Sow seed indoors in February; easily grown from cuttings (simple way to save favorite plant)

Uses: Middle or foreground of bed; edging

Notes: Many varieties are available; tallest grow to 15 inches, shortest to 8 inches. Requires rich, moist soil.

LOBELIA ERINUS
Lobelia

Half-hardy Annual ○ ◐ ◑

Zones: —

Height: 8 inches tall; 6-inch spread

Appearance: Blue (pink or white) flowers; small green leaves

Bloom Period: May to October

Propagation: Sow seed indoors late February to early March.

Uses: Foreground of bed; edging; good for fresh-cut or dried flower

Notes: Prized for clear blue color. Tends to die out in hot weather, so plant in cool northern exposure. Requires rich, moist soil.

Varieties: 'Cambridge Blue', light blue; 'Crystal Palace', dark blue.

LOBULARIA MARITIMA
Sweet Alyssum

Hardy Annual ○ ◐ ◑

Zones: —

Height: 4 to 8 inches tall; 6-inch spread

Appearance: White, rose or purple flowers; green foliage with fine texture

Bloom Period: May to October; faint sweet scent.

Propagation: Sow seed indoors in March or sow outdoors when soil can be worked in spring.

Uses: Foreground of bed; edging

Notes: Cut back, feed and water to rejuvenate and renew bloom. Start early indoors for use with spring bulbs. Tolerates poor, light, well-drained soil.

LUNARIA ANNUA
Honesty, Moneywort

Hardy Biennial/Annual ◐ ◑

Zones: 4 to 8

Height: 24 inches tall; 12-inch spread

Appearance: Purple or white flower spikes; large rounded green foliage

Bloom Period: April to May

Propagation: Sow seed outdoors for bloom the following year or start early indoors to treat as annual.

Uses: Middle or foreground of bed; good for cutting fresh or drying

Notes: Most prized for wide, rounded, papery seed-pods, but also valuable for early flower spikes. Best when grown as biennial. Prefers normal soil with adequate moisture.

Varieties: 'Variegata', leaves dusted and edged with white, both purple- and white-flowered strains, come true from seed, young seedlings usually green.

LYCHNIS CORONARIA
Mullein Pink, Rose Campion

Hardy biennial ○ ◐ ◑

Zones: 4 to 9

Height: 36 inches tall; 8- to 12-inch spread

Appearance: Deep magenta (to white flowers) atop branched stems with woolly gray foliage

Bloom Period: June

Propagation: By seeds sown spring to midsummer

Uses: Middle of border

Notes: Forms attractive rosette of gray foliage the first year. Sometimes lives for 3 years. Self-sows readily. Requires average soil.

Varieties: 'Alba', white flowers; 'Oculata', pale pink flowers with deeper centers, very attractive.

MELAMPODIUM DIVARICATUM

Tender annual ○ ◐

Zones: —

Height: 18 to 24 inches tall; 18- to 24-inch spread

Appearance: Golden-yellow daisy flowers with orange centers among fresh green foliage on bushy, compact plants
Bloom Period: June to frost
Propagation: By seeds sown indoors 6 to 8 weeks before last frost or outdoors when soil has warmed. Germinates in 7 to 14 days at 70°F.
Uses: Foreground to middle of border.
Notes: A still little-known annual that has the potential to become very popular. Very heat and drought resistant for good performance through summer. Native to Mexico and Central America. *M. paludosum* is an outdated synonym used in some seed catalogs. Requires average soil.
Varieties: 'Medallion', a more compact and floriferous cultivar.

MIRABILIS JALAPA
Four-o'clock

Half-hardy Annual ○ ◐ ◑
Zones: 8 to 9
Height: 30 inches tall; 24-inch spread
Appearance: Red, yellow, pink, lavender or white flowers; bright green heart-shaped foliage
Bloom Period: July to October; sweetly scented
Propagation: Sow seed indoors in late March, germinates in 10 days. May self-sow in garden.
Uses: Background or middle of bed
Notes: Flowers open around four o'clock. Store tuberous roots for the winter like dahlias. Guard against Japanese beetles. Very adaptable; drought tolerant.

MYOSOTIS SYLVATICA
Forget-me-not

Hardy Annual/Biennial ○ ◐ ◑
Zones: 3 to 8
Height: 9 inches tall; 6-inch spread
Appearance: Tiny blue (pink or white) flowers; narrow, green foliage
Bloom Period: April to June
Propagation: As annual, sow seed indoors in February; as biennial (in South), sow in July; often seeds itself in the garden.
Uses: Middle or foreground of bed; edging; good fresh-cut flower
Notes: Popular for clusters of tiny, sky blue flowers.

Early blooming, so often planted among daffodils, tulips and early perennials. Dies out in hot weather. Requires rich, moist, well-drained soil.
Varieties: 'Victoria', most popular blue variety.

NICOTIANA ALATA
Flowering Tobacco

Hardy Annual ○ ◐ ◑
Zones: —
Height: 36 inches tall; 24-inch spread
Appearance: Pink, red, white or green flowers; large green foliage
Bloom Period: June to October; sweetly scented
Propagation: Sow seed indoors in March.
Uses: Middle or foreground of bed; edging; good for fresh-cut or dried flower
Notes: Flowers open in evening, release sweet fragrance. Flowers close on hot days. Cut back for rebloom. Prefers shade protection from hot sun. Requires well-drained, moist soil.
Varieties: 'Nicki Series', short and compact, 16 to 18 inches by 12 inches; 'Domino Series', 10 to 14 inches by 10 inches, longer blooming than Nicki.
Related Species: *N. langsdorfii*, small nodding green flowers on well-branched 3 to 5 feet plants; *N. sylvestris*, long tubular white flowers of graceful appearance on 3- to 4-foot plants, very fragrant.

NIGELLA DAMASCENA
Love-in-a-mist

Hardy Annual ○ ◐
Zones: —
Height: 12 to 18 inches tall; 5- to 8-inch spread
Appearance: Light blue (rose or white) flowers with finely cut, feathery foliage
Bloom Period: May to June; later from late sowings
Propagation: Sow seed in fall or early spring; does not transplant well; self-sow readily year to year.
Uses: Foreground and middle of border; between late-flowering perennials
Notes: Although late sowings bloom later, best bloom is in early summer. Best when allowed to grow in masses. Requires average soil.
Varieties: 'Miss Jekyll', semidouble bright blue; 'Persian Jewels', mix of blue, lavender, rose and white.

ONOPORDUM NERVOSUM
Silver Thistle

Hardy Biennial ○ ◑

Zones: 5? to 8
Height: 6 to 9 feet tall; 3- to 4-foot spread
Appearance: Dramatic, spiny, white woolly plant, large leaves, branched stems, less notable purple flowers
Bloom Period: June to July
Propagation: Sow seed by midsummer for bloom next year; transplant when small; self-sows prolifically.
Uses: Background of border
Notes: Also called *O. arabicum*. Remove when plants begin to collapse by late summer. Requires average, well-drained soil.
Related Species: *O. acanthium*, very similar.

PAPAVER ATLANTICUM
Moroccan Poppy

Hardy Annual/Biennial ○ ◑

Zones: 6? to 8?
Height: 18 to 24 (12) inches tall; 12-inch spread
Appearance: Small pastel orange (to red) tissue paperlike flowers; light green foliage
Bloom Period: May to July, later in cool climates
Propagation: Sow seed in late summer or early fall *in situ* or transplant when small; does not transplant easily if taproot is disturbed.
Uses: Middle or background of bed; between late-blooming perennials
Notes: Wonderful border filler in early summer. Deadhead for prolonged bloom. Self-sows abundantly for future years. Best in cool weather, petals drop by noon on hot days. More perennial in cool climates. Requires well-drained soil.

PAPAVER RHOEAS
Flanders Poppy, Corn Poppy

Hardy Annual ○ ◑

Zones: —
Height: 30 to 36 inches tall; 12-inch spread
Appearance: Pink, red, salmon or white flowers; green foliage
Bloom Period: June to August

Propagation: Sow seed in fall where winters are mild, elsewhere in early spring, germinates in 15 days; does not transplant well.
Uses: Middle of bed; good fresh-cut or dried flower
Notes: Deadhead for prolonged bloom. Self-sows abundantly for future years. Repeat sowings for longer bloom. For arrangements, cut flowers in bud, sear stem. Best in cool weather. Requires light, well-drained soil.
Varieties: The Shirley poppies are strains of this species in mixed colors. Available in single and double strains.

PELARGONIUM ×HORTORUM
Zonal Geranium

Tender Annual ○ ◑ ◐

Zones: —
Height: 18 inches tall; 12-inch spread
Appearance: Rounded heads of red, pink, salmon, white or lavender flowers; rounded green foliage
Bloom Period: May to October
Propagation: Sow seed indoors in January; also by cuttings
Uses: Middle or foreground of bed; edging; good for fresh-cut or dried flower
Notes: Actually a tropical perennial. Old plants can be trained to several feet tall if kept indoors. Very adaptable; drought tolerant.

PENNISETUM SETACEUM
Crimson Fountain Grass

Half-hardy Annual/Tender Perennial ○ ◑

Zones: 8 to 9
Height: 36 to 40 inches tall; 24-inch spread
Appearance: Long pinkish inflorescences above dense, grassy foliage
Bloom Period: July to October
Propagation: Sow seed indoors in March; division where hardy
Uses: Foreground to middle of border; edging
Notes: Commonly sold as *P. ruppelii*; a unique and striking accent, also good in pots; combines well with pink flowers.
Varieties: 'Cupreum' ('Rubrum' or 'Atrosanguineum'), reddish foliage and plumes, not a seed strain, so roots must be overwintered in frost-free place.

Related Species: 'Burgundy Giant', similar to 'Cupreum' but taller and coarser with wider leaves, 6 to 8 feet, either an unidentified species, or hybrid, save roots in frost-free place.

PERILLA FRUTESCENS 'ATROPURPUREA'
Perilla

Hardy Annual ○ ◐ ◑

Zones: —

Height: 30–48 inches tall; 12-inch spread

Appearance: Insignificant flowers in spikes; deep reddish-purple foliage

Bloom Period: September; foliage effective all summer

Propagation: Sow seed indoors in March, germinates in 8 days. Sow seed outdoors after last frost.

Uses: Middle of bed; good fresh-cut foliage; good well into fall

Notes: Easiest purple-foliaged annual. Reseeds profusely for next year's crop. Foliage has herbal scent. Very adaptable; tolerates dry or moist soil.

PETUNIA ×HYBRIDA
Petunia

Half-hardy Annual ○ ◐ ◑

Zones: —

Height: 18 inches tall; 8- to 12-inch spread

Appearance: Purple, pink, red and white flowers; green foliage

Bloom Period: May to October; sweetly scented

Propagation: Sow seed indoors early March, germinates in 10 to 12 days

Uses: Middle or foreground of bed; edging

Notes: Flowers can be double, single or ruffled. Cascading forms available. Rejuvenate midsummer by cutting back, feeding and watering. Adaptable to most well-drained soils.

PHLOX DRUMMONDII
Annual Phlox

Half-hardy Annual ○ ◐ ◑

Zones: —

Height: 12 to 18 inches tall; 8-inch spread

Appearance: Pink, red, salmon, white or purple flowers; fine-textured green foliage

Bloom Period: June to September

Propagation: Best when seeds sown early indoors in March or sow outdoors when trees leaf out

Uses: Foreground of bed; edging; good fresh-cut flower

Notes: Use care in transplanting; won't last through hot summers.

PORTULACA GRANDIFLORA
Moss Rose

Tender Annual ○

Zones: —

Height: 4 to 8 inches tall; 8-inch spread

Appearance: Yellow, white, red, orange or pink flowers in single, semidouble or double forms; small, narrow green leaves give a very fine texture

Bloom Period: June to August

Propagation: Sow seed outdoors as soon as soil is warm, germinates in 18 to 20 days; also by cuttings

Uses: Foreground of bed; edging

Notes: Will self-sow for following year; easily transplanted. Water when young; very drought tolerant later. Good in pots. Flowers open in sun, close by evening. Requires poor, dry soil.

RUDBECKIA HIRTA HYBRIDS
Gloriosa Daisy

Hardy Annual ○ ◐

Zones: —

Height: 36 inches tall; 12-inch spread

Appearance: Yellow, orange and rust single or double daisies; green foliage

Bloom Period: June to September

Propagation: Sow seed outdoors when soil is warm or indoors 8 to 10 weeks before last frost, for earlier bloom

Uses: Middle of bed; good fresh-cut flower

Notes: Heat tolerant. Deadhead to prolong bloom. Tall varieties need staking. Young plants often overwinter, like biennials. Requires well-drained soil; drought tolerant.

RUDBECKIA TRILOBA
Three-lobed Coneflower

Hardy Biennial ○ ◐

Zones: 3 to 10

Height: 24 to 36 inches tall; 12- to 18-inch spread

Appearance: Small yellow daisies on branched plants with small three-lobed leaves

Bloom Period: July to September

Propagation: Sow seed outdoors when soil is warm or indoors 8 to 10 weeks before last frost, for earlier bloom

Uses: Middle of bed; good fresh-cut flower

Notes: Heat tolerant. Deadhead to prolong bloom. More likely to need staking in South, or pinch when 8 to 12 inches tall. May live more than 2 years. Requires well-drained soil.

SALVIA FARINACEA
Mealycup Sage

Hardy Annual/Tender Perennial ◯ ◑ ◐

Zones: 8 to 11

Height: 24 to 36 inches tall; 12-inch spread

Appearance: Bluish purple (or white) flower spikes; green foliage

Bloom Period: June to October

Propagation: Sow seed indoors in late February; also cuttings or division; may self-sow.

Uses: Middle or foreground of bed; good for fresh-cut or dried flower

Notes: Actually a perennial that is hardy in the South.

Varieties: 'Blue Bedder', an older variety preferred by some for its clearer blue, 24 to 30 inches; 'Rhea', blue, 15 inches tall; 'Victoria', popular blue variety for bedding and cutting, 18 inches tall; 'White Porcelain', white, 18 inches tall.

SALVIA SPLENDENS
Scarlet Sage, Salvia

Tender Annual ◯ ◑ ◐

Zones: —

Height: 8 to 36 inches tall; 8- to 12-inch spread

Appearance: Scarlet, salmon, purple or white flower spikes; green foliage

Bloom Period: June to October

Propagation: Sow seed indoors in late February.

Uses: Middle or foreground of bed; edging

Notes: One of the longest-blooming annuals, continuing well into fall. Very adaptable to most soils.

Varieties: 'Carabiniere', scarlet, 12 to 24 inches tall; 'Laser Purple', purple, 10 to 12 inches tall; 'Carabiniere White', white, 12 to 14 inches tall; 'Melba', salmon coral, 8 inches tall.

SANVITALIA PROCUMBENS
Creeping Zinnia

Hardy Annual ◯ ◑

Zones: —

Height: 6 inches tall; 12-inch spread

Appearance: Small deep yellow (or orange) daisies; small green foliage

Bloom Period: June to October

Propagation: Sow seed outdoors in late fall or early spring; reseeds; young seedlings may survive winter; thin in spring.

Uses: Foreground of bed; edging

Notes: Not necessary to start ahead indoors. Requires light, well-drained, dry soil.

Varieties: 'Mandarin Orange', orange flowers

SENECIO CINERARIA
Dusty Miller

Hardy Annual/Tender Perennial ◯ ◑

Zones: 7? to 10

Height: 12 inches tall; 12-inch spread

Appearance: Fernlike silver-gray foliage; insignificant yellow flowers

Bloom Period: —

Propagation: Sow seed indoors in April, germinates in 5 to 20 days; also by cuttings

Uses: Middle or foreground of bed; edging; good for fresh-cut or dried foliage

Notes: Prized for its silver-gray foliage. Actually a short-lived perennial, hardy south of Zone 7. Requires well-drained soil; drought tolerant.

SILENE ARMERIA
Catchfly

Biennial/Hardy Annual ◯ ◑ ◐

Zones: 4? to 9

Height: 12 to 24 inches tall; 6-inch spread

Appearance: Tiny hot-pink flowers in clusters on branched stems with narrow slightly blue-green foliage

Bloom Period: May to July

Propagation: Sow seed outdoors in late summer to early fall to grow as biennial or sow in early spring; also sow indoors in winter; self-sows readily

Uses: Middle to foreground of border; filler between perennials; good fresh-cut flower

Notes: Airy habit; very useful to fill gaps and blend colors in early summer; pinch when 8 inches tall to reduce height on rich soils; spring sowings bloom midsummer; old-fashioned plant.

TAGETES HYBRIDS
Marigold

Half-hardy Annual ○

Zones: —

Height: 8 to 48 inches tall; 8- to 12-inch spread

Appearance: Yellow, orange, rust or near-white double or semidouble flowers; green pinnately cut foliage

Bloom Period: June to October

Propagation: Sow seed indoors in early March, germinates in 1 week; easy to transplant; sow late spring for fall bloom

Uses: Background to foreground of bed; edging, depending on variety; good fresh-cut flower

Notes: Many varieties available, varying in color, height, flower size and foliage. Mostly trouble free, but watch for mites. Foliage scent unpleasant to some people. Adaptable but prefers rich, well-drained soil.

TITHONIA ROTUNDIFOLIA
Mexican Sunflower

Half-hardy Annual ○

Zones: —

Height: 48 to 72 inches tall; 48-inch spread

Appearance: Bright orange (or yellow) flowers; large wide green leaves

Bloom Period: July to September

Propagation: Sow seed indoors in April for earlier bloom, germinates in 10 days; sow outdoors as early as last frost date.

Uses: Background of bed; good fresh-cut flower if floral preservative added to water

Notes: Rich soils and excess water encourage overly large plants that break apart. Requires well-drained, moist to dry soil.

Varieties: 'Goldfinger' and 'Sundance' are more compact.

TORENIA FOURNIERI
Wishbone Flower

Tender Annual ◐ ◑

Zones: —

Height: 8 to 14 inches tall; 6- to 8-inch spread

Appearance: Bluish purple (rose or white) flowers; green foliage

Bloom Period: June to October; sweetly scented

Propagation: Sow indoors in early March. Sow outdoors after frost for later bloom. Often reseeds for following year. Transplants easily.

Uses: Foreground of bed; edging

Notes: Endures heat and humidity well. Rejuvenate by cutting back. Most useful as blue/purple addition to shade garden. Requires moist, well-drained soil.

Varieties: 'Clown Mix', rose, white, blue and violet flowers, 8 inches tall; 'Compacta', purple-blue, 8 inches tall.

TROPAEOLUM MINUS
Dwarf Nasturtium

Tender Annual ○ ◐

Zones: —

Height: 12 inches tall; 12-inch spread

Appearance: Yellow, red, orange or cream flowers; rounded green foliage

Bloom Period: June to October; some varieties sweetly scented.

Propagation: Sow seed outdoors after soil has warmed (too early and seeds rot); does not transplant well

Uses: Foreground of bed; edging; good fresh-cut flower

Notes: Flower buds and unripe seeds give peppery flavor to salads and pickles. Watch for black aphids. Dwarf types are best for most garden situations, see vines section for tall types. Grows best during cool weather, thriving in fall until frost. Tolerates poor, well-drained, dry soil.

Varieties: 'Alaska', foliage splashed with white, mixed colors, not so heat tolerant; 'Empress of India', scarlet flowers against purplish foliage; 'Jewel Mix', mixed colors, a good performer in heat; 'Whirlybird Mix', spurless flowers, mixed colors (all dwarf).

VERBASCUM BOMBYCIFERUM
Mullein

Hardy Biennial ○

Zones: 5? to 8
Height: 5 feet tall; 3-foot spread
Appearance: Branched spikes of yellow flowers above large felty white basal leaves
Bloom Period: June to July
Propagation: Seed; difficult to transplant
Uses: Background or accent in middle of border
Notes: Subject to basal rot from poor drainage and overrich soil. Requires well-drained, dryish soil.
Related Species: V. olympicum, Zones 6 to 8

VERBENA BONARIENSIS

Hardy Annual ○ ◑

Zones: 7 to 9
Height: 48 inches tall; 8- to 12-inch spread
Appearance: Tall wispy branched plant with widely spaced narrow leaves and small purple flower clusters
Bloom Period: July to October
Propagation: Sow seed after frost.
Uses: Background to middle of border; filler between perennials or spring bulbs
Notes: Best when allowed to grow in masses. A perennial where hardy in the South, farther north it self-sows freely. Requires average soil.

VERBENA × HYBRIDA
Verbena

Half-hardy Annual ○ ◑

Zones: —
Height: 8 to 12 inches tall; 10-inch spread
Appearance: Pink, red, lavender, purple or white flowers; finely cut green foliage
Bloom Period: June to September; some varieties sweetly scented
Propagation: Sow seed indoors 8 to 10 weeks before planting outdoors
Uses: Foreground of bed; edging; good fresh-cut flower
Notes: Heat tolerant, but watch for mites. Adaptable and will tolerate dry soils.

Related Species: V. 'Sissinghurst', lovely coral pink, must be grown from cuttings; V. tenuisecta, blue-lavender, white or pink flowers with finely cut foliage; both are good summer performers in southern heat.

VIOLA CORSICA
Corsican Violet

Hardy Annual ○ ◑ ◐

Zones: 6 to 9
Height: 8 inches tall; 8-inch spread
Appearance: Purplish blue pansylike flowers; green foliage
Bloom Period: Nearly all year
Propagation: Sow seed in late summer or early spring outdoors; also sow indoors during winter; self-sows freely
Uses: Middle or foreground of bed; edging; under spring bulbs; accent pots
Notes: Similar to pansy, but smaller flowered; very adaptable; heat tolerant with long bloom season, best bloom in spring and fall.

VIOLA × WITTROCKIANA
Pansy

Hardy Annual ○ ◑ ◐

Zones: 7(6) to 9
Height: 8 inches tall; 8-inch spread
Appearance: Blue, yellow, red, orange, white and purple flowers; green foliage
Bloom Period: April to June, longer where cool; sweetly scented
Propagation: Sow seed in August, grow over winter in cold frame (45.5 to 60.5° F), plant out in April. South of Zone 6, plant out in fall, mulch lightly with salt hay to protect foliage
Uses: Middle or foreground of bed; edging; under spring bulbs; accent pot; good fresh-cut flower
Notes: Will take moderate frost; thrives in cool weather; tends to die out in heat of summer. Requires rich, moist soil.
Related Species: V. cornuta hybrids, smaller flowered and longer lived, though scarcely perennial, as claimed, in most climates; 'Princess Blue' is a recent V. cornuta hybrid, compact with remarkable heat tolerance, Zones 4 to 9; V. tricolor, (Johnny-jump-up), smaller flowered and hardier than the pansy, yellow and/or purple flowers, self-sows freely, Zones 4 to 9.

ZINNIA ANGUSTIFOLIA
Zinnia

Tender Annual ○ ◑

Zones: —

Height: 12 inches tall; 12-inch spread

Appearance: Small-deep golden yellow (or white) flowers on rounded plants with narrow leaves

Bloom Period: June to October

Propagation: Sow seed indoors early March, germinates in 5 days. Sow in May for late-summer bloom.

Uses: Foreground of bed, edging

Notes: Also known as *Z. linearis*. A superior annual to associate with perennials. Mildew resistant. Requires well-drained soils, drought tolerant.

Varieties: 'Star White', white flowers

ZINNIA ELEGANS
Zinnia

Half-hardy Annual ○ ◑

Zones: —

Height: 12 to 36 inches tall; 8- to 15-inch spread

Appearance: Orange, yellow, pink, red or white flowers; green foliage

Bloom Period: June to October

Propagation: Sow seed indoors early March, germinates in 5 days. Sow in May for late-summer bloom.

Uses: Background to foreground of bed, depending on height; shorter varieties for edging; good fresh-cut flower

Notes: Hybridized into many shapes, sizes and heights. Cactus types have attractive, ragged petals. Good air circulation helps reduce mildew. Pinch young plants for bushiness. Adaptable to most well-drained soils.

Encyclopedia of Perennials

ACANTHUS SPINOSUS
Spiny Bear's-Breech

○ ◑ ◐

Zones: 7 (6) to 10
Height: 36 to 48 (24 to 30) inches tall; 36-inch spread
Appearance: Large deeply cut, slightly spiny leaves with spikes of mauve flowers
Bloom Period: June to July
Propagation: Division or root cuttings
Uses: Middle of border
Notes: Use for contrast where bold accent is needed; mulch for winter in Zone 6; can become weedy in the South; divide and replant to restrict vigor. Tolerates any soil that is not too rich.
Varieties: Var. *spinosissimus* is unnecessarily spiny
Related Species: *A. mollis*, less deeply cut leaves; Zones 8 to 10

ACHILLEA ×'CORONATION GOLD'
Fernleaf Yarrow

○ ◐

Zones: 3 to 8
Height: 36 inches tall; 18-inch spread
Appearance: Deep yellow flowers in flat head; green foliage with fernlike texture
Bloom Period: June to August
Propagation: Division
Uses: Background or middle of bed; good for fresh-cut or dried flower
Notes: In poor soil, shorter stems need no staking. Deadheading encourages rebloom with smaller flower heads. Requires well-drained, dry soil.

ACHILLEA GALAXY HYBRIDS
Yarrow

○ ◐

Zones: 3 to 8
Height: 24 to 36 inches tall; 18-inch spread

Appearance: Flat flower heads of clear salmon, pink, orange, red or yellow with ferny foliage
Bloom Period: June to August
Propagation: Division
Uses: Middle or foreground of bed; good fresh-cut or dried flower
Notes: New hybrids of *A. taygetea* and *A. millefolium* with a range of clear colors unique to the yarrows. Requires average to poor soil.
Varieties: 'Appleblossom', clear pink, 36 inches; 'The Beacon', bright crimson red, 30 inches; 'Great Expectations', light yellow, 24 inches; 'Salmon Beauty', light salmon.

ACHILLEA ×'MOONSHINE'
Moonshine Yarrow

○

Zones: 4 to 8
Height: 24 (12) inches tall; 18-inch spread
Appearance: Light yellow flowers in flat heads; fern-like silvery foliage
Bloom Period: June to August
Propagation: Division
Uses: Middle or foreground of bed; good for fresh-cut or dried flower
Notes: In light, poor soil, plant growth needs no staking; thrives in hot, dry locations; often re-blooms if old flower stems are removed. Requires well-drained, dry soil.

ACONITUM CARMICHAELII
Monkshood

◐

Zones: 2 to 7
Height: 48 inches tall; 12-inch spread
Appearance: Blue flowers in spikes; deep green pal-mately lobed foliage
Bloom Period: August to September
Propagation: Division
Uses: Background or middle of bed; good for fresh-cut or dried flower

Notes: Also called *A. fischeri*. Avoid hot afternoon sun and hot locations. Very poisonous if eaten. Requires rich, moist soil.

Varieties: 'Arendsii', deep rich blue flowers atop strong stems

Related Species: A. ×bicolor 'Spark's Variety', blooms midsummer

AJUGA REPTANS
Ajuga

◑ ●

Zones: 2 to 8

Height: 6 (2) inches tall; 8-inch spread

Appearance: Blue (pink or white) flowers; green, bronze or variegated foliage

Bloom Period: May to June

Propagation: Division or seed

Uses: Groundcover; foreground of bed; edging

Notes: Invasive groundcover but easily pulled to keep under control. Self-sows freely. Requires well-drained soil or plants will die out.

Varieties: 'Alba', white flowers; 'Atropurpurea', dark purple foliage; 'Burgundy Glow', variegated with white, bronze and green; 'Jungle Beauty', a tetraploid with large, deep green leaves; 'Pink Spire', pink flowers; 'Silver Beauty', grayish foliage edged with white

Related Species; A. *pyramidalis*, nonspreading, deep blue flowers

ALCHEMILLA MOLLIS
Lady's-Mantle

○ ◐ ◑

Zones: 3 to 9

Height: 18 (8) inches tall; 24-inch spread

Appearance: Greenish yellow flowers in billowy mass above rounded matte-green foliage

Bloom Period: June to July

Propagation: Division or seed

Uses: Foreground of bed; groundcover; edging; good for fresh-cut or dried flower

Notes: This unusual color combines well with pinks and blues. Requires rich, moist soil.

Related Species: A. *vulgaris* is very similar in appearance and growing requirements.

AMSONIA TABERNAEMONTANA
Amsonia

○ ◐ ◑

Zones: 3 to 8

Height: 24 inches tall; 18-inch spread

Appearance: Light blue flowers; narrow green leaves; yellow fall color

Bloom Period: May to June

Propagation: Division, seed or cuttings

Uses: Middle of bed

Notes: A native plant. Cut back about one-third after flowering to encourage compact growth. Very adaptable.

ANCHUSA AZUREA
Italian Alkanet

○ ◐

Zones: 3 to 8

Height: 3 to 5 feet tall; 2-foot spread

Appearance: Clusters of small blue flowers; large leaves

Bloom Period: May to June

Propagation: Division or root cuttings

Uses: Background or middle of the border

Notes: The best tall blue flower for late spring; usually needs staking; tend to be short lived. Requires well-drained soil.

Varieties: 'Little John', 18 inches; 'Loddon Royalist', 3 feet

ANEMONE ×HYBRIDA
Japanese Anemone

○ ◐

Zones: 5 to 8

Height: 60 (30) inches tall; 24-inch spread

Appearance: Pink, rose or white flowers with golden stamens; flowers taller than green foliage; coarse leaves

Bloom Period: September to October

Propagation: Division or root cuttings

Uses: Background or middle of bed; good fresh-cut flower

Notes: Provide winter mulch in North. May take two to three years to reach full vigor. Fall transplanting is often fatal. Requires rich, well-drained, moist soil.

Varieties: 'Honorine Jobert' (also called 'Alba'), white single flowers; 'September Charm', pink single flowers; 'Margarette', double rosy pink flowers; 'Prince Henry', double rose-red flowers
Related Species: *A. hupehensis*, pink, 36 inches tall, blooms about a month earlier, in August

AQUILEGIA LONG-SPURRED HYBRIDS
Long-Spurred Columbine

◑ ◐ ○

Zones: 3 to 8
Height: 24 to 36 inches tall; 18-inch spread
Appearance: Red, pink, white, yellow, blue and purple, often bicolored flowers; divided green foliage with small rounded segments
Bloom Period: May to June
Propagation: By seed
Uses: Middle or foreground of bed; good for fresh-cut flower and dried seedpod.
Notes: Replace this short-lived perennial yearly with seedlings. Poor drainage encourages rot. Short types need less staking. Requires well-drained soil.
Varieties: 'McKana Giants', 30 inches tall, available in single colors from seed; 'Music Series' F1 hybrid, mixed colors, 15 to 20 inches.
Related Species: *A. flabellata*, blue or white, short spurred, 8 to 15 inches, depending on variety; *A. vulgaris*, an old-fashioned, short-spurred species that persists in many old gardens, blue, purple, pink or white, 2 to 3 feet

ARTEMISIA LACTIFLORA
White Mugwort

○ ◐ ◑

Zones: 5 to 8
Height: 4 to 6 feet tall; 3-foot spread
Appearance: Creamy white plumes atop stems with green ferny cut leaves
Bloom Period: August
Propagation: Division or cuttings
Uses: Background of border, fresh cut flower
Notes: Unique tall astilbe-like plumes for late summer; always needs staking, more so in shade and rich soils; pinch and thin stems to control height and legginess. Requires average moist soil.

ARTEMISIA LUDOVICIANA
White Sage

○ ◐

Zones: 4 to 8
Height: 24 to 36 inches tall; 12-inch spread
Appearance: Fine-textured, silver foliage; insignificant flowers
Bloom Period: August to September
Propagation: Division or cuttings
Uses: Background or middle of bed; good for fresh-cut or dried flower
Notes: Needs staking to stay neat. Pinch for bushy shape. Roots especially invasive in light soils. Tolerates poor, well-drained, sandy soil.
Varieties: 'Silver King' and 'Silver Queen' are similar, but 'Silver King' has finer texture and is hardier, to Zone 3.

ARTEMISIA ×'POWIS CASTLE'

○ ◐

Zones: 5 to 8
Height: 24 to 36 inches tall; 36-inch spread
Appearance: Finely cut silver foliage; mounded habit; insignificant flowers
Bloom Period: August to September
Propagation: By cuttings
Uses: Background or middle of bed
Notes: Woody in the South, but herbaceous in the North. Pinch for bushiness. Tolerates poor, well-drained, sandy soil. Hybrid of *A. absinthium* and *A. arborescens*.

ARTEMISIA SCHMIDTIANA 'SILVER MOUND'
Silver Mound Wormwood

○

Zones: 4 to 8
Height: 12 inches tall; 18-inch spread
Appearance: Silvery foliage with fine, feathery texture; insignificant flowers
Bloom Period: August to September
Propagation: Division or cuttings
Uses: Foreground of bed; edging; good for fresh-cut or dried flower

Notes: A tight mound in early summer but stems may lean, leaving open center in summer; can be cut back when new growth shows at base. Requires poor, sandy, well-drained soil. Best when planted on mound of sandy soil. Good air circulation.

ARUNCUS DIOICUS
Goatsbeard

◑ ◑ ○

Zones: 4 to 9
Height: 6 feet tall; 3-foot spread
Appearance: Plumy white flowers; pinnately compound green foliage
Bloom Period: June to July
Propagation: Division or seed
Uses: Background or middle of bed; good dried
Notes: Native plant; resembles a huge astilbe. Requires rich, moist soil.
Varieties: 'Kneiffii', finely cut leaf segments, useful where a lacy texture is needed, 3 feet tall
Related Species: A. aethusifolia miniature with more finely cut leaves, recently introduced from Korea, 12 inches

ASARUM EUROPAEUM
European Ginger

◑ ●

Zones: 4 to 8
Height: 6 inches tall; 12-inch spread
Appearance: Insignificant flowers; rounded, kidney-shaped, dark green foliage
Bloom Period: April
Propagation: Division
Uses: Foreground of bed; groundcover; edging
Notes: Evergreen in the South. Spreads by creeping rhizomes. Not the same as edible ginger. Requires rich, moist soil.
Related Species: A. canadense, larger deciduous light-green leaves, Zones 3 to 8; A. shuttleworthii, evergreen native with attractively marbled foliage.

ASCLEPIAS TUBEROSA
Butterfly Weed

○

Zones: 3 to 8
Height: 24 inches tall; 12-inch spread

Appearance: Orange (yellow or red) flowers; narrow green foliage
Bloom Period: July to August
Propagation: Division; transplant only in spring as growth begins; also by seed
Uses: Middle or foreground of bed; fresh-cut flower
Notes: A brilliantly colored native sometimes available in yellow and red. Tolerates poor, well-drained soil; drought tolerant.

ASPERULA ODORATA
Sweet Woodruff

◑ ●

Zones: 4 to 8
Height: 8 inches tall; 12-inch spread
Appearance: White flowers; whorls of light green foliage
Bloom Period: April to May
Propagation: Division, cuttings or seed
Uses: Groundcover
Notes: Used to flavor May wine. Beware of spreading, invasive rhizomes. Looks like miniature pachysandra, but not evergreen. Requires rich, well-drained soil.

ASTER DIVARICATUS
White Wood Aster

◑ ●

Zones: 4 to 8
Height: 12 to 24 (8) inches tall; 18- to 24-foot spread
Appearance: Sprays of small white daisies on black stems above basal heart-shaped green leaves
Bloom Period: August to September
Propagation: Division, cuttings or seed
Uses: Middle to front of shaded border, groundcover
Notes: Very useful for late-summer bloom in dry shade; large basal leaves make good groundcover; pinch about a month before bloom to reduce height. Adaptable, drought tolerant.

ASTER ×FRIKARTII

○ ◑ ◑

Zones: 5 to 8

Height: 24 to 36 inches tall; 12-inch spread
Appearance: Lavender blue flowers; green foliage
Bloom Period: July to October
Propagation: Division or cuttings
Uses: Background or middle of bed; good fresh-cut flower
Notes: Pinch early for bushiness; good drainage and mulch needed to ensure winter survival in North. Adaptable to most conditions; good drainage.
Varieties: 'Monch' and 'Wonder of Staffa' are similar; 'Monch' is generally considered the best, with deeper color and stronger stems.

ASTER NOVAE-ANGLIAE
New England Aster

Zones: 4 to 8
Height: 36 to 60 inches tall; 18-inch spread
Appearance: Blue, purple, white, pink or lavender flowers; green foliage
Bloom Period: August to September
Propagation: Division, spring or fall or cuttings
Uses: Background of bed
Notes: Pinch twice before mid-July for bushiness. More compact and manageable if not grown in very rich soil. Most not good for cutting; 'Harrington's Pink' is an exception. Adaptable to most conditions; good air circulation reduces leaf diseases.
Varieties: 'Alma Potschke', glowing bright pink, almost too electric; 'Harrington's Pink', clear pink; 'Hella', deep violet-purple; 'Purple Dome', a new dwarf variety, forming a mound to only 20 inches tall, bright purple; all are good performers.

ASTER NOVI-BELGII
Michaelmas Daisy, New York Aster

Zones: 4 to 8
Height: 12 to 48 inches tall; 18-inch spread
Appearance: Blue, white, pink or lavender flowers; green foliage
Bloom Period: August to September
Propagation: Division, spring or fall, or cuttings
Uses: Background or foreground of bed; edging, depending on variety
Notes: Pinch tall varieties (36 to 48 inches) twice before mid-July for bushiness. Dwarfs (12 to 15

inches) are self-branching. Most not good for cutting. Adaptable to most conditions; good air circulation reduces leaf diseases.
Varieties: 'Mt. Everest', white, 36 inches; 'Pink Bouquet', pink, 15 inches; 'Professor Kippenburg', dwarf light lavender blue, 12 inches.

ASTER TATARICUS
Tatarian Aster

Zones: 4 to 8
Height: 4 to 6 feet tall; 2-foot spread
Appearance: Bluish lavender flowers; large green leaves
Bloom Period: September to October
Propagation: Division
Uses: Background of bed
Notes: Strong stems need no staking; pest free; rhizomes can be invasive, especially in the South; a beautiful color in the autumn light with *Solidago sempervirens*. Adaptable to most conditions.

ASTERMOEA MONGOLICA

Zones: 4(?) to 8
Height: 36 inches tall; 17-inch spread
Appearance: Double white flowers; small cut leaves on erect stems
Bloom Period: July to October
Propagation: Division
Uses: Background or middle of bed
Notes: One of the longest-blooming perennials; seldom needs staking; pest free; underground rhizomes are invasive. Adaptable to most conditions. The correct, but lesser-known name is *Kalimeris pinnatifida* 'Hortensis'.

ASTILBE ×ARENDSII
Astilbe

Zones: 3 to 8
Height: 24 to 48 inches tall; 24- to 36-inch spread
Appearance: Pink, white or red flowers; pinnately compound green (or bronze) foliage with ferny texture

Bloom Period: June to July
Propagation: Division
Uses: Middle or foreground of bed; groundcover; good fresh-cut or dried flower
Notes: Will grow in full sun only with constant moisture. Requires rich, moist soil. Many hybrids available with varying heights, colors and bloom times.
Related Species: *A. chinensis* 'Pumila' lavender, 18 (8) inches by 12 inches, the last astilbe to bloom in July; *A. taquetii* 'Superba', lilac-pink, 4 feet by 2 feet, blooms in July.

BAPTISIA AUSTRALIS
Blue Wild Indigo

Zones: 3 to 8
Height: 48 inches tall; 24- to 48-inch spread
Appearance: Blue pealike flowers; compound green foliage creates finely textured effect
Bloom Period: June
Propagation: Division or seed
Uses: Background of bed; good fresh-cut flower
Notes: Prefers not to be moved; a large, long-lived perennial, cut back about a third after flowering to encourage compact growth and avoid staking. Prefers moist soil with acid pH.

BEGONIA GRANDIS
Hardy Begonia

Zones: 6 to 10
Height: 2 to 3 feet tall; 1- to 2-foot spread
Appearance: Branched clusters of small pendant pink (or white) flowers above wide, light green leaves
Bloom Period: July to October
Propagation: By tiny bulbils produced prolifically along stems
Uses: Middle of border; edging
Notes: Tuberous roots are shallow. Avoid hot afternoon sun. Requires moist, rich soil. Excellent overplanting for spring bulbs. Also called *B. evansiana*.
Varieties: 'Alba', white flowers.

BERGENIA CORDIFOLIA
Bergenia, Megasea

Zones: 3 to 8
Height: 12 inches tall; 12-inch spread
Appearance: Pink (or white) flowers; coarse, round green foliage
Bloom Period: April to May
Propagation: Division
Uses: Foreground of bed; groundcover; edging
Notes: Large leaves provide bold textural contrast; may not bloom well due to tender flower buds.
Related Species: *B. crassifolia* is very similar.

BOLTONIA ASTEROIDES
Boltonia

Zones: 3 to 8
Height: 4 to 7 feet tall; 1- to 2-foot spread
Appearance: White or pink flowers; narrow green foliage
Bloom Period: August to September
Propagation: Division or seed
Uses: Background or middle of bed
Notes: Similar to the Michaelmas daisy, but disease resistant; pinch for compactness in windy or shaded locations.
Varieties: 'Pink Beauty', pink flowers, 3 feet; 'Snowbank', improved, now standard form only 3 to 5 feet tall that seldom needs staking, white.

BRUNNERA MACROPHYLLA
Siberian Bugloss, Hardy Forget-Me-Not

Zones: 3 to 8
Height: 15 inches tall; 18-inch spread
Appearance: Airy clusters of tiny blue flowers; coarse, heart-shaped green foliage
Bloom Period: April to May
Propagation: Division or seed
Uses: Foreground of bed; groundcover; edging
Notes: Also called *Anchusa myosotidiflora*; good groundcover in summer; reseeds freely in garden; foliage burns in hot summer sun. Requires rich soil.
Varieties: 'Langtrees', foliage splashed with silver, a good grower; 'Variegata', leaves edged with white, sensitive to sunburn.

CAMPANULA GLOMERATA
Clustered Bellflower

○ ◐ ◑

Zones: 3 to 8

Height: 12 to 36 inches tall; 24-inch spread

Appearance: Purple (or white) flowers; green foliage

Bloom Period: June to July

Propagation: Division in spring or just after blooming; also by seed

Uses: Middle or foreground of bed; good fresh-cut flower

Notes: Rhizomes less invasive in poor soil. Requires well-drained soil, kept on the dry side.

Varieties: 'Joan Elliot', deep violet-blue, 18 inches tall; 'Superba', violet-blue, 24 inches tall.

CAMPANULA PERSICIFOLIA
Peach-leafed Bellflower

○ ◐ ◑

Zones: 3 to 8

Height: 36 (8) inches tall; 12-inch spread

Appearance: Spikes of blue (or white flowers); narrow green foliage lower than the flowers

Bloom Period: June to July

Propagation: Division

Uses: Middle or foreground of bed; good fresh-cut flower

Notes: Will flower longer if dead blossoms are removed along spike. Prefers moist soil.

Varieties: 'Beechwood', pale blue; 'Caerulea', bright blue; 'Grandiflora Alba', larger white flowers.

CENTAUREA MONTANA
Hardy Cornflower

○ ◐

Zones: 3 to 8

Height: 24 inches tall; 24-inch spread

Appearance: Lacy blue flowers; green foliage

Bloom Period: May to July

Propagation: Division or seed

Uses: Middle or foreground of bed; good fresh-cut flower

Notes: Cut down as soon as new growth appears at base for substantial second bloom period, occasionally as late as August. Seeds itself freely. Requires poor, well-drained soil.

CERATOSTIGMA PLUMBAGINOIDES
Plumbago, Leadwort

○ ◐ ◑

Zones: 6 to 9

Height: 6 inches tall; 12-inch spread

Appearance: Small blue flowers; small green leaves

Bloom Period: August to September

Propagation: Division or cuttings

Uses: Foreground of bed; groundcover; edging

Notes: Turns bronze in fall before dying down. Plant spring bulbs underneath and cut to ground in winter for spring display. Rhizomes somewhat invasive. Requires well-drained soil; drought tolerant.

CHELONE LYONII
Turtlehead

◐ ◑

Zones: 4 to 8

Height: 36 inches tall; 18-inch spread

Appearance: Pink flowers; green foliage on straight stems

Bloom Period: August

Propagation: Division or seed

Uses: Background or middle of bed; good fresh-cut flower

Notes: Flower shape resembles a turtle's head. Requires rich, moist soil.

Related Species: *C. obliqua*, September blooming, deeper in color, but less hardy, Zones 6 to 9.

CHRYSANTHEMUM COCCINEUM
Painted Daisy, Pyrethrum

○ ◐

Zones: 3 to 9

Height: 24 inches tall; 12-inch spread

Appearance: Pink, red or white flowers; fernlike green foliage

Bloom Period: May to July

Propagation: By seed or division

Uses: Middle of bed; good fresh-cut flower

Notes: Also called *Pyrethrum coccineum*. Short-lived plant; divide every two to three years to prolong life span. Requires well-drained soil.

CHRYSANTHEMUM ×MORIFOLIUM
Chrysanthemum

○

Zones: 5 to 8
Height: 12 to 36 inches tall; 24-inch spread
Appearance: White, yellow, orange, red, salmon, lavender or pink flowers; green-lobed foliage
Bloom Period: August to October
Propagation: By cuttings, division or seed
Uses: Middle of bed; good fresh-cut flower
Notes: Pinch two or three times before mid-July for bushy, compact growth; best divided each spring. Provide winter mulch in North. Many types and colors available. Requires rich, well-drained soil.

CHRYSANTHEMUM ×SUPERBUM
Shasta Daisy

○ ◑ ◐

Zones: 5 to 9
Height: 24 to 36 inches tall; 12-inch spread
Appearance: White daisies; green foliage
Bloom Period: June to July
Propagation: Division or seed
Uses: Background or middle of bed; good fresh-cut flower
Notes: Divide every two to three years or plant will die out. Many varieties available, some with double or frilled flowers, some with shorter growth. Cut out stems after flowering for fresh basal foliage. Requires rich, well-drained soil.
Varieties: 'Alaska', commonly grown seed strain, variable growth habits, needs staking; 'Becky', also sold as 'Ryan's Daisy' and 'July Daisy', blooms a month later in July to August, vigorous strong stems need no staking; 'Starburst Hybrid', new hybrid with large flowers on strong, straight stems, unusually uniform from seed.

CHRYSOGONUM VIRGINIANUM
Green and Gold, Golden Star

Zones: 5 to 9
Height: 6 to 9 inches tall; 12-inch spread
Appearance: Small yellow daisies on leafy stems
Bloom Period: May to June, all summer in cool climates

Propagation: Division or seed
Uses: Front of border; edging; groundcover; good fresh-cut flower
Notes: A native plant that blends well with other shade plants. Requires rich, moist soil; somewhat drought tolerant in shade.
Varieties: Var. *australe*, shorter growing, spreads by rhizomes to make good groundcover, flowers only in early summer; 'Mark Viette', one of the longest-blooming varieties.

CIMICIFUGA RACEMOSA
Bugbane

Zones: 4 to 9
Height: 6 (3) feet tall; 4-foot spread
Appearance: White bottlebrush-like flower spikes; large, coarse, compound, ferny green leaves
Bloom Period: July; peculiar fragrance
Propagation: Division or seed
Uses: Background or middle of bed; good fresh-cut flower
Notes: A native plant that seldom needs division; avoid hot afternoon sun. Peculiar scent of foliage can be used to ward off bugs. Requires rich, moist soil; prefers acid pH.

CIMICIFUGA SIMPLEX
Kamchatka Bugbane

◑ ◐ ●

Zones: 3 to 9
Height: 4 (2) feet tall; 3-foot spread
Appearance: White bottlebrush-like flower spikes; large, coarse, compound, ferny green leaves
Bloom Period: October; peculiar fragrance
Propagation: Division or seed
Uses: Background or middle of bed; good fresh-cut flower
Notes: An Asian native that seldom needs division; avoid hot afternoon sun. Requires rich, moist soil.
Varieties: 'White Pearl', a commonly available improved variety
Related Species: C. ramosa, most useful for the purple-leaved variety *C. ramosa atropurpurea* 'Brunette' has leaves of an even deeper purple; both bloom in September to October with pale pink flowers, three to four feet tall.

CLEMATIS HERACLEIFOLIA
Blue Tube Clematis

○ ◐ ◑

Zones: 3 to 9
Height: 36 inches tall; 48-inch spread
Appearance: Pale to medium-blue flowers; coarse green foliage
Bloom Period: August to September
Propagation: By cuttings, division or seed
Uses: Background or middle of bed; good for cutting fresh or drying
Notes: Not a vine, but an almost woody perennial; long-lasting, sweet-scented flowers. Requires rich, well-drained soil.
Varieties: Var. *davidiana* is a reputedly showier variety.

CONVALLARIA MAJALIS
Lily of the Valley

◑ ●

Zones: 2 to 8
Height: 8 inches tall; 12-inch spread
Appearance: Nodding white or pale pink flowers; wide green foliage
Bloom Period: May to June; sweetly scented
Propagation: Division
Uses: Foreground of bed; groundcover; edging; good fresh-cut flower
Notes: Not evergreen, but a good, tight groundcover. Spreading, invasive rhizomes. Requires rich, well-drained soil; drought tolerant.
Varieties: 'Rosea', pale pink flowers, hard to come by; 'Striata', leaves streaked with yellow, tend to revert to green.

COREOPSIS GRANDIFLORA
Coreopsis, Tickseed

○ ◑

Zones: 4 to 9
Height: 12 to 24 inches tall; 12-inch spread
Appearance: Golden yellow daisies; narrow green foliage on bushy plants
Bloom Period: May to September, if deadheaded
Propagation: Division or seed
Uses: Middle or foreground of bed; good fresh-cut flower
Notes: Long-blooming, short-lived perennial; easily grown from seed and will bloom first year; similar to and much confused with *C. lanceolata*. Requires well-drained soil; drought tolerant.
Varieties: 'Early Sunrise', winner of All American and Fleuro Select awards, early and most continuously flowering variety.

COREOPSIS TRIPTERIS
Trefoil Coreopsis

○ ◑

Zones: 4 to 9
Height: 3 to 9 feet tall; 2- to 3-foot spread
Appearance: Small yellow flowers on tall branched stems; narrow three-parted green foliage
Bloom Period: August to September
Propagation: Division or seed
Uses: Background of bed; good fresh-cut flower
Notes: Useful tall yellow for late summer; pinch to reduce height. Requires average, well-drained soil.

COREOPSIS VERTICILLATA
Threadleaf Coreopsis

○ ◑

Zones: 3 to 9
Height: 24 inches tall; 18-inch spread
Appearance: Yellow flowers; finely cut, feathery green foliage
Bloom Period: June to August
Propagation: Division or seed
Uses: Middle or foreground of bed; good fresh-cut flower
Notes: Spreading rhizomes troublesome only in moist, sandy soils. Requires poor, well-drained soil.
Varieties: 'Golden Showers', golden yellow, tall, common, most likely to need staking; 'Moonbeam', among the best and longest-flowering perennials, pale yellow flowers, dark green foliage, 15 inches tall; 'Zagreb', golden yellow, 12 inches tall, but taller in the South.

CRAMBE CORDIFOLIA
Colewort

○ ◑

Zones: 6 to 9
Height: 4 to 6 (3) feet tall; 4-foot spread

Appearance: Masses of tiny white flowers on wide, stiffly branched stems above large kidney-shaped leaves
Bloom Period: June; strong, fresh honey fragrance
Propagation: Division or seed
Uses: Back or middle of large border
Notes: Wide-spreading foliage gradually deteriorates after bloom with heat and drought, so plan to underplant (*e.g.*, with fall-blooming bulbs) or hide space.

DELPHINIUM ×BELLADONNA
Belladonna Delphinium

○ ◑

Zones: 3 to 7
Height: 3 to 4 feet tall; 2-foot spread
Appearance: Blue flowers on spikes above dark-green palmately cut foliage
Bloom Period: June to September
Propagation: By seed
Uses: Middle of border
Notes: Hybrid of *D. elatum* and *D. grandiflorum*; more heat tolerant, longer blooming with more spikes, but less dramatic than *D. elatum*. Requires rich, well-drained soil.
Varieties: 'Belladonna', light blue; 'Bellamosum', dark blue.

DELPHINIUM ELATUM HYBRIDS
Delphinium, Larkspur

○ ◑

Zones: 3 to 7
Height: 3 to 6 feet tall; 2-foot spread
Appearance: Spikes of blue, purple, white, lavender or pink flowers; palmately cut green foliage
Bloom Period: June to July
Propagation: Sow seed in midsummer for fall planting or early winter indoors for spring planting
Uses: Background or middle of bed; good for cutting fresh or drying
Notes: Short-lived perennial; in areas with hot summers, grow as hardy annual; best results from setting plants out in fall or early spring; most need staking. Requires rich, well-drained soil.
Varieties: 'Blackmore and Langdon Strain', tall and magnificent, tends to be more perennial if divided regularly, single colors available; 'Connecticut Yan-

kee Strains', 30 inches tall; 'Fantasia Mix', 27 inches tall with strong stems; 'Pacific Coast Strains', elegant, 60 to 72 inches tall, available in single colors, notably short-lived.

DIANTHUS ×ALLWOODII
Allwood Pink

○ ◑

Zones: 4 to 8
Height: 12 inches tall; 8- to 12-inch spread
Appearance: Pink, salmon or white flowers on stems above fine-textured gray-green foliage
Bloom Period: Summer; sweetly scented
Propagation: By cuttings or layering
Uses: Foreground of bed; edging; good fresh-cut flower
Notes: *D. caryophyllus* × *D. plumarius*. Will continue to rebloom if deadheaded. Available in single or double (with extra petals) forms. A short-lived perennial, particularly with heat and humidity. Requires sandy, well-drained soil.
Varieties: 'Blanche', double, white-fringed petals; 'Doris', double, salmon pink with deep pink eye; 'Helen', deep salmon pink; 'Ian', compact, double, crimson.

DIANTHUS PLUMARIUS HYBRIDS
Cottage Pink

○ ◑

Zones: 3 to 9
Height: 18 to 24 (6 to 8) inches tall; 12-inch spread
Appearance: Pink and white flowers on stems above mats of fine-textured gray-green foliage
Bloom Period: May to June; spicy fragrance
Propagation: By cuttings and seed
Uses: Front of border; edging
Notes: A parent of many garden pinks, long-lived, mat-forming evergreen plants are attractive all year; many varieties. Requires average neutral or limy, well-drained soil.
Varieties: 'Bath's Pink', light pink with red center, particularly tolerant of heat and humidity as proven in Atlanta, Georgia, blooms about a month before others.
Related Species: *D. deltoides* (maiden pink), summer flowering; 6 to 12 inches tall, 18- to 24-inch spread

DIANTHUS SUPERBUS LONGICALYCINUS

◐ ●

Zones: 4 to 9
Height: 15 (4 to 5) inches tall; 12-inch spread
Appearance: Fringed pink flowers above mats of fine, narrow green foliage
Bloom Period: August to September
Propagation: By seed and cuttings
Uses: Foreground of border; edging
Notes: Welcome bloom in late summer. Pinch flower stalks at four inches, if needed, for stockier stems that stand up. Deadhead for prolonged bloom into fall. Requires average well-drained soil.

DICENTRA EXIMIA
Fringed Bleeding Heart

◑ ●

Zones: 3 to 7
Height: 12 inches tall; 12-inch spread
Appearance: Pink or white flowers; finely cut fernlike green or grayish foliage
Bloom Period: April to September
Propagation: Division or seed
Uses: Middle or foreground of bed; groundcover; edging; good fresh-cut flower
Notes: Blooms continuously with adequate moisture. Several named varieties, many are hybrids, some with grayish leaves. Requires rich, well-drained soil; prefers moist soil but can withstand summer drought.
Varieties: Var. *alba*, white flowers
Related Species: *D. formosa* (Pacific bleeding heart) similar, but with running rhizomes, freely hybridizes with the above; 'Luxurient', a hybrid, probably the best and most widely available. 'Stuart Boothman', particularly glaucous-gray finely cut foliage, deep pink flowers, possibly a hybrid with *D. eximia*.

DICENTRA SPECTABILIS
Common Bleeding Heart

◑ ● ○

Zones: 3 to 7
Height: 30 inches tall; 24-inch spread
Appearance: Pink or white flowers; green foliage with fernlike texture

Bloom Period: May to June
Propagation: Division or seed, often self-sows
Uses: Background or middle of bed; good fresh-cut flower
Notes: Dies down in summer, so plant behind later-flowering perennial to cover empty space. Cut down in early summer when foliage looks shabby. Dig deeply to transplant. Requires rich, moist soil.
Varieties: The common variety is pink; 'Alba' and 'Pantaloons' are white.

DICTAMNUS ALBUS
Gas Plant

○

Zones: 3 to 8
Height: 30 inches tall; 36-inch spread
Appearance: Spikes of pink or white flowers; moderately coarse, pinnately compound green foliage
Bloom Period: June
Propagation: By seed
Uses: Middle of bed
Notes: Very long-lived, nearly permanent perennial; avoid transplanting. On quiet days, match held below flowers will ignite volatile gas given off by flowers. Requires rich, well-drained, moist soil.
Varieties: The type is white flowered, but *D. albus purpureus* bears pink flowers.

DIGITALIS GRANDIFLORA
Yellow Foxglove

○ ◑ ◑

Zones: 3 to 8
Height: 24 to 36 inches tall; 12- to 18-inch spread
Appearance: Spikes of light yellow flowers with narrow green leaves
Bloom Period: June to July
Propagation: By seed or division; may self-sow
Uses: Middle to background of border
Notes: Also called *D. ambigua*. Requires average, well-drained soil.
Varieties: 'Temple Bells', 12 to 15 inches tall, comes true from seed.
Related Species: *D. ×mertonensis*, a hybrid of *D. grandiflora* and *D. purpurea*, strawberry pink flowers, a short-lived perennial unless divided every couple of years, 3 to 4 feet.

DORONICUM CAUCASICUM
Leopard's-Bane

◐ ○

Zones: 4 to 7
Height: 18 inches tall; 12-inch spread
Appearance: Yellow daisies; heart-shaped green foliage
Bloom Period: April to May
Propagation: Division or seed
Uses: Middle of bed; good fresh-cut flower
Notes: Foliage goes dormant in summer; cover spot with spreading perennials or annuals. While dormant don't let soil become too dry. Requires rich, moist soil. Also called *D. cordatum*.
Varieties: 'Miss Mason', a hybrid with somewhat longer-lasting flowers and foliage.

ECHINACEA PURPUREA
Purple Coneflower

○ ◐

Zones: 3 to 9
Height: 36 inches tall; 18-inch spread
Appearance: Pink (or white) daisy flowers with orange center; green foliage
Bloom Period: July to September
Propagation: Division or seed
Uses: Background or middle of bed; good for fresh-cut or dried flower
Notes: Also known as *Rudbeckia purpurea*. On poor, dry soils usually doesn't need staking. Requires well-drained soil, drought tolerant.
Varieties: 'Bright Star' and 'The King', more brightly colored selections; 'White Lustre', white flowers.

ECHINOPS 'TAPLOW BLUE'
Globe Thistle

○ ◐

Zones: 4 to 9
Height: 48 to 60 inches tall; 24-inch spread
Appearance: Spherical blue flowers; coarse green pinnately cut foliage
Bloom Period: July
Propagation: Division
Uses: Background or middle of bed; good for fresh-cut or dried flower

Notes: After first bloom, cut out old stems at soil level to encourage second bloom on shorter stems. Requires well-drained soil.
Related Species: *E. ritro* 'Veitch's Blue', a more diminutive variety with deeper blue flowers, 3 feet tall.

EPIMEDIUM GRANDIFLORUM
Barrenwort

◐ ●

Zones: 5 to 8
Height: 12 to 15 inches tall; 12-inch spread
Appearance: Masses of small pink, lavender, white or rarely yellow flowers; heart-shaped leaves on wiry stems. Deciduous
Bloom Period: March to April
Propagation: Division
Uses: Foreground of bed; edging; groundcover for dry shade; good fresh-cut foliage
Notes: Also called *E. macrantha*. Clump forming. One of the best groundcovers for dry shade. Largest flowered of the common species. Average to rich soil; drought tolerant in shade.
Varieties: 'Harold Epstein', pale yellow, larger leaves, has running rhizomes; 'Rose Queen', deep rose pink; 'White Queen', white.
Related Species: *E. ×rubrum*, a hybrid with *E. alpinum*, has spreading rhizomes that make an especially good groundcover, ruby red flowers, reddish foliage in spring.

EPIMEDIUM ×VERSICOLOR
Barrenwort

◐ ●

Zones: 5 to 9
Height: 12 to 15 inches tall; 12-inch spread
Appearance: Masses of small yellow flowers; heart-shaped leaves on wiry stems. Evergreen in mild climates, bronze young growth
Bloom Period: April
Propagation: Division
Uses: Foreground of bed; edging; groundcover for dry shade; good fresh-cut foliage
Notes: *E. grandiflorum* × *E. pinnatum colchicum*, somewhat rhizomatous, one of the best groundcovers for dry shade; cut damaged foliage to ground before growth starts in early spring. Requires average to rich soil; drought tolerant in shade.
Varieties: 'Sulphureum', most common, deep yellow.

EPIMEDIUM × WARLEYENSE
Barrenwort

◑ ●

Zones: 5 to 9
Height: 12 to 15 inches tall; 12-inch spread
Appearance: Masses of small orange flowers; heart-shaped leaves on wiry stems
Bloom Period: April
Propagation: Division
Uses: Foreground of bed; edging; groundcover for dry shade; good fresh-cut foliage
Notes: E. alpinum × E. grandiflorum, rhizomatous; one of the best groundcovers for dry shade. Cut damaged foliage to ground before growth starts in early spring. Requires average to rich soil; drought tolerant in shade.

EPIMEDIUM × YOUNGIANUM
Barrenwort

◑ ●

Zones: 5 to 8
Height: 8 to 12 inches tall; 12-inch spread
Appearance: Masses of small lavender or white flowers; small heart-shaped leaves on wiry stems
Bloom Period: April
Propagation: Division
Uses: Foreground of bed; edging; groundcover; good fresh-cut foliage
Notes: E. grandiflorum × E. diphyllum, most diminutive of the common species, good groundcovers for dry shade. Requires average to rich soil; drought tolerant in shade.
Varieties: 'Niveum' and 'Yenomoto' are both white; 'Roseum' is lavender-pink.

ERYNGIUM ALPINUM
Sea Holly

○ ◑

Zones: 3 to 8
Height: 30 (12) inches tall; 18-inch spread
Appearance: Stiff, spiny, steely blue flowers; coarse green foliage
Bloom Period: July
Propagation: Division or seed
Uses: Middle of bed; good fresh-cut or dried

Notes: Flowers stately and sculptural; most striking of the sea hollies. Requires poor, well-drained and dry soil. Difficult to find true plant in nurseries.
Related Species: E. planum, masses of smaller steel blue flowers, often supplied by nurseries as the above species, less sculptural.

EUPATORIUM COELESTINUM
Hardy Ageratum

○ ◔ ◑

Zones: 6 to 8
Height: 24 inches tall; 24-inch spread
Appearance: Light blue flowers; green foliage
Bloom Period: August to September
Propagation: Division, cuttings or seed
Uses: Middle of bed; good fresh-cut flower
Notes: Light blue flowers in early fall are good companions for chrysanthemums. Watch out for very invasive rhizomes and prolific seeding. Pinch midsummer for compact growth.

EUPATORIUM PURPUREUM
Joe-Pye Weed

○ ◔ ◑

Zones: 4 to 8
Height: 4 to 7 feet tall; 3- to 4-foot spread
Appearance: Dusky rose-pink flattish flower heads; whorled green foliage
Bloom Period: August to September
Propagation: Division or seed
Uses: Back of bed
Notes: Lanky in shade, pinch early summer for compact growth, but this reduces size of flower heads; bold accent for large gardens. Very adaptable, but needs moisture.

FILIPENDULA PALMATA
Siberian Meadowsweet

○ ◔ ◑

Zones: 3 to 8
Height: 4 feet tall; 3-foot spread
Appearance: Fluffy pink flowers; palmately lobed coarse green foliage
Bloom Period: June
Propagation: Division
Uses: Background or middle of bed

Notes: Stiff stems seldom need staking. Requires rich, moist soil.

Varieties: 'Elegans', most commonly offered form, pale pink; 'Nana', desirable short form, 18 inches tall, rich pink.

FILIPENDULA PURPUREA
Japanese Meadowsweet

◯ ◑ ◐

Zones: 6 to 8

Height: 4 feet tall; 3-foot spread

Appearance: Fluffy rich cerise-to-pink flowers; palmately lobed coarse green foliage on gracefully arching stems

Bloom Period: June

Propagation: Division

Uses: Background or middle of bed

Notes: Really attractive superior perennial, stiffer stems than *E. palmata* need no staking. Flower heads mature to reddish stems, attractive through summer. Perhaps the best species. Requires rich, moist soil.

FILIPENDULA RUBRA
Queen of the Prairie

◯ ◑ ◐

Zones: 3 to 9

Height: 6 to 8 feet tall; 3-foot spread

Appearance: Fluffy pink flowers; coarse green foliage

Bloom Period: June

Propagation: Division or seed

Uses: Background of bed; good for fresh-cut or dried flower

Notes: Rarely needs staking in spite of its height; moderately spreading rhizomes; watch for mites. Requires rich, moist soil.

Varieties: 'Venusta' ('Magnifica'), deepest pink, most common; 'Venusta Alba' ('Magnifica Alba'), white, shorter at 36 to 60 inches.

FILIPENDULA ULMARIA
Queen of the Meadow

◯ ◑ ◐

Zones: 3 to 9

Height: 3 to 6 feet tall; 2-foot spread

Appearance: Fluffy white flowers; pinnately compound green foliage

Bloom Period: June to July

Propagation: Division

Uses: Middle or front (for foliage only) of bed

Notes: Stiff stems need no staking; cut out stems after flowering for new basal foliage. Requires rich, moist soil.

Varieties: 'Aurea', the most notable and important form, golden foliage, particularly when rejuvenated after bloom, less important white flowers; 'Flore-Plena', double white flowers, superior to the species; 'Variegata', notable for the cream blotch in the middle of each leaf.

GAILLARDIA × GRANDIFLORA
Blanketflower, Gaillardia

◯

Zones: 3 to 9

Height: 12 to 30 inches tall; 12- to 18-inch spread

Appearance: Red and/or yellow daisies; green foliage

Bloom Period: June to October

Growing Requirements: Poor, sandy, well-drained, dry soil.

Propagation: Division, root cuttings or seed

Uses: Middle or foreground of bed; good fresh-cut flower

Notes: One of longest-blooming perennials. Sow seed early to grow as annual; must have lots of sun; needs good drainage to overwinter. Requires poor, sandy, well-drained, dry soil.

Varieties: 'Burgundy', wine red, 30 inches tall; 'Goblin', red and yellow, most popular variety, 12 inches tall; 'Yellow Queen', yellow, 30 inches tall.

GAURA LINDHEIMERI
White Gaura

◯ ◑

Zones: 5 to 9

Height: 3 to 4 feet tall; 3-foot spread

Appearance: An airy plant with masses of small white, pink-tinted flowers above narrow foliage

Bloom Period: June to October

Propagation: Division or seed

Uses: Middle to background of border

Notes: This native of Louisiana, Texas and Mexico tolerates drought, heat and humidity. Can have brilliant red fall color. Prefers sandy soil; tolerates well drained clay.

GERANIUM ENDRESSII
Hardy Geranium

○ ◐ ◑

Zones: 4 to 8
Height: 15 inches tall; 18-inch spread
Appearance: Pink flowers; palmately cut green foliage
Bloom Period: May to June; all summer in cool climates
Propagation: Division or seed
Uses: Middle or foreground of bed; groundcover; edging
Notes: Does best in cool, moist locations; combine with shrubs and roses. Requires moist, well-drained soil.
Varieties: 'Wargrave Pink' is an improved form and is the most available.
Related Species: G. ×oxonianum 'Claridge Druce', a distinctive and less showy hybrid, useful in dryish shade, rose-pink flowers, gray-green leaves.

GERANIUM HIMALAYENSE
Hardy Geranium

○ ◐ ◑

Zones: 4 to 8
Height: 18 inches tall; 18-inch spread
Appearance: Blue flowers; palmately cut green foliage
Bloom Period: June
Propagation: Division or seed
Uses: Middle or foreground of bed; groundcover; edging
Notes: Also called *G. grandiflorum*. Does best in cool, moist locations; combine with shrubs and roses. Requires moist, well-drained soil.
Related Species: 'Johnson's Blue', an excellent hybrid, very similar to *G. himalayense*, but blooming slightly later, nearly seedless.

GERANIUM MACRORRHIZUM
Hardy Geranium

◐ ◑

Zones: 4 to 9
Height: 15 inches tall; 15-inch spread
Appearance: Magenta, pale pink or white flowers; palmately lobed green foliage; red fall color
Bloom Period: May
Propagation: Division or seed
Uses: Foreground of bed; groundcover
Notes: Pungent scent to foliage; early blooming; good for dry shade; stoloniferous plants make tight groundcover. Requires average soil; drought tolerant.
Varieties: 'Album', white; 'Bevans', magenta; 'Ingwersen's Variety', pale pink.

GERANIUM MACULATUM
Hardy Geranium

◐ ◑

Zones: 4 to 9
Height: 24 inches tall; 18-inch spread
Appearance: Lilac-pink flowers; palmately lobed green foliage
Bloom Period: May
Propagation: Division or seed
Uses: Middle or foreground of bed; groundcover
Notes: Native to eastern North America; early blooming. Requires rich soil.
Varieties: Var. *albiflorum*, white flowers

GERANIUM SANGUINEUM
Hardy Geranium

○ ◐ ◑

Zones: 4 to 9
Height: 12 inches tall; 12-inch spread
Appearance: Rose-magenta, pink or white flowers; small palmate green foliage
Bloom Period: May to September
Propagation: Division, cuttings or seed
Uses: Foreground of bed; groundcover; edging
Notes: Long-flowering, very adaptable perennial; a variable species, so choose compact forms. Requires rich, well-drained soil.
Varieties: 'Album', white flowers with darker green foliage, 12 inches tall; 'Cedric Morris', rose-magenta,

earlier bloom that continues more effectively through summer, compact habit, 9 inches tall; Var. *striatum* (*lancastriense*), clear pink, 6 inches tall, compact bushy plant form; 'Shepherd's Warning', clear, rose-pink, 4 inches tall.

GEUM QUELLYON
Geum

○ ◑ ◐

Zones: 4 to 8
Height: 24 (10) inches tall; 12-inch spread
Appearance: Yellow, orange or red flowers; low-growing green foliage
Bloom Period: May to June
Propagation: Division or seed
Uses: Foreground of bed; edging; good fresh-cut flower
Notes: Short-lived perennial. Most available types are seed strains. Requires rich, well-drained soil.
Varieties: 'Lady Stratheden' (yellow) and 'Mrs. Bradshaw' (red) most common
Related Species: G. × *borisii*, good old garden variety with orange flowers; 'Georgenburg', April to May blooming, orange-yellow flowers followed by attractive seed heads, 12 (6) inches tall.

GYPSOPHILA PANICULATA
Baby's Breath

○ ◑

Zones: 4 to 8
Height: 3 feet tall; 2-foot spread
Appearance: Billowy masses of tiny white or pink flowers; glaucous gray-green, narrow leaves with fine texture
Bloom Period: June to August
Propagation: Division or direct-sown seed; dislikes transplanting
Uses: Middle of bed; good for fresh-cut or dried flower
Notes: Sprawling plant needs staking but can be used to cover bare spots of spring bloomers like poppies and bulbs. Requires light, well-drained soil with lime; prefers neutral to alkaline pH.
Varieties: 'Bristol Fairy', outstanding white double flowers, can spread 4 feet. Also double pink varieties available.
Related Species: G. *oldhamiana*, pale pink flowers, July to August; 30 inches.

HELENIUM AUTUMNALE
Sneezeweed

○

Zones: 3 to 9
Height: 24 to 72 inches tall; 18-inch spread
Appearance: Yellow, orange, rust and/or red daisies; narrow green foliage
Bloom Period: August to September
Propagation: Division, cuttings or seed
Uses: Background or middle of bed; good fresh-cut flower
Notes: Nonallergenic but blooms during hay fever season. If crowded by other plants, may die out. Pinch mid-June for compactness. Requires rich, moist soil.
Varieties: 'Bruno', mahogany red, 24 inches tall; 'Butterpat', butter yellow, 36 in. tall; 'Riverton Beauty', yellow with bronze center, 48 inches tall.

HELIANTHUS SALICIFOLIUS
Willow-leafed Sunflower

○ ◑ ◐

Zones: 3 to 9
Height: 6 to 8 feet tall; 3- to 4-foot spread
Appearance: Tall spikes of small, golden-yellow daisies above narrow foliage
Bloom Period: September to October
Propagation: Division or seed
Uses: Background of border in large gardens
Notes: A magnificent sight in October; a wonderful companion to late dahlias and grasses. May need staking in sun, definitely in shade, stems brittle at base. May be pinched in July. Perennial sunflowers lack the large heads of the annuals. Requires moist soil.
Related Species: H. *angustifolius*, equally magnificent in late October and November, only useful in the long falls of the South, Zones 6 to 9.

HELIOPSIS SCABRA
Heliopsis

○ ◑

Zones: 3 to 9
Height: 3 to 4 feet tall; 2-foot spread
Appearance: Golden yellow daisies; green foliage along stem

Bloom Period: June to September
Propagation: Division, cuttings or seed
Uses: Background or middle of bed; good fresh-cut flower
Notes: Color is very strong golden yellow. Watch for red aphids in midsummer. Many varieties available, all good and long blooming. Requires rich, moist, well-drained soil.
Varieties: 'Gold Greenheart', golden flowers with a cool green center, 3 feet tall

HELLEBORUS FOETIDUS
Stinking Hellebore, Bear's-foot Hellebore

◑ ●

Zones: 5 to 9
Height: 18 to 24 inches tall; 12- to 18-inch spread
Appearance: Branched clusters of small, light green flowers above dark green palmately compound leaves
Bloom Period: Winter to spring
Propagation: By seed
Uses: Foreground of border; edging; groundcover
Notes: A useful texture plant for dry shade; tends to be short-lived but self-sows prolifically. Requires well-drained soil.
Varieties: 'Wester Flisk', beet-red stems make a nice contrast to dark green leaves, comes mostly true from seed
Related Species: H. argutifolius (H. lividus corsicus), larger, coarser and more spectacular, Zones 8 to 9 as evergreen. (Root hardy to Zone 6 or 7.)

HELLEBORUS ORIENTALIS
Lenten Rose

◐ ◑ ●

Zones: 4 to 9
Height: 15 to 18 inches tall; 18-inch spread
Appearance: Cream, pink, purple, garnet and/or red speckled flowers; coarse palmately compound foliage
Bloom Period: March to April
Propagation: By seed
Uses: Front of border; edging; groundcover
Notes: The easiest species to grow; semievergreen; cut off damaged foliage before flowering in spring to improve appearance and reduce disease; self-sows. Requires rich, well-drained soil.

Related Species: H. niger (Christmas rose), may bloom early winter in warm climates, or as above in colder climates, pure white with golden stamens, sometimes tinged pink in bud, Zones 3 to 8.

HEMEROCALLIS HYBRIDS
Daylily

○ ◑ ◑

Zones: 3 to 8
Height: 12 to 48 (12 to 24) inches tall; 24-inch spread
Appearance: Red, pink, yellow, orange, cream and/or purple trumpet-shaped flowers on stalks above low, straplike green foliage
Bloom Period: June to September; a few varieties sweetly scented
Propagation: Division or seed
Uses: Middle or foreground of bed; edging; good fresh-cut flower
Notes: Many hybrids available with a range of bloom seasons and colors. Consult catalogs for desired colors. Perhaps smaller-flowered types blend into border more easily. Most flower about a month in midsummer (July in Philadelphia). Everblooming hybrids will be the wave of the future and are becoming more numerous, but so far are only available in limited color range.
Varieties: 'Fairy Tale Pink', 24 inches tall, very sensitive to drought; 'Krakatoa Lava', glowing orange with pink overtones, blooms late July to August; Everblooming Varieties: 'Forsyth Lemon Drop', 24 inches, soft golden yellow, one of the best rebloomers; 'Happy Returns', 18 inches, lemon yellow, repeat blooms best in the North; 'Pardon Me', 18 inches tall, red, repeat blooms best in South; 'Pink Recurrence', salmony pink with deep rose eye, Zones 6 to 9; 'Stella de Oro', 18 inches tall, golden yellow, the first repeat bloomer and very popular.

HEUCHERA MICRANTHA 'PALACE PURPLE'
Alumroot

○ ◑ ◑

Zones: 4 to 8
Height: 12 to 24 (12) inches tall; 12-inch spread
Appearance: Wide reddish purple leaves with spikes of tiny, almost insignificant, white flowers
Bloom Period: June to July

Propagation: Division and seed

Uses: Foreground of border, edging

Notes: Foliage color shows best in sun, or in South, light shade, and is best in spring; variable when grown from seed; wispy flower spikes are sculptural to some people, removed by others. Requires well-drained, moist soil.

Related Species: *H. americana* (Zones 4 to 9) and *H. villosa* (Zones 6 to 9), selected forms have marbled or reddish foliage, give partial shade.

HEUCHERA SANGUINEA
Coralbells

◯ ◑ ◐

Zones: 3 to 8

Height: 12 to 24 (8) inches tall; 12-inch spread

Appearance: Masses of tiny pink, white or red flowers on wiry stems above low, rounded green foliage

Bloom Period: May to July

Propagation: Division or seed

Uses: Middle or foreground of bed; edging; good fresh-cut flower

Notes: Low foliage and airy flower stems are nice featured toward front of bed. Requires rich, moist, well-drained soil.

Varieties: 'Chatterbox', pink, 18 inches tall; 'June Bride', white, 15 inches tall; 'Pluie De Feu', red, 24 inches tall.

HOSTA HYBRIDS
Hosta, Plantain Lily, Funkia

◑ ◐ ●

Zones: 3 to 8

Height: 18 to 60 (6 to 36) inches tall; 12- to 36-inch spread

Appearance: Spikes of white to purple flowers above lower, large, wide or narrow, green, blue-green or yellow foliage, often variegated

Bloom Period: June to August

Propagation: Division or seed

Uses: Middle or foreground of bed; groundcover; edging; good fresh-cut flower

Notes: Place in garden according to height of foliage, not flowers. Bloom season and size depend on variety. Requires rich, moist soil.

Varieties: *H. montana* 'Aureo-marginata', 24 to 36 (18) by 36 inches, gold-edged; *Hosta sieboldiana*, 24 by 36 inches, blue-gray foliage; *H. sieboldiana* 'Fran-

ces Williams', 24 by 36 inches, blue-gray edged in gold; 'Ginko Craig', 12 by 12 inches, white-edged; 'August Moon', 24 by 36 inches, chartreuse to gold; 'Krossa Regal', 60 (30) by 36 inches, blue-gray, stiffer, less arching than most hostas.

HOSTA PLANTAGINEA
August Plantain Lily

◑ ●

Zones: 3 to 9

Height: 24 to 30 inches tall; 24-inch spread

Appearance: Stocky spikes of long trumpet-shaped flowers above lower, wide, light green foliage

Bloom Period: August to September; sweetly fragrant

Propagation: Division or seed

Uses: Middle to foreground of border; edging; groundcover

Notes: One of the best hostas for late bloom, fragrance and overall form; a time-proven favorite. Requires average soil.

Varieties: 'Aphrodite', recently introduced, double flowers.

IRIS, BEARDED HYBRIDS
Bearded Iris

◯ ◑

Zones: 3 to 10

Height: 8 to 36 inches tall; 10- to 12-inch spread

Appearance: Classic iris flower with hairy beard on lower petals, in almost every color; straplike green foliage

Bloom Period: May to June

Propagation: Division

Uses: Middle or foreground of bed; edging; good fresh-cut flower

Notes: Bearded iris are the most popular and spectacular types; borers, soft rot and leaf diseases may be problems but are seldom devastating, though leaf diseases are usually disfiguring after bloom. Adaptable, prefers rich, well-drained soil.

Varieties: Available in every color of the rainbow. Intermediate-height bearded hybrids (15 to 28 inches tall) do best in garden because they need no staking, but the tall bearded iris (more than 28 inches tall) are the most popular because of their large flowers.

Related Species: *I. pallida* 'Albo-variegata', leaves variegated with white, purple flowers, 2 feet tall.

IRIS CRISTATA
Dwarf Crested Iris

Zones: 3 to 9
Height: 6 to 9 inches tall; 12-inch spread
Appearance: Light blue or white flowers with yellow crests on lower petals; narrow straplike foliage
Bloom Period: May
Propagation: Division or seed
Uses: Foreground of bed; edging, groundcover
Notes: Watch for slugs. Adaptable, but prefers rich soil.
Varieties: 'Alba', white

IRIS KAEMPFERI
Japanese Iris

Zones: 4 to 9
Height: 24 to 30 inches tall; 18- to 24-inch spread
Appearance: Wide spreading blue, purple, reddish purple, white, pink flowers, often attractively veined; straplike leaves
Bloom Period: June to July
Propagation: Division or seed
Uses: Middle of bed; edging; good fresh-cut flower
Notes: Correct name is now *I. ensata*; requires moist and rich lime-free soil, but rhizomes must not be submerged.
Varieties: Many, select favorites from catalogs

IRIS SIBIRICA HYBRIDS
Siberian Iris

Zones: 3 to 9
Height: 24 to 48 inches tall; 24-inch spread
Appearance: Blue, purple, reddish purple, white, pink flowers, often attractively veined; straplike leaves
Bloom Period: May to June
Propagation: Division or seed
Uses: Background or middle of bed; good fresh-cut flower
Notes: Good, tough, pest-free perennial, blooms with peonies. Requires moist, rich soil.
Varieties: Many, select your favorites from catalogs.

IRIS TECTORUM
Japanese Roof Iris

Zones: 4 to 9
Height: 12 inches tall; 12-inch spread
Appearance: Lavender-blue or white flowers with yellow crests; straplike foliage
Bloom Period: May to June
Propagation: Division or seed
Uses: Foreground of bed; edging; good fresh-cut flower
Notes: Tough and trouble free. Requires rich, well-drained soil.
Varieties: Var. *album*, white; 'Variegata', white variegated foliage, lavender-blue flowers

KIRENGESHOMA PALMATA

Zones: 5 to 8
Height: 3 to 4 feet tall; 4-foot spread
Appearance: Pale yellow, nodding, thick-petaled bells on arching plant with palmate leaves
Bloom Period: September
Propagation: Division or seed
Uses: Middle of border
Notes: Fussy but useful for late-summer bloom in shade; prefers cool location with constant moisture. Requires rich, moist well-drained soil.
Related Species: *K. koreana*, upright flowers, blooms August to September, 3 feet tall, rare.

KNIPHOFIA HYBRIDS
Red-Hot Poker, Tritoma

Zones: 5 to 9
Height: 24 to 60 (18 to 36) inches tall; 24- to 36-inch spread
Appearance: Tall orange, yellow, red and/or cream flower spikes above long, narrow, grasslike green foliage
Bloom Period: June to September, depending on variety
Propagation: Division or seed
Uses: Middle or foreground of bed; good fresh-cut flower
Notes: In northern areas mulch for winter protec-

tion. Leaves of some varieties can be tediously long, shorten if desired. Requires rich, moist, well-drained soil.

Varieties: 'Earliest of All', coral, 30 inches tall; 'Royal Standard', flowers have red top, yellow bottom, 36 inches tall; 'Primrose Beauty', pale yellow, 30 inches tall, blooms midsummer; 'Springtime', red top, cream bottom, 36 inches tall, blooms June; 'Wayside Flame', orange, 30 inches tall, blooms July to November.

LAMIUM MACULATUM
Dead Nettle

◐ ◑ ●

Zones: 4 to 9
Height: 8 inches tall; 12-inch spread
Appearance: Pink or white flowers; silver variegated leaves
Bloom Period: April to July
Propagation: By cuttings or division
Uses: Foreground of bed; groundcover; edging
Notes: Excellent groundcover, not invasive like the common dead nettle (*Lamiastrum galeobdolon*). Adapts to dry shade conditions in average soil.
Varieties: 'Beacon Silver', silver leaves with green edges, lavender flowers; 'White Nancy', a white-flowered sport of 'Beacon Silver'
Related Species: *Lamiastrum galeobdolon* 'Herman's Pride', leaves speckled with silver, yellow flowers

LIATRIS SCARIOSA
Gayfeather

○

Zones: 3 to 9
Height: 3 to 4 feet tall; 2-foot spread
Appearance: Spikes of purple or white flowers; narrow green foliage
Bloom Period: September
Propagation: Division or seed
Uses: Vertical accent in background or middle of bed; good fresh-cut or dried flower
Notes: Flowers on spike open simultaneously. Requires rich soil with good drainage, especially in winter; drought tolerant.
Varieties: 'September Glory', purple; 'White Spire', the best white cultivar

LIATRIS SPICATA
Spike Gayfeather

○

Zones: 3 to 9
Height: 2 to 3 feet tall; 2-foot spread
Appearance: Spikes of mauve, purple or white flowers; narrow green foliage
Bloom Period: July to August
Propagation: Division or seed
Uses: Vertical accent in background or middle of bed; good for fresh-cut or dried flower
Notes: Flowers on spike open at top first. Requires well-drained, but moist soil; poor drainage in winter can be fatal.
Varieties: 'Kobold', lilac, 2 feet, one of the most available and best

LIGULARIA DENTATA
Ligularia

◐ ◑

Zones: 4 to 8
Height: 4 (3) feet tall; 3-foot spread
Appearance: Clusters of yellow daisy flowers; large, bold, rounded, kidney-shaped, dark green leaves, purplish underside
Bloom Period: July
Propagation: Division or seed
Uses: Background or middle of bed
Notes: Protect from hot sun or leaves will temporarily wilt; requires constant moisture and rich soil.
Varieties: 'Desdemona' and 'Othello', both very similarly named forms
Related species: *L. hodgsonii*, smaller, 2 to 3 feet tall

LIGULARIA 'THE ROCKET'
Ligularia

Zones: 4 to 8
Height: 6 (3) feet tall; 3-foot spread
Appearance: Spikes of small yellow flowers along elegant dark stems above large, ragged heart-shaped, green leaves, purplish underside
Bloom Period: July
Propagation: Division or seed
Uses: Background or middle of bed

Notes: Morning sun only or leaves wilt distressingly; requires constant moisture and rich soil. Listed as either *L. przewalskii* or *L. stenocephala*, possibly a hybrid.

LINARIA PURPUREA
Purple Toadflax

○ ◑ ◐

Zones: 5 to 9
Height: 36 inches tall; 12- to 18-inch spread
Appearance: Spikes of tiny lilac (or pink) flowers on stems with narrow grayish green foliage
Bloom Period: June to October
Propagation: Division, stem cuttings or seed
Uses: Middle to foreground of border
Notes: Later bloom comes from side branches. May need staking, but can also be attractive when it has fallen over. Flowers resemble tiny snapdragons. Requires average soil.
Varieties: 'Canon Went', pink flowers

LIRIOPE MUSCARI
Lilyturf, Liriope

◑ ◐

Zones: 6 to 9
Height: 12 inches tall; 12-inch spread
Appearance: Spikes of purple (or white) flowers followed by black berries; evergreen grassy green foliage
Bloom Period: September
Propagation: Division or seed
Uses: Foreground of bed; groundcover; edging; good fresh-cut flower
Notes: Tough groundcover. Cut away winter-damaged leaves in March. Very adaptable and tolerant of dry conditions and virtually any soil.
Varieties: 'Lilac Beauty', lavender flowers held well above foliage; 'Monroe White', white flowers; 'Silvery Sunproof', leaves strikingly variegated with yellow, purple flowers

LOBELIA CARDINALIS
Cardinal Flower

○ ◑ ◐ ●

Zones: 2 to 9
Height: 3 to 5 feet tall; 1-foot spread

Appearance: Spikes of bright red (pink or white) flowers; narrow leaves
Bloom Period: July to September
Propagation: Division, stem cuttings or seed
Uses: Background or middle of border
Notes: Thrives in wet, rich soil, requires constant moisture; short-lived perennial unless divided every couple years; self-sows.
Varieties: 'Heather Pink', with soft pink flowers, is among several new pink forms; Var. *alba* is white.
Related Species: 'Bees Flame' and 'Queen Victoria' are less hardy, purplish foliaged seed strains, hybrids with *L. splendens*. *L. siphilitica*, blue, 2 to 3 feet tall; *L. siphilitica alba*, white flowers

LUPINUS RUSSELL HYBRIDS
Lupine

○ ◑ ◐

Zones: 3 to 8
Height: 36 inches tall; 18-inch spread
Appearance: Spikes of blue, pink, purple, white and/or yellow flowers; green palmately compound foliage
Bloom Period: June
Propagation: By seed
Uses: Background or middle of bed
Notes: Short-lived perennial; can be treated as an annual if seed is started early enough indoors. Provides afternoon shade in hot climates. Requires rich, well-drained soil, prefers acid pH.

LYCHNIS ×ARKWRIGHTII
Arkwright's Campion

○ ◑ ◐

Zones: 6 to 8
Height: 18 to 24 inches tall; 12-inch spread
Appearance: Orange-scarlet flowers; bronze foliage
Bloom Period: May to June
Propagation: Division or seed
Uses: Middle to foreground of border
Notes: Short-lived perennial; self-sows; striking color. Requires well-drained soil.
Varieties: 'Vesuvius', particularly deep colored
Related Species: *L. chalcedonica* (Maltese cross), old-fashioned, flat scarlet flower heads, June to July, 2 to 3 feet, Zones 3 to 9

LYSIMACHIA CLETHROIDES
Gooseneck

○ ◑ ◐

Zones: 3 to 8
Height: 2 to 4 feet tall; 2- to 3-foot spread
Appearance: Arched spikes of white flowers atop stems with green leaves of moderate size
Bloom Period: July
Propagation: Division or seed
Uses: Background or middle of border (if you dare); good fresh-cut flower
Notes: Tends to be quite invasive; shorter on poor, dry soils. Adaptable; moist to dry soil.

LYSIMACHIA EPHEMERUM

○ ◑ ◐

Zones: 6 to 8
Height: 3 feet tall; 1-foot spread
Appearance: Spikes of white flowers atop straight stems with gray-green leaves of moderate size
Bloom Period: July
Propagation: Division or seed
Uses: Background or middle of border; good fresh-cut flower
Notes: Not invasive like other species. Foliage is dull glaucous gray. Adaptable; prefers moist soil.

LYTHRUM SALICARIA
Purple Loosestrife

○ ◑ ◐

Zones: 3 to 8
Height: 3 to 5 feet tall; 2-foot spread
Appearance: Spikes of purple or pink flowers; narrow green foliage
Bloom Period: July to August
Propagation: Division or seed
Uses: Background or middle of bed; good fresh-cut flower
Notes: This European species can become a nuisance by seeding profusely and naturalizing in wetland habitats, now outlawed in some states. Adaptable; will even grow in very wet soils.
Varieties: 'Morden's Pink', pink, seedless when grown in isolation, 36 inches tall; 'Dropmore Purple', purple, 36 inches tall; 'Happy', dark pink, 18 inches tall; 'Fire Candle', rosy red.

MACLEAYA CORDATA
Plume Poppy

○ ◑ ◐

Zones: 3 to 8
Height: 8 to 10 feet tall; 6-foot spread
Appearance: Creamy white plumes on tall stems lined with large palmately lobed leaves
Bloom Period: July
Propagation: Division or seed
Uses: Background of border
Notes: Also called *Bocconia cordata*; invasive rhizomes need annual controlling
Related Species: *M. microcarpa* 'Coral Plume', pinkish bronze plumes, more rampantly invasive

MARRUBIUM CYLLENEUM
Greek Horehound

○ ◑ ◐

Zones: 6? to 9
Height: 8 to 12 inches tall; 12- to 18-inch spread
Appearance: Sprawling habit with rounded gray-green leaves; lax spikes of lavender flowers
Bloom Period: May to June
Propagation: Division, cuttings and seed
Uses: Foreground of border; edging
Notes: Requires poorish well-drained soil.

MERTENSIA VIRGINICA
Virginia Bluebell

◐

Zones: 3 to 8
Height: 36 inches tall; 12-inch spread
Appearance: Nodding blue flowers; moderate-size, oblong green foliage
Bloom Period: April to May
Propagation: Division or seed
Uses: Middle of bed; good fresh-cut flower
Notes: Early-blooming native plant; pink buds open blue. Foliage dies down in summer. Plant in late summer to early fall. Requires rich, moist soil.

MONARDA DIDYMA
Bee Balm, Bergamot

○ ◐ ◑

Zones: 3 to 9
Height: 36 inches tall; 18-inch spread
Appearance: Red, pink, purple or white flowers; green foliage
Bloom Period: June to July
Propagation: Division in spring (fall transplanting is risky) or by seed
Uses: Background or middle of bed; good fresh-cut flower
Notes: Shallow rhizomes spread rapidly but are easily pulled. Even mildew-resistant varieties will have some infection. Cut out old, unsightly stems when finished blooming for regrowth of low foliage. Requires rich, moist soil. Good air circulation reduces mildew on leaves.
Varieties: 'Gardenview Red', red, reputedly more resistant to mildew; 'Marshall's Delight', bright pink, also claimed mildew resistant; 'Mahogany', wine red; 'Prairie Night', bluish lavender; 'Snow White', white
Related species: M. fistulosa, more mildew resistant and drought tolerant, lavender

NEPETA ×FAASSENII
Faassen's Catmint, Faassen's Catnip

○ ◐ ◑

Zones: 4 to 8
Height: 18 inches tall; 24-inch spread
Appearance: Airy masses of small lavender-blue flowers above fine-textured gray-green foliage
Bloom Period: June to August
Propagation: Division
Uses: Foreground of border; edging
Notes: Seedless hybrid of N. mussinii and N. nepetella. Avoid rich soil; requires well-drained soil. Shear back after flowering for repeat bloom.
Related Species: N. mussinii, similar but with shorter bloom season and laxer habit, Zones 3 to 8; N. sibirica, blue spikes, 2 to 3 feet, blooms June to August, green leaves, spreading rhizomes

OENOTHERA TETRAGONA
Sundrops

○ ◐

Zones: 4 to 9
Height: 18 inches tall; 12-inch spread
Appearance: Yellow buttercuplike flowers, often red in bud, atop straight stems; green foliage
Bloom Period: June to July
Propagation: Division
Uses: Middle or foreground of bed
Notes: Also called O. fruticosa youngii. Shallow spreading rhizomes easily controlled. Cut back after flowering to low evergreen rosettes. Very adaptable to any well-drained soil.
Varieties: 'Fireworks', attractive red buds

OPHIOPOGON PLANISCAPUS 'NIGRESCENS'
Black Mondo Grass

◐ ◑

Zones: 6? to 9
Height: 6 inches tall; 12-inch spread
Appearance: Deep purple-black grassy foliage; less significant pale pink flowers followed by black berries
Bloom Period: August to September
Propagation: Division
Uses: Foreground of bed; groundcover; edging
Notes: Also called 'Arabicus'. Unique foliage for its deep color. Tough but slow growing. Very adaptable and tolerant of dry conditions. Cut away winter-damaged leaves in March.

PACHYSANDRA TERMINALIS
Japanese Pachysandra

◐ ● ◑

Zones: 4 to 8
Height: 8 inches tall; 8-inch spread
Appearance: White flowers; whorled dark-green foliage; white berries in fall
Bloom Period: April to May
Propagation: Division or cuttings
Uses: Foreground of bed; groundcover; edging
Notes: Among the best groundcovers; virtually weedproof; tolerant of root competition in shade. A mulch is essential for rapid establishment and health. Invasive rhizomes. Two clones required for

berries. Adaptable, but prefers rich soil with acid pH; somewhat drought tolerant.

Varieties: 'Green Carpet', low, compact habit, glossier foliage; 'Kingwood', deeply toothed foliage gives finer foliage effect; 'Variegata', white-edged leaves, brightens dark areas.

Related Species: P. procumbens (Allegheny pachysandra), semievergreen, clump-forming native.

PAEONIA LACTIFLORA
Peony

○ ◑

Zones: 3 to 8

Height: 24 to 48 inches tall; 18-inch spread

Appearance: Large pink, white, red (salmon or yellow) flowers; coarse, dark-green foliage

Bloom Period: May to June; sweetly scented

Propagation: Division; very long lived, so divide only to propagate. Cover eyes on tubers with no more than 1 inch of soil.

Uses: Background or middle of bed; fresh-cut flower

Notes: Large flowers, to 10 inches. In spring, remove mulch and debris to discourage botrytis, which kills shoots and flower buds. Foliage on many varieties becomes brown and unsightly by late summer and can be cut down without harm. Requires deep, rich soil; prepare 24 inches deep.

Varieties: Many varieties available in single, double, anemone and other forms. Recent herbaceous hybrids also include salmon and yellow shades.

PAPAVER ORIENTALE
Oriental Poppy

○ ◑

Zones: 3 to 8

Height: 24 to 48 inches tall; 18-inch spread

Appearance: Large red, orange, pink, salmon or white flowers; coarse, ragged green foliage

Bloom Period: May to June

Propagation: Division, root cuttings or seed

Uses: Background or middle of bed; good for fresh-cut flower or dried seedpods

Notes: Spectacular bloom period lasts only about two weeks. Foliage dies down in July, reappears in September; plan for other flowers to hide this gap. For arrangement, cut flowers in bud and sear stem. White varieties short-lived. Requires well-drained soil. Summer drought tolerant.

PENSTEMON BARBATUS
Common Beardtongue

○ ◑

Zones: 4 to 8

Height: 18 to 36 (8) inches tall; 12-inch spread

Appearance: Spikes of tubular scarlet or pink flowers above low narrow foliage

Bloom Period: June to July

Propagation: Division, cuttings or seed

Uses: Foreground to middle of border

Notes: One of the easiest species to grow; heat and drought tolerant; useful clear colors. Requires well-drained soil.

Varieties: 'Prairie Fire', orange-red; 'Rose Elf', rose-pink

PEROVSKIA ATRIPLICIFOLIA
Russian Sage

○

Zones: 3 to 9

Height: 36 inches tall; 18-inch spread

Appearance: Lavender-blue flowers; fine-textured silvery foliage

Bloom Period: July to August

Propagation: Division or cuttings

Uses: Middle of bed; good fresh-cut flower

Notes: Must have full sun and good drainage to do well; requires poor, dry soil. The plant usually sold as P. atriplicifolia is actually a hybrid.

Related Species: 'Longin', more compact and upright, particularly useful where rich soils may make P. atriplicifolia grow in an untidy manner; hybrid of P. abrotanoides and P. atriplicifolia.

PHLOX DIVARICATA
Wild Blue Phlox, Wild Sweet William

◑ ◑ ○

Zones: 3 to 8

Height: 15 inches tall; 12-inch spread

Appearance: Light blue (or white) flowers; fine-textured green foliage

Bloom Period: May to June

Propagation: Division or seed

Uses: Foreground of bed; edging; good fresh-cut flower

Notes: Native plant. Dies down in summer. Requires rich, well-drained soil.

Varieties: 'Fuller's White', good white-flowered form

PHLOX PANICULATA
Summer Phlox

Zones: 3 to 8
Height: 36 to 48 inches tall; 24-inch spread
Appearance: Pink, lavender, salmon, red or white flowers; green foliage
Bloom Period: July to August; very fragrant
Propagation: Division, cuttings or root cuttings
Uses: Background or middle of bed; good fresh-cut flower
Notes: Many varieties available in various colors. Provide good air circulation to reduce powdery mildew; some varieties more resistant than others. Requires rich, moist, well-drained soil.
Varieties: 'Bright Eyes', pink with red eye, considered to be among the most mildew resistant; 'Norah Leigh', leaves conspicuously edged with cream, lavender flowers, tends to sunburn in hot sun. The following varieties have been noted by various sources as possessing greater than normal mildew resistance: 'David', white, 2½ to 3 feet; 'Eva Callum', clear pink with red eye, 2 to 2½ feet; 'Franz Schubert', lavender; 'Sandra', scarlet.

PHLOX STOLONIFERA
Creeping Phlox

Zones: 3 to 8
Height: 6 (2) inches tall; 8-inch spread
Appearance: Blue, purple, pink or white flowers; small green leaves; foliage lower than flowers
Bloom Period: May
Propagation: By cuttings or division
Uses: Foreground of bed; groundcover; edging; good fresh-cut flower
Notes: Flowers with azaleas and likes the same growing conditions. Spreads by stolons but easily pulled if it creeps out-of-bounds. Good groundcover through summer. Not susceptible to mildew. Requires rich, well-drained soil; prefers acid pH.
Varieties: 'Alba' ('Bruce's White'), white; 'Blue Ridge', blue; 'Pink Ridge', best pink-flowered type; 'Sherwood Purple', purple, vigorous growth

PHLOX SUBULATA
Moss Pink

Zones: 3 to 8
Height: 4 inches tall; 12-inch spread
Appearance: Blue, pink or white flowers; fine-textured mat of green foliage
Bloom Period: April to May
Propagation: By cuttings or division
Uses: Foreground of bed; groundcover; edging
Notes: Very fine, stiff foliage forms low mat. Flowers appear among foliage. Best in sandy, well-drained soil; prefers alkaline pH, but adaptable.
Varieties: 'Brilliant', red; 'Coral Eye', pale pink, coral pink eye; 'Millstream Daphne', bright pink, yellow eye; 'Millstream Jupiter', blue

PHYSOSTEGIA VIRGINIANA
Obedient Plant, False Dragonhead

Zones: 2 to 8
Height: 24 to 36 inches tall; 18-inch spread
Appearance: Pink, purple or white flowers; narrow green foliage
Bloom Period: August to October
Propagation: Division
Uses: Middle of bed; good fresh-cut flower
Notes: Valuable for late bloom. Adaptable to a variety of sites; tends to be invasive. On poor, dry soils is shorter and on heavy soils is less invasive.
Varieties: 'Bouquet Rose', rosy pink, 24 inches tall; 'Summer Snow', white, 36 inches tall; 'Variegata', white-edged leaves, pink flowers, 36 inches tall; 'Vivid', lavender-pink, 24 inches tall

PLATYCODON GRANDIFLORUS
Balloonflower

Zones: 3 to 8
Height: 10 to 24 inches tall; 15-inch spread
Appearance: Deep blue (white or pink) flowers; green foliage along stems; yellow fall color
Bloom Period: July to August
Propagation: Division or seed
Uses: Middle of bed; good fresh-cut flower

Notes: Among the best midsummer blue perennials; cut back halfway a month before bloom or will need staking; dig deeply to transplant; remove seedpods to prolong bloom. Requires well-drained soil.

Varieties: Var. *albus*, white; 'Apoyama', 10 inches tall, deep blue, widely sold; Var. *mariesii*, 15 inches, deep blue; 'Shell Pink', 24 inches, pale pink

POLEMONIUM CAERULEUM
Jacob's Ladder

◑ ●

Zones: 2 to 7
Height: 2 to 3 feet tall; 1- to 2-foot spread
Appearance: Spikes of blue flowers above pinnately compound foliage
Bloom Period: June
Propagation: By seed
Uses: Middle of border
Notes: A strong grower in the North, but short-lived where summers are hot. Requires rich, moist soil.

POLEMONIUM REPTANS
Creeping Polemonium

◑ ●

Zones: 2 to 8
Height: 12 to 18 inches tall; 12-inch spread
Appearance: Light blue flowers above pinnately compound foliage
Bloom Period: May
Propagation: Division or seed
Uses: Foreground of border
Notes: The easiest species to grow, particularly where summers are hot in its native eastern United States. Requires rich, moist soil.

POLYGONATUM BIFLORUM
Solomon's Seal

◑ ●

Zones: 3 to 8
Height: 24 to 36 inches tall; 12-inch spread
Appearance: Small white flowers; broad green leaves; flowers hang along arching stems under foliage; yellow fall color

Bloom Period: May to June
Propagation: Division; may reseed in the garden
Uses: Background or middle of shady bed
Notes: Useful vertical accent in the shady garden. Adaptable, but prefers rich, well-drained soil.
Related Species: *P. commutatum*, similar, but larger, 3 to 7 feet by 2 feet; *P. odoratum* 'Variegatum', striking white stripes in foliage

POTENTILLA THURBERI
Thurber Cinquefoil

○ ◑ ◑

Zones: 4 to 8
Height: 18 (12) inches tall; 12-inch spread
Appearance: Small mahogany-red flowers in clusters on upright stems above radially compound leaves
Bloom Period: June to July
Propagation: Division or seed
Uses: Foreground of border; edging
Notes: One of the neatest and most upright of the herbaceous cinquefoils. Requires well-drained soil.
Related Species: *P. nepalensis* 'Miss Wilmott', carmine pink flowers with the more common habit of long, floppy flower stems.

PRIMULA ×POLYANTHA
Polyanthus Primrose

◑ ◑

Zones: 3 to 8
Height: 10 inches tall; 8- to 12-inch spread
Appearance: All colors of flowers, usually with yellow centers; rosettes of green oblong foliage
Bloom Period: April to May; sweetly scented
Propagation: Division or seed
Uses: Foreground of bed; edging; good fresh-cut flower
Notes: Prefers rich, constantly moist, but well-drained soil with afternoon shade in hot climates. The most common type of primrose, cultivated for centuries with many new and antique varieties.
Varieties: Barnhaven strains in wide range of colors are perennial and long lived; Pacific Giant strains are commonly available but tend to be short lived in garden.
Related Species: *P. japonica* (Japanese primrose), 12 to 24 (8) inches by 12 inch, tiered stalks of red, pink or white flowers above rosettes of green fo-

liage, May to June; *P. × tommasinii*, similar to polyanthus, light yellow flowers, antique hybrid, very heat tolerant and long lived in old, neglected gardens.

PULMONARIA SACCHARATA
Lungwort

Zones: 3 to 8
Height: 12 inches tall; 12-inch spread
Appearance: Pink buds open to nodding blue flowers; long green leaves speckled with silver
Bloom Period: April to May
Propagation: Division
Uses: Foreground of bed; edging; groundcover
Notes: A good, tight, weedproof groundcover. Requires rich, moist soil.
Varieties: 'Argentea', leaves predominantly silver; 'Highdown', flowers deep blue, leaves moderately spotted silver; 'Mrs. Moon', prominently silver-speckled leaves; 'Sissinghurst White', white flowers, prominently silver-speckled foliage.
Related Species: *P. angustifolia*, green leaves and gentian blue flowers, Zones 2 to 8; *P. rubra*, rich salmony pink, unspotted leaves, Zones 4 to 7.

RODGERSIA AESCULIFOLIA

Zones: 4? to 7
Height: 3 to 5 (2 to 4) feet tall; 2- to 3-foot spread
Appearance: Plumes of white flowers above large, radially compound leaves
Bloom Period: May to June
Propagation: Division or seed
Uses: Background to foreground of bed, depending on vigor
Notes: Prefers rich, cool and moist conditions, protected from hot sun; greatest vigor is in cool climates; one of the easier species.
Related Species: *R. podophylla*, perhaps the easiest species in the eastern United States, moderately rhizomatous for good groundcover.

RODGERSIA SAMBUCIFOLIA

Zones: 4? to 7
Height: 4 to 5 feet tall; 3- to 4-foot spread
Appearance: Plumes of cream flowers above pinnately compound leaves
Bloom Period: May to June
Propagation: Division or seed
Uses: Background to middle of bed
Notes: Prefers rich soil and cool, moist conditions, protected from hot sun; flower clusters mature to attractive garnet for summer.
Related Species: *R. pinnata*, smaller and more difficult to grow, 'Superba' is especially attractive with pink flowers and reddish new growth.

RUDBECKIA FULGIDA
Orange Coneflower

Zones: 3 to 9
Height: 24 (12) inches tall; 18-inch spread
Appearance: Bright yellow daisies with dark centers; broad-leafed green foliage
Bloom Period: July to September
Propagation: Division or seed
Uses: Middle or foreground of bed; groundcover; good fresh-cut flower
Notes: Broad, ground-hugging foliage forms tight groundcover to choke out weeds; doesn't need staking. Requires well-drained soil.
Varieties: 'Goldsturm', one of the best perennials available today.

RUDBECKIA LACINIATA
Cutleaf Coneflower

Zones: 3 to 9
Height: 6 feet tall; 3- to 4-foot spread
Appearance: Yellow daisies atop stems lined with coarsely cut foliage
Bloom Period: July to September
Propagation: Division, cuttings or seed
Uses: Background of border

Notes: Striking perennial for large gardens; the following variety is suitable for smaller gardens. Requires well-drained soil.

Varieties: 'Gold Drop', only 2 to 3 feet tall and self-supporting, good for middle of border; best variety for small gardens.

Related Species: *R. nitida*, similar species often confused with the above.

SALVIA GUARANITICA

◐ ◑ ◑

Zones: 6? to 10

Height: 4 to 6 feet tall; 3-foot spread

Appearance: Loose spikes of deep indigo-blue flowers above moderate-size bright green foliage

Bloom Period: July to frost

Propagation: Division, cuttings or seed

Uses: Background of border

Notes: Provide winter mulch in Zone 6; tuberous roots can be stored moist in cold cellar farther north or treated as annual from cuttings. Mildly rhizomatous. Except in poor soils, needs staking but may be cut back hard in summer to reduce height.

Varieties: 'Argentina Skies', light blue flowers, developed by the author.

SALVIA × SUPERBA
Violet Sage, Salvia

○

Zones: 4 to 8

Height: 18 to 36 inches tall; 18-inch spread

Appearance: Spikes of purple flowers; green foliage

Bloom Period: June to August

Propagation: Division or cuttings

Uses: Middle or foreground of bed

Notes: An excellent purple perennial for the sunny June border. Reblooms some if deadheaded. Prefers poor, well-drained soil.

Varieties: 'East Friesland' and 'May Night' ('Mainacht'), both excellent, 18 inches tall

SANGUINARIA CANADENSIS
Bloodroot

◐ ◑ ●

Zones: 3 to 8

Height: 6 inches tall; 8-inch spread

Appearance: White flowers; rounded green foliage

Bloom Period: April

Propagation: Division or seed

Uses: Foreground of bed

Notes: Prefers a site with deciduous shade for shelter from summer sun; goes dormant in summer. A native plant. Requires rich soil; prefers acid pH.

Varieties: 'Mutliplex', double flowers, blooms a week later, very vigorous in rich soil

SANGUISORBA CANADENSIS
Canadian Burnet

◐ ◑

Zones: 3 to 8

Height: 4 to 5 feet tall; 2-foot spread

Appearance: Spikes of white bottlebrush-like flowers on long stems above pinnately compound foliage

Bloom Period: September to October

Propagation: Division or seed

Uses: Background to middle of border

Notes: Avoid excess heat and provide afternoon shade in the South. Requires moist soil; more compact in a leaner, drier soil.

Related Species: *S. obtusa* (Japanese burnet), pink flowers July to August, 3 feet, Zones 4 to 8.

SEDUM × 'AUTUMN JOY'
Sedum

○ ◐

Zones: 3 to 9

Height: 24 inches tall; 15-inch spread

Appearance: Pink flowers in flat heads; fleshy green foliage

Bloom Period: August to September

Propagation: Division or cuttings

Uses: Middle or foreground of bed; good fresh-cut or dried flower

Notes: One of the best perennials available today. Performs best in poor, well-drained soil. Drought tolerant. Aging flowers deepen in color, ending in rust by winter and remaining attractive until spring.

Related Species: *S. maximum* 'Atropurpureum', purple foliage; *S. spectabile*, pink flowers on a shorter plant, blooms September, old-fashioned and still common in many old gardens, 2 feet, excellent companions to pink colchicum.

SMILACINA RACEMOSA
False Solomon's Seal

◐ ●

Zones: 3 to 7
Height: 2 to 3 feet tall; 1- to 2-foot spread
Appearance: Creamy white plumes, followed by red berries in fall, atop arching stems with moderate-size leaves
Bloom Period: May
Propagation: Division or seed
Uses: Middle of shaded border
Notes: Somewhat drought tolerant. Requires slightly acid, rich, moist soil.

SOLIDAGO CAESIA
Wreath Goldenrod

◑ ◐ ●

Zones: 4 to 8
Height: 24 to 36 inches tall; 24-inch spread
Appearance: Spikes of golden yellow flowers above moderately sized green foliage
Bloom Period: September to October
Propagation: Division, cuttings or seeds
Uses: Middle of border, good for fresh-cut or dried flower
Notes: One of the best plants for dry soils in shade, a native woodlander. Prefers average soil.

SOLIDAGO ×'PETER PAN'
Hybrid Goldenrod

○ ◑

Zones: 3 to 9
Height: 24 to 30 inches tall; 12-inch spread
Appearance: Yellow plumes on straight stems with moderate-size green leaves
Bloom Period: July to September
Propagation: Division or cuttings
Uses: Middle of border

Notes: Goldenrods don't cause hayfever, but bloom at the same time as the guilty ragweed. Hybrids have improved habits over the species; this is one of the best. Requires well-drained soil.

SOLIDAGO SEMPERVIRENS
Seaside Goldenrod

○ ◑

Zones: 4 to 8
Height: 4 to 6 feet tall; 2- to 3-foot spread
Appearance: Plumy, bright yellow flowers on tall stems lined with clean narrow green leaves
Bloom Period: September to October
Propagation: Division, cuttings, or seed
Uses: Background of border
Notes: Noninvasive clump forming; cut back halfway in midsummer to reduce height; a bright spot in early fall. Requires well-drained soil.

SOLIDAGO SPHACELATA 'GOLDEN FLEECE'
Golden Fleece Goldenrod

○ ◑

Zones: 4 to 8
Height: 12 to 18 inches tall; 12- to 18-inch spread
Appearance: Plumy, bright yellow flowers on arching stems lined with clean narrow green leaves, mounded habit
Bloom Period: September to October
Propagation: Division or cuttings
Uses: Foreground to middle of border
Notes: Noninvasive clump forming; compact habit needs no staking; drought resistant. Requires well-drained soil.

STACHYS BYZANTINA
Lamb's Ears, Woolly Betony

○ ◑ ◐

Zones: 4 to 9
Height: 15 (8) inches tall; 12-inch spread
Appearance: Prominent low-growing woolly, silver foliage; insignificant lavender flowers in silvery spikes
Bloom Period: June to July
Propagation: Division or seed
Uses: Foreground of bed; edging

Notes: One of few silver foliage plants for partially shady site. Many gardeners dislike flower spikes, but they give extra texture. Tends to die out in hot, muggy weather, fungicide will prevent this. Requires poor, well-drained soil; drought tolerant.
Varieties: 'Silver Carpet', a nonflowering variety with the same silvery foliage; 'Helene Von Stein', larger, vigorous, less woolly gray leaves, resists dying out in summer, seldom flowers, recent introduction of German origin.

SYMPHYTUM GRANDIFLORUM

◑ ◑ ●

Zones: 3 to 8
Height: 12 inches tall; 12-inch spread
Appearance: Pale yellow nodding flowers above low green foliage
Bloom Period: May
Propagation: Division or seed
Uses: Front of border; edging; groundcover
Notes: Useful for dry shade; resembles *Pulmonaria*; watch for slugs.
Varieties: 'Variegatum', leaves edged with cream

THALICTRUM ROCHEBRUNIANUM
Lavender Mist Meadow Rue

◑ ◑ ○

Zones: 4 to 8
Height: 36 to 60 inches tall; 24-inch spread
Appearance: Large, airy clusters of lavender flowers; compound green foliage with small rounded segments
Bloom Period: July to August
Propagation: Division or seed
Uses: Background of bed
Notes: Useful for its late summer bloom and contrasting foliage texture (leaves resembling those of columbine). Requires rich, well-drained soil.
Varieties: 'Lavender Mist', the common name, often wrongly listed as a cultivar
Related Species: *T. speciosissimum*, pale yellow flowers, June, glaucous gray-green foliage

TIARELLA CORDIFOLIA
Foamflower

◑ ●

Zones: 3 to 8
Height: 12 (6) inches tall; 8-inch spread
Appearance: White flower spikes above light green foliage
Bloom Period: May to June
Propagation: Division or seed
Uses: Foreground of bed; groundcover; edging
Notes: Spread by runners; may be invasive but is easy to pull out. Native plant. Requires rich soil, prefers acid pH; only slightly drought tolerant.
Related species: *T. wherryi*, similar to *T. cordifolia* but nonspreading; some variants have purplish foliage and pink flowers.

TRADESCANTIA ×ANDERSONIANA
Spiderwort

○ ◑ ◑

Zones: 4 to 9
Height: 24 inches tall; 18-inch spread
Appearance: Clusters of blue, white or pink flowers; grasslike green foliage along the stems
Bloom Period: June to August
Propagation: Division or seed
Uses: Middle or foreground of bed
Notes: Often sold as *T. virginiana*. Shorter forms are desirable because they are less likely to need staking; cut back after flowering for regrowth of shorter foliage.
Varieties: 'Blue Stone', deep blue, 12 inches tall; 'Pauline', pale pink; 'Innocence', white, 24 inches tall

TRICYRTIS FORMOSANA
Toad Lily

◑ ●

Zones: 5 to 9
Height: 3 to 4 feet tall; 1- to 2-foot spread
Appearance: Clusters of small white flowers, heavily speckled purple, atop straight or arching stems lined with moderate-size leaves
Bloom Period: September to frost
Propagation: Division, cuttings or seed
Uses: Middle of border

Notes: Also called *T. stolonifera*; rhizomatous, but not invasive; may need staking in very rich soil. Requires rich, moist soil.
Varieties: *T. formosana amethystina*, flowers tipped blue, earlier flowering in July to September.
Related Species: *T. dilatata*, similar to above but flowers August to September; 'Sinonome', a hybrid with *T. hirta*, larger flowers, very heavily speckled purple, vigorous, perhaps the best variety, 3 to 5 feet by 2 feet

TRICYRTIS HIRTA
Toad Lily

◑ ●

Zones: 4 to 8
Height: 2 feet tall; 1-foot spread
Appearance: Clusters of small flowers heavily speckled purple on white along straight or arching stems lined with moderate-size leaves
Bloom Period: September to October
Propagation: Division, cuttings or seed
Uses: Middle to foreground of border
Notes: Flowers occur along the stems as well as at the tip. Requires rich, moist soil.
Varieties: Var. *alba*, pure white flowers with yellow center

TRICYTRIS LATIFOLIA
Toad Lily

◑ ●

Zones: 6 to 9
Height: 2 feet tall; 1- to 2-foot spread
Appearance: Clusters of small yellow flowers lightly speckled purple atop arching stems lined with moderate-size leaves
Bloom Period: June to July
Propagation: Division, cuttings or seed
Uses: Middle to foreground of border
Notes: Also called *T. bakeri*, *T. puberula*; the earliest species to bloom in midsummer.

VANCOUVERIA HEXANDRA
American barrenwort

◑ ●

Zones: 5 to 8
Height: 12 inches tall; 12-inch spread

Appearance: Dark-green compound leaves of small rounded segments on wiry stems; small white insignificant flowers
Bloom Period: May to June
Propagation: Division
Uses: Foreground of border; groundcover
Notes: Of three species native to the Pacific Coast, this is the only one easily grown in the East; closely related to *Epimedium*, but with less showy flowers; very good for dry shade; spreads by rhizomes.

VERONICA ×'GOODNESS GROWS'
Goodness Grows Speedwell

○ ◑

Zones: 3 to 8
Height: 10 to 12 inches tall; 12-inch spread
Appearance: Spikes of deep blue flowers on lax stems with small green foliage
Bloom Period: May to hard frost
Propagation: Division or cuttings
Uses: Middle or foreground of bed; good fresh-cut flower
Notes: Probably *V. alpina alba* × *V. spicata*; one of the best and longest-flowering veronicas; low procumbent habit requires no staking; occasional deadheading improves appearance; divide every couple years to maintain vigor. Requires well-drained soil.

VERONICA INCANA
Woolly Speedwell

○ ◑

Zones: 3 to 8
Height: 12 (3) inches tall; 12-inch spread
Appearance: Procumbent spikes of blue flowers; low-growing silver foliage
Bloom Period: June to July
Propagation: Division, cuttings or seed
Uses: Foreground of bed; edging; good fresh-cut flower
Notes: Foliage is lower than flower; use in front of bed; procumbent flower stems seldom give effect of full height. Requires sandy, well-drained soil.

VERONICA SPICATA
Spike Speedwell

○ ◑

Zones: 4 to 8

Height: 1 to 3 feet tall; 1-foot spread

Appearance: Spikes of blue, pink (or white) flowers; green foliage along stems

Bloom Period: June to August

Propagation: Division, cuttings or seed

Uses: Middle or foreground of bed; good fresh-cut flower

Notes: Most varieties need staking or they will flop; deadhead to prolong bloom. Requires well-drained soil.

Varieties: 'Blue Peter', deep blue; 'Red Fox', the best pink variety, deep rose-pink; 'Sunnyborder Blue', a stocky long-blooming hybrid with deep violet-blue flowers, 18 to 24 inches.

VINCA MINOR
Periwinkle

◐ ●

Zones: 3 to 8

Height: 6 inches tall; 12-inch spread

Appearance: Blue, purple or white flowers; small, dark-green leaves on creeping stems

Bloom Period: April to May

Propagation: Division or cuttings

Uses: Foreground of bed; groundcover; edging

Notes: Useful groundcover and even denser and more effective in rich soil. Requires well-drained soil.

Varieties: 'La Grave' ('Bowles Variety'), with blue flowers, and 'Miss Jekyll', with white flowers, are the best varieties with a lower growth habit; 'Multiplex', double purple flowers; 'Variegata', leaves edged yellow, light blue flowers.

Encyclopedia of Ferns

ADIANTUM PEDATUM
Maidenhair Fern

● ◐

Zones: 3 to 9
Height: 1 to 2 feet tall; 1-foot spread
Appearance: Small rounded leaflets on dark wiry stems
Bloom Period: —
Propagation: Division or spores
Uses: Foreground of border, edging, groundcover
Notes: Unique foliage texture among the ferns; increases slowly into broad, tight clump; native to eastern United States. Requires rich, moist soil.

ATHYRIUM FELIX-FEMINA
Lady Fern

● ◐

Zones: 3 to 9
Height: 3 feet tall; 2-foot spread
Appearance: Light-green finely cut fronds
Bloom Period—
Propagation: Division or spores
Uses: Middle of bed; groundcover.
Notes: Stocky horizontal rhizomes form dense clumps; not the best fern as fronds often develop brown edges by late summer. Requires rich, moist soil.
Varieties: Many desirable dwarf and/or frilled foliage forms, including 'Congestum Cristatum', stocky crested fronds, 10 to 12 inches tall; 'Minutissimum', miniature, 5 inches tall

ATHYRIUM NIPPONICUM 'PICTUM'
Japanese Painted Fern

● ◐

Zones: 3 to 9
Height: 12 to 18 inches tall; 18-inch spread
Appearance: Fronds variegated with silver and maroon
Bloom Period: —

Propagation: Division or spores
Uses: Foreground of bed; edging; groundcover
Notes: Also called *A. goeringianum* 'Pictum'; one of the prettiest ferns; useful for brightening dark areas; clump-forming horizontal rhizomes. Requires rich, moist soil.

DRYOPTERIS ×CELSA
Log Fern

● ◐

Zones: 6 (5?) to 9
Height: 3 to 4 feet tall; 2-foot spread
Appearance: Deep-green upright glossy fronds; semievergreen
Bloom Period: —
Propagation: Division or spores
Uses: Background to middle of border
Notes: *D. goldieana* × *D. ludoviciana*; one of the most attractive ferns, superior to lady fern; clump-forming horizontal rhizomes.

DRYOPTERIS ERYTHROSORA
Pink Shield Fern

● ◐

Zones: 5 to 9
Height: 2 feet tall; 2-foot spread
Appearance: Deep green fronds; young fronds pink; semievergreen
Bloom Period: —
Propagation: Division or spores
Uses: Middle to foreground of border, edging.
Notes: One of the most colorful ferns; clump-forming horizontal rhizomes. Requires rich, moist soil.

DRYOPTERIS FELIX-MAS
Male Fern

● ◐

Zones: 3 to 9
Height: 3 feet tall; 3-foot spread

Appearance: Vase-shaped plant with deep green fronds
Bloom Period: —
Propagation: Division or spores
Uses: Middle of border
Notes: A sculptural fern with leaves radiating from a central point; rhizome upright, noncreeping. Requires moist, well-drained soil.
Varieties: 'Cristata', fronds crested or branched at tips.
Related Species: *D. marginalis* (marginal shield fern) deep green, 1 to 2 feet by 2 feet.

OSMUNDA CINNAMOMEA
Cinnamon Fern

Zones: 3 to 9
Height: 2 to 5 feet tall; 2- to 3-foot spread
Appearance: Vase-shaped plants with light green fronds with cinnamon-colored fertile (spore producing) fronds rising in center of plant
Bloom Period: May (for fertile fronds)
Propagation: Division or spores
Uses: Background to middle of border
Notes: One of the most sculptural of ferns; fronds rise neatly from central point. Requires rich, moist soil.
Related Species: *O. regalis* (Royal fern) coarser, less finely cut fronds provide a unique texture; spores are produced at ends of fronds rather than separate fronds in center as above; Zones 2 to 9.

POLYSTICHUM ACROSTICHOIDES
Christmas Fern

Zones: 3 to 9
Height: 2 feet tall; 2-foot spread
Appearance: Dark green fronds with rounded oblong segments; evergreen
Bloom Period: —
Propagation: Division or spores
Uses: Foreground of bed; edging; groundcover
Notes: Useful for dry shade. Adaptable, drought tolerant.

POLYSTICHUM SETIFERUM
Soft Shield Fern

Zones: 5 to 9
Height: 2 feet tall; 2-foot spread
Appearance: Lacy, finely cut, arching fronds arising from central point, midrib densely coated with brown "fur"; evergreen
Bloom Period: —
Propagation: Division or spores
Uses: Front of border, edging
Notes: Elegant, finely textured fern. Requires rich, moist soil.
Varieties: 'Divisilobum', leaves more finely divided

Encyclopedia of Grasses

FESTUCA AMETHYSTINA
Large Blue Fescue

○ ◑

Zones: 5 (4) to 8
Height: 18 to 36 (10) inches tall; 12-inch spread
Appearance: Tufted hairlike blue-green foliage; wiry stems with slender light-brown flower spikes
Bloom Period: June to July
Propagation: Division
Uses: Foreground of border; edging
Notes: More tolerant of heat and poorly drained clay soils than other blue fescues.
Related Species: *F. ovina glauca*, the best forms can be a very striking gray-blue, not so tolerant of heat and poor drainage as the above, 12 (6) inches by 9 inches; Zones 4 to 6.

HAKONECHLOA MACRA 'AUREOLA'

◑ ●

Zones: 6 (5) to 9
Height: 12 inches tall; 18-inch spread
Appearance: Lax, arching, grassy foliage striped with green and gold, sprays of tiny reddish flowers
Bloom Period: September to October
Propagation: Division
Uses: Foreground of border, edging, groundcover
Notes: Slightly spreading rhizomes slowly form a tight clump.

HELICTOTRICHON SEMPERVIRENS
Blue Oat Grass

○ ◑

Zones: 4 to 8
Height: 4 (2 to 3) feet tall; 2- to 3-foot spread
Appearance: Tufted narrow blue-green foliage, semi-evergreen; slender white or beige flower spikes
Bloom Period: June to July
Propagation: Division or seed
Uses: Middle to foreground of border; edging
Notes: One of the easiest blue grasses to grow; stands up well to summer heat and humidity.

IMPERATA CYLINDRICA 'RED BARON'
Japanese Blood Grass

○ ◑

Zones: 5 to 9
Height: 18 to 24 inches tall; 12-inch spread
Appearance: Upright narrow foliage develops blood-red color in midsummer through fall
Bloom Period: July to August
Propagation: Division
Uses: Foreground of border
Notes: Striking anywhere, but combines especially well with gray and silver foliage. Requires well-drained soil.

MISCANTHUS SINENSIS
Eulalia Grass, Japanese Silver Grass

○ ◑

Zones: 4 to 9

Height: 6 to 8 feet tall; 4- to 5-foot spread

Appearance: Pinkish plumes atop upright stems lined with long narrow foliage

Bloom Period: September to October

Propagation: Division or seed

Uses: Background of border

Notes: Striking foliage all summer, flower heads last through winter; cut to ground in early spring.

Varieties: 'Gracillimus' (maiden grass), very narrow foliage Zones 5 to 9; 'Morning Light', narrow leaves with white margins give silvery effect in landscape, Zones 5 to 9; 'Purpurascens', foliage becomes reddish in late summer, 3 to 4 feet tall, Zones 7 to 9; 'Strictus' (porcupine grass), gold bands across leaves, especially effective when backlit, Zones 6 to 9, superior to 'Zebrinus'; 'Variegatus', foliage prominently edged white, Zones 6 to 9.

PENNISETUM ALOPECUROIDES
Japanese Fountain Grass

○ ◑

Zones: 5 to 9

Height: 3 to 4 (2 to 3) feet tall; 3-foot spread

Appearance: Tufted plants with arching deep green foliage under pinkish purple bottlebrush-like flower clusters

Bloom Period: August to October

Propagation: Division or seed

Uses: Middle to foreground of border; edging

Notes: Not suitable for drying as flower cluster shatters with age.

Varieties: 'Hamlin', dwarf variety

Related Species: *P. setaceum*, continuous blooming, only hardy in Zones 8 to 11, so usually grown as annual.

Many grasses come into their own in autumn, lasting well into winter. The variegated foliage and plumes of Miscanthus sinensis 'Strictus' are especially striking when back-lit by the sun in September.

Encyclopedia of Vines and Climbers

ACTINIDIA KOLOMIKTA
Kolomikta Actinidia

Woody Twiner ○ ◐ ◑

Zones: 4 to 8

Maximum Height: 15 to 20 feet

Appearance: Deciduous heart-shaped leaves tipped with white in May and June, later tinted pink. Small white flowers among leaves

Bloom Period: May

Propagation: By softwood and hardwood cuttings, layering or seeds

Uses: Trellises; pergolas; walls with wire grid

Notes: Magnificent in early summer, fades to green by midsummer. Female plants bear small edible fruit. Male plants with showier foliage. Prune lightly to neaten in early spring and when needed. Requires average, well-drained soil.

Related Species: *A. polygama*, similar white-tipped leaves but less vigorous. Attractive to cats, which can cause damage; *A. arguta* (bower actinidia) deep green leaves with reddish petioles, 25 to 30 feet, edible fruit, Zones 4 to 8; *A. chinensis* (kiwifruit) egg-size edible fruit, light green fuzzy leaves with reddish hairs on petioles and stems, Zones 7 to 9.

CAMPSIS RADICANS
Trumpet Vine

Woody Clinger ○ ◐

Zones: 4 to 9

Maximum Height: 30 to 40 feet

Appearance: Deciduous pinnately compound leaves, clusters of orange trumpet-shaped flowers

Bloom Period: July to September

Propagation: By softwood and root cuttings, layering or seeds

Uses: Masonry walls; pergolas; tall poles

Notes: Extremely vigorous and can overrun nearby plants, root sprouts can overrun nearby shrubs. Attractive to hummingbirds. Spur prune back to main trunks in early spring. Adapts to any soil, but avoid rich soils.

Varieties: 'Flava', yellow flowers

Related Species: *C. × tagliabuana* 'Madame Galen', deep reddish orange flowers, a less rampant hybrid of the above, Zones 5 to 9.

CELASTRIS SCANDENS
American Bittersweet

Woody Twiner ○ ◐

Zones: 3 to 8

Maximum Height: 20 feet

Appearance: Deciduous dark green leaves, showy clusters of small orange and red fruit at ends of branches in October, fall foliage yellowish, insignificant cream flowers

Bloom Period: June

Propagation: By softwood cuttings, layering or seeds

Uses: Trellises; pergolas; fences; walls with wire grid

Notes: More decorative and less rampant with more persistent fruit than the Chinese bittersweet, need both male and female plants for pollination. Adapts to any soil, but avoid rich soils.

Related Species: *C. orbiculatus* (Chinese bittersweet), has become more common in many areas due to rampant weedy nature. Self-sows vigorously. Fruit smaller, less persistent, and borne in clusters along branches.

CLEMATIS, LARGE-FLOWERED HYBRIDS

Woody Grabber ○ ◐ ◑

Zones: 3 to 9

Maximum Height: 6 to 15 feet

Appearance: Large out-facing white, pink, red, blue, purple or striped flowers among matt green deciduous foliage

Bloom Period: May to October, depends on variety

Propagation: By softwood cuttings

Uses: Trellises; pergolas (taller varieties); fences; walls with wire grid

Notes: Height, color, flower size and bloom season depend on variety. Most have foliage too dense for roses and shrubs, but make good backgrounds. Pruning depends on bloom season and whether flowers originate from old wood or new growth; consult a clematis book. Requires moist, well-drained, rich soil.

Varieties: Hundreds of varieties include 'Barbara Jackman', bluish purple with striking magenta bar down each petal; 'Candida', large white; 'Hagley Hybrid', a good pink of moderate vigor, to 6 feet; C. ×jackmanii, popular, strong growing, dependable purple; 'Lady Betty Balfour', purple, needs sun to bloom, September; 'Vyvyan Pennell', large double lavender-blue.

CLEMATIS ARMANDII
Armand Clematis

Woody Grabber ○ ◐ ◑

Zones: 7 to 9

Maximum Height: 15 to 20 feet

Appearance: Clusters of white or pinkish flowers among deep green, glossy evergreen leaves

Bloom Period: April to May

Propagation: By softwood cuttings, layering or seeds

Uses: Trellises; pergolas; fences; walls with wire grid

Notes: In areas of marginal hardiness winter damage to evergreen foliage often mars bloom. Requires well-drained soil. Best in Zone 8, south.

Varieties: 'Apple Blossom', tinged pink, young foliage bronze; 'Snowdrift', pure white.

CLEMATIS 'DUCHESS OF ALBANY'

Woody Grabber ○ ◐ ◑

Zones: 4 to 9

Maximum Height: 10 feet

Appearance: Nodding or out-facing pink bell-shaped flowers among matt mid-green deciduous leaves

Bloom Period: June to July

Propagation: By softwood cuttings

Uses: Trellises; pergolas; fences; walls with wire grid; on shrub roses and large shrubs

Notes: A hybrid of *C. texensis*, which contributes unique flower form. Prune hard in spring for best growth. Requires well-drained, moderately moist soil.

Varieties: Other desirable hybrids include 'Gravetye Beauty', cherry red.

CLEMATIS MACROPETALA
Big-petal Clematis

Woody Grabber ○ ◐

Zones: 5 to 8

Maximum Height: 10 to 12 feet

Appearance: Masses of small, nodding blue or pink flowers, with a tuft of staminoides in center, among light green deciduous leaves, followed by fluffy seed heads

Bloom Period: May

Propagation: By softwood cuttings, layering or seeds

Uses: Trellises; pergolas; fences; walls with wire grid; good with late spring bulbs

Notes: A fine early clematis. Allow to grow into tangled mass for profuse bloom, prune after flowering only when necessary. Carefully remove dead stems in winter. Requires rich, well-drained soil.

Varieties: 'Markham's Pink', pink flowers

Related Species: C. alpina, hardier and earlier blooming, flowers lack the central staminoides, Zones 4 to 8; cultivars include 'Helsingborg' and 'Pamela Jackman', both good blues; 'Ruby', deep pink; 'White Moth', white.

CLEMATIS MAXIMOWICZIANA
Sweet Autumn Clematis

Woody Grabber ○ ◐ ●

Zones: 5 to 9

Maximum Height: 30 feet

Appearance: Masses of tiny white flowers and deep green glossy deciduous leaves

Bloom Period: August to September; very fragrant

Propagation: By softwood cuttings or seeds

Uses: Trellises; pergolas; fences; walls with wire grid; large shrubs

Notes: A prolific self-sowing weed in much of the eastern United States. Cut back right after flowering before seeds mature. Spur prune in early spring. Also called *C. paniculata*. Adaptable to any soil; requires warm summers to flower well.

CLEMATIS MONTANA
Anemone Clematis

Woody Grabber ○ ◐ ◑

Zones: 5 to 9

Maximum Height: 30 to 40 feet

Appearance: Masses of mid-size white or pink four-sepalled flowers on vigorous ropy vines with mid-green deciduous leaves

Bloom Period: May, often scented

Propagation: By softwood cuttings or seeds

Uses: Trellises; pergolas; fences; walls with wire grid; large trees with low branches

Notes: Can overrun a small tree. Allow to grow into tangled mass for profuse bloom, prune after flowering only when necessary. May be necessary to remove from tree every three years to prevent damage. Requires well-drained soil.

Varieties: Var. *rubens*, most common with pink flowers and reddish stems and new leaves; 'Tetrarose', larger flowered deep mauve-pink, tetraploid; Var. *wilsonii*, white, blooms 2 to 3 weeks later.

CLEMATIS TANGUTICA
Golden Clematis

Woody Grabber ○ ◐ ◑

Zones: 5 to 8

Maximum Height: 10 to 15 feet

Appearance: Small nodding yellow flowers among light green, fine-textured deciduous foliage, fluffy seed heads in fall

Bloom Period: July to August

Propagation: By softwood cuttings or seeds

Uses: Trellises; pergolas; fences; walls with wire grid; large shrubs

Notes: Most common yellow species but seems short lived where summers are hot. Normally dies back at least halfway in winter, prune severely in early spring for best growth. Requires well-drained, moist soil.

Related Species: 'Bill Mackenzie', hybrid with *C. orientalis*, profuse bloom and vigorous; *C. serratifolia*, similar but seems to grow better in hot summer climates.

CLEMATIS VITICELLA
Italian Clematis

Woody Grabber ○ ◐ ◑

Zones: 4 to 9

Maximum Height: 12 feet

Appearance: Small, nodding purple flowers dance on delicate wiry stems among fine textured mid-green deciduous foliage

Bloom Period: June to July or August

Propagation: By softwood cuttings or seeds

Uses: Trellises; pergolas; fences; walls with wire grid; on shrub roses and large shrubs

Notes: One of the best clematis for combining with roses, because its sparse foliage provides limited shade, also for honeysuckles and wall shrubs. Prune to 2 to 3 feet high each spring to allow for long growth before bloom. Requires well-drained, moist soil.

Related Species: Indispensable hybrids include 'Abundance', reddish pink; 'Alba Luxurians', white, often with green tips; 'Etoile Violette', rich purple, out facing; 'Mme Julia Correvon', rich wine red, out facing, very long blooming; 'Royal Velours', deep velvety purple.

COBAEA SCANDENS
Cup-and-Saucer Vine

Tender Annual Grabber ○ ◐ ◑

Zones: 9 to 11

Maximum Height: 12 to 15 feet

Appearance: Nodding bell-shaped flowers open yellow-green, deepen to purple among light green foliage

Bloom Period: Early summer to fall

Propagation: By softwood cuttings or seeds sown indoors 5 to 6 weeks before last frost

Uses: Trellises; pergolas; lattices; fences; walls with wire grid

Notes: Bell-shaped flowers with wide sepals resemble cup and saucer. Actually a tropical perennial, but flowers from seed rapidly. Provide afternoon shade in hot climates. Requires rich, moist soil.

Varieties: 'Alba', flowers fade to greenish white.

DOLICHOS LABLAB
Hyacinth Bean

Tender Annual Twiner ○ ◖

Zones: —

Maximum Height: 10 feet

Appearance: Racemes of lavender pea-shaped flowers followed by purple pods among large, deep green leaves with purple stems and petioles

Bloom Period: Summer to fall

Propagation: By seeds sown after last frost, germinates in two weeks

Uses: Trellises; pergolas; lattices; fences; walls with wire grid; tall poles; posts

Notes: Actually a tropical perennial to 30 feet. A striking, easy annual with flowers and pods simultaneously. Edible pods, beans and flowers. Requires hot summers and rich, well-drained soil. Also called *Dipogon lablab* and *Lablab purpureus*.

GELSEMIUM SEMPERVIRENS
Carolina Jessamine, Yellow Jessamine

Woody Twiner ○ ◖ ◑

Zones: 7(6) to 9

Maximum Height: 10 to 20 feet

Appearance: Small yellow trumpet-shaped flowers among small evergreen foliage

Bloom Period: February or March to May, may repeat later; fragrant

Propagation: By softwood cuttings or seeds

Uses: Trellises; pergolas; lattices; fences; walls with wire grid; tall poles; posts

Notes: Graceful native vine common in the woods and gardens of the southeastern United States. Adaptable, prefers moist, rich, well-drained soil.

Varieties: 'Pride of Augusta', double flowers

HEDERA COLCHICA
Persian Ivy

Woody Clinger ○ ◖ ◑ ●

Zones: 6 to 9

Maximum Height: 50 feet

Appearance: Large evergreen leathery leaves, sometimes variegated, greenish yellow flowers on mature plants not especially showy, followed by black berries in spring

Bloom Period: Fall

Propagation: By softwood cuttings

Uses: Walls; fences; tree trunks; groundcover

Notes: Celerylike smell of crushed leaves. Does not climb as readily as *H. helix*. Adaptable to almost any soil, very drought tolerant.

Varieties: 'Dentata', most common, dark green, slightly toothed edges; 'Dentata Variegata', edged white, Zones 8 (7) to 9; 'Sulphur Heart' ('Paddy's Pride'), prominent yellow blotch in middle of each leaf, most attractive

Related Species: *H. canariensis*; (Canary Island ivy) similar large, but less leathery leaves, Zones 8 (7) to 10; 'Gloire de Marengo' is edged with cream and most common, Zones 8 to 10.

HEDERA HELIX
English Ivy

Woody Clinger ○ ◖ ◑ ●

Zones: 5 (4) to 9

Maximum Height: 90 feet

Appearance: Evergreen palmately lobed leaves, sometimes variegated, greenish yellow flowers on mature plants not especially showy, followed by black berries in spring

Bloom Period: October

Propagation: By softwood cuttings

Uses: Walls; fences; tree trunks; groundcover

Notes: Clings tightly to almost any surface. Adaptable to almost any soil.

Varieties: Hundreds of varieties vary in leaf shapes, color, vigor and hardiness. 'Glacier', grayish leaf with white edge, good groundcover, brightens shady spot, Zone 7 (6); 'Gold Heart', hardy and vigorous, yellow blotch in leaf center. Hardiest cultivars (Zone 5) include 'Buttercup', hardy, young foliage gold, colors best in bright shade; 'Galaxy,' bird's foot type with narrow lobes; 'Tom Boy', bright green pointed egg-shaped leaves.

Related Species: *H. napaulensis* 'Marble Dragon'. This cultivar of Himalayan ivy has attractive silver veins, yellow fruit, Zones 7 to 9.

HYDRANGEA ANOMALA PETIOLARIS
Climbing Hydrangea

Woody Clinger ○ ◖ ◑

Zones: 4 to 7

Maximum Height: 60 to 80 feet

Appearance: Deciduous dark green heart-shaped leaves, white disk like flower heads surrounded by large sterile white blossoms composed of 4 sepals, shredding tan bark

Bloom Period: May

Propagation: By softwood cuttings

Uses: Walls; fences; tree trunks

Notes: Clings to almost any surface. Needs a couple years to establish roots. Requires rich, well-drained soil. Attractive on brick wall.

Related Species: *Schizophragma hydrangeoides* (Japanese hydrangea vine), similar to above but with single-sepalled sterile flowers, growth habit tends to stay closer to the supporting structure, Zones 5 to 8.

IPOMOEA ALBA
Moonflower

Annual Twiner ○ ◑

Zones: —

Maximum Height: 10 to 15 feet

Appearance: Night-blooming large white funnel-shaped flowers among light green, sometimes 3-lobed leaves

Bloom Period: All summer; sweetly fragrant

Propagation: By seeds, notch or file hard seed coat before sowing, germinates in two weeks

Uses: Trellises; pergolas; lattices; fences; walls with wire grid; tall poles; posts; nice near patios, decks and doorways

Notes: Prefers hot summers. Requires rich, well-drained soil. Actually a tropical perennial. Also called *I. bona-nox* and *Calonyction aculeatum*.

IPOMOEA QUAMOCLIT
Cypress Vine

Tender Annual Twiner ○ ◑ ◐

Zones: —

Maximum Height: 20 feet

Appearance: Small tubular starlike scarlet flowers among fine pinnately cut leaves

Bloom Period: All summer

Propagation: By seeds, notch or file hard seed coat

Uses: Trellises; pergolas; latices; fences; walls with wire grid, tall poles; posts

Notes: Prefers hot summers, but tolerates some shade. Requires well-drained soil. Also called *Quamoclit pennata*.

Varieties: Var. *alba*, white flowers

Related Species: I. ×*multifida* (I. ×*sloteri*, cardinal climber), similar larger flowers to 2 inches long, palmately cut leaves.

IPOMOEA TRICOLOR
Morning Glory

Tender Annual Twiner ○ ◑

Zones: —

Maximum Height: 12 to 15 feet

Appearance: Blue, pink or white funnel-shaped flowers

Bloom Period: All summer

Propagation: By seed, notch or file hard seed coat

Uses: Trellises; pergolas; lattices; fences; walls with wire grid; tall poles; posts

Notes: Flowers shrivel by evening. Watch for spider mites.

Varieties: 'Heavenly Blue', best known blue strain; 'Pearly Gates' (AAS), white; 'Scarlet Star', scarlet with white star and picotee.

JASMINUM NUDIFLORUM
Winter Jasmine

Woody Sprawler ○ ◑ ◐

Zones: 6 to 10

Maximum Height: 12 feet

Appearance: Yellow flowers along green stems, fine-textured deciduous leaves composed of three deep green leaflets

Bloom Period: Winter through early spring

Propagation: By cuttings any time or layers

Uses: Tied against walls, fences, trellises; cascading from above retaining wall.

Notes: Actually a lax shrub, but very attractive against a wall. Easy to grow with long winter flowering season in mild climates, especially with protection of a wall. Can grow in any well-drained soil; moderately drought tolerant. Thin out older wood after bloom is finished to encourage young blooming wood.

JASMINUM OFFICINALE
Poet's Jasmine

Woody Sprawler ○ ◑ ◐

Zones: 7 to 10

Maximum Height: 10 to 15 feet

Appearance: Clusters of small white flowers among semievergreen fine-textured pinnately compound leaves

Bloom Period: Summer; fragrant

Propagation: By cuttings

Uses: Trellises; pergolas; fences; walls with wire grid; tall poles; posts

Notes: Often needs to be tied in to its support. Spur prune early spring. Adaptable to many soils.

Varieties: 'Affine', pink-tinged buds; 'Grandiflorum', larger flowers; 'Aureo-variegatum' ('Aureum'), leaves with yellow blotches

LONICERA ×HECKROTTII
Goldflame Honeysuckle

Woody Twiner ○ ◐ ◖

Zones: 5 (4) to 9

Maximum Height: 10 to 12 feet

Appearance: Clusters of tubular flowers, carmine in bud, opening to cream, deciduous oval leaves

Bloom Period: Late spring to fall; fragrant at night

Propagation: By softwood cuttings or layering

Uses: Trellises; pergolas; fences; walls with wire grid; tall poles; posts

Notes: Does not reflower prolifically in shade. Adaptable; best in rich, moist, well-drained soil. A weak twiner. Watch for aphids in spring. Spur prune to main trunks in early spring, shorten long growth during summer.

LONICERA JAPONICA
Japanese Honeysuckle

Woody Twiner ○ ◐ ◖

Zones: 4 to 9

Maximum Height: 15 to 30 feet

Appearance: Creamy tubular flowers among light green, oval semievergreen leaves

Bloom Period: Late spring to fall; deliciously fragrant.

Propagation: By cuttings, layering or seeds

Uses: Trellises; pergolas; fences; walls with wire grid; tall poles; posts

Notes: The most fragrant species, useful in New England and Pacific Northwest, but in warm areas too rampant. Adapable to various soils. Has become a pest in many regions of the United States. Spur prune early spring.

Varieties: 'Halliana', very fragrant and vigorous; 'Aureo-reticulata', striking yellow-veined leaves, reddish stems, desirably less vigorous, flowers only sparsely.

LONICERA SEMPERVIRENS
Coral Honeysuckle

Woody Twiner ○ ◐ ◖

Zones: 4 to 9

Maximum Height: 15 to 30 feet

Appearance: Clusters of orange tubular flowers, followed by red berries, semievergreen oval leaves

Bloom Period: Late spring to fall

Propagation: By softwood cuttings, layering or seeds

Uses: Trellises; pergolas; fences; walls with wire grid; tall poles; posts

Notes: Attractive to hummingbirds. Watch for aphids in spring. Adaptable; best in rich, moist, well-drained soil. Spur prune to main trunks in early spring, shorten long growth during summer.

Varieties: 'Cedar Lane', resistant to aphids; 'Sulphurea' (often wrongly called 'Flava'), rich golden yellow flowers

Related Species: L. ×brownii 'Dropmore Scarlet', similar to above, but the hardiest type, developed in Manitoba, Canada; L. ×tellmanniana, hybrid with the large-flowered L. tragophylla, reddish buds open to coppery yellow flowers, useful in partial shade, which it requires, Zones 6 (5) to 9.

PARTHENOCISSUS HENRYANA
Silver Vein Creeper

Woody Clinger ◐ ◖ ●

Zones: 7 (6) to 9

Maximum Height: 25 feet

Appearance: Deciduous bluish green leaves with purple undersides, divided into five leaflets with central silver vein, red fall color; insignificant flowers followed by blue grapelike fruit in fall

Bloom Period: Spring

Propagation: By softwood cuttings

Uses: Walls; fences; tree trunks

Notes: Uniquely attractive for silver veins, which remain even with fall color. Fruit is not reliably produced. Adaptable, but prefers rich, well-drained soil. Clinging tendrils with suction cups can also adapt to twining.

Related Species: P. quinquefolia (Virginia creeper), native plant valued in New England for red fall color but too rampant for most warm-climate gardens, grows almost anywhere, Zones 3 to 9.

PARTHENOCISSUS TRICUSPIDATA
Boston Ivy, Japanese Creeper

Woody Clinger ○ ◑ ◐ ●
Zones: 4 to 8
Maximum Height: 60 feet
Appearance: Shiny, deep green, deciduous maplelike leaves, red fall color; insignificant flowers followed by bluish grapelike fruit
Bloom Period: Spring
Propagation: By softwood cuttings or seeds
Uses: Walls; fences; tree trunks
Notes: The ivy of northern Ivy League colleges. Fruit not reliably prolific. Adaptable to various soils.
Varieties: 'Lowii', small three- to seven-lobed leaves

PASSIFLORA INCARNATA
Native Passionflower, Maypop

Herbaceous Grabber ○ ◑
Zones: 7 (6) to 10
Maximum Height: 20 feet
Appearance: Lavender-blue flowers among palmately lobed leaves, followed by yellow egg-size fruits
Bloom Period: July to September
Propagation: By softwood cuttings, seeds or division of rhizomes
Uses: Trellises; pergolas; fences; walls with wire grid; tall poles; posts
Notes: The hardiest species. Dies to ground each winter. Spreading rhizomes easily controlled by pulling in North, may be troublesome in the South. Requires well-drained soil. Edible fruit. Native to southeastern United States.
Varieties: 'Alba', pure white flowers
Related Species: P. caerulea (blue passionflower), evergreen, Zones 8 to 11; 'Inncense', hybrid of *P. incarnata* bred for edible fruit with larger, more striking flowers, Zones 7 to 11.

PHASEOLUS COCCINEUS
Scarlet Runner Bean

Tender Annual Twiner ○ ◑
Zones: —
Maximum Height: 10 feet
Appearance: Spectacular clusters of scarlet pea-shaped flowers followed by long, flat, green pods among mid-green leaves
Bloom Period: All summer
Propagation: By seeds sown in place when soil is warm, germinates in 4 to 5 days
Uses: Trellises; pergolas; fences; walls with wire grid; tall poles; posts
Notes: Common in English vegetable gardens. Requires moist, rich, well-drained soil. Won't set pods above 80 ° F, so only for flowers in much of United States until fall. A tropical perennial from high elevations of South America. Roots can be stored like dahlias for winter.

TROPAEOLUM MAJUS
Tall Nasturtium

Tender Annual Grabber ○ ◑
Zones: —
Maximum Height: 8 to 12 feet
Appearance: Yellow, red, orange or cream flowers; rounded green foliage
Bloom Period: June to October; some varieties sweetly scented
Propagation: Sow seed outdoors after soil has warmed—too early and seeds rot; does not transplant well
Uses: Trellises; pergolas; fences; walls with wire grid; good fresh-cut flower
Notes: Not to be confused with dwarf nonclimbing types. Climbs by twining petioles. Flower buds and unripe seeds give peppery flavor to salads, pickles. Watch for black aphids. Grows best during cool weather, thriving in fall until frost. Requires poor well-drained soil.
Varieties: 'Fordhook Favorites', strong tall vines, single fragrant flowers, mixed colors; 'Gleam', semidwarf trailing types do not climb, 2 to 3 feet long, mixed colors.

TROPAEOLUM PEREGRINUM
Canary Vine, Canary Creeper

Tender Annual Twiner ◗ ◖

Zones: —

Maximum Height: 8 feet

Appearance: Bright yellow flowers with fringed upper petals, resembling a bird in flight, among deeply lobed, rounded leaves

Bloom Period: All summer

Propagation: By seeds

Uses: Trellises; pergolas; poles; fences; walls with wire grid

Notes: Grows poorly in hot weather, but thrives in cool climates and in autumn, until frost. Requires rich, moist, well-drained soil.

VITIS COIGNETIAE
Ornamental Grape, Glory Vine

Woody Grabber ○ ◗

Zones: 5 to 9

Maximum Height: 60 feet

Appearance: Large, dark green, rounded deciduous leaves, scarlet fall color, insignificant flowers and blue-black berries

Bloom Period: Spring

Propagation: By softwood cuttings, layers or seeds

Uses: Trellises; pergolas; fences; walls with wire grid; tall trees

Notes: The most decorative grape, particularly for fall color. Very vigorous. Adaptable. In limited space spur prune in fall or winter; spring pruning causes bleeding which is more alarming than harmful. Fruit is not edible. Prone to Japanese beetles.

WISTERIA SINENSIS
Chinese Wisteria

Woody Twiner ○ ◗

Zones: 5 to 9

Maximum Height: 25 feet

Appearance: Pendent clusters of purple, lavender or white flowers before pinnately compound light-green deciduous leaves appear

Bloom Period: April to May

Propagation: By softwood cuttings, layering, grafting or seeds.

Uses: Trellises; pergolas; fences; walls with wire grid; tall poles

Notes: Extremely vigorous, especially in the South. Adaptable to any soil, except waterlogged. In limited space prune four to five times a year, leaving only four to five basal buds, where close together, on each shoot. Strong twining trunks can easily strangle a tree. Perhaps this species is better than *W. floribunda* in limited space.

Varieties: 'Alba', white flowers

Related Species: *W. floribunda* (Japanese wisteria), longer flower clusters after leaves emerge, fragrant, Zones 4 to 9.

Encyclopedia of Flower Garden Shrubs

ABELIA × GRANDIFLORA
Glossy Abelia

○ ◑ ◐

Zones: 6 (5) to 9
Flower Garden Size: 3 to 6 feet tall; 3- to 6-foot spread
Maximum Height: 6 feet
Appearance: Dense rounded shrub with small funnel-shaped white, tinged pink flowers above small, dark, shiny green, semievergreen foliage
Bloom Period: June to frost
Propagation: By softwood cuttings or seeds
Uses: Background of bed
Notes: Prune moderately in early spring, only enough to control size and remove dead and winter damaged wood. Adaptable, prefers rich moist acid soil.
Related Species: A. ×'Edward Goucher', hybrid of above with pink flowers and smaller habit, 5 feet, Zone 6.

BERBERIS THUNBERGII
Japanese Barberry

○ ◑ ◐

Zones: 4 to 8
Flower Garden Size: 2 to 6 feet tall; 3- to 6-foot spread
Maximum Size: 6 feet
Appearance: Small green or redddish purple deciduous leaves on densely foliaged thorny shrub, small yellow flowers followed by small red berries in fall
Bloom Period: April to May
Propagation: By cuttings or seeds

Uses: Background, middle or foreground of bed, depending on variety
Notes: Only the colored foliage varieties, particularly purple, are of use in flower garden. Can be sheared or pruned to control size and density. Requires average to poor dry soils.
Varieties: Var. *atropurpurea*, tallest purple form; 'Aurea', golden foliage that withstands sun, slow growth to 3 feet; 'Crimson Pygmy', popular purple cultivar, to 2 feet; 'Rose Glow', purple form of moderate height with particularly attractive new growth, to 5 feet.

BUDDLEIA DAVIDII
Butterfly Bush, Summer Lilac

○ ◑

Zones: 5 to 9
Flower Garden Size: 5 to 10 feet tall; 5- to 8-foot spread
Maximum Height: 15 feet
Appearance: Loose, stiff shrub with spikes of lavender, purple, pink or white flowers, light green deciduous foliage.
Bloom Period: July to frost
Propagation: By softwood cuttings or seeds
Uses: Background of bed, good fresh-cut flower
Notes: Prune to 6 to 12 inches in early spring. Northern winters kill stems to ground like a perennial. Deadheading and summer pruning improves size of repeat flower spikes. Attracts numerous butterflies. Best in rich, well-drained soil.
Varieties: 'Black Knight', dark purple; 'Charming', large pink spikes; 'Empire Blue', violet-blue; 'Nanho Blue', lavender-blue, small gray-green fo-

liage, compact habit; 'Nanho Purple', purple, small gray-green foliage, compact spreading habit; 'Royal Red', wine red; 'White Profusion', white
Related Species: 'Lochinch', hybrid with gray foliage, lavender-blue flowers with orange eye and shorter habit, 3 to 5 feet, Zones 7 to 9

CARYOPTERIS × CLANDONENSIS
Bluebeard

○ ◑

Zones: 5 to 9
Flower Garden Size: 2 feet tall; 2-foot spread
Maximum Height: 2 to 3 feet
Appearance: Rounded shrub with spikes of blue flowers, small-toothed deciduous leaves
Bloom Period: August to September
Propagation: By softwood cuttings
Uses: Middle or foreground of bed
Notes: Prune to 4 to 6 inches in early spring. Requires well-drained soil.
Varieties: 'Blue Mist', light blue flowers; 'Dark Knight', deep blue-purple flowers, dark green foliage, upright habit; 'Longwood Blue', gray foliage

COTINUS COGGYGRIA, PURPLE-FOLIAGE FORMS
Purple Smoke Bush

○ ◑

Zones: 5 (4) to 8
Flower Garden Size: 6 to 8 feet tall; 6-foot spread
Maximum Height: 15 feet
Appearance: Deep purplish oval deciduous leaves of moderate size along upright stems
Bloom Period: June to July
Propagation: By softwood cuttings
Uses: Background of bed
Notes: Only purple foliage forms have value as flower garden shrubs and don't flower when pruned back in early spring to 6 to 12 inches. Adaptable, but prefers rich, moist, well-drained soil for best growth.
Varieties: 'Nordine', 'Notcott's Variety', 'Purpureus', 'Royal Purple' and 'Velvet Cloak' all have purple foliage. 'Velvet Cloak' is shorter and preferred in some schemes.

HIBISCUS SYRIACUS
Rose of Sharon, Shrub Althea

○ ◑ ◐

Zones: 5 to 9
Flower Garden Size: 5 to 6 feet tall; 5-foot spread
Maximum Height: 12 feet
Appearance: Upright shrub with large, wide, rounded flowers of lavender-blue to wine red or white, glossy deciduous foliage
Propagation: By softwood cuttings or seeds
Uses: Background of bed
Notes: Prune to 2 to 4 feet in early spring. Also suited to formal standards (straight single stem) in formal situations. Best with well-drained moist soil. Susceptible to Japanese beetles, but blooms well after beetles have disappeared. Often self-sows prolifically.
Varieties: 'Bluebird', lavender-blue flowers; 'Diana', pure white, seedless triploid; 'Helene', white with reddish purple center, seedless triploid.

HYDRANGEA PANICULATA
Panicle Hydrangea

○ ◑ ◐

Zones: 3 to 8
Flower Garden Size: 4 to 6 feet tall; 5-foot spread
Maximum Height: 20 feet
Appearance: Large, heavy pyramidal flower cluster on arching plants with dark-green deciduous foliage
Bloom Period: July to August
Propagation: By softwood cuttings or seeds
Uses: Background of bed; good dried flowers
Notes: Prune to 2 to 4 feet in early spring. Adaptable, but best in rich, well-drained soil. Flower heads are very coarse and a challenge to integrate into designs. Also suited to formal standards (straight single stem) in formal situations.
Varieties: 'Grandiflora', the ubiquitous "Peegee Hydrangea" with flower heads composed mostly of sterile flowers, striking, heavy and oversize; 'Floribunda', 'Praecox' and 'Tardiva' are less heavy looking as they have fewer sterile flowers, 'Tardiva' flowers in late summer.

HYDRANGEA QUERCIFOLIA
Oak-leafed Hydrangea

◗ ◖

Zones: 6 (5) to 9
Flower Garden Size: 4 to 6 feet tall; 3- to 5-foot spread
Maximum Height: 8 feet
Appearance: Large pyramidal heads of white flowers above large, deeply cut, oaklike deciduous foliage
Bloom Period: June to July
Propagation: By softwood cuttings, layers or seeds
Uses: Background of bed; fresh-cut or dried flower
Notes: Bold and exciting in the right location, but very coarse texture. Seems to grow almost anywhere, but prefers moist, well-drained soil. Will not flower if pruned in spring, thin out tall stems after flowers fade.
Varieties: 'Snow Queen', more large, sterile flowers than the species but heads still hold up straight; 'Snowflake', double flowers offer extended bloom into August, producing new petals on top of old ones but older petals look messy close-up.

LAGERSTROEMIA INDICA
Crape Myrtle

○ ◗

Zones: 7 (6) to 9
Flower Garden Size: 4 to 6 feet tall; 4-foot spread
Maximum Height: 25 feet
Appearance: Large clusters of red, pink, lavender, purple or white flowers on upright shrubs with small deciduous leaves
Bloom Period: August to September
Propagation: By softwood cuttings or seeds
Uses: Background of bed
Notes: Petals resemble bits of crepe paper. For flower garden, prune to ground in early spring, will behave as herbaceous perennial in North (Zone 6).

POTENTILLA FRUTICOSA
Bush Cinquefoil

○ ◗ ◖

Zones: 2 to 7
Flower Garden Size: 1 to 2 feet tall; 2-foot spread
Maximum Height: 4 feet
Appearance: Small rounded flowers on low mounded bush with small, palmately compound, deciduous leaves
Bloom Period: June to frost
Propagation: By softwood cuttings or seeds
Uses: Middle or foreground of bed
Notes: Blooms best where summers are cool, but tolerates a variety of growing conditions. Adaptable, but prefers rich, well-drained soil. Prune back about one-third and remove older stems in early spring.
Varieties: Many varieties, but some of the best are 'Abbotswood', white, Zones 5 to 7; 'Goldfinger', bright yellow; 'Primrose Beauty', light yellow; 'Royal Flush', rosy pink, fading to yellow in hot weather.

SAMBUCUS NIGRA 'AUREA'
Golden European Elder

○ ◗

Zones: 5 to 8?
Flower Garden Size: 6 to 8 feet tall; 6-foot spread
Maximum Height: 20 feet
Appearance: Golden, pinnately compound, deciduous leaves on upright and arching shrub; not flowering when cut back in spring.
Bloom Period: June
Propagation: By softwood and hardwood cuttings
Uses: Background of bed
Notes: Bright, golden foliage that does not fade or sunburn. Needs bright sun to color best. Rich, moist, well-drained soil for best growth. Prune to about 2 feet in early spring.
Related Species: S. racemosa 'Plumosa-aurea' (golden cut-leaf elder), a striking golden foliage but color tends to fade to green by midsummer and may sunburn in hot climates.

SORBARIA AITCHISONII
Kashmir False Spirea

○ ◗ ◖

Zones: 5 (6) to 8?
Flower Garden Size: 6 feet tall; 6-foot spread
Maximum Height: 9 feet
Appearance: White plumes above pinnately compound deciduous foliage; resembles a tall shrubby astilbe
Bloom Period: July to August

Propagation: By softwood and hardwood cuttings, division or seeds

Uses: Background of bed

Notes: Only for the large border, but spectacular in late summer. Prune severely to about 2 feet in early spring. Adapable.

Related Species: S. *arborea* (tree false spirea), similar to above, but hardier and potentially taller if not pruned back, Zones 5 to 8?; S. *sorbifolia* (Ural false-spirea), not recommended because of the propensity of running suckers, Zones 3 to 7.

SPIRAEA ×BUMALDA
Bumald Spirea

○ ◐

Zones: 3 to 8

Flower Garden Size: 2 to 3 feet tall; 2- to 3-foot spread

Maximum Height: 5 feet

Appearance: Deep pink, flat-headed flower clusters on bushy plants with green deciduous leaves, often variegated pink and cream

Bloom Period: June to August

Propagation: By cuttings or division

Uses: Middle to foreground of bed

Notes: Blooms on current season's wood, so can be pruned severely in early spring. If cut to ground, will behave as a perennial and bloom later in summer. Adaptable to most soils with adequate drainage.

Varieties: 'Anthony Waterer', common in old gardens, carmine-pink flowers, foliage often variegated with pink and cream, maximum height 2 to 3 feet; 'Froebelii', taller, with crimson flowers, not variegated; 'Gold Flame', shades of copper and orange on spring foliage, yellowish foliage continues through summer in cool climates, green where summers are hot, red and yellow fall color, not variegated.

VITEX AGNUS-CASTUS
Chaste tree

○ ◐

Zones: 7 (6) to 9

Flower Garden Size: 4 to 5 feet tall; 4-foot spread

Maximum Height: 20 feet

Appearance: Spikes of lavender-blue (or white) flowers above palmately compound, deciduous foliage on stiff upright stems

Bloom Period: July to September

Propagation: By softwood cuttings or seeds

Uses: Background of bed

Notes: Likes hot climates. Prune to about a foot high in early spring. May winterkill to ground in the North. Adaptable, but prefers well-drained, rich, moist soil.

Varieties: Var. *latifolia*, supposed hardier and more vigorous; 'Silver Spire', white flowers

Related Species: V. *negundo*, less showy flowers, hardier, Zones 6 (5) to 9

Bloom Seasons

PERENNIALS, BIENNIALS, HARDY
BULBS, FLOWER GARDEN SHRUBS
AND VINES BY MONTH AND COLOR

January to February

YELLOW
Crocus chrysanthus
Eranthis hyemalis
Jasminum nudiflorum

BLUE
Crocus chrysanthus

WHITE/CREAM
Crocus chrysanthus
Galanthus nivalis

GREEN
Helleborus foetidus

March

RED
Tulipa hybrids

ORANGE
Narcissus hybrids
Tulipa hybrids

YELLOW
Crocus chrysanthus
Crocus 'Yellow Mammoth'
Epimedium grandiflorum 'Harold Epstein'
Eranthis hyemalis
Gelsemium sempervirens
Jasminum nudiflorum
Narcissus hybrids
Tulipa hybrids

SALMON/APRICOT
Tulipa hybrids

PINK
Anemone blanda
Epimedium grandiflorum 'Rose Queen'
Helleborus orientalis
Narcissus hybrids
Tulipa hybrids

LAVENDER/MAUVE
Crocus tommasinianus
Epimedium grandiflorum
Tulipa hybrids

PURPLE
Crocus vernus
Helleborus orientalis
Tulipa hybrids

BLUE
Anemone blanda
Crocus chrysanthus
Scilla sibirica

WHITE/CREAM
Anemone blanda
Crocus chrysanthus
Crocus vernus
Epimedium grandiflorum 'White Queen'
Galanthus nivalis
Helleborus niger
Helleborus orientalis
Leucojum vernum

Narcissus hybrids
Scilla sibirica
Tulipa hybrids

GREEN
Helleborus foetidus

April

RED
Anemone coronaria
Bellis perennis
Fritillaria imperialis
Primula ×*polyanthus*
Tulipa hybrids

ORANGE
Epimedium ×*warleyense*
Fritillaria imperialis
Narcissus hybrids
Primula ×*polyanthus*
Tulipa hybrids

YELLOW
Crocus chrysanthus
Crocus 'Yellow Mammoth'
Doronicum caucasicum
Epimedium grandiflorum 'Harold Epstein'
Epimedium ×*versicolor*
Fritillaria imperialis
Gelsemium sempervirens
Geum 'Georgenburg'
Hyacinthus orientalis
Lamiastrum galeobdalon 'Herman's Pride'

Primula ×*polyanthus*
Tulipa hybrids

SALMON/APRICOT

Hyacinthus orientalis
Primula ×*polyanthus*
Tulipa hybrids

PINK

Anemone blanda
Anemone coronaria
Bellis perennis
Bergenia cordifolia
Chionodoxa luciliae 'Pink Giant'
Dicentra eximia
Epimedium grandiflorum 'Rose
  Queen'
Helleborus orientalis
Hyacinthus orientalis
Lamium maculatum 'Beacon
  Silver'
Narcissus hybrids
Phlox subulata
Primula ×*polyanthus*
Pulmonaria rubra
Pulmonaria saccharata
Tulipa hybrids
Wisteria floribunda
Wisteria sinensis

LAVENDER/MAUVE

Epimedium grandiflorum
Epimedium ×*youngianum*
  'Roseum'
Hyacinthus orientalis
Tulipa hybrids
Wisteria floribunda
Wisteria sinensis

PURPLE

Crocus vernus
Fritillaria meleagris
Helleborus orientalis
Hyacinthus orientalis
Primula ×*polyanthus*
Tulipa hybrids
Vinca minor
Wisteria floribunda
Wisteria sinensis

BLUE

Anemone blanda
Anemone coronaria
Brunnera macrophylla
Chionodoxa luciliae
Crocus chrysanthus
Hyacinthus orientalis
Mertensia virginica
Muscari armeniacum
Phlox subulata
Primula ×*polyanthus*
Pulmonaria angustifolia
Pulmonaria saccharata
Scilla sibirica
Vinca minor 'La Grave'

WHITE/CREAM

Anemone blanda
Anemone coronaria
Asperula odorata
Bellis perennis
Bergenia cordifolia
Chionodoxa luciliae alba
Clematis armandii
Crocus chrysanthus
Crocus vernus
Dicentra eximia alba
Epimedium grandiflorum 'White
  Queen'
Epimedium ×*youngianum*
  'Niveum'
Epimedium ×*youngianum*
  'Yenomoto'
Fritillaria meleagris alba
Helleborus niger
Helleborus orientalis
Hyacinthus orientalis
Lamium maculatum 'White
  Nancy'
Leucojum aestivum
Leucojum vernum
Muscari botryoides 'Album'
Narcissus hybrids
Pachysandra terminalis
Phlox subulata
Primula ×*polyanthus*
Pulmonaria saccharata 'Sissingh-
  urst White'

Sanguinaria canadensis
Scilla sibirica alba
Tulipa hybrids
Vinca minor 'Miss Jekyll'
Wisteria floribunda
Wisteria sinensis

GREEN

Helleborus foetidus

May

RED

Anemone coronaria
Aquilegia, long-spurred
  hybrids
Bellis perennis
Chrysanthemum coccineum
Geum quellyon
Lilium, Asiatic hybrids
Lonicera ×*brownii* 'Dropmore
  Scarlet'
Paeonia lactiflora
Papaver atlanticum
Papaver orientale
Primula japonica
Primula ×*polyanthus*
Tulipa hybrids

ORANGE

Geum ×*borisii*
Geum 'Georgenburg'
Geum quellyon
Iris, bearded hybrids
Lilium, Asiatic hybrids
Lonicera sempervirens
Lychnis ×*arkwrightii*
Papaver atlanticum
Papaver orientale
Primula ×*polyanthus*
Tulipa hybrids

YELLOW

Aquilegia, long-spurred
  hybrids
Chrysogonum virginianum
Coreopsis grandiflora
Doronicum caucasicum

Gelsemium sempervirens
Geum quellyon
Iris, bearded hybrids
Iris xiphium hybrids
Lamiastrum galeobdalon 'Herman's Pride'
Lilium, Asiatic hybrids
Lonicera sempervirens 'Sulphurea'
Lonicera × tellmanniana
Primula × polyanthus
Symphytum grandiflorum
Tulipa hybrids

SALMON/APRICOT
Aquilegia, long-spurred hybrids
Dianthus × allwoodii
Iris, bearded hybrids
Lilium, Asiatic hybrids
Papaver orientale
Primula × polyanthus
Tulipa hybrids

PINK
Anemone coronaria
Ajuga reptans 'Pink Spire'
Aquilegia, long-spurred hybrids
Aquilegia vulgaris
Bellis perennis
Bergenia cordifolia
Chrysanthemum coccineum
Clematis macropetala 'Markham's Pink'
Clematis montana
Convallaria majalis 'Rosea'
Dianthus × allwoodii
Dianthus plumarius
Dicentra spectabilis
Endymion hispanicus
Geranium endressii
Geranium macrorrhizum
Geranium maculatum
Geranium sanguineum
Heuchera sanguinea
Iris, bearded hybrids
Iris sibirica hybrids

Lamium maculatum 'Beacon Silver'
Lilium, Asiatic hybrids
Lonicera × heckrottii
Paeonia lactiflora
Papaver orientale
Phlox stolonifera 'Pink Ridge'
Phlox subulata
Primula japonica
Primula × polyanthus
Pulmonaria rubra
Pulmonaria saccharata
Rodgersia pinnata 'Superba'
Tulipa hybrids
Wisteria floribunda
Wisteria sinensis

LAVENDER/MAUVE
Allium aflatunense
Aquilegia, long-spurred hybrids
Iris, bearded hybrids
Lilium, Asiatic hybrids
Tulipa hybrids
Wisteria floribunda
Wisteria sinensis

PURPLE
Allium 'Purple Sensation'
Aquilegia, long-spurred hybrids
Aquilegia vulgaris
Iris, bearded hybrids
Iris sibirica hybrids
Iris xiphium hybrids
Lunaria annua
Phlox stolonifera 'Sherwood Purple'
Primula × polyanthus
Tulipa hybrids
Vinca minor
Wisteria floribunda
Wisteria sinensis

BLUE
Anemone coronaria
Ajuga reptans
Ajuga pyramidalis

Amsonia tabernaemontani
Anchusa azurea
Aquilegia flabellata
Aquilegia, long-spurred hybrids
Aquilegia vulgaris
Brunnera macrophylla
Camassia leichtlinii 'Blue Danube'
Centaurea montana
Clematis macropetala
Endymion hispanicus
Iris, bearded hybrids
Iris cristata
Iris sibirica hybrids
Iris tectorum
Iris xiphium hybrids
Mertensia virginica
Muscari armeniacum
Phlox stolonifera 'Blue Ridge'
Phlox subulata
Polemonium reptans
Primula × polyanthus
Pulmonaria angustifolia
Pulmonaria saccharata
Veronica × 'Goodness Grows'
Vinca minor 'La Grave'

WHITE/CREAM
Actinidia kolomikta
Ajuga reptans 'Alba'
Anemone coronaria
Aquilegia flabellata
Aquilegia vulgaris
Asperula odorata
Bellis perennis
Bergenia cordifolia
Camassia leichtlinii
Chrysanthemum coccineum
Clematis armandii
Clematis montana
Convallaria majalis
Dianthus × allwoodii
Dianthus plumarius
Dicentra spectabilis 'Alba'
Endymion hispanicus
Geranium macrorrhizum 'Album'

Geranium maculatum albiflorum
Geranium sanguineum 'Album'
Heuchera sanguinea
Hydrangea anomala petiolaris
Iris, bearded hybrids
Iris cristata 'Alba'
Iris sibirica hybrids
Iris tectorum album
Iris xiphium hybrids
Lamium maculatum 'White Nancy'
Leucojum aestivum
Lilium, Asiatic hybrids
Lonicera japonica
Lunaria annua
Muscari botryoides 'Album'
Pachysandra terminalis
Paeonia lactiflora
Papaver orientale
Phlox divaricata 'Fuller's White'
Phlox stolonifera 'Alba'
Phlox subulata
Polygonatum biflorum
Primula japonica
Primula ×*polyanthus*
Pulmonaria saccharata 'Sissinghurst White'
Rodgersia aesculifolia
Rodgersia pinnata
Rodgersia podophylla
Rodgersia sambucifolia
Smilacina racemosa
Tiarella cordifolia
Tiarella wherryi
Tulipa hybrids
Vancouveria hexandra
Vinca minor 'Miss Jekyll'
Wisteria floribunda
Wisteria sinensis

June

RED
Achillea Galaxy Hybrids
Aquilegia, long-spurred hybrids
Astilbe ×*arendsii*

Bellis perennis
Chrysanthemum coccineum
Clematis hybrids
Dianthus barbatus
Gaillardia ×*grandiflora*
Geum quellyon
Hemerocallis hybrids
Lilium Asiatic hybrids
Lonicera ×*brownii* 'Dropmore Scarlet'
Lychnis chalcedonica
Monarda didyma
Paeonia lactiflora
Papaver atlanticum
Papaver orientale
Penstemon barbatus
Potentilla thurberi
Primula japonica
Tropaeolum majus

ORANGE
Achillea Galaxy Hybrids
Geum ×*borisii*
Geum quellyon
Iris, bearded hybrids
Hemerocallis hybrids
Kniphofia hybrids
Lilium, Asiatic hybrids
Lilium Aurelian, Trumpet and Sunburst hybrids
Lonicera sempervirens
Lychnis ×*arkwrightii*
Papaver atlanticum
Papaver orientale
Tropaeolum majus

YELLOW
Achillea 'Coronation Gold'
Achillea Galaxy Hybrids
Achillea ×'Moonshine'
Aquilegia, long-spurred hybrids
Chrysogonum virginianum
Coreopsis grandiflora
Coreopsis verticillata
Digitalis grandiflora
Gaillardia ×*grandiflora*

Geum quellyon
Heliopsis scabra
Hemerocallis hybrids
Iris, bearded hybrids
Iris xiphium hybrids
Kniphofia hybrids
Lilium, Asiatic hybrids
Lilium, Aurelian, Trumpet and Sunburst hybrids
Lonicera sempervirens 'Sulphurea'
Lonicera ×*tellmanniana*
Lupinus Russell hybrids
Oenothera tetragona
Potentilla fruticosa
Thalictrum speciosissimum
Tricyrtis latifolia
Tropaeolum majus
Verbascum bombyciferum

SALMON/APRICOT
Achillea Galaxy Hybrids
Dianthus ×*allwoodii*
Hemerocallis hybrids
Iris, bearded hybrids
Lilium, Asiatic hybrids
Lilium, Aurelian, Trumpet and Sunburst hybrids
Papaver orientale

PINK
Abelia ×'Edward Goucher'
Achillea Galaxy Hybrids
Ajuga reptans 'Pink Spire'
Aquilegia, long-spurred hybrids
Aquilegia vulgaris
Astilbe ×*arendsii*
Bellis perennis
Chrysanthemum coccineum
Clematis 'Duchess of Albany'
Clematis hybrids
Convallaria majalis 'Rosea'
Dianthus ×*allwoodii*
Dianthus barbatus
Dianthus plumarius
Dicentra spectabilis

Dictamnus albus purpureus
Digitalis ×*mertonensis*
Digitalis purpurea
Filipendula palmata
Filipendula purpurea
Filipendula rubra
Geranium endressii
Geranium sanguineum
Gypsophila paniculata
Hemerocallis hybrids
Heuchera sanguinea
Iris, bearded hybrids
Iris kaempferi
Iris sibirica hybrids
Lilium, Asiatic hybrids
Lilium, Aurelian, Trumpet
   and Sunburst hybrids
Linaria purpurea
Lonicera ×*heckrottii*
Lupinus Russell hybrids
Monarda didyma
Paeonia lactiflora
Papaver orientale
Penstemon barbatus
Potentilla fruticosa
Primula japonica
Rodgersia pinnata 'Superba'
Silene armeria
Spiraea ×*bumalda*
Tradescantia ×*andersoniana*

LAVENDER/MAUVE
Acanthus spinosus
Allium christophii
Astilbe ×*arendsii*
Clematis hybrids
Delphinium elatum hybrids
Digitalis purpurea
Hemerocallis hybrids
Iris, bearded hybrids
Iris kaempferi
Lilium, Asiatic hybrids
Lilium, Aurelian, Trumpet
   and Sunburst hybrids
Linaria purpurea
Monarda didyma
Stachys byzantina

PURPLE
Allium giganteum
Aquilegia, long-spurred
   hybrids
Aquilegia vulgaris
Campanula glomerata
Clematis hybrids
Clematis viticella
Delphinium elatum hybrids
Hemerocallis hybrids
Hosta hybrids
Iris, bearded hybrids
Iris kaempferi
Iris sibirica hybrids
Iris xiphium hybrids
Lunaria annua
Lupinus Russell hybrids
Monarda didyma
Onopordum nervosum
Salvia ×*superba*

BLUE
Ajuga reptans
Amsonia tabernaemontani
Anchusa azurea
Aquilegia flabellata
Aquilegia, long-spurred
   hybrids
Aquilegia vulgaris
Baptisia australis
Campanula persicifolia
Centaurea montana
Delphinium ×*belladonna*
Delphinium elatum hybrids
Geranium himalayense
Geranium 'Johnson's Blue'
Iris, bearded hybrids
Iris kaempferi
Iris sibirica hybrids
Iris tectorum
Iris xiphium hybrids
Lupinus Russell hybrids
Nepeta ×*faassenii*
Nepeta mussinii
Nepeta sibirica
Phlox divaricata
Polemonium caeruleum
Tradescantia ×*andersoniana*

Veronica incana
Veronica ×'Goodness Grows'
Veronica spicata

WHITE/CREAM
Abelia ×*grandiflora*
Ajuga reptans 'Alba'
Aquilegia flabellata
Aquilegia, long-spurred
   hybrids
Aquilegia vulgaris
Aruncus aethusifolia
Aruncus dioicus
Astermoea mongolica
Astilbe ×*arendsii*
Bellis perennis
Campanula glomerata
Campanula persicifolia
Chrysanthemum coccineum
Chrysanthemum parthenium
Chrysanthemum ×*superbum*
Clematis hybrids
Convallaria majalis
Crambe cordifolia
Delphinium elatum hybrids
Dianthus ×*allwoodii*
Dianthus barbatus
Dianthus plumarius
Dicentra spectabilis alba
Dictamnus albus
Digitalis purpurea
Filipendula ulmaria
Gaura lindheimeri
Geranium sanguineum 'Album'
Gypsophila paniculata
Hemerocallis hybrids
Heuchera sanguinea
Hosta hybrids
Hydrangea quercifolia
Iris, bearded hybrids
Iris kaempferi
Iris sibirica hybrids
Iris tectorum album
Iris xiphium hybrids
Jasminum officinale
Kniphofia hybrids
Lilium, Asiatic hybrids

Lilium, Aurelian, Trumpet
and Sunburst hybrids
Lonicera japonica
Lunaria annua
Monarda didyma
Paeonia lactiflora
Papaver orientale
Phlox divaricata 'Fuller's
White'
Polygonatum biflorum
Potentilla fruticosa
Primula japonica
Rodgersia aesculifolia
Rodgersia pinnata
Rodgersia podophylla
Rodgersia sambucifolia
Schizophragma hydrangeoides
Tiarella cordifolia
Tiarella wherryi
Tradescantia × *andersoniana*
Vancouveria hexandra

GREEN
Alchemilla mollis

GRASSES
Festuca amethystina
Festuca ovina glauca
Helictotrichon sempervirens

July

RED
Achillea Galaxy Hybrids
Althaea rosea
Asclepias tuberosa
Astilbe × *arendsii*
Buddleia davidii 'Royal Red'
Campsis × *tagliabuana* 'Madame Galen'
Chrysanthemum coccineum
Clematis hybrids
Crocosmia hybrids
Gaillardia × *grandiflora*
Hemerocallis hybrids
Ipomoea × *multifida*
Ipomoea quamoclit
Lilium, Asiatic hybrids

Lilium, Oriental hybrids
Lobelia cardinalis
Lonicera × *brownii* 'Dropmore
Scarlet'
Lychnis chalcedonica
Monarda didyma
Penstemon barbatus
Phaseolus coccineus
Phlox paniculata
Potentilla thurberi
Tropaeolum majus

ORANGE
Achillea Galaxy Hybrids
Asclepias tuberosa
Campsis radicans
Crocosmia hybrids
Hemerocallis hybrids
Kniphofia hybrids
Lilium, Asiatic hybrids
Lilium, Aurelian, Trumpet
and Sunburst hybrids
Lonicera sempervirens
Phlox paniculata
Tropaeolum majus

YELLOW
Achillea 'Coronation Gold'
Achillea Galaxy Hybrids
Achillea 'Moonshine'
Asclepias tuberosa
Campsis radicans 'Flava'
Clematis tangutica
Coreopsis grandiflora
Coreopsis verticillata
Crocosmia hybrids
Digitalis grandiflora
Gaillardia × *grandiflora*
Heliopsis scabra
Hemerocallis hybrids
Kniphofia hybrids
Ligularia dentata
Ligularia hodgsonii
Ligularia 'The Rocket'
Lilium, Asiatic hybrids
Lilium, Aurelian, Trumpet
and Sunburst hybrids

Lonicera sempervirens
'Sulphurea'
Lonicera × *tellmanniana*
Oenothera tetragona
Potentilla fruticosa
Rudbeckia fulgida
Rudbeckia laciniata
Solidago 'Peter Pan'
Tricyrtis latifolia
Tropaeolum majus
Tropaeolum peregrinum
Verbascum bombyciferum

SALMON/APRICOT
Achillea Galaxy hybrids
Dianthus × *allwoodii*
Hemerocallis hybrids
Lilium Asiatic hybrids
Lilium, Aurelian, Trumpet
and Sunburst hybrids
Phlox paniculata

PINK
Abelia × 'Edward Goucher'
Achillea Galaxy Hybrids
Althaea rosea
Astilbe × *arendsii*
Astilbe taquetii 'Superba'
Begonia grandis
Buddleia davidii 'Charming'
Chrysanthemum coccineum
Clematis 'Duchess of Albany'
Clematis hybrids
Crinum × *powellii*
Delphinium elatum hybrids
Dianthus × *allwoodii*
Digitalis × *mertonensis*
Echinacea purpurea
Geranium sanguineum
Gypsophila paniculata
Hemerocallis hybrids
Heuchera sanguinea
Ipomoea tricolor
Iris kaempferi
Lilium, Asiatic hybrids
Lilium, Aurelian, Trumpet
and Sunburst hybrids
Lilium, Oriental hybrids

Linaria purpurea
Lobelia cardinalis
Lonicera × heckrottii
Lythrum salicaria
Macleaya microcarpa 'Coral
  plume'
Monarda didyma
Penstemon barbatus
Phlox paniculata
Platycodon grandiflorus
Potentilla fruticosa
Sanguisorba obtusa
Silene armeria
Spiraea × bumalda
Tradescantia × andersoniana

LAVENDER/MAUVE

Acanthus spinosus
Astilbe chinensis 'Pumila'
Buddleia davidii
Buddleia 'Lochinch'
Clematis hybrids
Delphinium elatum hybrids
Hemerocallis hybrids
Hosta hybrids
Iris kaempferi
Liatris spicata
Lilium, Asiatic hybrids
Lilium, Aurelian, Trumpet
  and Sunburst hybrids
Linaria purpurea
Monarda didyma
Phlox paniculata
Stachys byzantina
Thalictrum rochebrunianum
Tricyrtis formosana amethystina

PURPLE

Allium giganteum
Buddleia davidii 'Black Knight'
Campanula glomerata
Clematis viticella
Clematis hybrids
Cobaea scandens
Delphinium elatum hybrids
Dolichos lablab
Hemerocallis hybrids
Hosta hybrids

Iris kaempferi
Liatris spicata
Lythrum salicaria
Monarda didyma
Onopordum nervosum
Salvia × superba

BLUE

Aster × frikartii
Campanula persicifolia
Centaurea montana
Delphinium × belladonna
Delphinium elatum hybrids
Echinops 'Taplow Blue'
Eryngium alpinum
Hibiscus syriacus 'Bluebird'
Ipomoea tricolor
Iris kaempferi
Lobelia siphilitica
Nepeta × faassenii
Nepeta mussinii
Nepeta sibirica
Passiflora incarnata
Perovskia atriplicifolia
Platycodon grandiflorus
Salvia guaranitica
Tradescantia × andersoniana
Veronica incana
Veronica × 'Goodness Grows'
Veronica spicata
Vitex agnus-castus

WHITE/CREAM

Abelia × grandiflora
Althaea rosea
Aruncus aethusifolia
Aruncus dioicus
Astermoea mongolica
Astilbe × arendsii
Begonia grandis alba
Buddleia davidii 'White
  Profusion'
Campanula glomerata 'Alba'
Campanula persicifolia
Chrysanthemum coccineum
Chrysanthemum parthenium
Chrysanthemum × superbum
Cimicifuga racemosa

Clematis hybrids
Cobaea scandens 'Alba'
Crinum × powellii 'Album'
Delphinium elatum hybrids
Dianthus × allwoodii
Echinacea purpurea 'White
  Lustre'
Eryngium giganteum
Filipendula ulmaria
Galtonia candicans
Gaura lindheimeri
Geranium sanguineum 'Album'
Gypsophila paniculata
Hemerocallis hybrids
Heuchera sanguinea
Hibiscus syriacus 'Diana'
Hosta hybrids
Hydrangea paniculata
Hydrangea quercifolia
Ipomoea alba
Ipomoea quamoclit alba
Ipomoea tricolor
Iris kaempferi
Jasminum officinale
Kniphofia hybrids
Liatris spicata
Lilium, Asiatic hybrids
Lilium, Aurelian, Trumpet
  and Sunburst hybrids
Lilium, Oriental hybrids
Lobelia cardinalis alba
Lobelia siphilitica alba
Lonicera japonica
Lysimachia clethroides
Macleaya cordata
Monarda didyma
Phlox paniculata
Platycodon grandiflorus albus
Potentilla fruticosa
Sorbaria aitchisonii
Sorbaria arborea
Tradescantia × andersoniana
Vitex agnus-castus 'White
  Spire'

GREEN

Alchemilla mollis

GRASSES
Festuca amethystina
Festuca ovina glauca
Helictotrichon sempervirens
Imperata cylindrica 'Red Baron'

August

RED
Achillea Galaxy Hybrids
Althaea rosea
Asclepias tuberosa
Buddleia davidii 'Royal Red'
Campsis ×*tagliabuana* 'Madame Galen'
Chrysanthemum ×*morifolium*
Crocosmia hybrids
Gaillardia ×*grandiflora*
Helenium autumnale
Ipomoea ×*multifida*
Ipomoea quamoclit
Lagerstroemia indica
Lilium, Oriental hybrids
Lobelia cardinalis
Lonicera ×*brownii* 'Dropmore Scarlet'
Phaseolus coccineus
Phlox paniculata
Tropaeolum majus

ORANGE
Achillea Galaxy Hybrids
Asclepias tuberosa
Campsis radicans
Chrysanthemum ×*morifolium*
Crocosmia hybrids
Helenium autumnale
Hemerocallis hybrids
Kniphofia hybrids
Lonicera sempervirens
Phlox paniculata
Tropaeolum majus

YELLOW
Achillea 'Coronation Gold'
Achillea Galaxy Hybrids
Achillea 'Moonshine'
Asclepias tuberosa

Campsis radicans 'Flava'
Chrysanthemum ×*morifolium*
Clematis tangutica
Coreopsis grandiflora
Coreopsis tripteris
Coreopsis verticillata
Crocosmia hybrids
Gaillardia ×*grandiflora*
Helenium autumnale
Heliopsis scabra
Hemerocallis hybrids
Kirengeshoma koreana
Kniphofia hybrids
Lonicera sempervirens 'Sulphurea'
Lonicera ×*tellmanniana*
Potentilla fruticosa
Rudbeckia fulgida
Rudbeckia laciniata
Solidago 'Peter Pan'
Tropaeolum majus
Tropaeolum peregrinum

SALMON/APRICOT
Achillea Galaxy Hybrids
Chrysanthemum ×*morifolium*
Dianthus ×*allwoodii*
Phlox paniculata

PINK
Abelia ×'Edward Goucher'
Achillea Galaxy Hybrids
Althaea rosea
Anemone hupehensis
Aster novae-angliae
Aster novi-belgii
Begonia grandis
Boltonia asteroides 'Pink Beauty'
Buddleia davidii 'Charming'
Chelone lyonii
Chrysanthemum ×*morifolium*
Crinum ×*powellii*
Cyclamen hederifolium
Dianthus ×*allwoodii*
Dianthus superbus longicalycinus
Echinacea purpurea
Eupatorium purpureum

Geranium sanguineum
Gypsophila paniculata
Ipomoea tricolor
Lagerstroemia indica
Lilium, Oriental hybrids
Linaria purpurea
Lobelia cardinalis
Lonicera ×*heckrottii*
Lycoris squamigera
Lythrum salicaria
Phlox paniculata
Physostegia virginiana
Platycodon grandiflorus
Potentilla fruticosa
Sanguisorba obtusa
Sedum ×'Autumn Joy'
Spiraea ×*bumalda*
Tradescantia ×*andersoniana*

LAVENDER/MAUVE
Aster novae-angliae
Aster novi-belgii
Buddleia davidii
Buddleia 'Lochinch'
Chrysanthemum ×*morifolium*
Hosta hybrids
Lagerstroemia indica
Liatris spicata
Linaria purpurea
Phlox paniculata
Thalictrum rochebrunianum
Tricyrtis formosana amethystina

PURPLE
Aster novae-angliae
Aster novi-belgii
Buddleia davidii 'Black Knight'
Cobaea scandens
Dolichos lablab
Hosta hybrids
Lagerstroemia indica
Liatris spicata
Lythrum salicaria
Physostegia virginiana
Salvia ×*superba*
Tricyrtis dilatata

BLUE

Aconitum carmichaelii
Aster ×frikartii
Aster novae-angliae
Aster novi-belgii
Caryopteris ×clandonensis
Ceratostigma plumbaginoides
Clematis heracleifolia
Delphinium ×belladonna
Eupatorium coelestinum
Hibiscus syriacus 'Bluebird'
Ipomoea tricolor
Lobelia siphilitica
Nepeta ×faassenii
Nepeta sibirica
Passiflora incarnata
Perovskia atriplicifolia
Platycodon grandiflorus
Salvia guaranitica
Tradescantia ×andersoniana
Veronica ×'Goodness Grows'
Veronica spicata
Vitex agnus-castus

WHITE/CREAM

Abelia ×grandiflora
Althaea rosea
Artemisia lactiflora
Aster divaricatus
Aster novi-belgii
Astermoea mongolica
Begonia grandis alba
Boltonia asteroides 'Snowbank'
Buddleia davidii 'White
    Profusion'
Chrysanthemum ×morifolium
Chrysanthemum ×superbum
    'Becky'
Clematis maximowicziana
Cobaea scandens 'Alba'
Crinum ×powellii 'Album'
Cyclamen hederifolium album
Dianthus ×allwoodii
Echinacea purpurea 'White
    Lustre'
Gaura lindheimeri
Geranium sanguineum 'Album'
Gypsophila paniculata

Hibiscus syriacus 'Diana'
Hosta hybrids
Hosta plantaginea
Hydrangea paniculata
Ipomoea alba
Ipomoea quamoclit alba
Ipomoea tricolor
Jasminum officinale
Lagerstroemia indica
Liatris spicata
Lilium, Oriental hybrids
Lobelia cardinalis alba
Lobelia siphilitica alba
Lonicera japonica
Phlox paniculata
Platycodon grandiflorus albus
Physostegia virginiana
Polianthes tuberosa
Potentilla fruticosa
Sorbaria aitchisonii
Sorbaria arborea
Tradescantia ×andersoniana
Vitex agnus-castus 'White
    Spire'

GRASSES

Imperata cylindrica 'Red Baron'
Pennisetum alopecuroides

September

RED

Aster novae-angliae
Aster novi-belgii
Buddleia davidii 'Royal Red'
Campsis ×tagliabuana 'Ma-
    dame Galen'
Chrysanthemum ×morifolium
Gaillardia ×grandiflora
Helenium autumnale
Ipomoea ×multifida
Ipomoea quamoclit
Lagerstroemia indica
Lilium, Oriental hybrids
Lobelia cardinalis
Lonicera ×brownii 'Dropmore
    Scarlet'
Lycoris radiata

Phaseolus coccineus
Tropaeolum majus

ORANGE

Campsis radicans
Chrysanthemum ×morifolium
Helenium autumnale
Hemerocallis hybrids
Kniphofia 'Wayside Flame'
Lonicera sempervirens
Tropaeolum majus

YELLOW

Campsis radicans 'Flava'
Chrysanthemum ×morifolium
Coreopsis grandiflora
Coreopsis tripteris
Coreopsis verticillata
    'Moonbeam'
Gaillardia ×grandiflora
Helenium autumnale
Helianthus salicifolius
Heliopsis scabra
Hemerocallis hybrids
Kirengeshoma koreana
Kirengeshoma palmata
Lonicera sempervirens
    'Sulphurea'
Lonicera ×tellmanniana
Potentilla fruticosa
Rudbeckia fulgida
Rudbeckia laciniata
Solidago caesia
Solidago 'Peter Pan'
Solidago sempervirens
Solidago sphacelata 'Golden
    Fleece'
Sternbergia clusiana
Sternbergia lutea
Tropaeolum majus
Tropaeolum peregrinum

SALMON/APRICOT

Chrysanthemum ×morifolium

PINK

Abelia ×'Edward Goucher'
Anemone ×hybrida

Aster novae-angliae
Aster novi-belgii
Begonia grandis
Boltonia asteroides 'Pink
  Beauty'
Buddleia davidii 'Charming'
Chelone obliqua
Chrysanthemum × *morifolium*
Cimicifuga ramosa atropurpurea
Cimicifuga ramosa 'Brunette'
Colchicum species and hybrids
Crinum × *powellii*
Cyclamen hederifolium
Dianthus superbus longicalycinus
Echinacea purpurea
Eupatorium purpureum
Geranium sanguineum
Ipomoea tricolor
Lagerstroemia indica
Lilium, Oriental hybrids
Linaria purpurea
Lobelia cardinalis
Lonicera × *heckrottii*
Physostegia virginiana
Potentilla fruticosa
Sedum × 'Autumn Joy'
Sedum spectabile

LAVENDER/MAUVE
Aster novae-angliae
Aster novi-belgii
Aster tataricus
Buddleia davidii
Buddleia 'Lochinch'
Chrysanthemum × *morifolium*
Lagerstroemia indica
Linaria purpurea
Tricyrtis formosana amethystina

PURPLE
Aster novae-angliae
Aster novi-belgii
Buddleia davidii 'Black Knight'
Clematis 'Lady Betty Balfour'
Cobaea scandens
Dolichos lablab
Lagerstroemia indica

Liatris scariosa 'September
  Glory'
Liriope muscari
Physostegia virginiana
Tricyrtis dilatata
Tricyrtis formosana
Tricyrtis hirta
Tricyrtis 'Sinonome'

BLUE
Aconitum carmichaelii
Aster × *frikartii*
Aster novae-angliae
Aster novi-belgii
Caryopteris × *clandonensis*
Ceratostigma plumbaginoides
Clematis heracleifolia
Delphinium × *belladonna*
Eupatorium coelestinum
Hibiscus syriacus 'Bluebird'
Ipomoea tricolor
Lobelia siphilitica
Passiflora incarnata
Salvia guaranitica
Veronica × 'Goodness Grows'
Vitex agnus-castus

WHITE/CREAM
Abelia × *grandiflora*
Anemone × *hybrida*
Aster divaricatus
Aster novi-belgii
Astermoea mongolica
Begonia grandis alba
Boltonia asteroides 'Snowbank'
Buddleia davidii 'White
  Profusion'
Chrysanthemum × *morifolium*
Clematis maximowicziana
Cobaea scandens 'Alba'
Colchicum species and hybrids
Crinum × *powellii* 'Album'
Cyclamen hederifolium album
Echinacea purpurea 'White
  Lustre'
Gaura lindheimeri
Geranium sanguineum 'Album'

Hibiscus syriacus 'Diana'
Hosta plantaginea
Ipomoea alba
Ipomoea quamoclit alba
Ipomoea tricolor
Jasminum officinale
Lagerstroemia indica
Liatris scariosa 'White Spire'
Lilium, Oriental hybrids
Liriope muscari 'Monroe
  White'
Lobelia cardinalis alba
Lobelia siphilitica alba
Lonicera japonica
Physostegia virginiana
Polianthes tuberosa
Potentilla fruticosa
Sanguisorba canadensis
Vitex agnus-castus 'White
  Spire'

GRASSES
Hakonecloa macra 'Aureola'
Miscanthus sinensis
Pennisetum alopecuroides

October

RED
Buddleia davidii 'Royal Red'
Chrysanthemum × *morifolium*
Gaillardia × *grandiflora*
Ipomoea × *multifida*
Ipomoea quamoclit
Lonicera × *brownii* 'Dropmore
  Scarlet'
Tropaeolum majus

ORANGE
Chrysanthemum × *morifolium*
Kniphofia 'Wayside Flame'
Lonicera sempervirens
Tropaeolum majus

YELLOW
Chrysanthemum × *morifolium*
Gaillardia × *grandiflora*

Helianthus angustifolius
Helianthus salicifolius
Lonicera sempervirens
  'Sulphurea'
Lonicera × *tellmanniana*
Potentilla fruticosa
Solidago caesia
Solidago sempervirens
Solidago sphacelata 'Golden
  Fleece'
Sternbergia clusiana
Sternbergia lutea
Tropaeolum majus
Tropaeolum peregrinum

SALMON/APRICOT
  Chrysanthemum × *morifolium*

PINK
  Abelia × 'Edward Goucher'
  Anemone × *hybrida*
  Begonia grandis
  Buddleia davidii 'Charming'
  Chrysanthemum × *morifolium*
  Cimicifuga ramosa atropurpurea
  Cimicifuga ramosa 'Brunette'
  Linaria purpurea
  Lonicera × *heckrottii*
  Physostegia virginiana
  Potentilla fruticosa

LAVENDER/MAUVE
  Aster tataricus
  Buddleia davidii
  Buddleia 'Lochinch'
  Chrysanthemum × *morifolium*
  Linaria purpurea

PURPLE
  Buddleia davidii 'Black Knight'
  Cobaea scandens
  Dolichos lablab
  Physostegia virginiana
  Tricyrtis formosana
  Tricyrtis hirta
  Tricyrtis 'Sinonome'

BLUE
  Aster × *frikartii*
  Crocus speciosus
  Salvia guaranitica
  Veronica × 'Goodness Grows'

WHITE/CREAM
  Abelia × *grandiflora*
  Anemone × *hybrida*
  Astermoea mongolica
  Begonia grandis alba
  Buddleia davidii 'White
    Profusion'
  Chrysanthemum × *morifolium*
  Cimicifuga simplex
  Cobaea scandens 'Alba'

Crocus speciosus 'Albus'
Gaura lindheimeri
Ipomoea alba
Ipomoea quamoclit alba
Lonicera japonica
Physostegia virginiana
Polianthes tuberosa
Potentilla fruticosa
Sanguisorba canadensis

Grasses
  Hakonecloa macra 'Aureola'
  Miscanthus sinensis
  Pennisetum alopecuroides

November

ORANGE
  Kniphofia 'Wayside Flame'

YELLOW
  Helianthus angustifolius

LAVENDER/MAUVE
  Aster tataricus

PURPLE
  Tricyrtis formosana
  Tricyrtis 'Sinonome'

ANNUALS AND TENDER (ANNUAL) BULBS BY COOL OR WARM SEASON AND COLOR

Cool-Season Annuals
(Spring—until about June in most climates)

While many annuals have long bloom seasons, they deteriorate with the onset of warm weather and high temperatures. In climates with warm winters they can be started earlier and frost-tolerant varieties will often perform all winter long.

RED
Bellis perennis
Cheiranthus cheiri
Consolida orientalis (in hot climates)
Papaver rhoeas (in hot climates)
Phlox drummondii (in hot climates)
Viola cornuta hybrids
Viola × *wittrockiana*

ORANGE
Cheiranthus allionii
Cheiranthus cheiri
Viola × *wittrockiana*

YELLOW
Cheiranthus allionii
Cheiranthus cheiri
Viola cornuta hybrids
Viola × *wittrockiana*

SALMON/APRICOT
Papaver rhoeas (in hot climates)
Phlox drummondii (in hot climates)
Viola × *wittrockiana*

PINK
Bellis perennis
Centaurea cyanus
Cheiranthus cheiri
Consolida orientalis (in hot climates)
Lobelia erinus (in hot climates)
Myosotis sylvatica
Papaver rhoeas (in hot climates)
Phlox drummondii (in hot climates)
Viola × *wittrockiana*

LAVENDER/MAUVE
Consolida orientalis (in hot climates)
Lobularia maritima

PURPLE
Consolida orientalis (in hot climates)
Phlox drummondii (in hot climates)
Viola cornuta hybrids
Viola tricolor
Viola × *wittrockiana*

BLUE
Centaurea cyanus
Consolida orientalis (in hot climates)
Lobelia erinus (in hot climates)
Myosotis sylvatica
Nigella damascena
Viola cornuta hybrids
Viola corsica
Viola × *wittrockiana*

WHITE/CREAM
Bellis perennis
Centaurea cyanus
Cheiranthus cheiri
Consolida orientalis (in hot climates)
Lobelia erinus (in hot climates)
Lobularia maritima
Myosotis sylvatica
Nigella damascena
Papaver rhoeas (in hot climates)
Phlox drummondii (in hot climates)
Viola cornuta hybrids
Viola × *wittrockiana*

Warm-Season Annuals and Tender Bulbs (Summer—May to frost)

Most have long bloom periods, and many are suitable for late sowings for vigorous fall bloom.

RED

Amaranthus caudatus
Amaranthus hybridus erythrostachys
Antirrhinum majus
Begonia semperflorens-cultorum
Begonia × *tuberhybrida*
Canna × *generalis*
Celosia cristata plumosa
Dahlia hybrids (large flowered)
Dahlia merckii hybrids (bedding)
Dianthus barbatus
Dianthus chinensis hybrids
Gladiolus hybrids
Impatiens balsamina
Impatiens, New Guinea hybrids
Impatiens walleriana
Mirabilis jalapa
Nicotiana alata
Papaver rhoeas (in cool climates)
Pelargonium hortorum
Phlox drummondii (in cool climates)
Portulaca grandiflora
Salvia splendens
Tropaeolum majus
Verbena × *hybrida*
Zinnia elegans

ORANGE

Antirrhinum majus
Asclepias curassavica
Begonia × *tuberhybrida*
Calendula officinalis
Canna × *generalis*
Celosia cristata plumosa
Cosmos sulphureus
Dahlia hybrids (large flowered)
Dahlia merckii hybrids (bedding)
Eschscholzia californica (spring in South)
Gazania rigens
Gomphrena haageana
Helianthus hybrids
Impatiens, New Guinea hybrids
Impatiens walleriana
Portulaca grandiflora
Rudbeckia hirta
Sanvitalia procumbens 'Mandarin Orange'
Tagetes hybrids
Tithonia rotundifolia
Tropaeolum majus
Zinnia elegans

YELLOW

Abelmoschus manihot
Antirrhinum majus
Begonia × *tuberhybrida*
Calendula officinalis
Canna × *generalis*
Celosia cristata plumosa
Cosmos sulphureus
Dahlia hybrids (large flowered)
Dahlia merckii hybrids (bedding)
Eschscholzia californica (spring in South)
Gazania rigens
Gladiolus hybrids
Helianthus hybrids
Melampodium divaricatum
Mirabilis jalapa
Portulaca grandiflora
Rudbeckia hirta
Sanvitalia procumbens
Tagetes hybrids
Tropaeolum majus
Zinnia elegans

SALMON/APRICOT

Antirrhinum majus

Begonia × *tuberhybrida*
Canna × *generalis*
Celosia cristata plumosa
Dahlia hybrids (large flowered)
Dahlia merckii hybrids (bedding)
Gladiolus hybrids
Impatiens balsamina
Impatiens, New Guinea hybrids
Impatiens walleriana
Papaver rhoeas (in cool climates)
Pelargonium hortorum
Phlox drummondii (in cool climates)
Portulaca grandiflora
Salvia splendens

PINK

Antirrhinum majus
Begonia semperflorens cultorum
Begonia × *tuberhybrida*
Brassica oleracea (for fall only)
Canna × *generalis*
Catharanthus roseus
Celosia cristata plumosa
Cleome hassleriana
Cosmos bipinnatus
Dahlia hybrids (large flowered)
Dahlia merckii hybrids (bedding)
Dianthus barbatus
Dianthus chinensis hybrids
Digitalis purpurea
Gazania rigens
Gladiolus hybrids
Gomphrena globosa
Impatiens balfourii
Impatiens balsamina
Impatiens, New Guinea hybrids
Impatiens walleriana

Lobelia erinus (in cool
climates)
Mirabilis jalapa
Nicotiana alata
Papaver rhoeas (in cool
climates)
Pelargonium hortorum
Pennisetum setaceum
Phlox drummondii (in cool
climates)
Portulaca grandiflora
Verbena × *hybrida*
Verbena 'Sissinghurst'
Verbena tenuisecta
Zinnia elegans

LAVENDER/MAUVE
Brassica oleracea (for fall only)
Cleome hassleriana
Cosmos bipinnatus
Dahlia hybrids (large
flowered)
Dahlia merckii hybrids
(bedding)
Digitalis purpurea
Gladiolus hybrids
Impatiens balsamina
Impatiens walleriana
Lobularia maritima
Mirabilis jalapa
Pelargonium hortorum
Verbena × *hybrida*
Verbena tenuisecta

PURPLE
Ageratum houstonianum

Brassica oleracea (for fall only)
Cleome hassleriana
Cosmos bipinnatus
Dahlia hybrids (large
flowered)
Gladiolus hybrids
Gomphrena globosa
Impatiens walleriana
Lunaria annua
Phlox drummondii (in cool
climates)
Salvia splendens
Torenia fournieri
Verbena bonariensis
Verbena × *hybrida*

BLUE
Ageratum houstonianum
Browallia americana
Lobelia erinus (in cool
climates)
Salvia farinacea

WHITE/CREAM
Acidanthera bicolor
Ageratum houstonianum
Antirrhinum majus
Begonia semperflorens-cultorum
Begonia × *tuberhybrida*
Brassica oleracea (for fall only)
Browallia americana
Catharanthus roseus
Chrysanthemum parthenium
Cleome hassleriana
Cosmos bipinnatus

Dahlia hybrids (large
flowered)
Dahlia merckii hybrids
(bedding)
Dianthus barbatus
Dianthus chinensis hybrids
Digitalis purpurea
Gazania rigens
Gladiolus hybrids
Gomphrena globosa
Helianthus hybrids
Impatiens balsamina
Impatiens, New Guinea
hybrids
Impatiens walleriana
Lobelia erinus (in cool
climates)
Lobularia maritima
Lunaria annua
Mirabilis jalapa
Nicotiana alata
Papaver rhoeas (in cool
climates)
Pelargonium hortorum
Phlox drummondii (in cool
climates)
Portulaca grandiflora
Salvia farinacea
Salvia splendens
Tagetes hybrids
Verbena × *hybrida*
Verbena tenuisecta
Zinnia angustifolia 'Star White'
Zinnia elegans

GREEN
Nicotiana alata

Notable Foliage Colors

PERENNIALS, ANNUALS, BULBS, SHRUBS AND VINES

GRAY, SILVER OR BLUISH FOLIAGE

Achillea 'Moonshine'
Ajuga reptans 'Silver Beauty'
Artemisia species and hybrids
Athyrium nipponicum 'Pictum'
Buddleia 'Lochinch'
Buddleia 'Nanho Blue'
Buddleia 'Nanho Purple'
Caryopteris × *clandonensis* 'Longwood Blue'
Dianthus × *allwoodii*
Dianthus plumarius
Dicentra 'Stuart Boothman'
Festuca amethystina
Festuca ovina glauca
Gypsophila paniculata
Hedera napaulensis 'Marble Dragon'
Helictotrichon sempervirens
Hosta species and hybrids
Lamiastrum galeobdalon 'Herman's Pride'
Lamium maculatum
Linaria purpurea
Lysimachia ephemerum
Marrubium cylleneum
Miscanthus sinensis 'Morning Light'
Nepeta × *faassenii*
Nepeta mussinii
Onopordum nervosum
Parthenocissus henryana
Perovskia atriplicifolia
Pulmonaria saccharata
Senecio cineraria
Stachys byzantina
Thalictrum speciosissimum
Verbascum bombyciferum
Veronica incana

REDDISH, PURPLE OR BRONZE FOLIAGE

Ajuga reptans 'Atropurpurea'
Amaranthus hybridus erythrostachys
Astilbe × *arendsii* (several)
Begonia semperflorens cultorum (some)
Berberis thunbergii atropurpurea
Berberis thunbergii 'Crimson Pygmy'
Berberis thunbergii 'Rose Glow'
Brassica oleracea
Canna × *generalis*
Celosia cristata plumosa (some)
Cimicifuga ramosa atropurpurea
Cimicifuga ramosa 'Brunette'
Cotinus coggygria (purple foliage forms)
Dahlia 'Japanese Bishop'
Dahlia merckii hybrid 'Redskin'
Helleborus foetidus 'Wester Flisk'
Heuchera micrantha 'Palace Purple'
Hibiscus acetosella 'Red Shield'
Impatiens, New Guinea hybrids (some)
Imperata cylindrica 'Red Baron'
Lobelia 'Bees Flame'
Lobelia 'Queen Victoria'
Lychnis × *arkwrightii*
Miscanthus sinensis 'Purpurascens'
Ophiopogon planiscapus 'Nigrescens'
Perilla frutescens 'Atropurpurea'
Sedum maximum 'Atropurpureum'
Tropaeolum minus 'Empress of India'
Tulipa greigii hybrids

GOLDEN FOLIAGE

Berberis thunbergii 'Aurea'
Coleus × *hybridus* 'Golden Bedder'
Filipendula ulmaria 'Aurea'
Hakonecloa macra 'Aureola'
Hosta hybrids
Sambucus nigra 'Aurea'
Sambucus racemosa 'Plumosa-aurea'
Spiraea × *bumalda* 'Gold Flame'

WHITE, CREAM OR YELLOW VARIEGATED FOLIAGE

Actinidia kolomikta
Ajuga reptans 'Silver Beauty'
Brassica oleracea
Brunnera macrophylla 'Langtrees'
Brunnera macrophylla 'Variegata'
Convallaria majalis 'Striata'
Filipendula ulmaria 'Variegata'
Hakonecloa macra 'Aureola'
Hedera canariensis 'Gloire de Marengo'

Hedera colchica 'Dentata
  Variegata'
Hedera colchica 'Sulphur Heart'
Hedera helix (some cultivars)
Hedera napaulensis 'Marble
  Dragon'
Heuchera americana (some)
Hosta hybrids
Iris pallida 'Albo-variegata'
Iris tectorum 'Variegata'
Jasminum officinale 'Aureo-
  variegatum'
Liriope muscari 'Silvery
  Sunproof'
Lunaria annua 'Variegata'
Miscanthus sinensis 'Morning
  Light'
Miscanthus sinensis 'Strictus'
Miscanthus sinensis 'Variegatus'

Pachysandra terminalis
  'Variegata'
Phlox paniculata 'Norah Leigh'
Physostegia virginiana
  'Variegata'
Polygonatum odoratum
  'Variegatum'
Spiraea × bumalda
Tulipa hybrids (some)
Vica minor 'Variegata'

MULTICOLORED FOLIAGE

Ajuga reptans 'Burgundy
  Glow'
Amaranthus tricolor
Caladium × hortulanum
Coleus × hybridus
Impatiens, New Guinea hy-
  brids (many)

FALL FOLIAGE COLOR

Amsonia tabernaemontana
  (yellow)
Ceratostigma plumbaginoides
  (red)
Geranium macrorrhizum (red)
Hakonecloa macra 'Aureola'
  (red)
Hosta species and hybrids
  (yellow)
Imperata cylindrica 'Red Baron'
  (red)
Miscanthus sinensis 'Pur-
  purescens' (red)
Platycodon grandiflorus (yellow)
Polygonatum biflorum (yellow)
Vitis coignetiae (red)

Notable Flower Forms and Foliage Types (Textures)

PERENNIALS, ANNUALS, BULBS,
SHRUBS AND VINES

FLOWERS: SPRAYS

Alchemilla mollis
Begonia grandis
Brunnera macrophylla
Crambe cordifolia
Gypsophila species
Heuchera species and hybrids
Verbena bonariensis

FLOWERS: SPIKES

Acanthus spinosus
Antirrhinum majus
Camassia species
Campanula persicifolia
Cheiranthus cheiri
Dictamnus albus
Dolichos lablab
Endymion species
Kniphofia species and hybrids
Linaria purpurea
Lupinus Russell hybrids
Lysimachia species
Lythrum species
Penstemon barbatus
Polemonium caeruleum
Salvia species and hybrids
Sanguisorba species
Veronica species and hybrids
Vitex agnus-castus

FLOWERS: SPIKES,
PARTICULARLY TALL AND
DRAMATIC

Althaea rosea
Buddleia davidii
Consolida orientalis
Delphinium species and
   hybrids
Digitalis species and hybrids
Galtonia candicans
Gladiolus hybrids
Liatris species
Ligularia 'The Rocket'
Lobelia species and hybrids
Verbascum bombyciferum

FLOWERS: PLUMES

Amaranthus hybridus
   erythrostachys
Artemisia lactiflora
Aruncus dioicus
Astilbe species and hybrids
Celosia cristata plumosa
Macleaya species
Pennisetum setaceum
Phlox paniculata
Rodgersia species
Smilacina racemosa
Solidago species and hybrids
Sorbaria species

FLOWERS: CLUSTERS

Amsonia species
Anchusa azurea
Asclepias curassavica
Asclepias tuberosa
Aster species and hybrids
Boltonia asteroides
Campanula glomerata
Chelone species
Cleome hassleriana
Hydrangea paniculata
Hydrangea quercifolia
Lagerstroemia indica
Lunaria annua
Myosotis sylvatica
Pelargonium × *hortorum*
Phlox drummondii
Silene armeria

FLOWERS: NODDING OR
DOWN FACING

Campanula species and hy-
   brids (many)
Campsis species and hybrids
Clematis alpina
Clematis macropetala
Clematis tangutica
Clematis viticella
Cobaea scandens
Convallaria majalis

Fritillaria species
Galanthus species and hybrids
Galtonia candicans
Kirengeshoma palmata
Leucojum aestivum
Lilium species and hybrids
   (some)
Lonicera species and hybrids
Polygonatum species
Pulmonaria species and
   hybrids
Scilla sibirica
Symphytum species and
   hybrids

FLOWERS: FLAT HEADS

Achillea species and hybrids
Eupatorium species
Filipendula species
Hydrangea species and hybrids
Lychnis chalcedonica
Sedum × 'Autumn Joy'
Sedum spectabile
Verbena × *hybrida*

FLOWERS: DAISIES

Aster species and hybrids
Bellis perennis
Boltonia asteroides
Calendula officinalis
Chrysanthemum coccineum
Chrysanthemum × *morifolium*
Chrysanthemum parthenium
Chrysanthemum × *superbum*
Chrysogonum virginianum
Coreopsis species and hybrids
Cosmos bipinnatus
Cosmos sulphureus
Dahlia merckii hybrids
Doronicum species and hybrids
Echinacea purpurea
Gaillardia species and hybrids
Gazania rigens
Helenium autumnale
Helianthus species and hybrids
Heliopsis scabra
Ligularia species and hybrids
Rudbeckia species and hybrids

Sanvitalia procumbens
Tithonia rotundifolia
Zinnia angustifolia
Zinnia elegans

FLOWERS: PARTICULARLY LARGE, OFTEN SOLITARY

Abelmoschus manihot
Begonia × *tuberhybrida*
Dahlia hybrids
Helianthus hybrids
Ipomoea alba
Iris (tall-bearded hybrids)
Iris kaempferi
Paeonia species and hybrids
Papaver orientale
Rudbeckia hirta (large-flowered
   hybrids)
Tulipa hybrids

FOLIAGE: GRASSY OR STRAPLIKE

Festuca species
Hakonecloa macra
Helictotrichon sempervirens
Hemerocallis hybrids
Imperata cylindrica
Iris species and hybrids
Kniphofia species and hybrids
Liriope muscari
Miscanthus sinensis
Ophiopogon species and
   hybrids
Pennisetum species
Tradescantia × *andersoniana*

FOLIAGE: FERNY

Achillea species and hybrids
Artemisia lactiflora
Astilbe species and hybrids
Athyrium species
Chrysanthemum coccineum
Dicentra species and hybrids
Dryopteris species
Filipendula ulmaria
Osmunda species
Polystichum species

FOLIAGE: FINELY CUT, LACEY

Artemisia × 'Powis Castle'
Artemisia schmidtiana 'Silver
   Mound'
Coreopsis verticillata
Cosmos bipinnatus
Ipomoea × *multifida*
Ipomoea quamoclit
Nigella damascena
Potentilla fruticosa

FOLIAGE: WHORLED

Asperula odorata
Pachysandra terminalis

FOLIAGE: LARGE ROUNDED, OVAL OR HEART-SHAPED

Actinidia species
Begonia grandis
Bergenia species and hybrids
Brunnera macrophylla
Clematis heracleifolia
Crambe cordifolia
Digitalis purpurea
Helianthus hybrids
Hosta species and hybrids
Ipomoea alba
Kirengeshoma palmata
Ligularia species and hybrids
Lunaria annua
Macleaya species
Mirabilis jalapa
Nicotiana alata
Pulmonaria species
Stachys byzantina
Symphytum grandiflorum
Tithonia rotundifolia
Verbascum bombyciferum

FOLIAGE: SMALL ROUNDED, OVAL OR HEART-SHAPED

Abelia Hybrids
Adiantum pedatum
Alchemilla mollis

Aquilegia species and hybrids
Asarum europeum
Convallaria majalis
Epimedium species and hybrids
Heuchera species and hybrids
Hosta species and hybrids
Pelargonium × *hortorum*
Primula × *polyanthus*
Thalictrum species
Tiarella species
Tropaeolum majus
Tropaeolum minor
Vancouveria hexandra

FOLIAGE: SMALL NARROW

Dianthus species and hybrids
Gypsophila species
Liatris species
Linaria purpurea
Myosotis sylvatica
Portulaca grandiflora
Silene armeria
Zinnia angustifolia

FOLIAGE: PALMATELY LOBED AND COMPOUND

Abelmoschus manihot
Aconitum species and hybrids
Althaea rosea
Cleome hassleriana

Delphinium species and hybrids
Filipendula species
Geranium species and hybrids
Geum species and hybrids
Helleborus species and hybrids
Hibiscus acetosella
Ipomoea × *multifida*
Lupinus Russell hybrids
Parthenocissus henryana
Potentilla thurberi
Rodgersia species
Sanguinaria canadensis
Tropaeolum peregrinum
Vitex agnus-castus

FOLIAGE: PINNATELY LOBED AND COMPOUND

Acanthus spinosus
Artemisia lactiflora
Aruncus dioicus
Astilbe species and hybrids
Baptisia australis
Campsis species and hybrids
Chrysanthemum parthenium
Cimicifuga species
Clematis species and hybrids
Cosmos sulphureus
Dictamnus albus
Echinops 'Taplow Blue'

Filipendula ulmaria
Gazania rigens
Ipomoea quamoclit
Hydrangea quercifolia
Jasminum officinale
Papaver species and hybrids
Rudbeckia laciniata
Sambucus species
Sanguisorba species
Sorbaria species
Tagetes hybrids
Wisteria species

FOLIAGE: PARTICULARLY BOLD

Acanthus spinosus
Caladium × *hortulanum*
Clematis heracleifolia
Crambe cordifolia
Digitalis purpurea
Dolichos lablab
Echinops 'Taplow Blue'
Hedera colchica
Helianthus hybrids
Hydrangea quercifolia
Ligularia species and hybrids
Macleaya species
Rudbeckia laciniata
Verbascum bombyciferum
Vitis coignetiae

Horticultural Classification of Hybrid Tulips

Note: Bloom season is based on Zone 6 in the vicinity of Philadelphia.

Blooming Season	New Classification / Old Classification	Description
Early April	Kaufmanniana Hybrids / Kaufmanniana Hybrids	Often called waterlily tulips; large flowers on short stems, 6 to 8 inches; better garden plants than the Single Earlies in the North; red, cream, yellow, white or pink or a combination, hybridized from variants of *T. kaufmanniana* and *T. greigii*.
Early April	Single Earlies / Single Earlies	Usually fragrant, 12 to 14 inches, good for forcing, but garden performance is best in the South.
Early April	Double Earlies / Double Earlies	Double flowers, sometimes fragrant, 12 to 14 inches, good for forcing.
Late April	Mendel and Triumph / Mendel and Triumph	Most commonly used for forcing, also good for garden use, 16 to 20 inches; two classes are similar, both bred from Single Earlies × May-flowering classes.
Late April	Fosteriana Hybrids / Fosteriana Hybrids	Large flowers in clear colors on long stems, 14 to 24 inches; red, orange, yellow or white, hybridized from *T. fosteriana* and other classes.
Late April	Darwin Hybrids / Darwin Hybrids	Larger-flowered and earlier than Darwins, the most popular class today; large flowers on tall stems are less sturdy in bad weather, bred from Darwins × Fosteriana Hybrids, 20 to 26 inches.
Late April to May	Greigii Hybrids / Greigii Hybrids	Similar to Kaufmanniana Hybrids and hybridized with them, leaves mottled with purple, red, white or yellow, 8 to 16 inches.
May	Single Late / Cottage, Darwin Breeder combined	Classic egg-shaped tulips, wide range of colors, 20 to 26 inches.
May	Rembrandt / Bybloemens, Bizarres, Rembrandt combined	Broken forms (flamed and feathered) similar to the fashion of tulipomania period in Holland (circa 1630s), 20 to 26 inches.
May	Lily Flowered / Lily Flowered	Long pointed reflexed petals, derived from Cottage Tulips, 20 to 24 inches.
May	Viridiflora / Viridiflora	Partially green petals, 16 to 20 inches.
April to May	Fringed / Fringed	Petals delicately fringed, mostly derived from Single Lates but some derived from Darwin Hybrids, 20 to 24 inches.
Late April to May	Double Late / Peony Flowered	Includes double forms of Triumphs and May-flowering classes; some are very late flowering, 16 to 20 inches.
April to May	Parrot / Parrot	Sports of many classes with laciniate or deeply cut petals and exotic markings.

Horticultural Classification of Daffodils
(According to the American Daffodil Society)

Blooming Season	Division	Description
Early to mid-April	1. Trumpet	Trumpet is as long or longer than the perianth (petals), one flower per stem, colors more commonly yellow and white, but hybridizers have recently added pinks and reds to trumpets.
Mid- to late April	2. Long or Large Cup	Cup is more than one-third but less than the full length of the perianth, one flower per stem; most bloom slightly later than the Trumpets; petals are yellow or white and cups may be yellow, white, red, orange or pink. The great majority of hybrids fall into this division.
Late April	3. Short or Small Cup	Cup is less than one-third the length of the perianth, one flower per stem; petals are yellow or white and cups may be yellow, white, red, orange or pink.
Late April	4. Double	Extra petals replace or fill the cup or trumpet, one or more flowers per stem, wide range of colors.
Late April	5. Triandrus	Two to four (or rarely one) small, nodding bell-shaped flowers per stem, petals reflexed back, commonly white or yellow, but other colors have been hybridized into cups, hybrids of *N. triandrus*.
March and April	6. Cyclamineus	Long, narrow trumpet or large cup surrounded often by very reflexed petals, one flower per stem; colors include yellow and white and more recently red and pink trumpet, hybrids of *N. cyclamineus*. Most varieties are early blooming.
Late April	7. Jonquilla	Up to six small flowers per stem, sweetly fragrant, narrow rushlike leaves (rounded in cross section), the true jonquils, hybrids of *N. jonquilla*.
Late April	8. Tazetta	Up to 16 small flowers (sometimes more) per stem, strong fragrance, some not hardy in the North (above Zone 7) but commonly used for forcing indoors; paperwhites included here, hybrids of *N. tazetta*.
Late April to early May	9. Poeticus	White petals with small cups of yellow or green, edged with red or orange, one flower per stem, slightly fragrant, among the latest varieties.
February to May	10. Species	Wild species of narcissus, and hybrids that are presumed to have occurred in the wild.
April	11. Split Corona	Cup or trumpet (corona) split at least one-third of its length, often spreading almost flat against the petals; may be derived from any other divisions.
	12. Miscellaneous	Horticultural varieties and hybrids that do not fit into other divisions. Currently there are few varieties in this division.

Horticultural Classification of Lilies
(Adapted from the Royal Horticultural Society and the North American Lily Society)

Note: The average gardener will be primarily concerned with the following groups, which are most available in catalogs and together provide a long season of bloom in the garden:

May–July	I. Asiatic Hybrids
Late June–early August	VI. Trumpet and Aurelian Hybrids
July–late August	VII. Oriental Hybrids

Blooming Season	Division	Description
May to July	I. Asiatic Hybrids	Flowers may face upward, outward or downward (pendent) and come in white and almost any color or blend of colors except blue, often attractively speckled. Heights range from approximately 1 to 6 feet, most varieties in the range of 2 to 4 feet. The most popular division; includes 'Connecticut King' (yellow), 'Sterling Star' (white), 'Tiger Babies' (salmon-red), 'Viva' (orange-red).
May to June	II. Martagon and Hansonii Hybrids	Woodland lilies with small pendent flowers with recurved petals in "turk's-cap" form. Colors range from yellow to orange, rust and red, often speckled; 3 to 6 feet tall. Easy to grow and long-lived, but takes a couple of years to establish; includes 'Dalhansonii' (mahogany), 'Mrs. R. O. Backhouse' (yellow), 'Paisley Hybrids' (yellow-orange).
June to July	III. Candidum and Chalcedonicum Hybrids	Pendent (usually) flaring (widely trumpet shaped) flowers of white, yellow or buff; 2 to 4 feet tall. Most popular with specialists; includes 'Fragrance' (cream), *L. × testaceum* (buff), 'Uprising' (up-facing soft yellow-buff).
June to early July	IV. Hybrids of American Species	Pendent flowers in yellow, orange and red; 3 to 5 feet tall. Hybrids of West Coast species most easily grown in the West. Most popular with specialists; includes 'Afterglow' (crimson), 'Bellingham Hybrids' (orange and yellow), 'Shuksan' (yellow-orange).
Late June to July	V. Hybrids of Longiflorum and Formosanum	Fragrant trumpet-shaped flowers. Not many varieties nor widely available. Easter lilies included here.
Late June to August	VI. Trumpet and Aurelian Hybrids	Large fragrant flowers may be trumpet, bowl-shaped, flat or recurved. Colors include white, pink, yellow, apricot and orange; 3 to 6 feet. Strong and easy to grow; includes 'Gold Eagle' (yellow), 'Pink Perfection' (pink), 'White Henryi', (white with orange throat).
July to September	VII. Oriental Hybrids	Extremely fragrant flowers may be trumpet, bowl-shaped, flat or recurved in combinations of red, pink, white, and most recently shades of yellow; 2 to 6 feet. Includes *L. rubrum* and *L. speciosum* hybrids. Many are susceptible to virus infection and may not last more than a few years in the garden. Varieties: 'Black Beauty' (dark red), 'Casa Blanca' (white), 'Journey's End' (crimson).
Variable	VIII. Miscellaneous Hybrids	Hybrids not fitting into other divisions.
Variable	IX. Species, Varieties and Forms	Lilies that occur in the wild; includes *L. henryi* (orange, very tall, blooms in July to August), *L. superbum* (orange and yellow, blooms July).

THE USDA PLANT HARDINESS MAP OF THE UNITED STATES

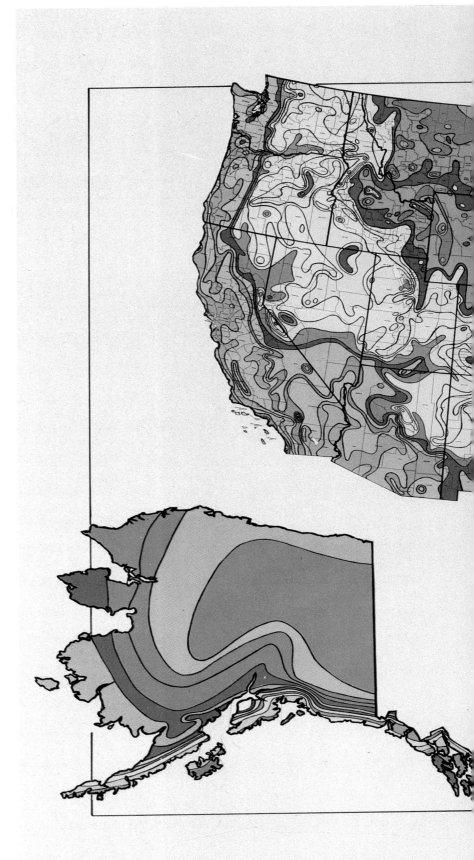

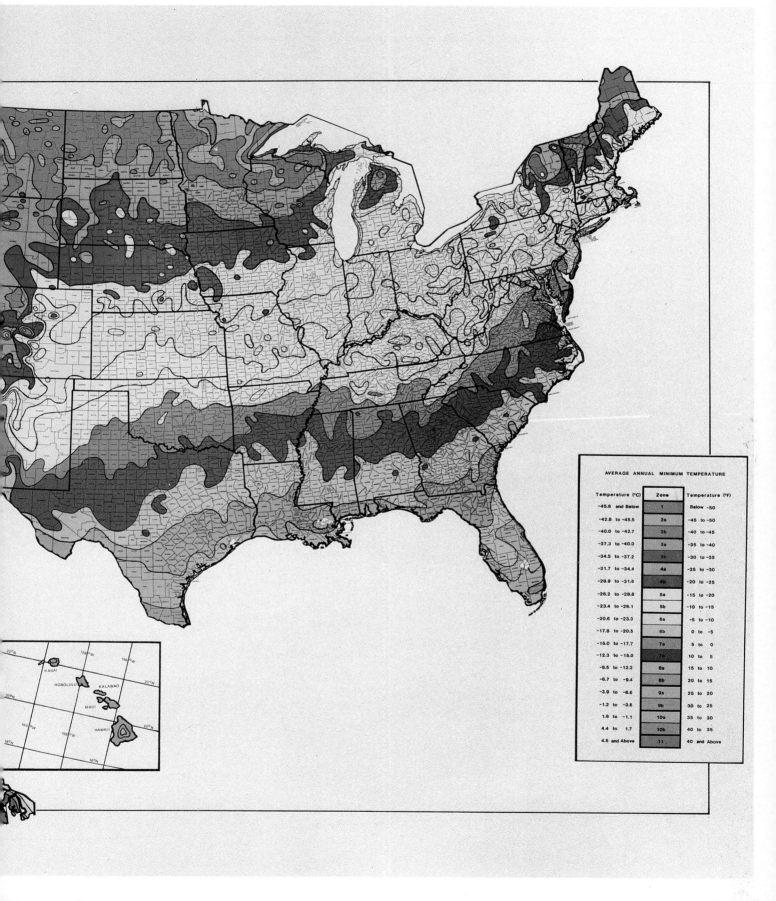

AVERAGE ANNUAL MINIMUM TEMPERATURE

Temperature (°C)	Zone	Temperature (°F)
-45.8 and Below	1	Below -50
-42.8 to -45.5	2a	-45 to -50
-40.0 to -42.7	2b	-40 to -45
-37.3 to -40.0	3a	-35 to -40
-34.5 to -37.2	3b	-30 to -35
-31.7 to -34.4	4a	-25 to -30
-28.9 to -31.6	4b	-20 to -25
-26.2 to -28.8	5a	-15 to -20
-23.4 to -26.1	5b	-10 to -15
-20.6 to -23.3	6a	-5 to -10
-17.8 to -20.5	6b	0 to -5
-15.0 to -17.7	7a	5 to 0
-12.3 to -15.0	7b	10 to 5
-9.5 to -12.2	8a	15 to 10
-6.7 to -9.4	8b	20 to 15
-3.9 to -6.6	9a	25 to 20
-1.2 to -3.8	9b	30 to 25
1.6 to -1.1	10a	35 to 30
4.4 to 1.7	10b	40 to 35
4.5 and Above	11	40 and Above

Books For Further Reading

ANNUALS:

Bales, Suzanne Frutig. *Annuals* (Burpee American Gardening Series). New York: Prentice Hall, 1991.

Nehrling, Arno, and Irene Nehrling. *The Picture Book of Annuals*. New York: Hearthside Press, 1966.

PERENNIALS:

Aden, Paul. *The Hosta Book*. 2nd ed. Portland, OR: Timber Press, 1990.

Armitage, Allan M. *Allan Armitage on Perennials* (Burpee Expert Gardener). New York: Prentice Hall, 1993.

Armitage, Allan M. *Herbaceous Perennial Plants*. Athens, GA: Varsity Press, 1989.

Bales, Suzanne Frutig. *Perennials* (Burpee American Gardening Series). New York: Prentice Hall, 1991.

Clausen, Ruth Rogers, and Nicolas H. Ekstrom. *Perennials for American Gardens*. New York: Random House, 1989.

Harper, Pamela, and Frederick McGourty. *Perennials: How to Select, Grow and Enjoy*. Tucson: HP Books, 1985.

Jelitto, Leo, and Wilhelm Schacht. *Hardy Herbaceous Perennials*. 3rd ed. Portland, OR: Timber Press, 1990.

Phillips, Roger, and Martyn Rix, *Random House Book of Perennials, vol. 1 Early Perennials*. New York: Random House, 1991. *Vol. 2 Late Perennials*. New York: Random House, 1991.

Thomas, Graham Stuart. *Perennial Garden Plants*. 3rd Edition, Millwood, NJ: Saga Press, 1990.

BULBS:

Barnes, Don. *Daffodils for Home, Garden and Show*. Portland, OR: Timber Press, 1987.

Let's Grow Lilies. A booklet available from Executive Secretary, North American Lily Society, P. O. Box 272, Owatonna, MN 55060. $3.50, including postage.

Rix, Martyn, and Roger Phillips. *The Random House Book of Bulbs*. New York: Random House, 1989 (Revised Ed.)

Scott, George Harmon. *Bulbs: How to Select, Grow and Enjoy*. Tucson: HP Books, 1982.

Wilder, Louise Beebe. *Adventures with Hardy Bulbs*. New York: Macmillan, 1990. Reprint of work originally published 1936.

WOODY PLANTS:

Dirr, Michael A. *Manual of Woody Landscape Plants*. 4th ed. Champaign, Ill.: Stipes Publishing Co., 1990.

Rix, Martyn, and Roger Phillips. *Shrubs*. New York: Random House, 1989.

ROSES:

Phillips, Roger, and Martyn Rix. *Roses*. New York: Random House, 1988.

Scanniello, Stephen, and Tania Bayard. *Roses of America*. New York: Henry Holt & Co., 1990.

VINES AND CLIMBERS:

Beckett, Kenneth A. *Climbing Plants*. Portland, OR: Timber Press, 1983.

Fretwell, Barry. *Clematis*. London: William Collins, 1989.

Harrod, Julie. *The Garden Wall*. New York: Atlantic Monthly Press, 1991. (American edition ed. Charles O. Cresson.)

Lloyd, Christopher, and Tom Bennet. *Clematis*. Deer Park, Wis.: Capability's Books, 1989.

SHADE GARDENING:

Schenk, George. *The Complete Shade Gardener*. Boston: Houghton Mifflin Co., 1984.

DESIGN:

Brooks, John. *The Small Garden*. New York: Macmillan, 1978.

Crowe, Sylvia. *Garden Design*. Chichester, U.K.: Thomas Gibson in association with Packard, Funtington, 1981.

Page, Russell. *The Education of a Gardener*. New York: Random House, 1983.

COLOR:

Jekyll, Gertrude. *Colour Schemes for the Flower Garden*. Rev. ed. by G. S. Thomas. Salem, N.H.: The Ayer Co., 1984.

Hobhouse, Penelope. *Color in Your Garden*. Boston: Little, Brown, 1985.

Wilder, Louise Beebe. *Color in My Garden*. Boston: Little, Brown, 1990. (Reprint of 1927 edition.)

PEST, DISEASE AND WEED CONTROL

Fogg, John Milton, Jr. *Weeds of Lawn and Garden*. Philadelphia: University of Pennsylvania Press, 1956.

Isely, Duane. *Weed Identification and Control in the North Central States*, Ames: Iowa State University Press, 1960.

Olkowski, William, Sheila Daar, and Helga Olkowski. *Common-Sense Pest Control*. Newtown, Conn.: Taunton Press, 1991.

Pirone, Pascal P. *Diseases and Pests of Ornamental Plants*. 5th ed. New York: John Wiley & Sons, 1978.

Smith, Miranda, and Anna Carr. *Rodale's Garden Insect, Disease and Weed Identification Guide*. Emmaus, Pa.: Rodale Press, 1988.

U.S. Department of Agriculture. *Selected Weeds of the United States*. Agriculture Handbook No. 366. Washington, D.C.: USDA, 1970.

SOILS:

Ortloff, H. Stuart, and Henry B. Raymore. *A Book about Soils for the Home Gardener*. New York: M. Barrows & Co., 1962.

Index

Note: Italicized page numbers refer to captions.